'A magnificent book . . . through the words of Richard Moore and the trail-blazing of the Scot who did, and continues to do, it his way, you will get a great understanding of much of the mystique of the sport' *Phil Liggett*

'An extraordinary tale of an extraordinary man' *Daily Telegraph*

'What really distinguishes the book, apart from the structural innovations, apart from the puzzle itself, is the tone: gentle, wise, vivid when it needs to be, and entirely compelling' *Robert Macfarlane, author of* Mountains of the Mind and the Wild Places

'As riveting a read as any detective story, as well as an intriguing attempt to separate myth from fact' *Metro*

'A bible to anyone aiming to be the best in their field . . . and the hardships and sacrifices it takes to get there . . . One can't but help find an insecure fragile man who deep down cared for every word spoken about him' *David Millar*

'The definitive portrait of one of Scotland's greatest sportsmen: obsessively driven, painfully shy' *Guardian*

'A wonderful story told with respect, affection, and a mastery of both research and subject' *Glasgow Herald*

'Moore is a gifted writer who covers the failed drugs test, Tours de France, sex-change rumours and escape from Scotland with panache . . .' *The Times*

'A gripping read' *Scottish Sunday Post*

D0193138

'Moore, almost paternally, paints an affectionate portrait of his subject . . . the anecdotes of Millar's tightness with money are worth the price of the book alone'   *Galloway Gazette*

'Trying to piece together the Robert Millar story is a little like rummaging around the Mary Celeste but Moore has done splendidly'   *Daily Telegraph*

'The standout sports biography of the year'
National Sporting Club

'[Moore's] text is littered with references which puts the main story into context and adds pace and depth to the narrative, making it read like a cracking novel'   *4sportsbooks.co.uk*

'Cycling is a sport that seems to inspire good writing: the pace, drama and characters lend themselves to an unfolding of tension on the page and this exhaustive account is written with genuine passion'   *Books Quarterly*

'An excellent book . . . as Moore peels away [Millar's] prickly exterior, there emerges a darkly humorous, fiercely intelligent man'
The Herald

'This year's must-read . . . Moore's meticulous but lively book skilfully steers the reader through the Gorbals-born Millar's early life, pro career and post-retirement disappearance'
Press Association

'Fascinating . . . earnest and lively'   *International Herald Tribune*

'The most intriguing of the Tour books this year'   *Bookseller*

IN SEARCH OF
ROBERT
MILLAR

Richard Moore

HarperSport

An Imprint of HarperCollinsPublishers

In loving memory of my mother, Katherine Moore
(1946–2005)

First published in hardback in 2007 by
HarperSport
an imprint of HarperCollins*Publishers*
London

First published in paperback in 2008

© Richard Moore 2007

1

A CIP catalogue record for this book is available
from the British Library

ISBN-13   978-0-00-723502-5
ISBN-10   0-00-723502-X

Printed and bound in Great Britain
by Clays Ltd, St Ives plc

The HarperCollins website address is
www.harpercollins.co.uk

Mixed Sources
Product group from well-managed
forests and other controlled sources
www.fsc.org Cert no. SW-COC-1806
© 1996 Forest Stewardship Council

FSC

Photographic acknowledgments

©: **Action Images/MSI** plates p 16 (bottom right); **Evening Express Glasgow** p 5
(centre); **Michel Coroir/Parc Naturel Régional du Haut-Languedoc** p 2 (top);
Granada TV p 7, p 8 (top); **Marcel Guerard** p 4 (centre); **Phil O'Connor** p 4
(bottom), p 5 (bottom), p 6 (top), p 13 (top left and right), p 16 (bottom left);
Offside/L'Equipe p 4 (top), 15 (bottom); **Popperfoto** p 6 (centre); **H.A. Roth** p 3
(bottom); **B. Smith** p 1; **Graham Watson** p 9, p 10 (all), p 11 (all), p 12 (both),
p 13 (bottom left and right), p 14 (all except top), p 15 (all except bottom), p 16
(top and centre). All other photographs supplied courtesy of *Cycling Weekly*
archives.

While every effort has been made to trace the owners of copyright material repro-
duced herein, the publishers would like to apologise for any omissions and will be
pleased to incorporate missing acknowledgments in any future editions.

Contents

'. . . remaining unknowable is the only true way to be known . . .'

Colum McCann, from *Dancer*

Prologue

I can remember, quite clearly, my first encounter with Robert Millar. It was at lunchtime on Saturday, 21 July 1984. I was 11 at the time. Robert Millar will remember the occasion more vividly, because while I was watching television with my dad in my family's living room, he was in the Haute-Ariège area of the Pyrenees, climbing a steep, winding road that ended at the ski station at Guzet Neige – the finish of stage 11 of the Tour de France.

We had recently moved to England from Scotland, and my Scottishness was being pointed out to me repeatedly. A PE teacher nicknamed me 'Jock', and it stuck. I hated being singled out. On the other hand, I quite liked it too. But I was desperately, urgently looking for allies – namely, fellow Jocks – wherever I could, even on television, even participating in obscure sporting events. I looked at the TV screen but couldn't really work out what was going on. There was a small group of sweating cyclists straining against a steep gradient and suffering in the blazing heat. So this was the Tour de France. It looked pretty boring.

I asked my dad, who was receiving his weekly fix of the Tour de France on ITV's *World of Sport*, whether any Scottish cyclists were competing in this strange event. 'There is one Scot,' he replied, a note of surprise in his voice. 'Robert Millar, from Glasgow. That's him there.'

Now I was interested. I was struck by the name, by its ordinariness. He didn't sound like he belonged there. 'Robert Millar' jarred alongside the exotic-sounding Laurent Fignon, Bernard Hinault, Pedro Delgado, even the American with the French-sounding name, Greg LeMond. And yet, although I didn't know it at the time, in the wiry, compact form of Robert Millar I had just stumbled upon someone who was not only Scottish but most certainly – and defiantly – different; someone who didn't just mind standing out, or apart, from the crowd, but actually seemed to want to.

'Will he win?' I asked.

'No,' said my dad, with good old-fashioned Scottish pessimism-realism.

But Dad was wrong, or at least partially wrong. I kept watching. I can vividly recall the footage of the Tour on that particular day, with commentary that sounded like it was coming from outer space. The grainy quality of the pictures and the sounds made the broadcast seem other-worldly. It was, in fact, less like watching sport and more like witnessing astronauts landing on the moon, or mountaineers arriving at the summit of Everest. And I remember Millar winning the stage, his second Pyrenean victory in consecutive years, on his way to claiming one of the race's three great prizes, the title of King of the Mountains. He was the first and to this day remains the only English speaker ever to wear the fabled polka-dot jersey awarded to the King of the Mountains all the way to the finish in Paris.

There was something about Millar, quite apart from his nationality and the fact that he was beating these foreigners at their own game, on their own turf, to the top of their own mountains, that was instantly fascinating. As he climbed the mountain his head bobbed gently and easily to the rhythm of the pedals. His style was unusual but fluid and efficient. His left knee flicked in and then out at the top of the pedal stroke, following a consistent, smooth pattern. His eyes were focused a few yards in front, yet they also appeared vacant, expressionless, drawn with the effort – 'the face of a hungry man', according to the commentator, Phil Liggett.

That Saturday afternoon Millar was in the company of three other cyclists, but when the slope reared up, he was the one doing most of the pace setting. He seemed to be teeming with nervous energy, repeatedly looking over his shoulder, checking the others, cajoling them even. While he was fleet of foot, they were leaden by comparison; the slender, lightweight Scot looked as if he might fly off at any moment, the others as if they would be dragged back down the hill by the pull of gravity. 'I hope he doesn't overdo it with his confidence,' said the partisan Liggett, as if trying to send the Brit subliminal messages.

Then, as they approached a sweeping left bend, Millar took flight. He stood up on the pedals and accelerated into the crowd, his bike swinging violently from side to side, his body bobbing up and down with urgency, releasing all that pent-up energy in a bid to shake off his companions, now down to two, a Frenchman and a Dutchman. Neither reacted; if anything, they seemed relieved to see him flee, glad of an excuse to slow down. Ahead of them Millar forged on, relaxing into that gentle, easy rhythm. In the commentary box, Liggett wasn't so calm: 'He's not a big-headed man at all, but when you speak to him confidence oozes out of him.' Several times he highlighted the incongruity of a cyclist from Glasgow excelling amid such company, and in such terrain. 'He was a little worried that this stage wouldn't be hard enough for him,' Liggett added with a chuckle.

Inside the final kilometre of the 226.5km stage, Millar's hand dipped inside the back pocket of his jersey and emerged clasping a white cap bearing the name of his team sponsor, Peugeot, which he then stuck on his head in one fluid movement. 'The little man from the Gorbals with the big heart and the powerful legs,' screamed Liggett, his voice crackling with emotion, as Millar climbed towards the finish. 'Millar has unleashed all his anger today on the Tour de France.'

Behind Millar, Luis Herrera and Pedro Delgado, late attackers, had leapfrogged his earlier companions; he had escaped at just the right time. But now they were chasing, and closing. They were within a minute; Millar had to sprint as if he was launching his initial attack all over again. But in the final metres, when he knew he had won, Millar appeared to relax, sitting upright, taking his hands off the handlebars, raising them, allowing his clenched fists to fall behind his head, then pumping them back into the air, palms open, eyes looking down rather than at the photographers, but face smiling. The clock stopped at seven hours, three minutes and forty-one seconds as he crossed the line. Seven hours! And he was sprinting! Uphill! It was inconceivable.

Then, his peaked cap framing his gaunt face, giving him the appearance of a jockey in need of a good feed, Millar faced what was for him the bigger ordeal: the post-race interview. Liggett asked the questions. What had gone through his mind on that final climb? 'That I was gonna win, that I knew I was gonna win, and that I was really happy,' mumbled Millar, wearing a blank expression apart from the thinnest of smiles forming on his lips. He had known virtually the whole stage that he was going to win, he added, and he was certain after the climb of the Col du Portet d'Aspet, when he was the strongest in the leading group. At the end of each sentence he seemed to add an 'eh' – virtually the only trace of a Scottish accent in his curious hybrid drawl. He proved as fascinating to watch during this interview as he had been during the race. He was a mass of contradictions, appearing self-assured yet nervous; possessed of steely confidence yet impossibly shy; in control yet awkward. He spent much of the interview looking away from the camera, away from his interrogator, but when he briefly glanced up his eyes burned with intensity. Or was it anger, as Liggett had suggested?

At the same time his face twitched and his brow contorted with apparent nervousness.

Cycling became my sport, Robert Millar my hero. His seemed to be the ideal identity for a displaced young Scot to assume in a strange foreign land: suitably different, possibly cool, certainly interesting. I was given a glossy coffee-table-style book, *The Fabulous World of Cycling 1984*. I still have it, though some of the pictures are missing, sacrificed to the covers of school jotters. I also wrote a letter:

Dear Jim,
Please will you fix it for me to go cycling with Robert Millar,
the Tour de France cyclist from Glasgow. I thought that, as a
former Tour of Britain cyclist, you might look kindly upon my
request.
Thank you.
Kind regards,
Richard Moore, 11, Cheshire (originally from Edinburgh).

Ordinarily, *Jim'll Fix It* fulfilled children's dreams of singing with Duran Duran, or playing football at Anfield. A plea to go cycling with a star of the Tour de France was, I fancied, sufficiently unusual to interest Jimmy Savile, who, after all, and as my dad pointed out encouragingly, really had been a Tour of Britain cyclist himself. There was no response.

What I didn't know at the time was that Millar had a reputation for being prickly and difficult. He also had a reputation for not always obliging fans seeking autographs or photographs, far less an approach from an eccentric, cigar-puffing, tracksuit-wearing children's TV personality. Sometimes he would politely refuse; more often the response would be a more direct 'fuck off'. As one of Millar's former managers noted, 'The challenge with Robert was to get him to tell people to fuck off in a courteous way.' Yet Millar was – is – nothing if not a walking, (occasionally) talking paradox. He could also, as countless people will testify, be obliging, generous and funny, specializing in a wry, dry and often black sense of humour.

My first real-life encounter with him was in January 1988, when he returned to Scotland for a hotly anticipated 'Robert Millar Training Weekend'. For this camp, intended to help his aspiring young countrymen, Britain's greatest ever cyclist gave his time freely, asking only for travelling expenses. And, as a committed vegetarian, for enough beans and toast to last him the weekend. When Millar appeared in Stirling it represented the first real opportunity for the latest generation of hopeful (as well as some pretty hopeless) young cyclists to learn from someone we all aspired to emulate – and in one or two cases, judging by the hairstyles and contrived reticence, actually to *be*.

At that first camp there was massive disappointment when we learned that he couldn't accompany us on training rides because he was recovering from a minor operation in a place 'where it affects cyclists most', as it was reported. 'Where the sun don't shine' would also have been accurate. The next year he was back, and fit. Towards the end of the first training ride I found myself splashing through puddles on back roads near Stirling in a small group of five riders that had become detached from the larger groups. One of the riders in the group, even smaller than he looked on the television, was Robert Millar. We took it in turns to ride at the front alongside him. But when it came to my turn, and my front wheel drew level with his, a very strange thing happened. Fate, or a gust of wind, intervened. My woolly winter training hat was whisked clean off my head, and deposited in a puddle. I don't think Millar had seen that one before. He kept his cool, but half turned and said, almost inaudibly, 'A wet hat's better than no hat, eh?' To which I nodded silently before peeling away from the group to go back and get it.

The chance to ride alongside Millar had disappeared in a freakish puff of wind. All those questions loaded with self-interest – How many miles should a 15-year-old ride in a week? What races should a 15-year-old aim for? If you're going to turn professional, how good should you be at, say, 15? – would have to wait.

But not for long, because the training ride was followed by a question-and-answer session. We shuffled nervously into a lecture theatre, and then Millar appeared. The questions flowed, while Millar's eyes darted around, rarely focusing on his audience. His answers were brief and to the point, and they were characterized by that steely assurance that seemed so at odds with his diffident manner. Most of the questions, inevitably, were about the Tour de France. Millar looked a little puzzled. 'I think you should ask some different questions,' he said in that curious mid-Atlantic-Scottish-French accent, wearing that half smile. 'None of you are riding the Tour de France, so I don't think it's relevant me talking about it, eh.' That was us, a roomful of teenagers, told. He did have a point though.

Nine years later, three years after his retirement, he managed the Scotland team in the Prutour, the nine-stage Tour of Britain. I was in that team, and my abiding memory is of Millar as shy, friendly, modest, with a vast knowledge of the sport, and almost always ready with a witty, often dark one-liner. Perhaps he was too shy to be a truly effective manager. But that was handy in our case: we were rubbish.

There was an incident before the start of one of the later stages. One of the Scotland riders had misplaced his race numbers. This was a disaster: without them, he wouldn't be allowed to start. The rider in question was infamously disorganized, always late, always leaving something behind at the hotel. Yet with barely a minute left before the start, the numbers miraculously appeared . . . from where Millar had hidden them.

He smiled that thin smile as he handed them over and said nothing. The rider got the message.

There is no debate over whether or not Robert Millar is Britain's greatest ever Tour de France cyclist – and that, in many people's eyes, makes him Britain's best-ever cyclist. Supporters of Tom Simpson, the Englishman who died on the slopes of Mont Ventoux during the 1967 Tour de France, might disagree. But Simpson was a one-day specialist: he excelled in the 'classics' and the world road race championship, which he won – the only British rider ever to do so – in 1965. Millar, on the other hand, was a man for the major tours, of France, Italy and Spain. For many, these three races are the pinnacle of the sport, and in these events Millar stands head and shoulders above any other cyclist from these islands, which is not bad for someone who grew up in Glasgow, whose frame extended (when he wasn't crouched over his bike) to five feet six inches, and who tipped the scales at just nine stone.

Millar was an outstanding cyclist, clearly, but he also had style and class. He was cool, enigmatic, aloof, and quietly determined. His obsessive quest for perfection was awesome. It could be quite terrifying, too. After one stage of the Tour de France the television cameras caught him removing his racing jersey to reveal a painfully skinny upper body, arms as brown as barbecued steak, and torso, with ribs protruding, translucent white. 'Ooooh,' said my mum, recoiling in horror. Not mock horror. Everything about him – his self-contained manner, his appearance – screamed absolute dedication, and of an extreme way of living.

When, in the early 1980s, Millar emerged as one of the world's leading cyclists, his sport, to most in Britain, was as colourful, intriguing and impenetrable as a foreign language, and those who enjoyed it were fed only on scraps of coverage. It couldn't have been further removed from the arenas where we traditionally watched and enjoyed sport: football grounds, athletics tracks, tennis courts. The Tour de France was on another scale; it belonged in a different dimension; it represented something other, something more, than sport. You didn't enjoy the Tour de France, you marvelled at it. The mountains, especially, were where the Tour de France was transformed from being merely a sport into something bigger, more significant. And it was here, in the thin air and against the jagged backdrop of the Alps and the Pyrenees, that Millar excelled. His gifts in such an environment, his ability to dance with smooth grace up such steep mountains, seemed an extravagantly, exotically impressive, not to say surreal talent for somebody raised in one of Europe's most industrialized and impoverished cities. The Tour's profile in Britain increased throughout the 1980s, thanks in large part to the growing impact of English speakers such as Millar.

There are those who claim that in his apparent desperation not to engage with the media, Millar was his own worst enemy. Many said that he lacked charisma; others complained that he had no personality. They were wrong. He was the Morrissey of the sporting world: enigmatic, complex, sardonic; unconventional yet cool; hopelessly shy but at the same time absolutely sure of himself. Oh, and a vegetarian. Confidence, as Phil Liggett said, oozed from Robert Millar, but it was a curious kind of confidence. He was an outsider, always. Watching him race could be as exasperating as it could be exhilarating. He lost the 1985 Tour of Spain on the penultimate day, having been the outstanding rider in the race, when the Spanish teams ganged up to ensure a home victory, but also, and equally importantly, to deny Millar. He was certainly alone there. At the roadside the Spanish fans held up banners expressing their contempt for the strange Scot, for the crimes of (in no particular order) not being Spanish, wearing an earring, and having permed hair. Millar *was* different. He rubbed people up the wrong way. The director of the Tour de France nicknamed him the *asticot* – maggot – of professional cycling. To professional observers he was the 'weedy Woody Allen lookalike, with spectacles, pony tail, and balancing chips on each shoulder'; he looked 'more like a Dickensian chimney sweep' than a man who made his name and his fortune in such a brutal and unforgiving sport.

The career of Britain's best-ever cyclist ended abruptly, ignominiously, and without fanfare. His French team went bust on the eve of what would have been his twelfth Tour de France, and that was it. The end. Millar disappeared.

He didn't literally disappear, at least not at first. He hovered around the cycling scene for a few years; he was appointed British national coach, and he wrote, with flair and humour, for cycling magazines. But his spell as national coach ended just as ignominiously when he was told, less than a year into the job, that he was surplus to requirements.

In the midst of this some rumours began to swirl around Millar. Some were cruel, some were downright vicious, but they were fuelled by gossip, not least because they went unchecked by Millar. One tabloid newspaper, upon hearing the rumour that this famous cyclist might be having a sex change, camped outside his door for a week. In 2000 the story was published and Millar was, according to some who knew him, devastated. Yet, in keeping with the cyclist who had pursued his career with singular focus and stubborn self-containment, he did not respond. He said nothing.

Then he really did disappear. All his ties with the cycling world were severed. He appears to want nothing to do with the sport any more. He has next to no contact with any of the people he knew through cycling, only the occasional email – usually one or two lines, often terse, cryptic, sometimes humorous. Every year, especially before the Tour de France, hordes of people try to get in touch with Millar, wanting to speak to him about the race, or wanting him to write about it. If they ever manage to reach him – and email is the only known method – he doesn't respond.

Initially I felt a little uneasy about trying to find Robert Millar – not just the Millar of today, but the young Millar who grew up in Glasgow; who in his teenage years sought escape on his bicycle; who finally left the city for good, and used his bike to pursue a cycling career on the continent; who lived in France, on and off, for fifteen years, most of them with his wife and son, from whom he fled when his career ended in 1995; who then went to England, where he lived for several post-retirement years before disappearing from the sport and the public spotlight. Perhaps my unease came from the oft-stated understanding that you should never meet your heroes, far less try to write a book about them.

Nevertheless, I made email contact with Millar through a third party, one of only two people I knew who were still in very occasional contact with him, and who were as exasperated as others by his apparent 'disappearance'. In the initial email I floated the idea of a book, and ended with this: 'Modesty might prevent you from agreeing that such a book is overdue, but I hope you will be happy for me to progress with the project . . . in any case, I'd like to hear your initial thoughts.' I wasn't seeking Millar's approval exactly because I didn't think he'd willingly endorse a book, but the response, through the third party, was surprisingly positive. By which I mean that he didn't tell me to fuck off. Yet all it amounted to really was that he knew I was trying to write a book. He let it be known that he did not object to – or, as he put it, could not stop – a book being written about Robert Millar the cyclist. But a book about Robert Millar the cyclist was not really what I had in mind. I wanted to know what Millar was like, where the dedication (or anger) that drove him to the top of world cycling had come from. It was Robert Millar the person I really wanted to get to know.

I met people, and spoke to them about Millar. Many said the same things. Yes, he was a bit strange, eccentric, stubborn, likeable when you got to know him – and special, that was the word that kept being repeated. I lost count of the number of times a former team-mate said 'Robert's special' with a knowing, enigmatic smile. Naturally, this only made me more curious, but also slightly wary. It was a euphemism, but for what?

Then I travelled to Ninove, in Belgium, to see Allan Peiper, one of the more thoughtful and articulate of Millar's former team-mates. Initially Peiper didn't adjust well to retirement, as he explains in his autobiography. But after staring into the void of life after cycling and eventually finding a new sense of purpose, it was clear that he had been thinking quite a bit about Millar too. 'Rob was very intellectual compared to most cyclists,' said Peiper. 'He thought about life and had it figured out, to some extent, but that didn't make him any less complicated. There was anger inside him. It's the same with a lot of top sportsmen, especially top cyclists. They have some emotional chinks that create the drive to want to be good. Whether it's Lance Armstrong growing up in a trailer park, or Robert Millar growing up in Glasgow, I think for a lot of us there was a definite cause there, something that caused them to be angry. Something that made them need to succeed and prove themselves. Or just be accepted.'

For some reason, Peiper's words, and his obvious enthusiasm for the task of trying to decipher the character of his old team-mate, fired my own enthusiasm. Somehow, talking to Peiper also made me less wary, less scared of the task of trying to unravel the Robert Millar enigma. I returned to my hotel room and wrote a second email, hoping that he would reply to this one directly.

Hi Robert,

I wanted to finally email you directly rather than going through [the third party] – hope you don't mind. As you know, I'm planning to write a book about you to coincide with the Tour starting in London next year; it seems the right time given your status as Britain's best ever Tour rider.

Over the last few months I've met with quite a few people who knew you growing up in Glasgow, and others who raced with you later. I've been putting off contacting you directly, to be honest, because, although I followed your career very closely at the time, I still felt there were gaps in my knowledge. Basically, I didn't want to ask daft questions. However, now I feel that I'm getting there, and that I am less likely to ask daft questions. I really wanted to establish contact to see how – or indeed if – you would like to answer my questions. Of course I'm aware that you may have some questions for me as well, and I'd be pleased to answer them.

For your interest I am in Belgium just now and met with Allan Peiper, who spoke with great fondness of you and sends his best.

I look forward to hearing from you.

Best wishes,

Richard.

1

It's the Grit that Makes the Oyster

Glasgow is all grey. It's not that I'm ashamed of being a
Glaswegian, I most certainly am not, but abroad you find
out what you have been missing.

Robert Millar put Scotland on an international stage it had
never previously graced, but as an ambassador for the country,
and in particular for his home city of Glasgow, he could not
have done a worse job. At times it could seem, especially to
some of those he'd left behind, that he derived some perverse
satisfaction from sticking a knife into the city of his birth, or
applying a kick to its head – both appropriate metaphors for a
city that is not unfamiliar with violence.

Millar spent twenty years in Glasgow before leaving – or, as
he would have seen it, escaping. After disappearing to the continent he rarely returned for more than a few weeks at a time.
Initially he came back to his parents' home for the winter,
training with the same group of cyclists he'd trained with in
previous years, selling some of the season's racing kit, telling
stories of continental racing and its stars, against whom he was
now racing, and speaking in a French/American-tinged accent
that was markedly different to a guttural Glasgow brogue. But
after the death of his mother, Mary, in 1981, Robert's visits
home became fewer and further between.

Millar left nobody in any doubt as to why his trips home became shorter, and less frequent, until they stopped altogether. The impression of Glasgow that he shared with the wider world – 'abroad, where you find out what you have been missing' – was unequivocal, even if his own feelings towards Glasgow, and Scotland, have at times appeared ambiguous. In an interview in 1987 he blamed the weather, declaring it 'disgusting' and continuing, 'Know any place else where it rains during the day, but not at night? I like the people, not the place: grey, grey, grey. But remember, I spent the first few years of my life in the Gorbals before moving to the city outskirts – a modern housing estate built on a razed slum and fast turning back into one.' In the city where he grew up, said Millar, the first lesson learned was that 'Fellow who can't climb tree fast enough gets eaten.'

It was too much for some Glaswegians. That same year, 1987, a letter appeared in *Cycling* magazine: 'Well done, Robert, you've done it again. You have just put off many would-be visitors from coming to Glasgow. I've been listening to you moaning and whining for years now, it's pathetic. Glasgow is no worse than any other big city in Britain, and a lot better than some. Can you possibly think of anything worse to say? No – I think you've said it all. On your bike, Robert.' And when an extract of a chapter on Millar in Robin Magowan's *Kings of the Road* appeared in *Cycling*, it provoked this response from a Scottish reader: 'The suggestion that Millar was a "dead end kid" who was lucky not to be "behind bars, if not dead at 15" is amazing. Robert Millar was raised in Pollok. Unlike the Gorbals this is a very average housing estate just like any other city around the globe, and is not particularly unpleasant . . . Strange indeed that the son of an engineer, raised in an average area and educated to a high standard should be described in this way . . . I am suspicious of the seemingly verbatim quotes of Millar's, such as "I had the A- and O-levels to have gone to university." In Scotland we do not sit A-levels.'

And yet, and yet . . . 'I don't feel Scottish,' he told a journalist in 1998, 'I am Scottish.' A sense of resignation is perhaps detectable here, but also some pride – and, typically of Millar, defiance. There are other examples of his paradoxical attitude towards Scotland. In 1992, during a Tour de France that visited all the member countries of the European Union that bordered France, the riders' daily race numbers were adorned with the blue EU flag with its twelve small stars; each morning, Millar painstakingly coloured in the stars with a blue biro before scratching a cross – thus creating a Saltire, Scotland's national flag. Yet it is clear that Millar felt oppressed and held back by Glasgow and its people. Being small in height and build, in a city renowned for its proliferation of 'hard men' and its admiration for the 'big man', he might also have felt that he didn't fit in. But 'grey' was the word he seemed to prefer, using it repeatedly to describe the city. In stark contrast was Europe, colourful and alive with possibilities.

It was to Europe that he travelled, as soon as he could. When Millar arrived in that promised land, he bumped into an Australian cyclist whose ambitions, if not his middle-class upbringing, mirrored his own. Phil Anderson would later go on to become the first non-European ever to wear the yellow jersey of the Tour de France leader. But four years before that he was, like Millar, lost and alone in Paris. At the airport, Millar looked in vain for the representative from the Athlétique Club de Boulogne-Billancourt (ACBB) who had (or so he understood) been sent to meet him. When it became clear that there was no such person, Millar got a taxi to Boulogne-Billancourt, the Paris suburb where he, Anderson and four other exiles were to be barracked in apartment blocks. These were Spartan, and hardly glamorous. For Millar, the contrast with Glasgow can't have been as stark as he might have anticipated, or hoped for.

Though Millar was quiet and reserved, Anderson, who arrived in Paris from Melbourne within hours of Millar, soon learned about his new club-mate's upbringing in Glasgow. 'I remember him saying to me, early on, that he saw cycling as a way out,' says Anderson. 'For him, I think it was a way of getting out of a depressed situation. I don't think he had a very good home life or family life, and he saw cycling not so much as a way to make wealth, but a way to get out. He spoke a little bit about Glasgow and he didn't paint a very good picture; he came from the rough side of town, I think. I certainly understood, from what he told me, that he came from the wrong side of the tracks.'

There was some truth in Millar's description of Glasgow and of his upbringing. But it wasn't the whole truth. Willie Gibb, who attended secondary school with Millar, began cycling with him, and also went on to become one of Scotland's leading cyclists, winces at some of Anderson's comments. 'I wouldn't have said that he came from the wrong side of the tracks,' he says. 'Robert came from a working-class background, but it wasn't impoverished. His parents had originally lived in the Gorbals, which was a rough area of Glasgow, but they moved to Pollokshaws. It was Pollokshaws where I was born and bred. I knew his parents, I knew his sister, and I would say he probably had a similar upbringing to me. My parents were the same as his. They didn't have a lot of money, but most people lived like that then.'

The Gorbals, until parts of it were demolished and families like the Millars were moved into suburbs or out of Glasgow altogether, was notorious as one of Europe's worst slums. Millar was born there, and began primary school there, but he moved out to the suburbs – another promised land – when he was 8.

Gibb wonders if the myth of growing up in the Gorbals might have suited his old friend, then comes up with a more plausible explanation. 'I don't think he'd have gone out of his way to correct people if they had the wrong impression of his upbringing. Not because he wanted people to think that he grew up in a slum. I think it was more likely that he just didn't care what people thought.

'Another thing that I noticed was that when he did start to do really well, and he'd be interviewed on the telly, he wouldn't promote himself or Scotland. He'd say Glasgow was this grey place where it never stopped raining. That switched a lot of people off, including my father. And he started talking in this strange accent. My dad used to say, "He's been in France a year and he's got this stupid Anglo-American-French accent." God knows where that came from.'

As much as Millar tried to dismiss the city and its people, and as much as he tried to move on, it is impossible to untangle Millar and Glasgow. The more he disparaged the place with his put-downs, the more obvious it became that his relationship with it was more complex than it might appear. To begin to understand Millar, then, it is necessary to understand Glasgow, and then to ponder the question: how might a small, introverted boy, a rebellious maverick and, to use his own description, 'an individualist', have experienced growing up in such a place? Apart from learning, very early on, how to climb metaphorical trees.

If a city's character is reflected by the books that are written about it, then the image of Glasgow is unambiguous: it has a reputation as a tough, macho, often violent city dominated by the hard men of the factories, shipyards and pubs. Even today, this is the Glasgow that is depicted in many of the books displayed prominently on promotional stands in the city's airport: *Gangland Glasgow*, *Glasgow's Hard Men*, *Glasgow Crimefighter*, *Glasgow's Godfather*. Then there is the poverty, which tends to be reinforced by films (*Red Road*, *My Name is Joe*, *Small Faces*), and the reality of which is not in doubt. In Glasgow there are, and there certainly were in the 1950s and 1960s, pockets of serious deprivation, some of them among the worst in Europe.

A report in 2005 claimed that men living in some parts of Glasgow have the lowest life expectancy of anywhere in Europe. Castlemilk, Possilpark, Ruchill, the Gorbals: even for people only vaguely familiar with the city, these are names evocative of poverty, of social problems, and of violence.

Yet it is also a place renowned for the humour of its people, and for the outgoing, friendly, 'gallus' Glaswegian. On one of my visits a taxi driver gave me a running commentary as we travelled through the city. It was an alternative tourists' guide, and it was delivered in a thick, almost impenetrable accent, accompanied by resigned shakes of the head and expressive shrugs of the shoulders. If my guide's body language was anything to go by – it wasn't so easy to make out what he was actually saying – as we left one housing scheme and entered another, the city got progressively worse the further we travelled from the centre. Then we drove into a particularly bleak housing scheme, with no shops or even pubs, only high-rise flats packed tightly against one another – a 'desert with windows' as Billy Connolly, who perfectly sums up the love/hate relationship many Glaswegians have with their city, once referred to some of Glasgow's housing schemes. Here, however, there was sheet metal where many of the windows should have been. We picked up speed after narrowly avoiding a bucket of water – at least I think it was water – that appeared to have been thrown in the direction of the taxi. The driver shrugged again, scowled, and commented, 'Ah widnae let a dog oot here.' Which was funny, of course. Much Glasgow humour is delivered with a self-consciously casual attitude towards some of the uglier aspects of life there, and it is rarely accompanied by a smile. As a consequence, not everybody gets it.

This is the Glasgow that Millar professed to despise and which he was desperate to escape, but which clearly shaped his dry, often dark sense of humour, among other things. And perhaps in Millar too there was a perverse sense of pride, of kudos, in coming from and surviving such a place – from the wrong side of the tracks, as he allowed Phil Anderson to believe. The Scottish playwright John Byrne, who came from another estate, in nearby Paisley, with 'aspirations' to the title of 'worst slum in Europe', has expressed this well: 'I felt vastly superior, smugly superior, to everyone who went to art school because I came from the worst slum in Europe! We were in the thick of it.' The notion may not be far removed from another frequently levelled accusation, that there is a tendency in cities such as Glasgow to romanticize poverty and violence. But Byrne is hardly alone in suggesting that great art can flourish and that great artists can thrive in such conditions – because of, rather than despite, the environment. 'It's the grit that makes the oyster,' Byrne remarked, and so it is with sports people. You needed to be tough to survive in such a place. And as Millar quickly realized, you needed to be tough – and to be seen as tough – to make it as a cyclist, too.

Robert Millar was born to William and Mary Millar in the family home, 4 Wellcroft Place in the Gorbals area of Glasgow, at 6.15 a.m. on 13 September 1958. Mary and Bill, as he was known, already had a son, Ian, born on 29 December 1955, nine months after they were married. A daughter, Elizabeth, would follow in January 1962.

The Gorbals had once been a village on the south side of the River Clyde, separate from the sprawling city. In medieval times it was designated as Glasgow's leper colony: the leper hospital was opened in 1350, five years after the building of a first bridge to connect the village to the city. The Gorbals was annexed by Glasgow in 1846. By then its composition and character were already changing, thousands of Ireland's poor having settled there from around 1840. It wasn't yet the slum it would become, but neither was it the place it had once been. The population of the Gorbals swelled with the arrival of these immigrants, from Eastern Europe as well as Ireland, then from the 1930s by Jews fleeing the Nazis, though the influx of Jewish immigrants predated Hitler. By 1885, over half of the Gorbals' primary school population was Jewish. The Gorbals even had its own Jewish newspaper.

The Gorbals in which Millar spent the first few years of his life was bursting at the seams, its population having mushroomed to some fifty thousand by 1950. It had been fictionalized in the 1930s in an iconic Glasgow novel, *No Mean City*. As the title suggests . . . actually, it's not altogether clear what the title suggests. The subject matter was less ambiguous: it was all violence and gangs and knives, with a main character known as the 'Razor King'. Less well known but also evocative of the area is *A Gorbals Tale*, billed as 'a nostalgic and light-hearted story of post-war Gorbals', starring a policeman whose beat includes 'razor-carrying thugs, illicit bookies, drunks and prostitutes'. Our hero is thus immersed 'in the violent culture of the Gorbals – an area of grim tenement buildings with a foreboding culture of violence. Angus [the policeman] meets his first challenge when a local prostitute, Laughing Mary, is murdered. Later, when he rescues young Lilly Grant from the grip of evil shebeeners [who ran unlicensed drinking establishments], he is ambushed and savagely beaten in an act of revenge.' And this, remember, is a nostalgic and light-hearted story of the Gorbals. It is difficult to imagine what might feature in a tale of gritty reality.

But it is too easy to caricature the area; it was not so unremittingly grim. The Millars' home was typical of the area: a four-storey sandstone tenement with one large living room, a kitchen, a bedroom, and a toilet, but no bath. Many praised the elegance and grandeur of the grid-iron pattern of these four-storey tenements, and, rather than violence, the community spirit that was always so evident in the Gorbals, particularly, and despite the overcrowding, in the inter-war period. Certainly the primary school attended by Robert Millar, just around the corner and a couple of hundred metres from his front door in Wellcroft Place, was (still is) a strikingly impressive building. Abbotsford Primary School is the oldest surviving school building in the Gorbals, though it ceased to be a school in 1996. Built in 1879, the classrooms – now offices – were organized around an open central hall, above the doors the sculpted heads of eminent Scots including the Church reformer John Knox and the explorer David Livingstone. Fellow pupils at Abbotsford describe the young Robert Millar as a 'smart, funny but occasionally intense kid'. It was there that he acquired his first nickname, 'Eskimo', on account of his playground trick of pulling his blue anorak over his head while running around making a prolonged 'Wheeeeeeeee!' noise. There are few signs here of the introverted, shy persona Millar adopted later.

Millar attended Abbotsford for four years, until the family found itself subject to Glasgow Corporation's policy of 'displacement'. Notwithstanding the overcrowding, and the decay that became particularly acute between the wars, it was as much because of the Gorbals' reputation as one of Europe's worst slums that it was chosen as the first area in Glasgow to be redeveloped – i.e. demolished. As far as the Corporation was concerned, the solution to the population explosion crisis – by the early 1950s an estimated six hundred thousand of the city's 1.08 million people required rehousing – was to create new housing schemes on the periphery of the city. Communities were broken up, and some were shunted out to the new towns of East Kilbride, Cumbernauld or Irvine. For others, the only way was up. High-rise flats were, the Corporation decided, the future. They were certainly futuristic, especially in the artists' impressions – no less inaccurate, or idealistic, in the 1960s than they are now. The flats were known as 'vertical streets', which, probably intentionally, lent an air of glamour and excitement. It was to one such high-rise, in Pollokshaws, no more than a couple of miles to the south of the Gorbals, that the Millars moved in the summer of 1967 when the Wellcroft Place tenements fell victim to the wrecking ball.

I visited the 'vertical street' where Millar lived – on Shawbridge Street, in Pollokshaws – and found a twenty-two-storey tower block surrounded by quiet residential streets, and beyond them, acres of green parkland: Pollok Park. Other than the tower blocks – there are a dozen of them, jutting into the sky like sore thumbs – it is a leafy, pleasant place. And it was a pleasant place when the Millars moved there, the tower blocks modern, shiny and new. For a young child in particular it would no doubt have been an exciting place to live. The Millars occupied a flat on the eleventh floor, with views across Glasgow, the green expanse of Pollok Park and, to the west, out across rural Renfrewshire.

Many of Glasgow's tower blocks have now been knocked down, but those in Pollokshaws survive – just. Decay has set in, just as it had taken hold of the Gorbals by the 1950s, and today the blocks seem to remain standing solely to provide people seeking emergency housing with a temporary place to stay. I met a young Asian boy in the stairwell and, a little naively, asked whether anyone had lived there for any length of time. I had imagined that neighbours of the Millars might still be living there; they might even remember young Robert squeezing his bike into the metal-doored lift to take it up to his bedroom, which was where, according to neighbours, he kept it.

'Yes, there are some people who've been here a long time,' said the boy.

'Really?' I replied. 'Would anyone have been here for thirty, forty years?'

The boy smiled – out of pity, I think. 'No way! No one stays here that long. When I said long, I meant about a year.'

When the Millars moved from the Gorbals to Pollokshaws, Robert was transferred to the Sir John Maxwell Primary

School, spending three years there before moving into one of the city's more famous secondary schools, Shawlands Academy. The academy is an old sandstone building which, even today, has none of the trappings of so many other large inner-city secondary schools, some of which can be quite forbidding. There are no coils of barbed wire or broken glass encrusting the tops of the walls; no graffiti scarring the walls; no outward signs of violence, or means of deterring it. Rather, the impression is of nothing less than respectability. In fact, Shawlands is now considered one of Glasgow's most up-and-coming suburbs. The school has one dark secret, though. Robert Millar is not the only former pupil who went on to achieve fame – or, in the case of one individual, infamy.

John Martyn, the celebrated folk musician, was Millar's elder by ten years and two days. Although there is no reason other than the fact that they attended the same school to draw any comparisons between Martyn and Millar, it is impossible to resist the temptation. Martyn, like Millar, displayed a healthy disregard, verging on contempt, for authority. The future musician walked barefoot to school; the future cyclist – by now known to many of his fellow pupils as Bobby – went to war with his teachers over his insistence on wearing a denim jacket instead of the school blazer. Martyn railed against the city's obsession with football; and so, in a more subtle way, did Millar, by virtue of his preference for cycling. Like Millar, Martyn didn't really fit the Glasgow stereotype of the hard man; he was really too Bohemian and cerebral for violence. Plus, fighting might have been difficult with bare feet. He did once claim, however, that 'You went out and kicked a few heads or you were looked on as a pansy.' A more infamous ex-pupil of Shawlands Academy, to whom an especially virulent form of violence became familiar, is someone the school and the city would rather keep a secret: the Moors murderer Ian Brady. With Myra Hindley, Brady abducted and murdered five children in the

1960s, burying four of them on the moors surrounding Manchester. He also spent his early years in the Gorbals before moving out to the suburbs.

Willie Gibb confirms that the description of Millar as a 'quiet rebel' was accurate. If he was asked something in class he'd offer a yes or a no, without elaboration, even – or especially – when the teacher was looking for a little more. 'It was like he couldn't be bothered,' suggests Gibb. 'But he didn't go out his way to make trouble. I mean, he got up to mischief. There was one occasion at school when he brought a quarter bottle of Crawford's Four Star whisky and he was drinking it in the school toilet. I know, because I found him.' According to Gibb, it was not uncommon for some of the older pupils to ostentatiously display their bottles of beer at school. A delivery lorry would appear at the bowling club beside Shawlands Academy, usually loaded with crates of beer, some of which would inevitably find their way into the possession of the pupils. Fortified wine was another popular tipple. But whisky was not. In this respect, notes Gibb, 'It was typical of Robert to up the ante a little bit.' Gibb also recalls an incident that could have ended in more serious trouble. When he was 15, Millar and another friend, Tom Brodie, broke into a local joinery workshop, entering through the roof. 'But they couldn't get back out,' says Gibb with a smile. 'When the guys came and opened the shop the next day they found them and had them arrested. I think Brodie spent the night in Barlinnie [the Glasgow prison], but Robert, because he hadn't turned 16 yet, got away with it.'

At a school like Shawlands, or any state school in Glasgow, football was a core, or compulsory, activity. Alongside poverty and violence, it was an aspect of Glasgow life that was, and is, difficult to escape. To say that Glasgow is obsessed by football is like observing that in Dublin they are partial to a pint or two of Guinness. The city is both defined and divided by football, more accurately by the Celtic–Rangers rivalry and the tribalism inherent in this. It is a rivalry that has its roots in religion – Celtic represent the Catholic community, Rangers represent the Protestant community – and inevitably, games between the two halves of the 'Old Firm' have tended, historically, to perpetuate the city's violent reputation. Millar, Gibb told me, didn't feature in the school football team, but not because he couldn't play. 'Although he was skinny and small, he was strong. You couldn't knock him off the ball. He certainly wasn't bad. But he didn't seem to show a lot of interest in it.'

In fact, much like his father, whose big passion seems to have been ballroom dancing, at no stage in his life does Millar appear to have shown any interest in football, which more likely owed to a lack of interest, or rebelliousness, than to his small build. Indeed, some of the city's finest footballers have been small – Jimmy 'Jinky' Johnstone, of Celtic's 1967 European Cup-winning team, being, at 5ft 4ins, the most obvious example. Such players, though, tended to be fast as well as skilful. It is interesting that Gibb cites Millar's strength as his main attribute. As a cyclist it would be this, along with his endurance, that allowed him to excel. Millar, according to Gibb, was a decent footballer rather than an outstanding one. He could hold his own but he didn't dazzle. Moreover, he showed no interest in it – which would count as an act of rebellion in Glasgow, or at least as an example of not following the pack. When in 1985 he returned to Glasgow, having scaled the heights of the Tour de France, he was asked by the city's paper, the *Evening Times*, whether he craved more recognition in his home country. 'Football and rugby are the two main sports here so the top men must come from them,' he acknowledged. 'However, it's nice to be appreciated.'

By the 1960s, however, there was an alternative weekend pursuit to watching football. In Glasgow, as in many working-class cities throughout Europe, the bicycle was becoming a reasonably popular, if marginal, pastime. Initially it was a handy and cheap mode of transport for the working man, getting him to the factory or the shipyard, and then home, often in wobbly fashion, from the pub. And for a few, perhaps those who weren't wedded to the football culture, it also provided a means of escape at the weekends.

Surrounding Glasgow in all directions were more or less traffic-free roads that skirted spectacular lochs, climbed remote hills, hugged the coast, and delved into secluded parts of the country, all of which were perfect for cycling. Large groups of club cyclists began to meet on the outskirts of the city on Saturday and Sunday mornings to explore these roads, usually stopping for a 'drum-up' – a fire would be lit upon which soup could be heated and tea brewed – by the banks of Loch Lomond. Many of those who were drawn to cycling preferred solitude to crowds, such as football crowds. They also preferred green space to the urban environment. 'Off to find some green bits,' Millar would remark later of a 1980 photograph that showed him riding through Glasgow, heading out on a training ride. Cycling provided, literally and metaphorically, an escape for those such as Millar and another famous Glaswegian who eventually managed to move away from the city and his working-class roots, the comedian Billy Connolly.

For Connolly, humour was an effective way of surviving life as an apprentice welder in the Clyde shipyards, as well as eventually providing his means of escape. But cycling also provided him with more fleeting 'escapes'. In an interview with *The Independent* in 2000, Connolly, agreeing with the description of himself as a 'sociable loner', explained, 'I was never a joiner [of clubs or organizations]. Even when I cycled I never joined a cycling club, I just cycled around on my own and sometimes joined lines of other cyclists.' He was referring to the club runs, which were organized and designed for socializing, down to the fact that riders went two abreast, as an aid to conversation.

Indeed, contrary to the image of the cyclist as only a loner or escape artist, cycling, especially club cycling, was often a social activity that appealed to sociable types – or 'sociable loners', perhaps. The sport could therefore satisfy two apparently conflicting sides of a personality, the desire both for solitude and for mixing with others, especially those who were like-minded.

The proliferation of clubs reflected the interest in cycling in Glasgow at this time. There were touring clubs and racing clubs, men-only clubs and clubs for Christians, where Sunday rides would include a visit to church. The 1960s and 1970s constituted a peak period; the club scene has perhaps never been stronger. Jimmy Dorward, a leading light in this club scene for more than five decades, compares the clubs to clans. When, as a young boy, he showed an interest in joining a club he was told simply to ride up to Loch Lomond on a Sunday and find the spot where that club met. Each club had a different and clearly defined 'drum-up' spot by the banks of the loch. Dorward went in search of the Douglas club but couldn't find them. 'I found the Clarion instead and ended up joining them,' he recalls. 'The Douglas, which had been a very strong club, took a nosedive after that.' Smiling, he adds: 'But I don't think that had anything to do with me not joining them.

'Cycling was a way of life for a lot of people. It was more than a sport, and there was a tremendous social aspect. If you wanted to join a club you just turned up at the "drum" and someone would come and speak to you. If the newcomer got dropped [left behind] there was always someone who'd look out for them and go back for them. After the drum-up the scraps would start; in these big groups of thirty, forty or fifty, we'd race back to Glasgow and it would be every man for himself. But someone would still look out for the newcomer. You'd say, "Just stay with me, I'll get you back." And there was tremendous club loyalty. If you were even seen cycling with another club you'd be asked what you were doing. You'd be seen as a traitor.'

One of Robert Millar's first cycling expeditions, before he became involved in the club scene, was when he was only 11, in the company of three friends, among them Willie Gibb, who had been inspired to take up cycling by the example of his racing father. The youngsters cycled away from Pollokshaws in the direction of East Kilbride, around ten miles away, though Gibb turned home early while the remaining trio of intrepid 11-year-olds continued in an easterly direction, with the benefit of a generous tailwind. It wasn't just the stiff headwind that made things difficult on the way back. There was also the matter of taking the wrong road, which meant they came back into Glasgow through Rutherglen. To them, it might as well have been a different city. When they managed to stumble upon Bridgeton they were able to find their way home, late, but with their parents none the wiser.

It was with Gibb and Tom Brodie that Millar began to cycle on a more regular basis. 'We used to run about on bikes that were like Raleigh Choppers,' remembers Gibb. 'We were on bikes all the time.' The three young cyclists began to venture out of the city with greater frequency. They were beginning to enjoy going far and fast, and an element of competition was being introduced, not through racing one another but thanks to the buses that trundled up and down the main road to Ayr, a seaside town thirty miles south of Glasgow. 'At that time the buses were pretty slow,' explains Gibb, 'so we used to tuck in behind them, sheltering in their slipstream. They could probably get up to about forty miles an hour, but they had no acceleration. So you could get in behind them as they left the bus stop and sit behind them all the way to Kilmarnock [twenty miles away] or even as far as Ayr, then turn around and catch another bus back to Glasgow.'

The bicycles were put to other uses as well, such as fishing. Illegal fishing, naturally. Gibb knew of a small loch owned by a syndicate comprising some of the movers and shakers of

Glasgow society – 'legal folk, judges, people like that'. 'We'd go up and do all-nighters, especially during the school holidays,' he recalls. 'It would get light about three in the morning. We used to cycle there with our fishing rods strapped to the top tube of our bikes, and then hide the bikes in the long reeds. The loch was about eight or nine miles from where we lived. We caught loads of good-sized brown trout. There was an old folks' home near where I lived and I'd keep a couple of fish myself then give the rest to the old folks. I don't know what Robert did with his. The old folk never asked where they came from.'

One of the early stories that attached itself to Millar as he climbed the cycling ladder was the claim that he had become hooked on the sport of cycling after seeing the Tour de France on a television in a shop window. It's a story that has been told and retold, but it isn't true. In fact, Millar set the record straight as early as 1984. 'That [story] upset me because it made it sound as if I lived in a cave,' he said. 'It made out that as I came from Glasgow I was poor and depressed.' As Gibb confirms, it wasn't by watching the Tour de France but simply through riding his bike with friends that Millar became interested in the sport. In the same interview in 1984, in *Cycling*, Millar described his first bike as 'a wreck: it was made from plumber's tubing. I used to paint it every six months or so.'

When they were 15, Millar, Gibb and Brodie enquired about joining a cycling club at Riddle Cycles, a shop situated in the shadows of Hampden Park, the national football stadium, that was owned by a couple of elderly brothers, always immaculately turned out in brown overalls. It was the Eagle Road Club the trio had their hearts set on; they were impatient to race, and the Eagle had a reputation as one of Glasgow's top racing clubs. The Riddles put them in touch with Jim Paton, the Eagle Road Club's treasurer, but when Paton met them they were left, according to Gibb, feeling 'dismayed'. Paton told them that to go straight into a racing club would be too big a leap; to go from chasing buses up the Ayr road to mixing it with racing men would be sheer folly. But Paton wasn't discouraging. He was also a member of the Cyclists' Touring Club, and advised that the boys join another local club, the CTC-affiliated Glenmarnock Wheelers, instead. They might have felt disappointed and frustrated, but they took Paton's advice.

The Glenmarnock club, which had been established in 1941, owed its popularity, especially among those just starting out in the sport, to John Storrie. Storrie had just turned 50 when he first encountered the 15-year-old Millar, but the small, skinny boy was one of many who received their first cycling lessons under Storrie's tuition. Though the three boys came to the club via Jim Paton's recommendation, Storrie favoured a direct approach to recruitment. While out cycling he would approach youngsters on their bikes, ask them if they enjoyed their cycling and whether they might be interested in joining a club. Then he would give them his business card. It is unlikely that such methods would be successful now, or even acceptable. As Storrie himself says: 'That probably wouldn't be allowed nowadays. Someone would complain. But I just wanted to introduce them to the bike.'

Most of the boys who joined the Glenmarnock, like Millar, Gibb and Brodie, wanted to race, and were impatient to do so. But for Storrie the club scene, and the ritual of the weekly club run, was just as important. It provided an informal education. It was where youngsters could learn how to cycle in a group, riding two abreast and sticking as close as possible to the back wheel of the rider in front in order to gain shelter and conserve energy for when it was their turn to take the pace at the front. When they stepped up to road racing, in large bunches of cyclists, the experience of training in a group would stand them in good stead.

The club runs were largely ordered, organized outings governed by an informal code of etiquette. To many newcomers to the sport the first club run can be quite intimidating, the experience of riding in such close proximity to other cyclists a nerve-shredding ordeal. And there had not so far been any obvious signs that Millar was blessed with a gift for cycling. Of the three friends, it was Tom Brodie who appeared to be the strongest, perhaps on account of his being a little older, and physically much bigger than the other two. Yet when all three joined the Glenmarnock Wheelers it became clear that it wasn't just Brodie who had talent. Millar, his speed and bike-handling skills perhaps honed by chasing the rear bumpers of buses up and down the Ayr road, appeared to take to the club runs like a duck to water. 'We quickly realized that we were as strong and fast as a lot of the guys who were racing quite regularly,' said Gibb. 'That came as a surprise to us.'

Gibb states that Millar, at this time, displayed none of the aloofness or the reluctance to engage with people that he showed later – at least not with him or Brodie. 'It was a different kind of relationship he had with us than with most people. I'm not saying it was better or worse, but I think he was more relaxed in our company because we did so much cycling together. We did other things – going to the park, climbing into people's gardens, stealing apples, all those kinds of things – but we just really enjoyed riding around on our bikes.'

Ten years after Millar's induction to cycling, when he had already started to shine in the Tour de France, John Storrie wrote to *Cycling* magazine recalling his first impressions of Millar. 'He was not a hooligan,' he said, 'but the best way to describe him at that age was that he was the "James Dean of cycling" – a bit of a rebel, but with one cause in mind: cycling. Like James Dean, he had a dislike for authority, probably stemming from his school days. He was not happy at work [Millar started an engineering apprenticeship after leaving school] but he could not take his mind off cycling. Cycling was in his thoughts night and day.' Even so, when Jimmy Dorward came to give a lecture to the club, Storrie noted that 'it was typical of Robert's make-up that when it came to the technical part he became bored and had to be told off for reading *Cycling* in the middle of the lecture'. Storrie concluded his article by stating that the youngster was 'quite a loner and conversation was confined to a few words'.

Storrie, now in his early eighties, suffered a stroke in 2002. While he struggles to recall some recent events his memories of the young Millar remain vivid. In particular he remembers some of the quirks of his personality. 'When he first appeared he was a raw boy, a rough boy,' he says. 'He had shoulder-length hair, which no one else had at the time. He liked to be different. He was very quiet. He didn't make friends easily. On the club runs we would have drum-ups by the side of Loch Lomond, so we'd all stop and make a fire and sit down together. But Robert would go away on his own, maybe fifty yards away, and light his own fire. He did that every time. I didn't try to bring him into the group. I just let him get on with it. We joked about him wanting to be on his own but he never gave us an explanation. I don't remember him not liking people; he was just a loner.'

Jimmy Dorward, who was running the Scotia club at the time and encountered Millar on occasional club runs, recalls a similar incident. 'We stopped for the drum-up and the young lads arrived with Robert Millar,' he explains. 'We got the fire going, and after a while I realized Millar wasn't there. "Where's Millar?" I asked. "Oh, he's away," someone said. That was unheard of. If you went to a club's drum-up you collected a few sticks and when you left you said, "Thanks for the drum." But that was Millar's nature. He just drifted off.'

Another strange episode that Storrie remembers was a club run that ended with a stop on a private beach by the banks of the Lake of Menteith, around twenty miles north of Glasgow. It was a glorious summer's day and Storrie, having obtained the permission of the house owner, allowed his young charges to go swimming. The condition stipulated by the land owner was that they behaved themselves, and all complied, except one: the rebel. While everyone else stripped off and went swimming, Millar kept his racing clothing on and stepped into the water until it was up to his knees. 'He was a devil,' says Storrie, smiling now. 'He collected a pile of stones, holding them in his jersey, and he started throwing them at the boats. He kept throwing stones into one boat; he had so many stones in his jersey that I thought he was going to sink it. I kept saying "Robert, stop that!" but he just laughed. I couldn't get a word out of him. Eventually I paddled out to where he was and tipped him into the water. He wasn't happy. He came out the water shouting, "They were my fucking good cycling shorts!" They were soaking wet.'

Storrie declares himself unsure whether Millar might have got into more serious trouble had cycling not provided an outlet for his energy, allowing him to channel his rebellious streak. But he does point out that Millar would not be unique had he been 'saved' by cycling. 'That was the good thing about what I was doing. I was taking people away on the bike, getting them out of Glasgow, away from trouble. It was the ambition of a lot of kids to own a bike and I let them come along whatever bike they had. Some clubs would have said, "Away you go, that's not suitable." But if someone came out with us, as long as they could pedal, I'd let them come. I made allowances. I waited for them at the top of a hill. Others didn't.'

The other thing Storrie remembers is Millar's burgeoning ability as a cyclist, in particular his apparent fondness for hills. 'When you hit a hill he loved to jump away and get up it first. He was competitive. He was naturally strong, really outstanding.'

Though he could be difficult, Storrie retains fond memories of the teenaged Millar, and even fonder ones of watching his career blossom on the biggest stage of all, the Tour de France. As he wrote in *Cycling* in 1984, 'What a great thrill it was to see

Robert on TV in 1983, winning the Pyrenean stage, then winning the same stage in 1984 against heavy odds . . . I am not ashamed to say that I shed tears of emotion as he danced away to victory, and even now, on the video re-run, I still get glassy-eyed. Knowing Millar, I can safely say, quoting Al Jolson, "We ain't seen nothin' yet."'

2

Mammy's Boy

Once you stop school there's nothing to do. I had the [exams]
to have gone to university. For what – an engineering degree?
Like my dad, they're all on the dole.

Robert Millar walked out of the large iron gates of Shawlands
Academy for the final time on 27 May 1975, at the age of 16. He
had spent five years at the school and had just completed his
'Highers' – Scotland's equivalent of A levels – performing well
enough in those exams to earn a three-year engineering
apprenticeship at Weir's Pumps, a sprawling factory in
Cathcart on the eastern fringes of Glasgow that provided
employment for a few thousand young men – almost exclusively
men. Willie Gibb remembers his classmate as 'not studious' but
'smart', 'able to pass exams without really trying'.

By then the Millar family had moved up in the world, not
literally but metaphorically, having swapped the eleventh floor
of the high-rise flat in Shawbridge Street for 73 Nithsdale
Drive, a ground-floor flat in a sandstone tenement building
that is a copy of a design by the nineteenth-century Glasgow
architect Alexander 'Greek' Thomson. Today it's a B-listed
building, and the flats, with their views towards the north of
Glasgow and the Campsie Hills, are much sought after. If it was
a Thomson original, like the building housing flats around the

corner, they'd be even more sought after. 'You can't touch them without permission from Rome,' joked one of the Millars' old neighbours when I paid a visit to 73 Nithsdale Drive.

Millar had also graduated from the Glenmarnock Wheelers club runs to full-blown racing, riding time trials and mass-start road races. Though race outings were still comparatively rare – he said later that he competed in only four events in his first year's racing – he seemed, after finishing 'sixth and last' in his first ever race, to make rapid progress. Three months after leaving school he achieved his most significant result so far, if only for the fact that it gained him his first name check in the publication that had proved such a distraction in the classroom and in what he considered to be dull lectures: *Cycling* magazine. For cyclists aged between 16 and 18 it was the biggest date on the calendar, the national junior road race championship, held over forty-two miles on a circuit in Dundee, some seventy miles to the north-east of Glasgow. The race was won by a rider who was a year older than Millar, and who at that time dominated the junior racing scene in Scotland. Bobby Melrose of the Nightingale Cycling Club sprinted in at the head of a small group of riders, leading for the final two hundred yards and crossing the line a convincing three lengths clear. In fourth place, just out of the medals but in the same time as Melrose, was, reported *Cycling* on 16 August, R. Miller (*sic*) of Glenmarnock Wheelers. Sixth was Tom Brodie, given the same time of one hour, fifty-two minutes and fifteen seconds. It would be around eighteen months before *Cycling* consistently began to spell Millar's name correctly.

By this stage Millar had also started training on Saturdays with a group known as the Anniesland Bunch (it still meets, incidentally, every Saturday at 10 a.m, at Anniesland Cross, riding a circuit of between seventy and eighty miles known as the 'Three Lochs', taking in Loch Goil, Loch Long and Loch Lomond). One of the regulars in the Anniesland Bunch was another rider who was showing considerable promise, and who was a year younger than Millar. His name was David Whitehall. Whitehall remembers Millar appearing at the meeting point at Anniesland Cross and having him pointed out. 'I remember someone saying, "There's that new guy, Robert Millar from the Glenmarnock,"' shrugs the quietly spoken Whitehall. 'Right away you could see that he had a bit of power. He didn't have much experience following the wheels in the group, but after a few weeks it shone through that he had class.'

Another member of the group was Ian Thomson, a strong rider in the 1960s and 1970s who also served as Scotland's national team manager between 1969 and 1986. Thomson recalls his first impression of the 16-year-old Millar. 'At the bottom of the old Whistlefield, a steep climb fairly near the start of the Three Lochs, he just took off. I thought, "Who is this kid?" There were forty or fifty of us out in the group – the roads were quiet in those days – and on this steep climb this boy took off and immediately put five or six lengths into us. It was February or March. And it was a miserable day, I remember that.'

Gibb says that Brodie was still the strongest of the three friends, but he was beginning to sense a change in Millar's attitude towards cycling. He had been bitten by the racing bug. While Gibb and others would attach panniers to their bikes and pedal out of the city on touring and youth hostelling excursions at weekends, for Millar, cycling quickly became centred on training and racing rather than riding for fun. Although he hadn't been studious at school, he applied his brain to this training, and to plotting the progression of his cycling career. It was natural, then, that he should turn to Billy Bilsland.

In 1997, after he had retired, a tribute to Millar's career was paid by *Cycle Sport* magazine in the form of an issue devoted to, and guest-edited by, Millar. In it, he was asked who had been the biggest single influence in his career, and he named two people, Arthur Campbell and Billy Bilsland. 'Arthur helped me find a team and meet the right people, while Billy was my first serious coach. Just saying "thank you" doesn't seem enough when I think of how much they've helped me.'

Campbell's first encounter with Millar was on a Sunday club run in, to the best of his memory, early 1976. He certainly remembers being struck by both Millar's natural ability and his reticence. 'It was a hard, hard Sunday. Billy was there; a lot of the best riders in the west of Scotland were there. It was harder than a race! Robert and Willie Gibb turned up, we met in the centre of Glasgow, and I said to them, "Be careful." We rode to the highest village in Scotland, Wanlockhead, and after that, climbing up Glen Taggart, he was beside me. The road went up and up, and I said, "Go easy, son, this is really too far for you" – it was about 120 miles. And he just rode away from me, never said a word.' Campbell still seems perplexed by the Millar enigma. 'Was it shyness? I don't know. I always tried to analyse it myself. Most people couldn't put up with it, or you got the idea that he couldn't put up with you. One got the impression that he didn't suffer fools – at all, not even gladly. I don't think anybody got to know him.'

Bilsland, who is married to Campbell's daughter, was a giant of the Scottish scene, with stage wins in the 1967 Peace Race (held behind the Iron Curtain and known as the world's toughest amateur race), the Milk Race and the Tour de l'Avenir. By the time he emerged Ken Laidlaw was still the only Scot ever to have finished the Tour de France, in 1961; only one other, Ian Steel, had even started the great race; indeed, only a handful of Scots had ever gone to the continent and not returned within a season, their bodies – and confidence – shattered. It is a measure of Bilsland's ability, as well as his mental fortitude, that he stayed for seven years and only missed out on riding the Tour in the most bizarre circumstances. He turned professional for Peugeot in 1970 but when he failed to make the team for the 1971 Tour de France he returned, disappointed, to Britain. Then one of the riders selected instead of Bilsland suffered an injury. A letter was dispatched to his Paris address but he never saw it. He read about his selection in a newspaper, returned immediately to Paris, but he was too late. By then a young Frenchman, Bernard Thevenet, had been selected instead. It proved a stepping stone for him: Thevenet went on to win the Tour twice in the mid-seventies, while Bilsland, who rode for Peugeot for three years, never did get his chance at the Tour.

It is impossible not to wonder how different Bilsland's career might have been if only his Peugeot team had managed to contact him. But Bilsland would prefer not to. 'I don't talk about that,' he says. And the silence that follows suggests he's not joking.

Despite that disappointment he enjoyed a relatively long and moderately successful professional career on the continent, finally retiring and returning to Glasgow for good in 1976, when he was still only 30. Bilsland was a renowned hard man, able to survive any race, no matter how tough. He didn't win many of them, but it hardly mattered. Such riders were of great value to the continental professional teams, where they fulfilled the role of *domestique*, or team helper. In his seven years on the continent Bilsland was a much-respected *domestique* for the Peugeot team before moving to the Dutch-based TI Raleigh squad. Coincidentally, his protégé Millar would go on to ride for both teams in their later guises.

Millar first encountered Bilsland in the winter of 1975, at a circuit training class. The following year, with Millar feeling that he had outgrown the Glenmarnock Wheelers, the pair talked. Millar felt ready to move up to the next step, and the next step, as he saw it, was the Glasgow Wheelers. Bilsland's connections with the club, as well as those of Arthur Campbell, the president of the British Cycling Federation and a leading light in the world governing body, the Union Cycliste Internationale (UCI), convinced Millar that a move to the

Glasgow Wheelers would allow him to climb the rungs of the ladder he could now see in front of him, stretching all the way to the continent and, eventually, the Tour de France. It was at this time that he and Willie Gibb went their separate ways, though Gibb also said goodbye to John Storrie and the Glenmarnock Wheelers and joined another club, the Regent CC. Tom Brodie, meanwhile, went with Millar to the Glasgow Wheelers, though his racing career was destined never to reach full flight.

Gibb says that by this stage it was obvious to him that Millar was determined 'to give cycling a right good go'. They still cycled together, but there was no more chasing buses down the Ayr road, or all-night fishing trips. Millar was not one to talk openly about his ambitions, but Gibb remembers that 'he started to come up with all these changes to our training. Robert read a lot of books, but there was one in particular, *Cycle Racing: Training to Win* by Les Woodland. He followed what was in that to the letter.' When Gibb recalls the severity of these sessions it can bring him out in a cold sweat, even now. 'When I think back to the training we did, it was way over the top. It was brutal. We were basically over-training, but because we were young we were able to do it and recover from it. Robert was doing all kinds of weight training – he was getting some guidance from Billy Bilsland by now – and I just did the same as him. We did a lot of double sessions, training during the day and again in the evening.' Gibb was a strong rider himself, representing Scotland at the 1982 Commonwealth Games and winning several national championships. He retired from racing in the mid-eighties to concentrate on earning a living. Then, in the mid-nineties, having established a successful career in the electronics industry, he made a comeback. 'I tried to do the same kind of training that I'd done with Robert in the 1970s,' he says, 'but I couldn't do it. I couldn't cope with the intensity of it.'

By 1976 Millar was racing every weekend and, though still a junior, he was placing regularly in the top three, even in events open to senior riders. After several near-misses he scored his first win on 15 May in the Chryston Wheelers fifty-six-mile road race; two weeks later he won his second bunched race, the Glasgow Road Club fifty-mile road race. In August, in the junior road race championship, he improved from fourth twelve months earlier to first, 'justifying his Billy Bilsland training', according to *Cycling*, 'with an inches victory from Dave Whitehall, Ivy CC, in the championship over 45 miles in Aberdeen'. He was still appearing as 'Miller', and perhaps here, in his apparent unwillingness to point out the mistake to the *Cycling* correspondent, was the first example of his reluctance to engage with the media. Whitehall gained revenge on his rival in the time trial Best All-Rounder (BAR) competition, which was decided by a rider's best times over twenty-five and fifty miles. A missing marshal in a time trial in Glasgow cost Millar a chance to overhaul Whitehall, an incident that 'prompted a furious outburst from Arthur Campbell'.

By now Campbell and Bilsland had seen Millar's potential and were beginning to assume mentoring roles. 'I had just stopped racing so I went out training with Robert and the boys,' says Bilsland. 'My wife and I didn't have kids at that time, so Robert would come and stay with us before races, and we'd be up early in the morning and away.' To this day, Millar is the only rider who has enjoyed such close attention from Bilsland. Despite his years on the continent, in the tough school of professional racing, Bilsland has rarely actively sought to help promising young Scottish cyclists, though he has remained involved with the sport through his bike shop in the east end of Glasgow, and by holding various roles with his beloved Glasgow Wheelers. He has been the club chairman for more than a decade. The most likely reason for his reluctance to mentor other riders is that he would be too realistic about their chances. He knew that most, if they tried their luck abroad, would fail, and fail spectacularly. He didn't want to waste his time, or theirs. But in Robert Millar he very quickly identified someone who would not fail.

There is a parallel here with Millar himself. As his professional career blossomed he quietly helped several young Scottish cyclists to find clubs or teams on the continent, but there was only one who seemed to enjoy Millar's unqualified support. His name was Brian Smith, and, while not enjoying as spectacular a career as Millar, Smith did ride as a professional for the best part of a decade, the high point of which was a season with the American Motorola squad alongside a young Lance Armstrong. Millar's attitude appeared to be identical to Bilsland's. For both men, a sense of realism prevailed, and at times that could be devastating for those whose dreams were crushed by a cold, hard dose of it – such as me and my fellow young cyclists when, at the training camp in Stirling in 1989, Millar advised us not to ask him about the Tour de France because it wasn't 'relevant' to us. But underpinning this apparently insensitive remark was the conviction of someone who knew what he was talking about, and knew he was right.

When he was in his late teens, on the other hand, Millar seemed convinced that he would be different – that he knew how to make it, and would succeed if he applied certain principles. In an interview in 1991, Bilsland observed, 'Millar was one in a million. He always knew where he was going.' He had, he added, 'an inner hardness'. Bilsland's conviction on this point has not changed in the years since then. 'From day one he said he wanted to go to the continent and turn professional,' he says. 'That was his aim. And it's always easier if your father's gone before you.' When pressed on his use of the word 'father', Bilsland rejects the suggestion that he was a father figure to Millar. 'Not really, because I wasn't that much older than him,' he explains. 'It was more a case of me saying to him, "Any way

I can help you, I will."' Bilsland must have been fond of Millar. 'Yeah, I like him. I think he's a great guy.'

Bilsland speaks in the present tense sometimes, at other times referring to his former protégé as if he is no longer around. The reason is that he is uncertain about the current state of their relationship. Like everyone else, and despite their previous closeness, he has no idea where Millar is. He has heard rumours, but nothing concrete, and nothing from Millar himself. When Millar was inducted into the Scottish Sports Hall of Fame in 2003 it was Bilsland who attended the ceremony on his behalf, at the request of the organizers. He didn't hear from Millar, and he still has the small trophy presented to Millar, in absentia, on the night. Yet he remains fiercely protective of someone he remembers with great fondness. So much so that when I initially contacted him he refused to talk about him. 'Robert's a private person,' was Bilsland's response. 'He wouldn't want a book written about him.' Although no one else refused to discuss Millar, I did sense, in the case of one or two of his old acquaintances, an initial hesitation, and guardedness. Some seemed to want to protect Millar, though from what, and for what reason, they did not know. That much became clear when they all asked the same questions. Where is he? What's he doing?

Bilsland's refusal to talk about his former protégé, however, was a big problem. And one of the difficulties, quite apart from the fact that I considered his input essential, was that I could see his point. Millar had given his consent to my writing a book by email through a third party, which, I had to admit, hardly constituted a ringing endorsement. But it was all I had, it was all I was likely to get; and I felt strongly that the story of Britain's greatest ever cyclist, the man who had single-handedly turned thousands of us on to the sport, deserved to be written. Bilsland's knockback was therefore a hard blow. So I wrote to him, outlining my plans for the book and the motivation that lay behind it – and thankfully, he relented. When we met, he couldn't have been more helpful.

Neither could he have been more convincing in his respect and admiration for Millar. He appears genuinely upset by some of the stories that have circulated around Millar, particularly in relation to his legendary inability to get on with people. 'I never found that,' Bilsland insists. 'He was shy, and OK, to try to speak to him was like drawing teeth sometimes, but I could chat to him. When he came home for the winter he always came into the shop [Billy Bilsland Cycles] and he could be chatty.' And anyway, suggests Bilsland, to focus on how Millar interacted with people who in many cases were complete strangers is to completely miss the point – or the point of his cycling career at least. 'Robert did it for himself,' he says. 'He didn't do it for adulation.' And then he adds, making a clear distinction between romantic notions – or delusions – of the sport and the cold reality of the business of professional cycling, 'Robert did it for money, which might be the root of all evil, but it's handy to have.'

Bilsland is matter-of-fact rather than sentimental. A well-built, stocky man who turned 60 in 2006, he is cheerful and friendly. He has a permanent twinkle in his eye and he laughs a lot, a silent laugh that begins deep in his stomach and eventually overcomes him, causing his shoulders to shake. But while he appears more genial and good-humoured than Millar, he can be a straight talker, too. 'Robert didn't suffer fools, never did,' he says. 'Big words were a thing with Robert. He doesn't do bullshit. Some people are egotistic, but Robert didn't have a big ego. I can imagine him now, wherever he is, if he meets someone out on his bike and they say, "You do a bit of cycling?" He'll say, "Aye, I do a bit of cycling." That would be it. End of conversation. He's a downbeat, unassuming guy. A very bright guy. When I think about chatting to him, he was just a good guy. It's a pity.'

'If you speak to Robert, tell him I'm still alive,' he smiles when I leave him at the station in Glasgow.

Apart from Bilsland, Millar was also hugely reliant on his father, Bill, for transport to races. However, although he was close to his mother, his relationship with his father was, by all accounts, strained. Those who knew the family say that father and son were similar: physically small, slightly built, quiet. Bill walked with a limp, often with the aid of a walking stick, as a result of polio.

'Robert was a great mammy's boy,' says Arthur Campbell. 'His father had a bit of a limp and I think he was a bit . . . I wouldn't say Robert was disgraced by it, but he didn't appear to have the same respect for his father as he did for his mother. His mum was a seamstress, and she never kept very well.' Willie Gibb gently disputes Campbell's suggestion, recalling journeys to London and Manchester with Bill Millar at the wheel. 'He was good,' says Gibb. 'He went out of his way to help Robert. He was a quiet guy but helpful. I never picked up that Robert was embarrassed by his father's limp, though he didn't always appear grateful for the help he gave him. I think it could be as simple as the fact that his father would have been the sterner of his parents, the disciplinarian of the family. Robert wouldn't have liked that.'

David Whitehall remembers one exchange between Robert and his father at a race in Aberdeen to which Bill had driven. 'Robert seemed ashamed to be seen with him; he'd kind of usher him away. It was like his father was the delivery man, taking him to races, and then that was his work done until it was time to drive him home. I remember he put the wrong wheels on Robert's bike. Robert was furious. "Dad, you put on the wheels with the big tubs [tyres]!" He gave him a right dressing down. And his dad just took it, you know, in a mea culpa type way. He'd kind of be saying, "You know what Robert's like." Others found it quite awkward.'

Neighbours of the Millars on Nithsdale Drive remember Bill with affection. Contrary to Millar's quote at the head of this chapter, they don't recall him ever being out of work. Rather, he had risen from being an ironmonger's assistant at the time of Millar's birth to become a salesman. Describing Bill Millar as the 'perfect neighbour' and 'always well dressed, very dapper', they explained that his passions were ballroom dancing – which he did with aplomb, despite his limp – and gardening. He tended a small patch in front of the Millars' flat. Though quiet, he was cheerful, he could be outgoing, and he was, according to those neighbours, 'quite proud of his boy'.

Bill Millar was occasionally sought by the media for a comment as his son's career blossomed, though he didn't appear to be effusive. When in 1984 Robert really hit the heights in the Tour de France his father was approached by Channel 4 and asked for a reaction. 'We tried to get his father to give comment,' recalls the Channel 4 commentator, Phil Liggett, 'but he said, "I've got more children than just the one who rides the Tour de France. It's very good that he's done it, but I like my other children just as much." It was a strange interview. His dad didn't seem to want to know.' Even later, when a journalist phoned the house to arrange an interview with his son, Bill Millar replied, 'He is difficult . . . you had better check with Robert himself.'

It is possible, perhaps, to read too much into Millar's apparent behaviour towards his father, particularly since most of the anecdotes date from when Millar was a teenager. It is not unknown for teenagers to be unpleasant towards their parents, after all. Millar was perhaps no worse, or better, than Harry Enfield's horrific adolescent creation Kevin the Teenager. Nonetheless, in the few words Millar ever uttered about his family, when he was well into his twenties, he could be disarmingly frank about his poor relationship with his father. In 1984, in an interview with Jean-Marie Leblanc, then a journalist but the future director of the Tour de France, he was asked if he'd had the support of his family when he left Scotland for France. 'More or less,' Millar replied. 'In fact, I have never got on very well with my father and I decided to live my life as I wanted. I only go back to Scotland for a few days each year since my mother died. Eventually, I won't go back at all. I will live in Australia or Canada, or I may stay in France, where the standard of living is better than in Britain.'

Speaking in 1985, four years after the death of his mother, he told a film crew that her loss had come as 'a bit of a let down'. *The High Life* was a documentary about Millar made by Granada TV and broadcast on the eve of the 1986 Tour de France, and in a sequence filmed so late that it almost didn't make the final cut, Millar finally opened up about his family. 'I was a lot closer to my mother than I was – than I am – to my father,' he said. 'I don't know if that's natural, or what. In our family it was like that.' He looked down and quietly added, 'Kind of a disappointment.' Then the heavily furrowed brow was replaced by a nervous smile. 'I don't really miss my family much.'

'So your mother never saw you reaching the heights?' asked the film's director, Peter Carr.

'Nuh . . . nuh,' Millar responded. 'I saw my father when I went home to race but I might only see him twice a year if I go home again in the winter. I don't really . . . I don't really miss him that much. I have my life here and it's like a different thing. It's like going home to something else. It's like being on holiday.'

The camera lingered on Millar as he stared silently at the ground. A smile flickered across his face but the heavy furrow and the frown quickly returned. Today, Carr, who spent the best part of a year making *The High Life*, remembers Millar as 'enigmatic, mysterious, laconic . . . I thought he was troubled'.

As for Millar's brother, Ian, and sister, Elizabeth, only scraps are known. Ian worked with Robert at Weir's Pumps, David

Whitehall recalls, though he found this out quite by chance. 'His brother was the opposite personality, and I knew him, but I didn't know he was Robert's brother. Robert never told me; he never spoke about his family at all. One day someone said, "You know that's Robert's brother?" He was quite open and outgoing, quite friendly.' Several of Millar's cycling friends met his sister, to whom he was closer in age and, according to Gibb, virtually identical in appearance. Elizabeth trained as a nurse and got married. 'I remember when his sister got married,' says Whitehall. 'Robert didn't go to the wedding because he was doing his weight training that night. There was only me and one other guy who he spoke to at work, and it was this other lad who told me. The wedding was in January, I remember that, so it wasn't even during the season. I mean, you could understand if it was in June or something . . . But there was more to it than him snubbing his sister's wedding. It was an excuse not to go, I think. He didn't relish social situations. Even cycling club prize presentation dinners. He was just very shy.'

Following the death of Millar's mother, Mary, in 1981, Bill Millar remarried and moved out of Glasgow, to the small town of Kirkintilloch, a few miles north of the city, by the Campsie Hills, where he died in the early 1990s. Several people told me that Elizabeth still lives in Glasgow, working as a nurse. Billy Bilsland said that she called into his shop a couple of years ago, but he had no idea how to find her. She was married – though the marriage ended – and possibly no longer uses the Millar name. My efforts to find Elizabeth and Ian included dispatching more than two hundred emails through the Friends Reunited website, which drew many replies but only one positive response. 'You were fortunate to find me,' read the email. 'I knew the Millars very well. Elizabeth was a close friend of mine for a long time and Ian was best man at my wedding in 1981 . . . We all stayed in Wellcroft Place in the Gorbals and [attended] Abbotsford Primary . . . Ian now lives in the Aberdeenshire area and I keep in touch with a Christmas card every year. I have his address if you need it. I think Elizabeth still stays in Glasgow, but as I said, I don't know where Robert is now.'

I wrote to Ian Millar on two occasions, but he didn't respond. Had I managed to speak to either Ian or Elizabeth, I would have asked them about Millar's paradoxical relationship with his father, who, by most accounts, was a pleasant, gentle, even docile man. Yet he was also his father, and therefore a figure of authority. And, given that Millar seemed predisposed from an early age to dislike and distrust authority figures, Bill might not have needed to be especially strict, or very much of a disciplinarian, to earn his younger son's disapproval. The question is, was Millar's personality forged through his difficult relationship with his father, or did his relationship with his father become strained because of his attitude towards authority figures? It might be revealing, in this context, to note that those who knew something of the three siblings report that neither Ian nor Elizabeth shared Robert's hostility towards authority figures, or, for that matter, towards their father. They were, in the words of one, 'pretty normal and easy-going in comparison with Robert'.

I do not know whether there was any specific cause for the rift in Millar's relationship with his father, and those who knew him – Bilsland, Campbell, Gibb, Whitehall – are confident there wasn't. My inclination is to agree, and to conclude that Millar's indifference towards his father was simply Robert Millar being Robert Millar. He was fiercely independent, and he wanted to be seen as being independent, so what better way to assert your independence, especially at a young age, than to alienate your father?

It was towards the end of the 1976 season, Millar's first with the Glasgow Wheelers and his first under the tutelage of Billy Bilsland, that he started to produce the results that would gain him wider attention. It was one thing to win the junior road race title, quite another to finish second in a field containing the best senior riders in the country in one of the classic time trials held at the tail end of the season. On 9 October, in torrential rain and heavy mist, the Tour of the Trossachs, a twenty-seven-mile hilly time trial that climbed the Duke's Pass by Aberfoyle, was won by Sandy Gilchrist, one of the stars of the British amateur scene. Millar, who had turned 18 the previous month, was second. This and other results earned him a call-up to the Scottish senior squad for the following season. Also in that squad were Gilchrist and Bobby Melrose, another young rider, who became Millar's regular training partner.

Melrose and Millar were drawn together by circumstance as much as anything else. Melrose was pursuing a career as a professional cyclist, and he made frequent forays to Belgium, sometimes visiting Bilsland. He only worked occasional part-time hours and was therefore able to train during the day. Millar, meanwhile, was also able to train most days. In his case, that was because he was spending less time at work than he should have done.

Weir's Pumps of Cathcart, the factory that employed around eighteen hundred workers in the late 1970s, was the natural first step on the career ladder for hordes of school leavers in Glasgow. More importantly, it was the only place that could provide many of them with a pay packet. As a first-year apprentice doing an ONC in mechanical engineering as part of his employment, Millar was paid £26 a week. It was enough to keep many 18-year-olds off the streets during the day and in the pub in the evening, but Millar was miserable there. It soon became clear that he was unsuited to work, and, perhaps just as significantly, to the working environment.

By coincidence, one of his contemporaries at Weir's, starting out on the same engineering apprenticeship, was his main rival in the Scottish junior races, David Whitehall. Whitehall was a year younger, but he and Millar had much in common. First and foremost, both were cyclists. Both were reserved and quiet, too; neither really fitted the stereotype of the garrulous 'west of Scotland male', as Whitehall puts it. But there was one crucial difference: Whitehall was conscientious and serious about gaining his apprenticeship at Weir's, Millar was not. Some days he didn't turn up; other days he went missing in the afternoon. Even when he was there, it was in body rather than mind, spirit or application. He appeared to relish the challenge of devising ingenious new ways of skiving, of getting one over on the management, or anyone, for that matter, who told him what to do and when. 'There was a pipe room,' explains Whitehall. 'Robert had a very black sense of humour, and he'd say he went in there for a sleep, so he'd be well rested for training. He'd also come out with things like, "I've perfected a new way of sleeping in the toilets", then he'd demonstrate how he could lie, with his head resting on the cistern. Sometimes I wouldn't know if he was serious. I'd think, "Are you having a laugh?" But he was serious.'

The first twelve months of the three-year apprenticeship included basic skills, using drilling machines and fitting machines, all geared towards the manufacture of water pumps. After the first year the apprentices were 'let loose' in the factory, working in castings or assembly. 'You tended to get moved around every six months,' continues Whitehall. 'As a technician apprentice, which is what Robert and I were, you were seen as being a potential manager in years to come. So there was a bit of an "us and them" divide between the apprentices and the workers on the shop floor.' Whitehall describes the atmosphere on the shop floor as 'male-dominated, typical west of Scotland', in the sense that there were two preoccupations among most of the workers, 'ragging and shagging'. 'There was a lot of smut, and I think Robert felt ill at ease among all of that, especially among lads his own age. "What did you do at the weekend?" they'd ask, really goading him. "Did you get a burd?"'

Apart from drinking, football and girls, Glasgow's religious divide was another preoccupation, and it manifested itself at Weir's in strange ways. The Protestant–Catholic schism was not overt, says Whitehall, 'but it seemed more than a coincidence that in one particular office everyone would either be a non-believer or a Protestant, while next door it would be the other way round. It seemed to be arranged like that. I don't think it was an accident.' Although Millar came from a Protestant family, he showed no religious leanings, says Whitehall. 'Cycling was his religion.' Interestingly, one of Millar's team-mates from his days riding professionally in France, Ronan Pensec, makes a similar observation: 'He was almost religious in his dedication to training.'

It was another of the unwritten rules of Glasgow life – in fact, it must be written in the city charter – that in places of work nicknames are compulsory, even if it is only, and most commonly, 'Big Man' or 'Wee Man'. Often one will be used as a prefix to someone's name – hence 'Big Davie' or 'Wee Rab'. But inevitably there was cruelty in the nickname assigned to 'Wee Rab' Millar. He was known in the factory as 'Eagle Beak', Whitehall reveals, 'because of his large nose'.

It would appear that every Billy Connolly-inspired carica-ture of the Glasgow working-class male was reinforced on the shop floor at Weir's. Connolly told tales of the shipyards, but by the seventies many of these had closed and factories like Weir's developed a similar culture, with rigidly applied rules concern-ing what was acceptable for young males. Working hard, going to the football and the pub, and 'pulling burds' was not only standard but required behaviour; falling asleep in the toilets while dreaming of riding the Tour de France was not. 'Weir's was Robert's worst nightmare,' says Whitehall. 'It was just like a Billy Connolly sketch – there were these dominant characters, people you'd be a bit afraid of. And Robert was different, not because he was a cyclist, but more because of his demeanour.

He was perceived as a weirdo. He didn't talk much, which was what struck most folk. When people did try to communicate with him they got the impression that he didn't want to talk to them. I think he just felt he had absolutely nothing in common with them. Robert talked to me a bit, about cycling and races, never family or anything like that. The only other thing he talked about was the boredom of the factory, and how he couldn't wait to get out. He used to say he found it mind-numbing. "The only reason I'm doing this is to make money to buy bike equipment," he said. His attitude was that he didn't want to go to college and he didn't want to be at Weir's either, but he had to do something until he could go over to France to get the professional contract. It was a means to an end.'

Racing provided more than a weekend diversion. As 1977 approached Millar took to training with even more gusto. He was now following a programme of weight and circuit training as well as cycling, with Bilsland providing guidance. Bilsland took him to his old interval training circuits, timing Millar and Brodie as they made repeat efforts. 'There were guys who were better as juniors,' comments Bilsland, 'but you could see that Robert had a big margin for improvement. He was so consistent when we were doing interval training and mile reps [repetitions]: he could bang out more or less the same times sprint after sprint, even at 16.'

For the last two winters Millar had also been attending circuit training classes run by Bilsland's old coach, Jimmy Dorward, held in a large school in the Springburn area of Glasgow. The classes were held on Tuesday and Thursday evenings and they always followed the same routine: a twenty-minute warm-up followed by a session of circuit-type exercises – squat thrusts, sit-ups, press-ups – designed to improve strength and overall fitness. The hall was divided in two, with cyclists training at one end and footballers – among them several who would go on to play for Rangers, and one, Walter

Smith, who was eventually appointed Scotland coach, and who attended the class at the same time as Bilsland – at the other. Bobby Melrose was a regular. 'The warm-up was severe, never mind the circuit training,' he recalls with a grimace. 'The footballers only did the warm-up, then they would lie at the back of the hall on mats while we did our training. Then we played football with them at the end. It was brutal.'

'It was a great night,' says the ageless Jimmy Dorward, now in his fifth decade of coaching cyclists. His description of the warm-up doesn't quite tally with Melrose's – actually, it is amusingly at odds with it. 'General callisthenics,' is how he describes the class, his hands flailing dismissively, 'limbering up, stretching, a little jogging and so forth. I drew cyclists from all over Glasgow for those classes. But it was a great night and the lads loved it. I tried to get the footballers to join in when Alex Willoughby, a midfielder with Rangers, came along. But they said, "No chance, we don't want to be shown up." But then, cyclists have tremendous dedication to training.' To illustrate the point, Dorward, who was Bilsland's coach, told me what his pupil told him on his return from the 1968 Olympics in Mexico. 'He came back and said that the cyclists hadn't really mixed with the other athletes, many of whom seemed to be there to enjoy themselves. The ones they mixed with best were the boxers. The boxers know that if they don't train they're going to get a leathering. The cyclists were the same. So the cyclists and the boxers behaved impeccably – they had that in common.'

Dorward is modest about the significance of his role in running the legendary Springburn circuit training classes. 'It wasn't on my account that it was a fantastic class. Billy used to go, and he sent Robert. I watched him in circuits and he stood out there. He drove round, you know? He was a very good example to everyone. I remember Robert as being special, even when he was 16, 17. You don't get many of that calibre.' Dorward didn't coach Millar, but he would have liked to. 'It's like a cabinet maker,' he reasons, 'if you see a nice piece of wood you'd like to work with it.'

Almost certainly as a result of all this dedicated training, Millar made an immediate impact in 1977, his first senior year. In the first event of the season, a handicap race in Ayrshire in mid-March, he sprinted in first, just beating Whitehall. Two weeks later, the Tour of the Shire provided a sterner test. According to *Cycling*, 'Sandy Gilchrist and Dave Brunton [both seniors, who tied for first place] were red-faced when junior road race champion Robert Miller [*sic*] was only ten seconds down' in a race run off 'in tough conditions, with an icy cross-wind'. Next up was one of the biggest events on the Scottish calendar, the Easter weekend Girvan 3-Day in Ayrshire. With his performance here, in the colours of Strathclyde, Millar offered 'hope for the future', according to *Cycling*; 'a fine fifth place by Scottish junior champion Robert Millar [clearly he was making an impact: it was the first correct spelling of his name] on the final stage'. But the revelation of the weekend was another young rider, an Englishman by the name of John Parker. His and Millar's paths would cross again two years later.

Millar continued to perform well and earned selection to the Scottish team for July's Scottish Milk Race, which was certainly the biggest race in Scotland and second only to the Milk Race – the two-week stage race held in England – in Britain. At 18, Millar was the youngest in an international pro-am field that included the leading British professional riders and amateur teams from Switzerland, Czechoslovakia and Poland. Five days long, the stages ranged from 83 miles to 105 miles, and took the riders the length and breadth of the country, from Glasgow to Aberdeen and Ayr.

Millar's race almost came to a disastrous end on stage 3, Arbroath to Aberdeen, when he skidded on a gravelly bend and broadsided into a bridge parapet, colliding with a spectator who was sitting there. Rider and spectator disappeared over the side of the bridge, falling twelve feet, though Millar was able to use the unfortunate gentleman 'as a cushion', reported *Cycling*. Unhurt, Millar got back up and rejoined the field. (It is not known what happened to the man who'd provided a soft landing.) Early the next day, 'his left thigh red from the crash', Millar attacked repeatedly on the 103-mile stage from Stonehaven to Aberdeen. It got him nowhere, but it did get the Scottish team talked about, prompting *Cycling* to hail them as 'the best band of triers the host country has recently produced, forcing their attentions on the race and taking the suffering that went with it'.

On the final day, Millar produced a sensational performance, placing second on the ninety-four-mile stage having attacked with seven miles to go. 'The field was shredded and patched up many times over the 900-foot moors,' *Cycling* reported. 'With 30 miles left in the unabating wind [where] horizontal bars of driving rain replaced the brief sunshine, a long gradual climb to exposed moorland cut the field to 31.' With fifteen miles to go, and a Swiss rider out in front, Millar punctured, but he quickly rejoined the group of thirty-one riders and at seven miles to go launched an attack. 'It promised the waiting crowds something to hope for, but his gallant attack, like so many made by the Scots, was to fail. Second place was still a superb ride, Scotland's best.' In his first international race, in his first year as a senior, Millar finished seventeenth overall. Ninth was Gilchrist, the top-placed Scot. 'We had been under a lot of pressure to do well in the Scottish Milk Race,' recalls Melrose, another member of the team. 'There was always the threat that they'd pull the plug on the race if the home riders didn't do well. Generally we were struggling, but that day that Robert got second, I couldn't believe it. The wind was unbelievable. I was nearly crying. It was some ride.'

Several weeks later Millar again shone in a field containing riders several years older than him, placing second in the Scottish road race championship, held over a ninety-one-mile course in Dundee. Having been in a late escape with Sandy Gilchrist, and despite being hailed 'the most courageous of the Scottish under-20s', he was beaten to the line by another prodigious talent. Jamie McGahan, just 18 and thirteen days younger than Millar, was the new Scottish senior champion. Clearly Millar was not the only young Scot with huge talent.

Unlike Millar, McGahan really could claim that he came from the wrong side of the tracks. He was brought up in Possilpark, one of Glasgow's most notorious districts, in a tenement flat with no hot water. 'It was one of the things that motivated me,' he says, 'I'd come in from doing 120 miles in the cold and then I'd have to heat a big pot of water for a wash. I remember thinking that everyone had a shower except me, but I didn't think it was a big deal. Poverty's relative, isn't it?' McGahan had been on the same Strathclyde team as Millar at the Girvan Easter stage race, earlier in 1977. On the first stage he crashed heavily, bent his bike and was swept up by the 'broom wagon' – the vehicle that follows the race, picking up crash victims and stragglers. Though it was early in the stage there was another rider in the broom wagon, with a functioning bike. McGahan asked if he could borrow it, then followed roads that he didn't know until, quite by chance, he came to a junction on the race course some ten miles from the finish. A plan was instantly hatched in his 18-year-old brain. 'I hid behind a wall,' he recalls. 'I must have been there three quarters of an hour. The leading group came past and I thought, "I'll let them go." It would have been too obvious. Then the next group came along, and I jumped out and joined them. But because I was so fresh I decided they were going too slow for me, so I jumped up to the next group. I really just wanted to stay in the race. But at the finish the guy in the broom wagon reported me. I remember this guy, in front of everyone, shouting, "Stand up, Jamie McGahan! You took a short-cut!" I was really, really embarrassed.'

Like Millar, McGahan realized in 1977 that he wanted to turn professional. But, again like Millar, he learned that in his path would be various obstacles, some real, others existing in the minds and attitudes of others. 'I was aware straightaway what Robert's ambition was. It was mine, too: we wanted to be pros. But people told us, "The best thing you can do, son, is go and get a job." That was definitely the prevailing attitude in Scotland.' There had been an indication from Millar earlier in the season that he would not only resist but rail against prevailing attitudes, and that he would repeatedly place himself in opposition to the authorities, no matter the consequences. A bizarre example of this is a Millar story that has passed into Scottish cycling folklore, concerning an extraordinary 'double disqualification' during one weekend in 1977.

It was a weekend when Millar contested two one-day events, both in the vicinity of Glasgow. On the Saturday, in a circuit race in Bellahouston Park, Millar was in the lead group, but he could only watch as one of his fellow competitors – most likely Tom Brodie – sprinted clear to win the race, crossing the line with arms held aloft in the traditional celebration, just like the professional stars did when they won big races on the continent. Unfortunately, this being amateur racing, there was a rule against taking your hands from the bars when it was deemed by the commissaire (race referee) to be dangerous. The rule wasn't always applied, but on this occasion it was, and Brodie was disqualified.

The next day, in a race on the outskirts of Glasgow, Millar found himself in the lead group as they hurtled towards the finish, and this time he won the sprint and unashamedly raised both hands in the air to celebrate the 'win'. The commissaire, Jock Shaw, was aghast. 'There was a substantial bunch of riders and Millar shot out of it with two hundred metres to go,' says Shaw. 'Then he sticks both his hands in the air, the day after his pal has been disqualified for doing so. I said, "What did you do that for? I've no choice but to disqualify you." And he just shrugged. "My pal did it yesterday. I was checking you knew the rules.'" What he really wanted to do, suggests Shaw, was to catch him out. Perhaps another motivation was to give him a stick with which to beat the commissaire who'd disqualified Brodie the previous day. The race was of secondary importance. 'He was neither up nor down about being disqualified,' suggests Shaw. 'He didn't seem to care.'

This couldn't-care-less attitude is seen time and again with Millar; it was either this or its polar opposite, righteous indignation, that he tended to display towards officials. But the question is, was there any basis, beyond his innate rebelliousness, for Millar to be suspicious of the motives and actions of others, in particular fellow riders or race officials? Later in his career there was - spectacularly so. But later in that same year, 1977, there was an incident that he consciously committed to memory, in the same way, perhaps, that Lance Armstrong would later claim to 'store on the hard drive' any perceived wrongs by perceived enemies.

One of Millar's final events of the 1977 season was the Tour of the Peak, a prestigious 90-mile road race in the Peak District. Millar made it into the race-winning break, but, as they raced into a driving headwind, he suffered a puncture. He made a quick stop and was handed the spare bike from the service car while the mechanics repaired his machine. He chased and re-captured the break; but a little later, on the approach to a climb, the service car drove alongside Millar to offer him his own bike back. Gerry McDaid, a Scottish official on duty at the Tour of the Peak, observed this and was horrified to see Millar accept the invitation to stop and swap bikes. In fact, McDaid suspected that the mechanics, knowing that a steep climb was approaching, might have been toying with the unknown and inexperienced young Millar. Having lost his momentum at such a critical point, Millar never regained contact with the break. McDaid reproached him at the finish: 'You made a big mistake there, Robert.'

'I know,' Millar replied. 'It's in my little black book. I'll not do it again.'

3

The Smaller They Are, the Harder They Fight

I realized that only Arthur Campbell and Billy Bilsland knew anything about where I wanted to go as a bike rider; everyone else was of the 'You'll never do that' school of thought. It was as if they believed you had to be born in Europe to be a pro bike rider.

Cycling is a summer sport, but to racing cyclists it can seem that winter is the more important period. It is during the winter months that dreams are dreamt and goals are set. Rather than being a period of hibernation, it is a time of transition, when the hard work is done, long miles are accumulated, and real improvement, even transformation – from bad to mediocre, average to respectable, good to great – can seem possible. It is also the time of year that separates those who are serious about their dreams and goals from those who are not. The Christmas Day test is a useful barometer. Top cyclists say that they train on 25 December not because it will necessarily do them good, but because they know that some of their rivals will not. Similar tests of dedication, or character, can apply to days of torrential rain and interminable cold, and in the most extreme cases, when the roads are blocked with snow. At the highest level, it is all about attitude and the scoring of psychological points, even, or possibly especially, for your own benefit. And it is an area in which Robert Millar excelled.

It was over the winter of 1977/78 that he seems to have set a goal he knew would gain him a foothold on the ladder that would lead, eventually, to a professional career. He realized that the foundations, psychological as well as physical, needed to be laid during the cold months. Naturally, he trained on Christmas Day, riding the seventy-mile 'Three Lochs' circuit in the company of Jamie McGahan. For good measure, they did the same on New Year's Day.

Willie Gibb remembers Millar telling him, in the middle of that winter, his main goal for the following season. It was out of character for him to talk about his ambitions, which is one reason why Gibb can recall this statement of intent. A second reason was its sheer audacity: Millar told Gibb that he would win the British road race championship. 'It was bizarre, and I thought he was just being daft,' says Gibb. 'He wasn't even the best in our little group in Glasgow. I couldn't comprehend it. I thought he was talking nonsense because I would never even have dreamt of saying something like that. I think I put the top guys on a pedestal – not consciously, but I assumed they were better than me and I couldn't beat them. But Robert had this attitude, I think, of believing that if he wasn't strong enough now, he'd become strong enough. And that was obviously what he was determined to do that winter.'

There is a third reason why Millar's winter prediction remains lodged so firmly in Gibb's memory. To the astonishment of Gibb and everyone else – everyone except Millar, that is – he fulfilled it.

For the season-opening Girvan stage race over Easter weekend in 1978, Millar was selected to represent the Scottish 'A' team, alongside Sandy Gilchrist and Jamie McGahan. It was a race run off in, according to *Cycling*, 'the worst conditions ever for

Girvan' – which was saying something. It was freezing cold, and it snowed, making one climb impassable, which instead of shortening the race added five more miles to the course, taking the distance for the stage up to a hundred miles and reducing the main bunch of riders to just nine. Tellingly, Millar was one of the survivors, placing fifth on the stage and eighth overall. In terms of scoring psychological points, he was already in credit.

From there he travelled to England for the Sealink International, a five-day stage race, where he finished eighth, with third-placed Des Fretwell the only other British rider in the top ten. His run of good form continued a couple of weeks later when he was fifth behind Fretwell in Llangollen-Wolverhampton, a counting event towards the Pernod series – effectively the national road race series. It was a result that earned Millar a quote in *Cycling*, and an unusual one at that, since it found him in confident, cocky mood. 'Call me the flying Scotsman,' Millar instructed the reporter, adding of the season that stretched ahead of him, 'I'll be riding the Milk Race and the Scottish Milk Race and I hope to ride the Commonwealth Games.'

The Milk Race represented a huge step up for Millar and some of his other young Scottish team-mates, including McGahan. Curiously, they had come in for some criticism in the midst of a tug-of-love between the Scotland and Great Britain teams over Sandy Gilchrist. The experienced Gilchrist, noted *Cycling*, would 'do better in the GB squad than when "supported" by young Scots who lack stage-race experience'. How those inverted commas, dripping with sarcasm, wounded the young Scots' pride! Who were those people at *Cycling*, mocking their aspirations to support a team leader such as Gilchrist in the Milk Race? A fortnight before the Milk Race started in Brighton, Bobby Melrose placed second in another Pernod event, the Lincoln GP, with Millar fifth. 'Significantly, in every break there was a Scot,' reported *Cycling*. 'Such was their determination to answer detractors of their ability with actions as eloquent as a thumbed nose.'

The manager of the Scotland team for the Milk Race was that stalwart of the Scottish scene Jimmy Dorward. He had also managed Millar at the Girvan stage race, which provided him with an introduction to some of the teenager's more curious behaviour, and his unwillingness to conform. When they left the guesthouse to go for a meal, Dorward and his riders walked down one side of the road, while Millar, alone, opted for the other. 'The other side was more interesting, I suppose,' Dorward, who presumably thought he had seen it all, remarks with a shrug.

But that was nothing. Before the Milk Race, Dorward encountered Millar's stubbornly independent streak again, though this time he found it difficult to laugh off. The team had assembled in Glasgow for the flight to London. 'I gave them a wee talk,' explains Dorward. 'The Milk Race was a major international race, fourteen days long, and they were a young team, so I was telling them what I was expecting and what I wasn't expecting. I told them they weren't going to win the race. I didn't want them going up the road with the Czechs and Poles only to get an absolute hammering that would take two days to recover from. I suppose I was trying to calm them down, so they wouldn't be overawed by the situation. But after I'd said my piece, Robert spoke up: "You're talking a lot of fucking nonsense."' Dorward says that he was close to telling the 19-year-old to pack his bags. 'But I thought I'd give him another chance, particularly since we hadn't actually started the race yet.'

It turned out to be a wise decision. It was to prove an eventful Milk Race for the Scottish team and for Dorward, but, ironically, Robert Millar was the least of his problems.

By the time of the Milk Race, in late May, Millar's working arrangements had changed radically. Having been little more than a virtual employee of Weir's Pumps for some months, on account of his cat naps in the toilets and mysterious afternoon disappearances, he finally made the arrangement official and permanent by resigning. And, in keeping with the increasingly professional approach he was adopting towards cycling, this was no reckless decision financially. In an interview with *Cycling* later in the season, Millar said that he'd received £500 from Lorimer's Brewery, which supported several Scottish athletes though, in Millar, only one cyclist. Given that his £26 a week from Weir's was no longer coming in, it was his only significant income, prize money in races being modest. The money, he said, had come in handy in the light of his decision to leave work – which hadn't been taken lightly, he added. But, as the 19-year-old explained, 'You've got to commit yourself some time in your life.'

Millar did in fact have one influential ally among the senior members of the factory staff in Peter Johnstone, the union convenor. In just about every respect, Johnstone, who had previously worked in the Clyde shipyards, fitted the bill of the west of Scotland working-class male. A big, gruff, garrulous man, Johnstone's accent leaves absolutely no doubt in your mind as to where he is from. He speaks as if he has nails in his mouth. He is a stereotypical Glaswegian, too, in being a good talker and a natural story teller. Crucially for Millar, Johnstone was also a cyclist, and as the convenor at Weir's his role was to represent and fight for the interests of the workers. He admits that, because of their shared interest in cycling, he was perhaps more sympathetic to Millar's quirks and foibles than he might otherwise have been – though only to a point. 'I never really got to know him because he wasn't a great communicator,' he says. 'Why would I bother talking to him? I had better things to do! I had everyone's problems to deal with at that time.'

In the early months of 1978 Millar approached Johnstone with a request: he wanted time off for training. Which, in its own way, was almost as audacious as his stated ambition to win the British championship. 'Nobody ever had time off at Weir's for anything,' states Johnstone, though he went nevertheless to try to negotiate some time off for Millar and Whitehall, both of whom were targeting selection for the Commonwealth Games in Edmonton, Canada. 'I got them two and a half days a week,' says Johnstone, a note of triumph still detectable. 'Davie was tickled to death with that, but Robert came back and said he wasnae happy at all. I said, "Well, Robert, I cannae dae any better than that." And he said, "Well, I think I'm gonnae have to leave." I advised him against it. His apprenticeship finished in August – he only had aboot three months left.'

Arthur Campbell, by now taking an increasing interest in Millar, and beginning to play the role of mentor, also advised him against leaving. 'Robert didn't know it, but Peter Johnstone was keeping an eye on him on my behalf,' he reveals. 'When he told me he was thinking about leaving I told him to do his time and get his apprenticeship. Get your papers, I told him, and then you can go to France and try to be a cyclist. I told him to speak to his parents, at least, but he shook his head and said, "It's my decision."'

Ian Thomson, the Scotland team manager, remembers when Millar packed in his apprenticeship at Weir's. 'We were on a Sunday training run in early April and he was talking to me about it. I said, "You've not got long to go, do your time, make the effort, then you've got something behind you and you can do what you want." And then he went in the next day and resigned. I thought, "So much for my powers of persuasion . . ."'

It is revealing to note that the language of working in the factory so closely resembles that of being in prison. But Millar didn't care much for doing his time, or finishing his sentence, which was how he probably regarded the apprenticeship. He might even have derived some satisfaction from completing two years, eight months of a three-year apprenticeship –

another gesture 'as eloquent as a thumbed nose'. But a deeper reason was surely his unhappiness at Weir's, and, more than that, the thought that working there might inhibit his cycling ambitions over a crucial period, starting with the Milk Race, continuing with the British championship and the Commonwealth Games, and concluding, if he could gain selection to the British team, with the world championship in West Germany. He knew that success in any of these events could be his passport to Europe, and that Europe, in turn, could be his passport to a way of living, and a way of earning a living, infinitely preferable to working in a factory.

In the background, partly offering a counter-voice to the pleas of caution from Campbell, Johnstone and Thomson, was the calm reassurance of Billy Bilsland. He was the one man, after all, who had done what Millar wanted to do: he had ridden as a professional on the continent. Wittingly or not, Bilsland provided tangible evidence that it could be done. 'Back then there was a mentality that you needed a trade,' says Bilsland. 'I said to him, "You'll be out of cycling a lot longer than you're in it, so you have to think of the future. But at the same time, it's a short time in your life and you've got to make the most of it."'

Peter Johnstone certainly recognized that Millar was unhappy at Weir's. 'You could tell his heart wasn't in it, and the better he got at cycling, you could see the direction he was going in. It was obvious to me, anyway. The last job Robert had was working in the test department with me. It was all big water pipes and steam pipes, and Robert would go in there and hide. There was plenty of heat in there so it was a good place for a wee kip.' Lowering his voice to a whisper, he adds, 'I know because I sometimes did it myself. You'd be "between jobs", you know? But nobody would find Robert in there unless they went looking.'

'But would they not go looking?' I ask Johnstone. 'Wasn't Millar supposed to be doing something?'

'Ach no,' Johnstone replies with a laugh. 'Robert widnae be missed.'

So Millar left Weir's, and he wasn't missed.

Johnstone, meanwhile, was left wondering if his fellow apprentice David Whitehall, whom he considered to be just as talented as Millar, might be tempted to follow the same path. 'I asked wee Davie, was he not thinking about doing it,' says Johnstone. 'But Davie said, "I don't think I'm good enough." And wee Davie was the man, a multi-Scottish champion. Strange that Millar thought he was good enough.'

The Milk Race opened with a two-mile time trial in Brighton, before winding up the country in one-hundred-mile stages taking the riders into Wales, on to Birmingham and into Yorkshire before eventually finishing, two weeks later, in Blackpool. Bobby Melrose crashed out on stage 4, between Aberystwyth and Great Malvern, and on the same stage Robert Millar made his first appearance at the head of the race, making it into a short-lived four-man escape with an Irishman, a Swede and a Pole.

It was on the eve of the race's rest day that the Scottish team, which had been performing respectably if not spectacularly, made the headlines. 'Things had been going great,' insists Dorward, his face falling and his head shaking slowly as he relates the story. 'The team had great spirit, always laughing. But there was a stage that finished in Scarborough, with a rest day the next day, and the boys were wanting to go out on the town. We had a wee chat and I told them that if they went out they had to be back by eleven. I could see their faces light up – they were expecting me to say nine. Three in the morning, that's when they came in. Robert Millar, by the way, was the first back – just before eleven. Jamie [McGahan] was close behind him. But the others I had to send home, and for all the wrong reasons I became a celebrity on the race.' Millar and

McGahan were thus the only Scots to finish the Milk Race, with Millar placing a fine twenty-first overall. It was, reckons the unfortunate Melrose, the making of both riders. 'They came back from the Milk Race totally different riders,' he says. Melrose still wonders whether he might have achieved his ambition of turning professional had it not been for the crash on stage 4. 'It was a bit of a sickener for me.'

After the decidedly shaky start to their manager–rider relationship, Dorward could only admire Millar's approach to and aptitude for stage racing. He seemed to have an uncanny knack of doing the right thing. 'It's something I always say to riders,' says Dorward, 'that in a stage race, when you cross that line, you head straight for your digs. No matter what anyone says, you head straight for your bed, and get in. But I didn't need to tell Robert. When I got to the hotels after stages on that Milk Race there'd always be one key missing – Robert's. He was always first to the hotel. He was completely focused on rest and recovery.'

Millar's meticulous attention to detail was also apparent in his habit of surreptitiously removing ashtrays from the hotel bars – not for a sly cigarette, but to prop up the legs at the foot of his bed. Arthur Campbell had observed the top cyclists doing this on the Peace Race, the equivalent of the Tour de France for amateurs, and had recounted the story to the young Millar. The theory was that the blood would flow from the legs towards the heart, to be recycled and replenished. Millar took note. He began sleeping on a bed tilted at an angle, feet sloping down towards his head. It might have been uncomfortable at first, but if it worked, it was worth persisting. Millar persisted, and team-mates report that he was still propping up the end of his bed on ashtrays several years into his professional career.

The 1978 Milk Race left Dorward with another vivid memory of Millar, this one from the journey home. 'Robert finished as the top young rider: the harder it got the better he did. But I remember coming home from Blackpool in the train with Robert and Jamie. We were talking, and what was strange – very strange, given what he went on to become – was that Robert was doubting his climbing ability. I said, "But you were climbing well, Robert." Yet he was comparing himself to the very best climbers in the race, the real mountain goats. He was only 19, but here he was comparing himself to world-class riders, most of them much older than him.' Dorward remains struck by this today and considers it to be enormously revealing, both in the sense that it provided the drive to work hard and improve, and also because it sheds a powerful light on one aspect of his personality: 'He never made allowances for anything, and that was one of his problems, I think, in not getting on with people. He couldn't make any kind of compromise.'

Now a full-time cyclist, and training most days – and often evenings too – with Bobby Melrose, Millar raised even more eyebrows with his performance at the end of June in the Manx International, one of the toughest and most prestigious races in the UK, held on the famous TT circuit (the world's oldest surviving motorcycle racing circuit) and featuring a significant obstacle: Snaefell mountain, possibly the closest equivalent in the British Isles to an Alpine or Pyrenean pass. Coming near the end of the 37.75-mile lap, Snaefell rears sharply up from the town of Ramsey. The road winds up the mountain in a series of bends, in the process rising from sea level to a height of 1,300 feet (396 metres). It might not sound much, but it is a serious and, at close to five miles, a long climb. To anyone who has ridden the TT circuit (on a push bike rather than a motorbike) the names of its sections are highly evocative: May Hill (climbing out of Ramsey), Whitegate, Ramsey Hairpin, Gooseneck, Mountain Mile, Mountain Box, Black Hut. Adding considerably to its difficulty, Snaefell is climbed three times in the Manx International.

In 1978 the race largely held together over the first two laps, but on the third ascent of Snaefell, as the riders left Ramsey and were beginning the steep section of the climb, the 19-year-old Millar put in a sudden acceleration that carried him clear of the leading group. Only one rider reacted, or was able to react. Steve Lawrence, a prolific winner of the top British races, sprinted after Millar and had made contact with him by the Ramsey Hairpin, after which the slope levels slightly. Ian Thomson was in the Scotland team car that day, and he drove up alongside Millar to give instructions. 'I remember saying, "Alter your pace." If you ride steady a guy will always hang on and hang on; if you alter the pace, like the real good climbers can, you'll lose him.' Millar left it too late, only trying the tactic when the slope levels slightly, but for Thomson his perform-ance on Snaefell was significant. 'I was beginning to realize then what Robert might be capable of.' According to *Cycling*, the Manx International confirmed Millar's 'growing stature', even if he was beaten in the sprint by Lawrence. 'The slightly built Scot, looking small against the well-built Lawrence, did his fair share of work until the closing miles when an England victory became a formality.'

An opportunity for revenge came just nine days later, at the British championship. Lawrence was the defending champion, but this was the race Millar had been targeting all season, the one he had told Gibb more than six months earlier, in the depths of a Glasgow winter, that he would win. Yet it seems that he neglected to tell his parents that he was even going, never mind that he was planning to win it. Indeed, Arthur Campbell seems as incredulous today as he was on the Saturday that he met Millar's parents, the day before the national championship was held in Lincolnshire. 'I met Robert's mother and father in the centre of Glasgow,' Campbell recalls, 'and I said to them, "I hope Robert does it tomorrow." His mother said, "Why, where is he?" I said, "You don't know? Are you kidding me?" "No," said his mother, "he never said where he was going. He never says where he is going." Robert analysed everything, and he had a very retentive memory. If I said something that contradicted something I'd said a year earlier, he'd tell me. But his lack of communication, even with Billy and me, was a problem. He's never had the acclaim he deserves, but a lot of it is his own fault.'

The national championship, held over 117 miles on a tough nine-mile circuit on the edge of the Lincolnshire wolds, began in drizzle, but Millar demonstrated his confidence by attacking as early as the second of thirteen laps. Jamie McGahan followed him, as did four others, and this six-man group stayed clear for thirty miles. When it was caught, Millar remained vigilant, and near the head of the race, refusing to panic when one rider built a lead in excess of two minutes. With twenty-eight miles to go, when most of the riders were no longer capable of making sudden bursts, Millar made his move. He was joined by Steve Lawrence, and the pair pursued the lone escapee, who was caught and dropped, leaving the defending champion and the young Scot to contest the title. The sprint, at the conclusion to a race described as 'pulsating', proved a formality: Millar 'soared up the finishing hill well clear of Lawrence'. It wasn't so much a sprint as a test of who could still, after almost five hours in the saddle, squeeze any remaining energy and strength from their legs. Lawrence, as he admitted afterwards, had nothing left, and he was full of admiration for his young rival.

The victory that Millar had forecast six months earlier led to conjecture that he was the youngest ever national road race champion. The records were inconclusive, but it was a record day for the Scots. Behind Millar, Sandy Gilchrist was fourth and Jamie McGahan fifth. 'From novice to national champion in four years' began the first ever profile of Millar in *Cycling*. Billy Bilsland's opinion had been sought for the article. 'He's got tremendous determination and a really single-minded approach to his racing,' said the recently retired professional. 'He's ambitious and knows exactly where he's going.' Yet Bilsland played down his part in the 19-year-old's progress. 'I give him advice, that's all. The only person who deserves any credit for his success is himself.'

For his part, Millar explained that the Milk Race had given him the form that carried him to second in the Manx International and first in the national championship. 'I found the first few days very hard. But then I started to find my feet and just seemed to get stronger every day.' Of his win over Lawrence, he said, 'I knew Steve was very tired, he'd worked hard early on, but I was feeling very good and I thought I'd stand a much better chance in an uphill sprint.' His sudden improvement, he said, could be attributed to racing regularly in England. 'We have to travel if we want competition. In Scotland you're only racing against four or five riders of your own ability. In England there are fourteen or fifteen, and it makes it that much harder.'

Overseas travel followed. As a reward for finishing the Milk Race, Millar and McGahan were sent on their first international racing excursion, to represent Scotland in the Star Race in Roskild, Denmark. Millar excelled once again to place fourth, but it is not the result that McGahan, who was twenty-second, recalls most clearly. 'It was a strange race – a Mickey Mouse event really. But what I remember most is Robert being gregarious, which was very unusual. After the race we went on these helter-skelters, big dippers . . . and Robert let fly. It was really out of character. He was roaring and laughing. I suppose we were let off the leash a little bit in Denmark. But I never saw him like that before or after.'

A much more significant international event, not involving Millar, occurred just a fortnight later, at the Tour de France. In what was one of the most newsworthy of the numerous drugs scandals to afflict the sport of cycling, the Tour leader, Michel Pollentier, was caught trying to cheat doping control following one of the mountain stages. The Union Cycliste Internationale (UCI) and the French Ministry of Youth and Sport seized 'apparatus consisting of a bulb and tube, which was operated from the armpit through the shorts . . .' Pollentier had strolled into the doping control caravan with several capsules of old ('clean') urine concealed under each armpit. A plastic tube led from each bulb and was wrapped around his body before finally running through the groove between his bum cheeks to his penis. 'It took the medical team fifteen minutes to dismantle the apparatus,' reported *Cycling*. 'I had no intention of defrauding,' explained Pollentier, 'but with all these new products that one uses, one never knows . . .'

Though the Pollentier case had an irresistibly humorous aspect to it – it still does – it also highlighted an issue that, even then, cropped up with alarming regularity on the pages of *Cycling*. Quite simply, nobody who followed the sport could be oblivious to the suspicion that, at the top level, the use of performance-enhancing products was prevalent. Whether it was Jacques Anquetil, the five-time Tour de France winner, claiming that the Tour was impossible on bread and water, or Pollentier pleading that his bulbs of old urine amounted only to a policy of prudence and caution, the association between drugs and cycling – continental cycling especially – has always seemed uncomfortably close.

Though news of positive tests and scandals tended to disappear as rapidly as they appeared, the issue did prompt the occasional bout of soul-searching. In a post-mortem of the 1978 Milk Race, *Cycling* dwelt on some of the 'concerns' of the home-based riders. With the exception of the young Millar, they had under-performed, or been outperformed by their overseas rivals, and the analyses and explanations were couched in euphemisms and mysterious dark utterances. The riders, said the magazine, were 'wary of the dangers of speaking out'. Specifically, they were 'concerned about their rivals, particularly the East Europeans, drawing further and further ahead. They talk of the Russians, Poles, Czechs and East Germans being "on something" . . . They worry about dope testing – not about being tested themselves, but about the efficiency of the tests. They hear about miraculous "blockers" which hide proscribed substances from the testing procedures. And they get twitchy about anabolic steroids.'

Their fears were not unfounded, as history has demonstrated. But it was also recognized, even accepted, that professional cycling in the European heartland – France, Belgium, the Netherlands, Italy and Spain – was no stranger to *le dopage*. Again, history, particularly recent history, has demonstrated that such beliefs had more than a little basis in fact, though it is difficult, now, to know how widespread this knowledge was, and whether those who believed it – or think now, with the benefit of hindsight, that they believed it then – had anything more than hearsay and rumour to go on. The tales of drug taking did, after all, add another layer of intrigue, as well as a certain mystique, to the exotic world of continental cycling.

David Whitehall says today that the reputation of the continental scene was one reason for his not giving up his apprenticeship at Weir's and following Millar to France. 'I was tempted, but the drugs and all that . . .' He tails off. 'I remember someone saying that if Robert didn't take the stuff he'd be back on the next boat – but that was the kind of thing people said. I don't know how true it was. I did think I could make a go of it. But I wanted to have a normal life as well, and be attuned to what was happening in the world. These guys are so wrapped up in what they're doing that they don't know if there's an earthquake or a war going on. They think what they're doing is real life. But they're in a bubble.' Whitehall also recognized that, though he might have had the talent, he possibly didn't possess the hunger. 'You have to have the will to win in your stomach,' said Millar in 1985. Whitehall admits he didn't have that; he had doubts instead. 'Robert was a wolf on the bike,' he adds, with a mixture of admiration and bewilderment.

With his national title, Millar's 1978 season could already be declared a success. A 19-year-old winning the country's senior road race was exceptional, and news of his sudden emergence reached some of the British riders who were pursuing careers on the continent. They included Paul Sherwen, a professional with the French Fiat team, and Graham Jones, a leading amateur with France's top club, the ACBB of Paris. It was Millar's desire to join them, but there were other ambitions to fulfil first. First up, in July, was the Scottish Milk Race, the race that had represented something of a breakthrough for him the previous season with his second place on the final stage.

A very strange thing happened at the start in Strathclyde Park, to the east of Glasgow. The opening stage was a prologue, a short individual time trial, but as the clock ticked towards Millar's start time he was nowhere to be seen. The meticulously organized and thus far utterly professional 19-year-old had gone AWOL. The unfolding of events was reported in *Cycling*. '"Where is Millar?" officials shouted as the timekeeper counted down to one, and the 400-crowd waited. It was a late flying start for him, handlebars on automatic as arms struggled to rid himself of tracksuit top, but he stormed out and came back . . . gasping like a fish out of water.'

The five-day pro-am race, dubbed the 'Race of Friendship', ended with Millar the best British amateur, in tenth overall. He rode a characteristically aggressive race, but the event was also notable for the fact that he was on a new bike: a Harry Hall, built by the legendary Manchester-based frame-builder whose bikes were graced by so many of the top British cyclists. Hall was perhaps the biggest benefactor in the country, though his reasons weren't entirely altruistic: he knew that if the top British riders were seen riding his bikes, other cyclists would follow suit. 'I didn't know Robert before he contacted me,' says Hall, who had also worked as mechanic to numerous British teams over the years, including that of Tom Simpson at the 1967 Tour de France. When Simpson collapsed and died on Mont Ventoux, Hall was first on the scene. 'Robert wrote a letter to me,' Hall explains. 'He said he'd seen one or two riders on my frames and he fancied one. So I looked around to see what he'd done and I was quite impressed. He obviously had some ability. I said, "I'll build you a frame and won't charge you. Give me your old frame and we'll do a swap."'

Hall's sponsorship arrangement with riders was as original as it was ingenious. He allowed his sponsored riders to build up a 'tab' in the shop, which they would settle at the end of the year. However, the bill was reduced significantly if the riders got their pictures in *Cycling* magazine, as John Herety, one of the riders sponsored by Hall, told me. 'Harry gave you a frame and you had to hand it back at the end of the year, but if you got your picture in *Cycling* you got £30 off your tab. If you got your picture on the front cover then it was worth £100.' Herety, showing the cunning that later took him to a successful professional career on the continent and in Britain, was quick to work out how best to profit from this arrangement – and it wasn't necessarily to win big races. 'What I did was create really good relationships with the photographers.'

Millar's relationship with Hall continued until he left for France, but it was resumed in 1985 when he made regular visits to Manchester to assist with *The High Life*, the documentary film made by Granada TV. 'He was what you might call a canny lad,' chuckles Hall, 'a quiet lad. There were times he'd come into the shop before I got in, and he'd stand waiting in the back. I'd come in and say to the lads in the shop, "Have you offered Robert a tea or coffee?" And they'd say, "Robert who?" And I'd say, "Robert Millar!" He was very well known by then but he wouldn't say who he was, just that he'd come in to see Harry. He was very unassuming.'

There were two big engagements left in 1978, both of which would take Millar overseas again. The first trip he took in the company of, among others, Ian Thomson, Sandy Gilchrist and David Whitehall, as a member of the Scottish team for the Commonwealth Games in Edmonton, Canada. They were to be away for three weeks, which gave Thomson an opportunity to get to know Millar a little better. Thomson was already sensing that he might not have as long to work with him, and select him for his teams, as he would wish; he recognized that Millar was destined to leave for France sooner rather than later.

This was a source of regret for Thomson. 'He shone so brightly and so quickly that he was in and out of the national squad in no time,' he says. 'There was a limit to what you could do for him anyway. I remember I took him to the Girvan that year [1978] and he arrived on the Friday night with his bike in bits. I said, "Robert, you shouldn't be building your bike the night before the race," but he did it. Robert would not look for you to do things for him.' What stood out, according to Thomson, was Millar's focused determination to succeed. He possessed a singleness of purpose that others simply didn't have, which led to charges that he was selfish, even ruthless, in pursuing his ambition of a career as a professional cyclist. But Thomson professes only admiration for Millar's application, and doesn't have much time for the theory that Millar sought escape from circumstances, at work or at home, which made him unhappy. 'Unless you became one of the crowd it could be quite tough, but Robert wouldn't become one of the crowd – that was his choice. He wouldn't mix because he was focused on what he wanted to do. He was unique for someone that age in resisting peer pressure.' Yes, agrees Thomson, Glasgow was a tough place. But the idea that the small, slightly built Millar might have been put upon, or bullied into leaving, doesn't make sense to him. 'I've got a theory,' he says, 'that the smaller the Glaswegian is, the harder he is. Because they're smaller they have to fight harder. If you ever see a fight, it's often the wee guy being the most aggressive.'

Unfortunately, the Commonwealth Games did not see Millar at his best. 'He blew it,' Thomson recalls. While the big favourite, the Australian Phil Anderson, made it into the break and won the race, Millar was left chasing shadows all day – though torrential rain made shadows unlikely, and turned the circuit into a skating rink. 'He should have been there with Anderson,' Thomson adds, 'but he was still young.'

The Commonwealth Games might have been Millar's first big international appearance, but his poor performance there doesn't seem to have troubled him. He was relaxed for the three weeks they were there, according to Thomson. He even had a go at track riding, with a view to taking part in the pursuit – though in the end he didn't. But it is probable that Millar wouldn't have been unduly worried by his relative failure in Edmonton, and for two reasons. One was that the Commonwealth Games were unimportant as far as the European racing scene was concerned, and that was where his ambitions lay. His attitude towards the next major gathering, the 1980 Olympics, was even more blasé: 'Why would I want to go to Moscow?' he said. Like the Commonwealth Games, the all-amateur Olympics, though meaningful back home in Britain, were of little consequence to the professional road cycling scene. Some riders delayed turning professional until after the 1980 Olympics, but the possibility didn't even cross Millar's mind.

The second reason was that he already had a clear idea about whom he'd be racing with the following year, even if he kept this information to himself.

Other than the race itself, Thomson has only positive memories of the weeks spent with Millar and the rest of the team. 'I remember going and playing snooker with him one afternoon. I'd never played before; Robert obviously had. It was good; I never had any trouble with the boy at all. He knew by the time of the Games that he'd be going to France the following year, but he never, ever talked about what he was going to do. Other boys would say, "I'm going to do this, I'm going to do that," and you thought, "Fuck off! You've never even been to the continent!" It's another world over there, a hard game.'

Millar's room-mate in Edmonton was Sandy Gilchrist, with whom Millar had travelled to races over the past couple of seasons. Gilchrist was the senior rider in Scotland, and Millar seemed to respect him. Years later, when Gilchrist was national coach, he asked Millar to return to Scotland to help run training camps. Millar, he says, was 'only too happy to help'. Still, Gilchrist admits that he found Millar hard work at times. He didn't say much, for a start. He would instead sit and listen to the conversation before 'coming out with a couple of one-liners'. He could be funny. He had a way with words – his own way, naturally. Gilchrist, like Jimmy Dorward, remembers Millar complaining that he wasn't a very good climber. 'He thought he was mediocre,' says Gilchrist, 'but, in his words, he could "sprackle" over the top. I always remember him saying that. I think he meant that he would struggle up the climb and make a last desperate effort over the top to stay with the other riders. It was a good word, though, sprackle. Only Robert could come out with that. He would totally refute the idea that he was special. He just thought that he put a lot into his cycling, so he expected to get a lot out.' And Gilchrist has a theory that his quietness, his reluctance to engage with people, might have been part of a carefully calculated strategy. 'He put a lot into his mental preparation, and being anti-social, cutting himself off from people, was part of that. He would probably see that as being part and parcel of becoming a good rider.'

After managing only twenty-third in the Commonwealth Games road race, from Edmonton Millar flew to the world championship on West Germany's motor racing circuit the Nurburgring, in late August. His first world amateur road race championship ended with him as Britain's best finisher in fifty-ninth.

One of Millar's last events in a busy season was the Raleigh Dunlop Tour of Ireland, which he rode for a composite 'All Stars' team that included Gilchrist and Phil Anderson and was sponsored by British Airways. The revelation of that race was a young Irishman called Stephen Roche. But Millar did well too, finishing fourth overall. A week later he won the Tour of the Peak by more than three minutes – a nice postscript to the previous year's race, when a poorly timed bike change cost him his place in the leading break. Harry Hall still possesses a picture from *Cycling* showing Millar out of the saddle and climbing towards victory, resplendent in his British champion's jersey, which was white with red and blue bands around the chest. Alas, the picture was on the inside pages rather than the cover and therefore would have been worth only £30 rather than £100 to Millar. He finished an outstanding season by winning the Tour of the Trossachs time trial, ending a seven-year run of wins by Sandy Gilchrist, and shattering the course record, set in 1964 by Ian Thomson.

A more significant item appeared in *Cycling* magazine on 7 October. 'Millar Gets Paris Call' read the headline. The story was reputedly prompted by a phone call to the offices of the magazine from Claude Escalon, deputy director of the Paris-based Athlétique Club de Boulogne-Billancourt (ACBB). 'I'm

very interested in taking an Englishman [*sic*] called Millar,'
Escalon told the staff at *Cycling*. 'Have you any idea what kind
of a rider he is, and where I could contact him?'

4

A Jungle

You don't get anywhere being nice. Not in bike racing.

Claude Escalon was not alone in trying to fix Millar up with a French club. Through his international contacts as a high-ranking UCI official, Arthur Campbell had been sounding out US Créteil, the club with which Billy Bilsland raced before he turned professional, when the call came from Escalon. In fact, his phone call to the offices of *Cycling* wasn't quite as coincidental as implied in the magazine. Over the past two seasons a tradition had started whereby the Athlétique Club de Boulogne-Billancourt, based in the western suburbs of Paris, would cherry-pick the best British talent. It was a ritual that started after Paul Sherwen's move to the Paris club in 1977.

As an English speaker at the ACBB, Sherwen, from Cheshire, was an anomaly, a one-off, but he made such an impact that he was invited, when he left after a year to turn professional, to nominate one of his countrymen. For the 1978 season Sherwen had suggested that his replacement should be another rider from the north-west of England, Graham Jones. With Sherwen and Jones, the ACBB struck gold. And, not surprisingly, the success of these two riders fostered in those running the club a belief that on the other side of the English Channel lay a rich and untapped seam of talent. By the start of 1979, when Millar arrived in Paris, Sherwen had ridden his first Tour de France, with Fiat, and Jones had signed his first professional contract, with Peugeot. Jones had even finished 1978 with the prestigious Merlin Plage Palme d'Or trophy, awarded annually to the best amateur in France. According to the new tradition, he had been asked by the ACBB which British rider should replace him. Jones had responded that there was one outstanding candidate: Robert Millar.

Back in Glasgow, Millar was also doing all that he could to fix himself up with a move to the continent, which would be a step closer to a professional contract. There was a clearly defined pathway to that end. Millar had already worked out that the place to shine was not the Commonwealth Games, the Olympics, or the Milk Race; it was by racing with the best amateurs in France, Belgium, Holland and Italy, where most professional teams were based. The teams' recruitment process was straightforward: they plucked the best talent from the domestic amateur racing scene. The only way to turn professional, then, was to live there. And, the really difficult bit, to win there.

Apart from giving up work and winning the races that would alert people such as Jones to his talent, the 20-year-old had been preparing for his departure in other ways, too. With the help of Arthur Campbell, he had been studying French. 'I had made all the arrangements for him to go to France,' says Campbell, 'but when the offer from the ACBB came I kept out of it. At that time I became inundated with riders wanting to go to France to try and turn professional. I ended up saying, "No problem. Go to Central Station [the railway station in Glasgow] and make your way from there." It wasn't as easy as they thought, and I had been let down by every one of them – for various reasons. When you go there, you have to be prepared to give everything.' After trying and failing to persuade

Millar to finish his apprenticeship, Campbell didn't hesitate in encouraging him to move to France, but with the same proviso: 'Speak to your parents.' The advice was met with an identical response: 'It's my decision.'

Campbell had been teaching Millar French for almost a year as 1978 drew to a close. When the lessons started, Millar hadn't even been outside the country. But Campbell was impressed by his commitment to learning the language, noting that he started from scratch, but 'did it the way it should be done'. Campbell adds that 'though Robert didn't say much, he had a good grasp of the English language. If you have that, you have a head start.' He gave him homework, which was done every time, on time. Still, Campbell felt duty bound to warn him, 'All you're learning from me is the grammar. I speak French to you in a way that I don't speak to French people, articulating every word, overemphasizing every sound. When you go to France you won't know what's hit you.' Despite his rebellious track record when it came to educational matters, according to Campbell Millar was a model pupil, though he scoffs at the suggestion that he might have enjoyed learning French for its own sake. 'Oh no, oh no – it all came from his ambition to be a cyclist. It wasn't that he wanted to speak French!'

Given his feelings towards Glasgow, which he would articulate later, it seems likely that Millar regarded his imminent departure as decisive and final. Some of those who knew him were certainly left with that impression, recalling that he seemed to be preparing to cut his ties completely. For the past year, and especially since he had finished working at Weir's, he had trained regularly with Bobby Melrose. Of course, even before he left work he'd still managed to join the out-of-work Melrose with surprising regularity. 'He very seldom went to work,' Melrose recalls with a smile. 'In the winter we went out training during the day and in the summer we'd train during the day and then go out with the bunch at night. And we had an arrangement, even though we weren't in the same club, that we would help each other in races and then split the prize money. You were always looking to make as much as you could.' Despite their friendship – Melrose says he got on well with Millar and was fond of him – he was under no illusion that it would survive a move to France. 'I think he realized that when he went to France he didn't want to be missing his pals,' Melrose says. It was a conscious decision, Melrose thought, for the purely pragmatic reason that he 'didn't want anything to come back for, or it would have been too easy for him to pack it in and come home. He didn't want to feel lonely or missing anything about home. I can't remember if he told me that, though I'm sure he did. But that was the impression I had, anyway.'

Willie Gibb recalls Millar's 'tunnel vision' once his heart was set on moving away and pursuing a career as a cyclist. 'It was almost like he didn't care what other people thought of him. He was very obstinate and he was totally focused on where he wanted to go, but there was never any big-headedness about it. It was very matter of fact with Robert.'

There are marginal differences of opinion, but many people who were involved in the British cycling scene in the late 1970s make more or less the same observation: that Robert Millar was one among an unusually large group of talented riders – at 19, they say, he had comparable ability to Bobby Melrose, Jamie McGahan, Willie Gibb and the top young rider in England, John Parker – but that he was different. 'Special' is the word many used to describe him at various stages of his career, so that it became a euphemism for different, original, talented, unusual, eccentric, maverick. Many – a surprising number, perhaps – offered their appraisal with obvious and unconcealed affection.

Listening to what they had to say, and reading Millar's own words, I was reminded of another iconic Scottish sportsman and cult hero, the climber Dougal Haston. Like Millar, Haston was aloof and economical with words, but also prodigiously talented and ferociously driven. Like Millar again, Haston divided people: some found him engaging company and became fiercely protective of his reputation after he died, others reckoned he had the social skills – and also the sting – of a wasp. When he died in a skiing accident in 1977, Haston was writing a novel, *Calculated Risk*, whose hero, John Dunlop, was very obviously based on the author. In one passage, Dunlop makes a distinction between himself, a serious career climber, and a female friend, whom he describes as a 'weekend climber':

> For you [climbing's] one of the dozens of beautiful facets of life that are there to be enjoyed: it doesn't rule your life as it does mine . . . Maybe you're right, maybe I'm obsessive. But Jackie Stewart didn't become world champion just by pottering around vaguely in cars. He had one singular urge and that was to be the best Formula 1 driver in the world. Racing was his life, just as climbing is my life . . . there is a group that's recognised as the world's best and that's where I want to be. God knows I'm far enough away from it now, but I'd never have the remotest chance of reaching it with your attitude. It's difficult for most people to understand a singular strong urge to do something well. You only really take out of something the amount you put in; you get small amounts of pleasure out of many things, whereas I get a huge amount of pleasure out of one.

Haston, just as Millar would do, also repeatedly made a distinction between people like him and 'normal people', the implication being that to be considered normal would be construed as a grave insult; and, taking the theory to its natural conclusion, that normality, including any evidence of normal behaviour, was to be resisted and avoided. Normality could only hold you back; the key was to be different, not to fit in, to set yourself apart from your peers.

Millar flew into Charles de Gaulle airport in January 1979 with an address, Rue de Sèvres, in his pocket. 'No one came to meet me, so I took a taxi,' Millar told Rupert Guinness for his 1993 book *Foreign Legion*, which documented the extraordinary impact on world cycling made by the English-speaking 'exiles' in a relatively brief period, from Paul Sherwen in 1977 to Stephen Roche, Sean Yates, John Herety and Allan Peiper, all of whom represented the ACBB in the years after Millar. 'We drove to Paris,' Millar continued, 'and came to this place with huge doors. There was no sign, but I walked through to ask a lady there, who came up and asked what I wanted.' Then, a claim that would have shocked Arthur Campbell: 'I couldn't speak any French at all. But I worked out that what she was saying was that the Rue de Sèvres I wanted was on the other side of Paris.'

In *The High Life*, the hour-long documentary film about Millar, he talks engagingly, if slightly awkwardly, about his first impressions of Paris, confessing that he had been 'scared to speak at first'. Millar then reveals that as well as the French lessons with Campbell, he had also purchased a cassette course. 'I did three hours a day until the end of the course,' he says. He continues, falteringly, 'It's a bit kind of difficult at first, when you get off the plane . . . you're in the airport in Paris, and you show the taxi driver the address you want to go to, and he takes you there. It's kind of a letdown. Because you think that everyone's going to look after you. They see so many guys come [to France] that they don't really look after you so well. You have to do it all yourself and you feel kind of . . . let down. It's a bit of an anti-climax.'

Phil Anderson was settling into his apartment when Millar arrived, to be met by Claude Escalon. The deputy director explained that, with four riders already ensconced in the

ACBB-owned apartment, there was no room for Millar. He was shown instead to a nearby gymnasium, which would provide temporary accommodation. There was a not unreasonable assumption, suggested Guinness, that at least one of the four riders in the apartment would crack before too long and head for home, thus freeing up a bed for Millar. 'There were so many good riders that to survive you needed to be special,' Millar told Guinness. Four years later, reflecting again on his move to France, he explained, 'It was like a mercenary thing. You just took yourself there and you did it.' When asked why the club was prepared to take on so many foreigners at that time, Millar's response was characteristically glib and self-denigrating: 'We didn't ask for so much. If you didn't speak French you couldn't ask questions, and you couldn't understand the answers. What you don't know you can't ask about.'

The ACBB had begun life as the Vélo Club de Billancourt in October 1924, though four years later it was absorbed by the Association Cycliste Boulonnaise and renamed the Association Cycliste de Boulonnaise-Billancourt. In 1943 it changed again, becoming the Athlétique Club de Boulogne-Billancourt, with other sports coming under the club's umbrella, at the behest of the local council. Six years later, Paul Weigant was appointed to direct a professional ACBB team, which lasted until the 1960s. When the professional branch of the operation folded, Weigant turned his attention to the amateur team, and simply ran that as if it was a professional set-up, with predictable results: they became the most formidable and feared amateur racing club in France. In 1979 Weigant was still in charge. 'They used to call it the Armada coming,' said Millar. 'Everybody would be looking at you and going, "Those sods are here. Which one of them is going to win?" And you'd be walking about trying to look confident.'

By the time Millar arrived at the ACBB the club was run by the local council. Directors for each of the thirty-four sports in its portfolio were appointed by the Boulogne-Billancourt Town Hall, with each sport responsible for attracting its own sponsorship. Cycling, as France's national sport, had no problems in this regard: Peugeot, Adidas and Le Coq Sportif all poured money and equipment into the amateur team. It was an impressive set-up, but the question asked by many concerned their motivation for signing foreign riders – the question, of course, being why, other than the fact that, as Millar observed, they came cheap. In fact, there was kudos in being represented by 'exotic' overseas talent. Clubs throughout France, not only the ACBB, began to appreciate that they could attract extra column inches in the newspapers, thereby raising the profile of the club, and the area they represented. In Boulogne-Billancourt, the policy also fitted into an impressive forward-thinking strategy to promote sport and healthy living within the community. As Michael Coleman, writing in *Cycling*, noted after a trip early in 1979 to visit the ACBB exiles, 'The success of [Boulogne-Billancourt's] sports teams helps residents to acquire municipal pride and hence a willingness and a desire to raise the level of sports facilities even higher. While the ACBB's first priority is to cater for the recreational needs of its citizens, it sees nothing unusual in importing British talent to help achieve this.'

Back in Britain as well, of course, a mythology and mystique began to grow around the legendary ACBB, even if the name caused some confusion, simply because very few had any idea what the letters represented. ACCB, ABCB . . . ACDC. Easier to remember was the ACBB racing jersey, which became as familiar to cycling fans as those of the top professional teams, featuring a distinctive, if suitably understated, grey and orange with black-and-white chequered pattern on the sleeves, acknowledging the sponsorship from Peugeot. The ACBB jersey wasn't the flash, colourful get-up of some of the professional squads, whose jerseys were often a confusing mass – or mess – of indecipherable sponsor names; it was more serious, more sombre, more like a uniform. *Petit gris* was the name given to the ACBB rider, on account of his lowly amateur status and drab grey outfit.

The Irishman Shay Elliott was the first notable English speaker to go through the ACBB 'system', in the 1950s, but two decades later it was Paul Sherwen who opened the floodgates – and consciously so. 'I was the first, so I tried to open the door up to as many English-speaking guys as possible,' explains Sherwen today. Paul Weigant, known to everyone as 'Mickey', reputedly because he'd worn a Mickey Mouse badge in his racing days, was, in stark contrast to his cartoon nickname, a formidable presence, with his shock of white hair and serious, solemn air. 'Weigant was very old-fashioned,' Sherwen confirms. 'It was very difficult for us guys going over there, especially when we had just rocked up off the boat, because we didn't understand French. He would speak in very old-style French, in the third person. He'd say, "Monsieur Weigant, he tells you that . . .", and you'd think, "Hang on, I thought *this* was Monsieur Weigant." It was very confusing. Weigant was an old, respectable gentleman and Claude [Escalon] was his heir, if you like. He was the mechanic when I rode there but he took more responsibility as Weigant got older.'

Even after he had established himself as a professional, Sherwen felt a responsibility, almost a duty of care, towards the latest English-speaking ACBB recruits. Because Sherwen had personally recommended Graham Jones, who in turn recommended Millar, the established professional took far more than a casual interest in the amateurs' progress. 'I used to go back to the ACBB apartment to visit the guys whenever I was in Paris,' Sherwen says, 'because it was important for them to have a link to a guy who was a pro, which is what they were all working towards. I did feel that it was my legacy, my heritage. I'd just drop in and say hello, to Graham Jones, then Phil Anderson, Stephen Roche – and of course Robert. Robert was very quiet, but he impressed me with his dedication to the job. That was the amazing thing about Robert. He was very, very dedicated to being a professional, probably more than the rest of us. He was the first one to be dead serious about his food. Some people might have thought he was a bit eccentric. But results were the most important thing. And he got them.'

Millar didn't have to stay long in the gymnasium. Weigant owned a smaller apartment in the same block as the one occupied by Anderson and co., and he allowed Millar and another young British cyclist to move in there. This other rider, who appeared from Calais having travelled across by boat, was John Parker, from Southport. Parker cannot initially recall the circumstances that led to his sharing an apartment with Millar. 'I must have drawn the short straw,' he suggests. And he isn't joking. He took an instant dislike to the taciturn 20-year-old from Glasgow. 'I tried to spend as much time as I could in the other apartment.'

The first duty the young ACBB recruits had to fulfil involved reporting to the *service des courses* – the club's HQ, a depot, lined with pictures of ACBB 'graduates', with office and workshop situated in the rear of a municipal sports hall – to be measured for bikes and clothing. John Herety, a *petit gris* in 1981, recalls a sign displayed prominently in the *service des courses*: 'If you want to win races you'll win money; if you want to win money you'll lose races.' As for the pictures, in effect the ACBB hall of fame, Millar would later reveal that he felt a mixture of intimidation and inspiration. 'You'd walk in and the bikes were all hanging up in a row,' he told *Cycle Sport* in 1997. 'You'd go into the little office round the side and there were all these photos of the guys who'd been before you. There were some pretty famous names there, so you'd think, "Jeez, am I good enough to do this?"' He was certainly in distinguished company; and even if that company existed only in 2D form, it could still bring a lump to the throat, or send a chill down the spine – or both at the same time. 'Look at my boys there,' said Weigant, glowing with pride, as he showed *Cycling*'s Michael Coleman around ACBB HQ. 'Anquetil, Darrigade, Graczyk, Elliott, Stablinski . . .'

Parker remembers that when they reported to the *service des courses* to be given their team kit, Millar had his Harry Hall bike with him. 'But they said, "No. You ride for this club, you ride this bike," and handed him a bog-standard, off-the-peg Peugeot.' Soon after this, Parker began to realize that, although they were all ACBB team-mates, two sets of rules applied: one for the foreigners, another for the French riders. According to Parker, the French riders would be allowed to ride their own, superior bikes; they would simply have them resprayed in Peugeot colours and transfers. 'Not that it made a difference,' Parker adds. 'We still stuffed them.'

The club could exert considerable control over the foreign riders, primarily because all the prize money was pooled, to be distributed at the end of the season. This had two significant consequences: first, that the riders were largely at the mercy of the club; second, that they had to live off what money they had managed to save before they arrived. Which, for each of them, was not very much. Life on a budget with the ACBB, in an apartment described as 'a bedsit' by Parker, was Spartan, to say the least. Parker likened it to university life, but with less social-izing, less, or no, female contact, and more physical pain and suffering. The army might be a more accurate comparison, though with more of an emphasis on self-discipline. Parker arrived in Paris with £150 and returned home with £150. Anderson says the same, that he returned to Australia at the end of the season with the same amount he'd arrived with. The prize money had covered his year, just. And it turned out that they didn't need to wait until the end of the year for all their prize money: mid-race prizes, or 'primes', would be given directly, in cash, to the rider at the end of the race. On such occasions they could splash out. As Millar said later, 'They'd say, "You're skint, aren't you?" And you'd say, "Yeah. Can I do that crit [criterium – a town-centre circuit race] in the week?" You'd be sick of eating pasta and bread all week, and you wanted something decent to eat, so you'd ride a crit and get a prime . . . you could go to the pictures or something, get a pizza, get a paper. It's sad to think about it, but that was life back then.'

In 1985, in a feature interview in *The Face* magazine, Millar opened up a little more about this period. 'It was a jungle,' he said, 'you either made it or you didn't. You got the impression that the roads were going to be paved with gold, and they weren't. It was shit. They put you in an apartment with two or three other guys and for the first two or three months I got very depressed. There were a lot who could not take it, living in a strange country, and just went home. Your life came down to that ten or fifteen seconds at the end of a race, when you either won or lost and either had something to live on or not. If I had not been good enough then I knew I would be back in the factory, being just another number in a time box.'

Parker paints a bleakly humorous picture of life with Millar in Monsieur Weigant's small apartment. When he turned professional, Millar became infamous for his attitude towards food, which in cycling terms was as unconventional as you could get. He became a strict vegetarian in a country that still considered steak as a de rigueur breakfast for the racing cyclist. But Parker says that his flatmate couldn't afford to be too fussy in 1979. 'We lived on liver and rice. In France you get grade A, B, C, D, E steak . . . and we'd buy grade E, when we could afford it. But we ate a lot of liver, because it was cheaper. We'd boil a pan of rice and that would be our main meal plus our dessert – we'd just add jam to it.' Another incentive to race came through the knowledge that the ACBB provided a pre-race meal, and, for the major classics, breakfast as well. 'So you were generally guaranteed one good meal a week,' says Parker.

With cunning ingenuity, and perhaps also a sense of prag-
matism, Millar and Parker actually managed to turn their
circumstances into a positive scenario. They realized, with the
help of French riders who mocked them for being 'fat and
unfit', that by eating less they could become better cyclists. 'We
got into this mad dieting thing,' says Parker, shaking his head.
'We had this competition to see who could eat the least, to get
as lean and mean as possible. I got down to nine stone, and
Robert was less than that. We were bloody going well, I'll tell
you that, but I don't think it did us any favours. I don't think
we were healthy.' Parker runs through a typical day's menu:
porridge for breakfast, salad and some form of cheap meat at
lunchtime, then pasta or rice and a bit more cheap meat for tea.
'But we'd have very, very small portions, so we'd be going to
bed hungry. And of course we were training four or five hours
in the day as well. It was obviously a sign of our determination
to succeed. But you look back now . . .' Parker shakes his head.

As well as the dieting, there was another doomed attempt
to 'better' themselves through competition. To improve their
French they introduced a rule: between nine in the morning and
five in the afternoon they were banned from speaking English;
only French was allowed. The result was not as intended. 'We just
didn't speak to one another . . . until five came along, then we
started speaking to each other again, in English.'

Not, of course, that Millar was the most talkative of flat-
mates, even in his native tongue after the 5 p.m. watershed. 'He
didn't talk about Glasgow or his family,' says Parker. 'He didn't
get on with his dad, I knew that. He was a loner – but most
cyclists are, to be fair. And we had to be pretty selfish: we all
wanted to turn pro. I suppose that's why there was always a
little bit of conflict between everybody.' Parker thinks this was
fuelled by the ACBB, and he likens the situation to the *Big
Brother* house. 'We had to get on but we were also competing
with each other. But there's a balance between selfishness and

getting on with people.' But Parker reckons Millar didn't, or couldn't, strike that balance. 'With Robert, everything was focused around himself. He would just sit there, not saying anything and basically ignoring you, but I think he was going through everything he needed to do: working out what he needed to do to get ahead. He'd sneak out training sometimes. I'd go down to go out with him and he'd gone. It was like he didn't want you to find out what he was doing. Fifty per cent of the time Robert was normal, the rest of the time he'd become very secretive, as if he was working on something or doing something that he shouldn't have been doing, or didn't want anyone to know he was doing.'

In the other apartment was Phil Anderson, another young Englishman, Neil Martin, and assorted French riders – the apartment could officially accommodate four, but this was flexible. Anderson, who spent the year sleeping in the living room, laughs as he recalls training rides with Millar. Confirming that he was a loner, the Australian says, 'I found this out early. You'd go training with him, and you'd be yapping away. He didn't say much, so he'd always be pretty quiet anyway. But then you'd turn round and he wasn't there! He'd just stop for a slash without saying that he was stopping for a pee. Yeah, he was a loner. He was focused, that's how he came across.'

There was tension between the foreigners and the French members of the ACBB, who still formed the large majority in a club of 150 cyclists. Anderson says that the riders, unlike the management, were resistant to the 'outsiders', who were viewed with the same suspicion as immigrants who arrive from poorer countries looking for work – which, in a sense, is what they were. 'They knew we could be used as cheap labour. They possibly wouldn't have minded us being there if we did a good job for them, helping their arses . . . getting them to the finish. But I think there was some resentment when some of us started showing leadership qualities – when we showed we could win, and weren't just making up the numbers in the team.' For his part, Parker offers a characteristically blunt analysis of his French team-mates: 'They were bastards.'

Certainly it must have been strange for the French riders, who'd pretty much had things their own way, suddenly to be confronted with this battalion of foreigners, all utterly focused on turning professional, and hungry – literally hungry in the case of Parker and Millar – for success. It was the beginning of the internationalization of the sport of cycling, which contin-ued throughout the 1980s with the arrival on the European circuit of Colombians, more and more Australians, and, eventu-ally, entire squads of Americans, who came with their own teams, their own sponsors, and their own way of doing things. French cycling seemed to wobble in the face of these challenges, and it has never truly recovered. But even back in 1979, in the eyes of a Frenchman, Claude Escalon, the seeds of the downfall were being sown. He could see a marked difference in attitude between the determined foreign riders and the spoiled French cyclists. 'The British always give 100%, exactly as they promised,' he told *Cycling*. 'The French promise 100% and deliver 50.'

A couple of years later, Escalon returned to this subject after being asked why there was such a high success rate among the British riders who came to the ACBB. 'Because, contrary to the French, they know what they want and they make all the necessary sacrifices. It is as simple as that. [The British] do what they are told. They have come here to turn professional, to learn, and they do so with a seriousness that I admire . . . From the start they listen to the advice that one gives them and they watch what goes on around them. Generally, when they arrive here, they ride very badly – it is a common fault with all of them. They do not know how to ride in a peloton and they attack at the wrong moment, wasting time and energy. After five or six weeks over here they have learnt their lesson and rarely make the same mistakes again. But it must be that they come from a type of racing that is much less tactical than ours.'

Millar, looking back on his year with the ACBB nearly two decades later, reckoned the success of the English speakers had everything to do with the effort and the commitment they were forced to make just to be there in the first place. 'The French guys can go home to their mum at the weekend and they take bike racing differently. They treat it as a passion, whereas if you go there because you want it to be your job you're more professional about it when you're an amateur. They would just like to be a pro bike rider, but when you went as a foreigner it was because you wanted to be one. It's a little bit different. You didn't want to fail, whereas if they didn't make it they could go home to their parents. If we went home everybody would say, "You weren't good enough."'

Millar and his ACBB team-mates weren't long in Paris before they left for the club's traditional training camp on the Côte d'Azur. For four weeks, from early February 1979 to the first week in March, they were put up in a small out-of-season hotel at Les Issambres in the south of France. It was also their introduction to racing, and Anderson made an immediate impact, finishing second in the season-opening Grand Prix de St Maxine, and winning the second, the GP de Sanary.

Millar's start was less certain, in part because he sensed that Paul Weigant didn't like him. 'Weigant didn't like little guys like me,' Millar told Rupert Guinness, admitting that at that point he feared he might be on his way home. 'If you didn't win one of the races on the Côte d'Azur you were sent home. That was it.' Whether that was true or not, Millar saved his skin by winning the final race contested by the ACBB in the south, the GP de Grasse, alone and by over a minute, with Parker second. He also managed to finish second to Neil Martin in the GP Roquebrune-sur-Argens. As they prepared to return to Paris,

Martin revealed that they had been told that their month in the south of France had been a trial period. 'But I think they've been pleased with our riding so far, and now we're accepted.'

On their return to Paris they contested the first amateur classic of the season, Paris-Ezy. In this race of 128km, against an enormous field of 220 riders, Millar demonstrated the talent he'd shown the previous year for raising his game for the big occasions: he was fifth. And, crucially, he played a part in a team win, with the victory going to another foreign ACBB man, Loube Blogojevic.

Later that month, in the second classic of the season, Paris-Evreux, it was Millar's turn to benefit from having strong team-mates. This time he won, making an English-speaking double after Graham Jones's victory the previous year. One hundred and ninety riders started the 162km race, with 'the 20-year-old lightweight Scot in the thick of every vital move', *Cycling* reported. He made it into the first ten-man break, which was joined by another eight riders, and then, as they tackled a 30km circuit of Evreux, he waited until a long climb that came with just eight kilometres to go, attacking his breakaway companions to cross the line alone, fifteen seconds ahead of his pursuers.

What separated the ACBB from many of the other French clubs was the fact that they raced not as individuals but as a unit. In this sense a year with the ACBB could provide a vital education for life as a professional, too. The first and only priority in any race was that an ACBB rider should win; it didn't matter who. What it did mean was that if you managed to get yourself into a winning position, either by attacking alone or by making it into the leading break, then you would have an entire team of riders working on your behalf in the bunch behind you. But as Millar later explained, 'If you couldn't win, you had to say you couldn't, then work for somebody else who could.'

Or you could bluff it, which could be a gamble. With typical self-deprecation, mixed with calculating ruthlessness, Millar told Bobby Melrose, when he returned to Glasgow in the winter of 1979, that he had figured out how he could benefit from the team system. 'He would say he was the worst guy in the ACBB, and we said, "How the hell did you win that race then?" And he'd say, "I was dying, but I managed to get away and ten guys blocked for me."' Millar was being modest, of course. Even Parker concedes that he was 'phenomenally powerful – he could get up the climbs, he could time trial, he could go along the flat at some horrendous speed if he wanted to'.

What Millar certainly realized was that physical ability could be of secondary importance to cunning. Strength alone would not win you many races; you needed a shrewd tactical brain, and perhaps a ruthless streak, too. In a later interview with *Cycle Sport* he said something that suggested that any ruthlessness, or selfishness, or apparent unfriendliness, owed simply to his understanding that others would do the same to him, if he gave them half an opportunity. You needed to have 'an attitude', claimed Millar, 'and not the kind of attitude that's friendly to everybody. In the amateurs you didn't have friends; they were all rivals. It was only when you turned pro that you had a few friends, but they were still people who could take the bread out of your mouth.' Even team-mates, Millar explained. 'Anybody – it didn't matter what language they spoke. You didn't have the experience [as an amateur] to use people for what good they could be to you, like you would later. You'd be friendly, but when it came to a race you'd cut their throat like anybody else.'

Millar was called back to Britain at the end of April to ride the Sealink International five-day stage race for the British national team. Parker was also in that team, and so was a future ACBB rider, John Herety. 'All eyes will be on Robert Millar,' *Cycling* stated. 'If Britain is to have a winner, he's the likely one.'

For Herety, the race provided a 'rude awakening to someone who was very patriotic'. Given his apparent antipathy towards

Glasgow and Scotland, it seems surprising that it was Millar's patriotism that struck Herety, yet it was on the final stage, as they tackled a climb, that Herety got the message. Millar was protecting a slender lead in the King of the Mountains competition over an Englishman, Steve Wakefield. Herety, as Millar's team-mate, was providing the Scot with a lead-out, pacing him up the climb until close to the top, when Millar should sprint past him to take the points. 'I had to rough Wakefield up a bit,' confesses Herety, 'to make sure he didn't beat Robert – just getting in his way, that kind of thing. But as we crossed the line at the top he rolled up alongside Robert and said, "Come on, that's not British!" And Robert, very aggressively, turned round to him and said, "Fuck off, I'm not British – don't you forget it."'

In the event, Millar, suffering from a bug, could only manage a disappointing ninth overall. And in the review of the race in *Cycling*, though he won praise for his aggressive riding, Millar gave the magazine's editor, Ken Evans, some cause for concern. 'Millar doesn't look healthy at all,' wrote Evans. 'His legs look fine, but his upper body seems puny in comparison, and his face looks undernourished. I don't know whether he should see a doctor or a dietician.' The diets of Parker and Millar seemed to be worrying the ACBB management as well. In front of Parker, Weigant urged *Cycling*'s Michael Coleman to 'tell John he must eat lots of green vegetables and salads'. When Parker opened the fridge door to demonstrate that he did, Weigant was horrified. 'But that salad has been there five days – it's lost all its value. You must buy fresh each day from the market.' Millar would later become so diet conscious, and fastidious about what he would and wouldn't eat, that it seems strange that he ate so apparently badly in his first year in France – notwithstanding the lack of money. He reckoned he spent £14 a week on food at that time.

But however he was fuelled, it didn't seem to matter in the races. Anderson and Millar were emerging as the two star pupils of the ACBB school in 1979, though it took Millar some weeks to fully recover from the illness he picked up at the Sealink International. In early May he appeared to be returning to form. He featured prominently in the Paris-Mantes classic, though he confessed to still being off-colour. 'I'm my own doctor,' Millar told Ken Evans, who had presumably enquired about his health. Evans remained to be convinced, adding to his race report this SOS: 'nurse/cook still needed at 108 Rue de Bellevue, Boulogne-Billancourt, Paris'.

Yet a month later, just before he was due to return to Britain to defend his national road race title, Millar achieved the outstanding victory of his career to date: the five-stage Route de France. Not only did he win, but he dominated to such an extent that he all but guaranteed himself a professional contract for the following season. It was the first time a foreigner had won the twenty-nine-year-old race since Peter Crinnion in 1962. It was also enough to give him the overall lead in the season-long Merlin Plage Palme d'Or trophy, awarded to the best amateur in France. But perhaps most significantly of all, it was here, in a race based around the city of Vichy, that he first showed his talent for racing in the mountains, displaying 'extraordinary climbing powers', according to *Cycling*.

And so he returned to Britain, to Bradford, once again to put on his Glasgow Wheelers shirt to defend his national title. It wasn't the only shirt he had in his baggage, however. This time he had told his parents – or his seamstress mother, at any rate – that he was riding the national championship. For the title race, his mother had altered the champion's jersey he'd been awarded the previous year, to make sure it was a proper fit for her small, lightly built son when, once again, he stood on the top step of the podium. Assuming he won. And Millar, clearly, did assume. According to Gerry McDaid, a Scottish official in attendance at the championship, Millar handed 'a small package' to the race organizer before the event started, telling him, 'When I win the race, present me with this jersey, it's tailored to fit and better than that bag you've got there.' The shirt had presumably been brought by Millar's father. Jamie McGahan can recall Bill Millar being in Bradford to watch the race, and he remembers him shouting after his son, following the race, 'Don't forget to write to your mother!' Millar had travelled from Paris to Bradford by train, in the company of Parker. He also stayed with Parker's family for the weekend.

The race, over 113 miles, was held on a hilly 6.7-mile circuit in front of large banks of spectators, many of them camped out around a pub midway up a hill that ascended in three stages, each one a little steeper than the last. The championship was, like the previous year, hailed as an epic race, featuring numerous attacks and counter-attacks, with the top finishers, down to Parker in eighth place, hailed as 'hard men' by *Cycling*, 'but harder still, Millar and [Joe] Waugh'. Millar won again, beating Waugh in a close two-man sprint, crossing the line with one arm in the air.

What made this victory arguably even more impressive than his first national title was that Millar was a marked man. Every time he tried to break clear he was chased down. So doggedly did his challengers pursue his every move that they were dubbed 'shadows' by *Cycling*: 'When Millar unhitched his numerous shadows, casting them adrift with a spot of stardrive, no one could live with him . . . his flight to connect with [lone escapee] Waugh was champion stuff, savoured by spectators all around the circuit, torn between supporting him and the tiring Waugh, who began his solo with seven laps to do.' Millar's audacity, and his attention to detail, were also noted. After riding alone for two laps to close the two-minute gap to Waugh he eased up just before he caught him, carefully removing the hat he wore beneath his leather crash hat, then making sure the crash hat was sitting properly on his head. Adjustments completed, he then – and only then – caught his rival, working with him to the finish. Waugh attacked Millar on the final climb; then he tried again inside the final kilometre. But Millar waited, biding his time, tightening his toe straps, watching his rival. Into the finishing straight and Waugh jumped to the right, forcing Millar to come round him on his left, and into the wind. Millar dived to the other side of the road, seeking the shelter of the crowd, and he pulled clear to win – but only by inches.

On the podium he declined the standard-issue, and standard-sized, jersey of national champion, producing instead the one altered by his mother. In fact, the prize presentation was delayed while Millar made absolutely sure that the race officials had the correct garment. When the formalities were over he was asked if he would be turning professional the following season. 'When I won the Route de France it was more or less certain that I would be turning pro,' he replied. 'Now I think I'll be pro by the end of the year, probably for Peugeot.'

The national championship hadn't been the best race for Parker, who had also started with the ambition of winning, even if his confidence didn't extend to having a customized jersey prepared for the podium. He was, nevertheless, happy for Millar. He didn't have a problem with his ACBB club-mate winning; on the contrary, they threw a small celebration for him back at the family home. And Parker had a suggestion: 'I said, "Look, there's no way you're getting back on the train after winning that. You fly and I'll go on the train – give yourself a treat." So my dad took him to the airport and I got the train with the bikes.' Parker still seems flabbergasted by what happened next. 'If that were you, what would you do?' he asks me. I hesitate, so he prompts me. 'I'm travelling back to Paris with your bike . . . you'd meet me at the station, wouldn't you? Did he heck! He left me to get a taxi back to the apartment. That might seem a silly little thing, but for me it summed him up.' He slumps back in his chair in exasperation. 'What an arsehole.'

Parker now runs a bike shop in the Lancashire village of Burscough, between Preston and Southport, and he has the look of a former athlete, with not an ounce of fat – he must still be on the liver/rice diet – and skin stretched taut over his skull.

But there was also an air of disappointment about Parker. When they were on the Côte d'Azure in February 1979 he and Millar had been earmarked for professional contracts, according to Weigant. But Parker, perhaps not surprisingly given his diet, fell ill and struggled to regain his form. The illness was diagnosed as glandular fever, and though he returned the following season, a career as a professional – the only reason for going to France, as he made clear – eluded him. He stayed away from the sport for several years. 'I basically failed, I suppose, so I didn't want anything to do with it. Because I'd see Millar and Anderson and think, "They've done it and I've not." There was maybe a bit of jealousy there. I mean, they were far better riders than me and I accepted that. What really used to frustrate me was watching some of the French lads, who were shite, riding the Tour. That pissed me off. If I'd been French I'd have got a contract.'

Parker now wonders if his 'failure' proved a mixed blessing, however. Several years later, when he worked in the cycling trade, he bumped into Phil Anderson at a show in Germany. 'I couldn't believe how bad he looked – he looked knackered. He'd been a bubbly kind of guy, but his eyes were sunk into his head.' Parker also tells a poignant story about an encounter with his former flatmate in 1986 on the slopes of Alpe d'Huez. Initially your sympathy, or empathy, is with Parker, the 'failed' cyclist standing with a group of friends on the steep slopes of the Alpe, where stage 18 of the Tour finished after 162km. Watching the heroes of the Tour pass, on a stage that would be hailed by *Cycling* as 'one of the greatest days in Tour history', might have prompted a profound feeling of failure in Parker. But as the riders passed, struggling up the hill in ones and twos and small groups, there was no sign of Millar, who was wearing the polka-dot King of the Mountains jersey. In fact, Millar, suffering from illness, was in grave trouble that day, toiling even to stay with the backmarkers. Later Millar revealed that he received abuse that day from sections of the crowd; they seemed to take exception to the King of the Mountains being so far down, and accused Millar and his fellow backmarkers of being idle and overpaid. When he did finally appear to Parker he was twenty minutes down and, according to Parker, 'just completely out of it'. He didn't recognize Parker. With his thousand-yard stare, Parker thinks that he probably didn't even see him. 'He was gone – he wasn't on this planet. There he was, with the permed hair and everything, the big star, and me with my baggy shorts. So I got behind him and started pushing him, going, "Come on, you bastard!" There's a picture of me pushing him. I'd have loved to send it to *Cycling*, saying, "I was pushing the bastard as an amateur and I'm still pushing him now!" But no, he was completely wasted. It were quite sad really.' This, like his encounter with Anderson, might also have helped put Parker's 'failure' into perspective.

By September, with the season drawing to a close, Millar was placed second in the Merlin Plage Palme d'Or competition, with Anderson fourth. At the start of that month it was all but confirmed that both riders would sign for Peugeot for 1980, joining Graham Jones. First, however, there was the world amateur road race championship, which produced another extraordinary performance by Millar – one that grabbed the attention not just of the British and the French but also the international media.

In Valkenburg in Holland Millar made it into the four-man break that contested the world title in front of a crowd of fifty-five thousand, many of them lining the famous Cauberg climb, the focal point for the race. It was also to prove Millar's undoing. He was in that race-deciding break of four riders, with

Italy's Gianni Giacomini, Jan Jankiewicz of Poland and Bernd Drogan of East Germany, having moved through a strung-out, stretched field in the closing stages of an exceptionally gruelling race, even by world championship standards. Halfway up the Cauberg for the eleventh and final time and Drogan attacked, switching to the other side of the road. Jankiewicz was first to spot him and immediately responded, gaining his back wheel; then Giacomini followed. But where was Millar, who earlier in the race, according to *Cycling*, had 'thrashed' his companions on this climb? In fact, the Scot had suffered a minor disaster at the most crucial point of the 178km race: as he jumped out of the saddle in response to Drogan's acceleration, he pulled his foot out of the pedal. With five hundred metres to go, after a frantic chase – or 'sprackle' – over the top of the Cauberg, Millar caught the leaders, but he was exhausted, and tactically at a disadvantage in the four-man sprint. Though he attacked with three hundred metres to go he was overwhelmed and crossed the line fourth, and out of the medals, behind the victorious Italian, Giacomini. 'All the way for nothing,' said Millar at the finish. 'I messed it up.' He rued the moment his foot became detached from the pedal, which cost him valuable seconds and momentum, and left him with a strength-sapping chase. 'Maybe I wouldn't have been world champion, but I think I would have been on the podium, at least.'

Consolation for Millar came with victory in the Palme d'Or. It meant that the lightweight Scot with the poor diet, who had initially been dismissed by the ACBB *directeur général*, Paul 'Mickey' Weigant, as too small, was officially the best amateur in France. He won an international time trial in Lille in late September, then placed fifth in the biggest time trial in the world, the Grand Prix des Nations, behind Anderson; he also partnered the Australian to sixth in a two-man time trial, the Baracchi Trophy, in Italy in mid-October, in what would be his last race as an amateur.

Millar returned to Glasgow for the winter, and to an unexpected accolade from his home city: in late December he was
declared Glasgow Sportsman of the Year. The title came with a
handsome trophy, which was presented to a fresh-faced, crop-
haired and smiling Millar at the awards dinner. He had much
to smile about: before leaving Paris for the winter he and
Anderson had signed contracts with Peugeot, worth the
princely sum of 4,250 francs a month. The ACBB chapter was
closed, but it left a lasting impression on Millar, who in 1997
offered this: 'We [the English speakers] were part of something,
an entity. If you went over to Europe now and mentioned the
names, people would recognize it as something that existed.'

There remained only one final act for Millar as an ACBB
rider: to nominate his replacement. He plumped for a young
Dubliner who'd impressed him at the Tour of Ireland. With his
thatch of dark curls and sparkling eyes, Millar's successor
made an instant impression, as much for his effervescent personality as for his undoubted class as a cyclist. His name was
Stephen Roche.

Roche, who had also made a favourable impression on the
French national coach during the 1979 season, went on to win
the Palme d'Or trophy for best amateur in France in 1980.
Following Graham Jones's success in 1978 and Millar's a year
later, this was the final straw as far as the French were concerned. They took the logical step, adhering – almost – to one
of life's famous maxims: if you can't beat them, ban them.
Foreign riders, they ruled, would no longer be eligible for the
Palme d'Or.

5

The Y Team

One [British] journalist asked me what I did when I wasn't
cycling. Like, did I have a full-time job? [Response unknown.]

From an early age Robert Millar seems to have looked upon his
cycling career as a journey. 'A long journey of progression' as he
put it, with each step to be 'taken seriously', and 'each level
requiring more work'. The notion of the journey had been
instilled by Arthur Campbell and Billy Bilsland, and it went, as
Millar later explained, 'something like: Scottish champion,
British champion, race in France, start pro contract, average
pro, good pro, great pro'.

When he turned professional with Peugeot in 1980, then, he
would have considered himself to be stepping onto the middle
rung of the ladder. It is an interesting perspective, and one that
certainly sets Millar apart from those who might have considered the moment of signing a professional contract as confirmation that they'd made it, or arrived at the summit.
Undoubtedly some, perhaps the majority, would reckon they'd
done the hard part, and now they could enjoy the riches. That
possibly explains why the average professional career lasts only
two or three seasons.

But as pragmatic and measured as he was, Millar was in for a shock on turning professional. What he was about to realize, as he embarked on the next phase of his career, was that the gap between the third and fourth rungs of the ladder – racing as an amateur in France and turning professional – was considerably bigger and more difficult to negotiate than the lower steps had been. Up to this point Millar doesn't seem to have broken stride, but now he contemplated not so much a gap, more a yawning chasm, so big that he must have wondered whether one of the rungs was missing.

It was as a professional that his size and physique first became an issue. At the ACBB he knew he wasn't Mickey Weigant's favourite, principally because he was small. Weigant favoured big, strong riders, especially time trial specialists, or *rouleurs* who could turn a big gear and motor along the flat, usually in the service of the team. But because Millar won races, Weigant had little choice but to forgive him the crime of being small. He got away with it as an amateur. With Peugeot, and his new *directeur sportif*, Maurice de Muer, it was different.

The Peugeot team was, in Millar's own words, 'a French institution where you got the immediate impression that foreigners were merely tolerated and that to earn your place you had to be a better rider than a Frenchman costing the same money'. The team for 1980 comprised thirteen Frenchmen, one Belgian, one Dutchman, one Australian (Phil Anderson), a South African and two British riders – Millar and Graham Jones. Despite being a 'French institution' – the company had been involved with cycling since 1896, and had won the Tour de France as long ago as 1905 – Peugeot had stronger links with British cyclists than any other team. Tom Simpson was a Peugeot rider when he died in 1967; a few years later Billy Bilsland was a Peugeot rider, of course. But it was, unmistakably, a team with a strong French flavour; and the suspicion was that the arrival of foreign riders didn't dilute this. If any-thing, it made the French element, which included older, established professionals, a stronger unit, even more resistant to the foreign arrivals. What happened, at least initially, was not so much a dilution of the old Peugeot blend, more a reac-tion akin to adding oil to water.

On the face of it, efforts were made to integrate the foreign riders. When Millar arrived on the Côte d'Azure for the team's first training camp in February his room-mate wasn't Jones or Anderson, but one of the most senior of the Peugeot riders, Roger Legeay. 'To help or make you learn the language quicker you only roomed with French speakers,' explained Millar. But the arrangement didn't last long. 'Things went quietly for the first few days but I was quickly moved on to another place when [Legeay] realized that I objected to his smoking in the room.' Legeay, who went on to become Peugeot *directeur sportif*, later admitted the smoking habit to Rupert Guinness, though he insisted it was occasional. 'Just one, now and then.' (Millar's aversion to smoking, and his intransigence towards smokers, had also been in evidence a couple of years earlier, when he accepted a lift from an older cyclist to a race in Inverness. On the way home, Millar's driver asked if he would mind him smoking. He wound down the window as he spoke, anticipating that his seventeen-year-old passenger would say no. Millar's response, however, was a def-inite 'Yes, I would mind.')

As understandable as Millar's stance was, it might also be interpreted as an early sign of his independence, and his stub-born refusal to compromise for the sake of team harmony, or to fit in. Legeay's status in the team, as a respected and trusted *domestique*, cut little ice with the resolutely unsycophantic Millar. While other 21-year-old neo-pros might have been pri-vately irritated by Legeay's smoking, Millar was unafraid to risk creating a rift. He would later claim that 'though the younger guys in the team were friendly enough, there was a definite "them and us" mafia among the older guys, who would never accept you'.

Though these older riders wielded considerable power, it was Maurice de Muer – nicknamed Napoleon, said Millar, on account of his 'size and manner' – who was in overall charge. Aged 59 when Millar joined the team, he had been a *directeur sportif* since 1961, and had led the Peugeot team since 1975. Jean-Marie Leblanc, a French professional cyclist-turned-journalist, who later became director of the Tour de France, described de Muer as a boss who favoured 'attacking, forceful' riding. 'It was an education to see de Muer at the start of a race,' wrote Leblanc in 1981, 'with his team huddled round a Michelin map, on which he had marked the day's route, the wind direction and the points to attack, like a general directing an army.' With Peugeot, de Muer won the Tour de France in consecutive years with Bernard Thevenet – the rider who stood in for the AWOL Billy Bilsland at the Tour in 1973. But since 1977 Peugeot had been in decline. 'The climate in the team was degenerating,' wrote Leblanc. 'De Muer was less attentive in his recruitment. Cliques formed. Doping scandals hit the team, and for two years de Muer lost his enthusiasm.' By 1980, de Muer had removed some of the disruptive elements, though it was unclear whether his enthusiasm had returned. 'Today's riders begin by speaking of money before they speak of the bicycle,' he complained to Leblanc, 'and they do not follow their profession with as much strictness. They do not seem to be away from home for a day before they are phoning their wives to come to them. It is only an example, but it shows they lack a certain attitude. Cycling requires a spirit of sacrifice, which today seems to be crumbling, and no one can do anything about it. It is the age we live in.'

In this sense, it is puzzling that he didn't take to Millar, whose dedication and professionalism, even then, were exemplary.

In fact, according to Millar, de Muer didn't merely dislike him. 'I know he hated my guts,' he told Rupert Guinness in 1993. 'Like Weigant at ACBB, he liked big guys and I was small.'

De Muer's attitude manifested itself in his refusal to select Millar for teams – or the 'A' team, at least. Instead, he was bundled off to lesser races, including events that were completely unsuited to a rider of his build and ability. While Anderson was selected for Paris-Nice, the 'Race to the Sun' that was traditionally the first big rendezvous of the continental road season, Millar was left at home. When asked about Millar's absence, Anderson told *Cycling*, 'Oh, he's back in Paris. There's only room for eight in a team in Paris-Nice. Millar is a little small in the bunches and he gets knocked around. You have to learn to fight your way to the front. I guess it's the same for all new pros.'

One of the Peugeot mechanics, Patrick Valcke, recalls that Millar used to visit him, to ask whether he had been selected for races. Since riders' bikes had to be prepared in advance, the mechanics usually knew before the riders who had made de Muer's A team. Millar had worked this out, so he would approach Valcke and his colleagues for inside information. Invariably he left them chastened, resigned again to competing in what he christened the 'Y' team. 'The Y team was the number two team, which in other teams is often labelled the B team,' Millar told *Cycle Sport* in 1997. 'It was full of wankers really. And we called it Y because Y is so far off from A that it's not worth worrying about. I always thought it was because when you got in the A team there was this attitude of why [Y?] the hell are you here?'

Graham Jones, embarking on his second season as a professional in 1980, had no such problems. Though he was similar in build and ability to Millar – in fact, many maintain that Jones was the more naturally talented of the two British riders – de Muer appeared to like Jones. He was certainly willing – too willing, as Jones recognizes now – to throw him into races. Mainly this seems to be because Jones was obliging: he took orders and never said no, to the detriment of his career in the long term. Jones now appreciates that he was over-raced by Peugeot.

In contrast, Millar was desperate to ride, but unwilling to compromise. Jones reckons that it was Millar's personality, rather than his size, that counted against him. 'Robert wasn't getting into teams because he made himself unpopular,' he says. 'He was quiet and he could be awkward. I always got on all right with him; in fact, I found he had a good, dry sense of humour. But he had an attitude that came out at times and he couldn't get away with it. He'd say things and I could see the older riders in the team thinking, "Who's this little twat?" I think he rubbed people up the wrong way.' With Millar's build – Jones says that 'he had nothing on his upper body and big, muscular legs' – he was ideally suited to being a specialist climber. But if de Muer realized this, he didn't oblige the young Scot, often sending him instead to flat races, where he would be buffeted by cross-winds and wouldn't stand a chance of putting in a performance that might earn him promotion from the Y team. Millar was miserable. 'He had a hard time,' says Jones. 'I'm sure he got really depressed about it. I saw him get some hammerings that first year, even in races that would eventually suit him. I can remember him in tears after a team time trial, he'd taken that much of a battering.'

Possibly adding to Millar's misery was the lightning-quick progress of his fellow neo-pro, Phil Anderson. Anderson also says he felt like an 'alien' in the Peugeot squad, but he seems to have adapted more easily to professional racing – perhaps because he was bigger, and more of an all-rounder, or possibly simply because de Muer liked him. Like Jones, Anderson was aware that Millar was struggling. 'I didn't mind being with the French guys, it didn't matter to me, but Robert would be in his room by himself. He had a very dry sense of humour that I think came out more in English. He was definitely very talented, but he didn't seem happy; he felt he should get a better deal. All of a sudden I was doing the Tour de France, and doing well, and I was climbing out of the four-thousand-franc bracket, and he was left behind.'

But Millar's first year with Peugeot wasn't a complete disaster; if it had been, he wouldn't have had a second year. At the end of March he finished a respectable twelfth overall in the second of the two prestigious early-season French stage races, the Criterium National, after placing third in the mountainous second stage and thirteenth in a final time trial won by French legend Bernard Hinault. A month later he came close to victory in the lesser Tour of the Vaucluse, a five-stage pro-am race based around Avignon, finishing second to his Peugeot teammate Michel Laurent. Then in June, in the six-day Tour de Romandie, he placed eighth, behind Hinault, but he missed out, of course, on the Peugeot team for the Tour de France, which included both Anderson and Jones.

Instead he travelled to Belgium to prepare for the world championship, which followed the Tour, on a course in Sallanches, in the French Alps, reckoned by many to be the hilliest and toughest for many years. It was the one occasion in the year when riders represented their country instead of their professional team. Millar could thus prepare properly, in the knowledge that his ability to ride the race wouldn't depend on the whimsical selection policy of Maurice de Muer.

Nevertheless, it was a daunting prospect. The end-of-August title race was the biggest date on the professional calendar, with the winner entitled to wear for the next twelve months the rainbow jersey of world champion, which vied with the Tour de France yellow jersey as the most prized garment in world cycling. Millar would be up against riders 'fresh' from the Tour, with three weeks' hard racing in their legs. Indeed, the Tour was, in those days, considered essential preparation for the world championship. Making things even more difficult for Millar was a ruling in France that in the period leading up to the world championship all races were for nationals only; foreigners were banned. Which is why he spent six weeks in Belgium riding 160km races on flat, windswept courses that were not remotely to his liking. It was hardly the best preparation for Sallanches, which would see the riders complete twenty laps of a 13km circuit, with 54km of climbing in a race of some 260km.

The race, on a course described even by the great Hinault as 'frighteningly hard', is still hailed as one of the best ever world championship battles. In a rain-lashed race of attrition that saw most of the favourites fall away on the steep slopes of the 2.7km Domancy hill, Hinault made the decisive move on the fourteenth lap. Only four riders could go with him: the lanky Italian climber Gianbattista Baronchelli, Jorgen Marcussen of Denmark, Michel Pollentier and, astonishingly, an unknown young rider from Scotland, Robert Millar. Following this quartet was the French team car, whose passengers included the great Jacques Anquetil, the first man ever to win five Tour de France, and a more unusual guest - Millar's countryman, Gerry McDaid, by now following in Arthur Campbell's footsteps as a top ranking international official. 'I had a ringside seat for one of the greatest ever championships,' says McDaid, 'and I remember Anquetil's surprise at Millar's presence in that four-man break. At one point he turned and said, "Who is that guy? He's far too young - he shouldn't be there." The attitude in the car was very much that Robert had no right to be there; that it was audacious of him even to be attempting to keep such company. This was a course for the old horse, Hinault.' When Hinault had launched his first attack a lap earlier, he 'ripped the already dwindling bunch to tatters', reported *Cycling*, 'setting a withering rhythm at the front, and showing in a matter of minutes which men still had strength in their legs. It was a vicious display, and the snarl on his face was one of savoured revenge as so many great riders dropped back.'

Pollentier, the Belgian ejected from the 1978 Tour for attempting to cheat doping control with the rubber bulb in his armpit, was dropped on lap fifteen, but Millar remained in the leading quartet as they ascended Domancy for the sixteenth time. By now he was struggling. The formidable Hinault, who by 1980 had already won the first two of his five Tours de France, dropped back to have words with the 21-year-old Scot, whose contribution to the pace setting was becoming more erratic as fatigue set in. According to Millar, Hinault simply asked him how he was feeling. 'Bad,' replied Millar. But Le Blaireau (the Badger), as Hinault was known, had little sympathy. He didn't want a passenger, especially a rider of whom he knew little.

On lap seventeen it was Marcussen's turn to fall out of the leading group. Near the summit Millar was also dropped, losing twenty yards to Hinault and Baronchelli, but he put in a lung-busting effort, 'sprackling' over the top, to regain contact with the leaders on the descent. The effort seemed to finally drain Millar's last reserves, for next time up the hill he was dropped for good. With the chasing group more than three minutes down, Millar, still riding towards a bronze medal, continued alone, but he was exhausted. 'My head was spinning,' he said afterwards. 'I couldn't do anything.' The chasing group caught and dropped him, leaving him to trail in eleventh. Confirming that the Sallanches title race was perhaps the toughest in history, only four more riders finished the race – fifteen from 150 starters.

'It was one lap too long, wasn't it?' was Millar's reaction. *Cycling* noted that 'for the second year running the little Scot with the outsize heart had come heartbreakingly close to a medal' in a race that was won by Hinault in seven and a half hours. 'It was just untrue the way I felt when they dropped me,' continued Millar, who managed a half smile. 'For this race I tried just to ride my bike like in any other one, but it does something to you when you see riders like [that year's Tour de France winner Joop] Zoetemelk crack and you're sitting there comfortably. I'm not too disappointed. There was a time when I really thought I might get the bronze – not before the race, of course. With a lap to go I felt all right, but then everything went.'

Sitting at home in Glasgow, in a state of disbelief as he watched the epic title race unfold on television, was Millar's old school and cycling pal Willie Gibb. 'He kept attacking and he was giving Hinault a hard time. Robert seemed to bust that race apart and I remember Hinault having words with him. I can imagine he would have said, "Who the hell are you to attack me?" Robert didn't seem scared of Hinault, like a lot of guys were. To Robert he was just a French guy, you know? Just a bike rider. It was incredible to watch.'

For Hinault, the world title was indeed revenge, after he'd been forced to abandon the Tour de France with a knee injury. Rumours surrounded his retirement from the great race, including one that he had fled late at night because he feared a dope test, having allegedly taken cortisone to treat the injury. Hinault was incensed. The Badger was known as such for his willingness to fight, and fight ferociously, when backed into a corner. By the time the Sallanches title race came around, Hinault certainly felt that he'd been backed into a corner, his 'honour sullied time and time again in the newspaper columns', as he later put it in his autobiography. 'As the day approached I was so excited that I went three nights without sleeping. I was on the boil . . . I almost struck a woman who wanted my autograph and picked a bad moment to ask me. She insisted, and I gave her a mouthful. If she'd carried on I don't know what I might have done.' Not a man to be messed with, clearly. And not too surprisingly, in Hinault's account of that 1980 world championship race, the upstart Millar does not earn a mention. Which is a tribute, of a kind.

His ride in the world championship marked Millar as a cyclist of huge potential, and it rescued a disappointing season. It might even have kept him in a job, and saved him from making a humiliating return to Glasgow. As it was, he returned to his home city for the winter possibly feeling marginally more confident about his ability, but still racked by doubts over whether he was cut out for survival in the tough and complicated world of professional cycling.

He was interviewed by *Cycling* in December and admitted that 'it was very difficult at first. I was meant to ride many of the early-season races, but I wasn't up to it. The racing was a different rhythm. Amateur racing would start faster, but the pros finish faster. We'd ride at 40kph for a long time, then for the last hour, or hour and a half, at 50, or even 60kph.' Millar said he couldn't comment on the rough-and-tumble of the finishing sprints in professional racing. 'I don't know – I was never there.' He also admitted that he was concerned that some of the racing might be taking too much out of him, digging into his reserves. He struggled with the longer distances of professional racing. And he had ridden fewer races than many of his fellow professionals – fewer than a hundred. (By way of comparison, Graham Jones rode 140 in 1981.) He explained that Maurice de Muer had told him that he needed to add some bulk to his nine stone, and Millar seemed to agree. 'Towards the end of races I start to fall off a bit, and it must be a lack of resources.' In 1981, added Millar, his ambition was to ride the Tour de France.

In Glasgow Millar added a dash of glamour to the winter club runs, which he joined wearing the familiar white-and-black-chequered kit of the Peugeot team. But neighbours didn't know what to make of the boy who had returned from France and who dressed exclusively in Peugeot-branded clothing, on and off the bike. 'We thought he must work for Peugeot, in their factory or something,' says one. But one of the benefits of being a professional, especially a neo-pro on a modest salary, was the surfeit of clothing. Training tops, racing shirts, shorts, tights, socks, mitts, caps – being in a professional team meant that by the end of the season you had accumulated more kit than you knew what to do with, with the prospect of being equipped with the same again the following season. For Millar, as for many professionals in a similar position, this provided an opportunity to supplement his income. The gear was sold off, some of it from Billy Bilsland's newly opened bike shop, and some by Millar from the family home in Nithsdale Drive. Jamie McGahan remembers calling there to buy some of Millar's old Peugeot gear.

People like McGahan, David Whitehall and Bobby Melrose don't recall Millar being much changed on his winter visits home after he'd turn professional. There was no boasting, no big-headedness; if anything, he could appear quite down about his prospects. Two things, however, stood out: his changing accent, and his diet. Whitehall says that Millar 'wouldn't eat anything, only nuts'. Contrary to de Muer's advice, he was losing weight, not gaining it. 'People told him he looked awfully gaunt,' Whitehall continues, 'but Robert would say, "If you're a climber, that's what you've got to do." I also remember him coming out on winter runs and he kept stopping for a pee, every fifteen minutes or so. He said it was because he was taking diuretics to help lose weight – proper medical diuretics, not just tea or coffee.'

With obvious pride, Billy Bilsland tells his favourite Millar story, which dates from this winter of 1980. 'Five of us went for a ride round the coast and we ended up in public toilets, getting changed into dry clothes. The attendant came in and I said to

him, "OK, you've got a champion here – which one of us is it?"
Of course Robert was the last guy he picked. There wasn't an
ounce of fat on him. "See that wee thin guy?" I said. "He's the
man." He had a six-cylinder engine; he had the engine to do the
job, and that's what it comes down to.'

Yet Bilsland concedes that a rider's 'engine' isn't the only
factor, and he recalls Millar's doubts about whether he'd be able
to 'hack' it. 'When he was back one winter he asked me, "How
much money do you think I'd need to open a shop?" I said I'd
help him, but then he hacked it.' Bilsland never doubted that he
would, and for one very simple reason: 'When you go over
there you've got to be able to be on your own.' Laughing,
Bilsland adds, 'He told me he could be at a table with all the
French guys jabbering away while he sat there reading *Readers'
Digest*! Robert didn't need other people. When Jamie McGahan
went to France he went with another rider from Scotland – a
good enough rider, but not in the same class. That's almost like
taking baggage with you. You can't do it.'

McGahan, who had two spells racing in France, and about
whom Bilsland once said that he had 'muscles on his muscles',
will admit this now. He says he was intimidated by French
amateur racing – a natural enough reaction given that the
races were 'neurotic: hyper, erratic, nervous. You could be as fit
as you like, but if you didn't know how to position yourself,
how to hold your position, and if you didn't have the concentration and awareness, you didn't stand a chance.' There was
also a 'mafia' of older riders, many of them former professionals, who carved up races between them. Yet the racing was, in
many respects, the easy part, McGahan adds. 'I felt I had to go
over there to give it a try, but I knew I'd miss other people's
company. I didn't like the idea of living like a monk. Actually,
living like a monk wouldn't have bothered me, it was counting
the dots on the wallpaper that was the problem. It was a lonely,
lonely existence. I remember on my second stint in France that

I won a race, and that was when I discovered that there was only one thing worse than going badly and going home to an empty flat, and that was winning and going home to an empty flat. There was no one to share it with, no one to talk to. You went home, shut the door, and that was it. Robert could handle that.'

McGahan's second period in France took him to the city of Troyes, in the Champagne region, which had also become Millar's base towards the end of 1980. The two Scots lived in the city at the same time. 'The only time I saw him when I was there was in a supermarket,' says McGahan. 'I had really given up on the idea of turning pro by then, and he was struggling as a professional. We chatted a bit. He said being a pro was better than working in a factory. It looked like he was giving up at that stage, it really did. He didn't seem too down about it, just resigned.' McGahan expresses surprise now that when they met in the supermarket that day Millar didn't invite his fellow Scot to his flat for dinner, or suggest that they catch up over a coffee, though he admits that at the time he didn't expect such a gesture. 'I'd have been taken aback if he'd suggested we meet up, so I didn't really think about it. It's just now, looking back on it as a mature person, that I think it was a bit odd.'

Peugeot made a new signing for the 1981 season – another English speaker, further diluting the French influence, or adding yet more oil to the water. The newcomer was Stephen Roche, who was thus following an identical path to Millar. The 21-year-old made an immediate and quite astonishing impact on the professional ranks, winning the Tour of Corsica and Paris-Nice, for which Millar was once again overlooked by de Muer. But it wasn't solely as a result of his ability that Roche made a favourable impression. As Jean-Marie Leblanc reported in April 1981, 'The French press has adopted this likeable boy who has made considerable progress in our language in just one year and who has everything to become a star . . . he has lost his shyness and has developed a personality that endears him to all.'

Today, Roche retains the amiability that so endeared him to the French press. I have arranged to meet him in the lobby of a hotel in central Paris. He is an hour late, and counting. As I wait, I find myself gazing through the hotel's enormous windows, focusing on the street, watching people stream past, studying each face until satisfied it isn't Roche. A familiar commentary begins to run on a loop in my head: 'And just who is that? That looks like Roche. [now shouting] That looks like Stephen Roche! It *is* Stephen Roche!' I think that if I keep going it might become a self-fulfilling prophecy.

The voice (in my head) belongs to Phil 'Voice of Cycling' Liggett and it's arguably his most famous piece of commentary, dating from the 1987 Tour de France. On the mist-shrouded summit of La Plagne, Roche seemed to be losing the Tour to the Spaniard Pedro Delgado. After Delgado crossed the line a long wait was anticipated for Roche, but then, miraculously, and catching Liggett and everyone else completely off guard, the Irishman materialized through the mist, crossing the line to keep the yellow jersey before collapsing, having an oxygen mask attached to his face, and being loaded into the back of an ambulance. He recovered to do it all again the next day – and of course he went on to win the Tour.

When Roche does finally arrive, half an hour after calling to say he'd be ten minutes, I am aware, because he had warned me in advance, that he has another appointment in fifteen minutes. 'It's OK,' he reassures me before I can say anything. 'I was late for you, so I can be late for my next meeting.' Everyone says this about Roche: he is instantly charming and likeable, with no pretensions. As the reporter Dennis Donovan once wrote of Roche, 'He still amazes me for he looks like a choir boy, and with those blue eyes he's the sort of son every mother wants, every girl would like to have for a boyfriend, and every man would like to have for a pal.'

When he rode for the ACBB in 1980, Roche got to know Millar a little and revised his first impression of him, formed at the previous year's Tour of Ireland where the Scot had proved to be a stubborn, aloof opponent. During Roche's year as an amateur in Paris, Millar occasionally visited, continuing the tradition started by Paul Sherwen. Millar said later that they were encouraged to make such visits by the ACBB, though he seems to have doubted the wisdom of the tradition, or at least viewed it with customary cynicism. 'It was a motivation thing, that's why ACBB used to get the guys who'd turned pro to come back to the apartment every now and again,' recalled Millar. 'The funny thing was, when you went back to the flat there'd be two or three English-speaking guys left and half the French, and you'd be a wretched little pro, just about keeping your ass in a job, and they'd all have like stars in their eyes: "A pro!"' On those occasions Roche and Millar would sometimes train together.

Initially, Roche – unusually for him – struggles to articulate his thoughts. 'Robert, like, was always the kind of guy you love, because he's a nice guy, but you also love to hate, because he was very complicated. But when you realized that, you just had to accept him and appreciate the guy. Accept him for what he does and how he does it.'

At the beginning of February 1981, Millar and Roche travelled together in Millar's Peugeot 306 to the traditional Côte d'Azure training camp. When they arrived, Maurice de Muer was playing cards. He looked up briefly, acknowledged Millar, and exchanged a few words with him. Then, addressing Millar, while Roche hovered in the background, he said, 'Tell your chauffeur to go away now, Robert.'

'My chauffeur?' replied Millar. 'Oh, you mean Stephen. It's Stephen Roche.'

The journey down to Narbonne had given Roche an introduction to another aspect of Millar's personality that was to gain him a notorious reputation among team-mates. As they approached the final *péage* (toll) barrier – 'the expensive one' Roche points out – Millar pulled into the slip road, stopped the car, got out, opened the boot, and removed a set of heavy-duty bolt cutters. With these he sheared straight through the metal chain, lifted the barrier, left the road, and then rejoined it, just beyond the *péage*. The Scots carefully cultivated reputation for being, euphemistically speaking, prudent with their money – or, if you prefer, tight, mean, thrifty – was clearly in safe hands with Millar. But Roche argues that Millar wasn't a spendthrift for the sake of it. 'Professional cycling was all about surviving,' he says. 'It was about looking after yourself, and being intelligent.' Cutting through *péage* barriers was, suggests Roche, just one manifestation of this, a necessary evil in the business of surviving life in the jungle.

Because even Roche, who won as many friends as he did races, describes the professional milieu as a jungle. He rejects the notion that, as a foreigner in a French team, he felt resentment. 'It wasn't a *feeling*, it was a reality. But you had to accept that. I was there to do a job, I was on a mission. By being there I was taking the bread off a Frenchman's table, if you want to put it like that, but there was no bread to be had in my own country. I never took the resentment to heart, but I can imagine Robert taking it to heart.'

Here is the Millar paradox laid bare – or one of them, at least. Roche seems to have detected – perhaps only now, on reflection – that Millar wasn't as tough or invulnerable as he appeared, or as he made himself appear. At the time, Roche and others were struck not by his vulnerability but by the opposite: his apparent determination to be different, his stubborn refusal to compromise, his having the courage of his convictions, however strange they appeared. Even in the matter of what he ate he would not budge, which could cause enough problems before his conversion, not long after he turned professional, to an exclusively vegetarian diet.

Vegetarians were virtually unheard of in professional cycling. 'The Knowledge', as Millar himself would later refer to the various codes and informal yet unchallengeable rules of professional cycling, dictated what riders did and didn't do. The Knowledge was handed down from old pros to young pros, and a central tenet was that one must eat meat. Lots of it. There was one other known vegetarian in the professional peloton, Jonathan Boyer, who in 1981 became the first American ever to ride the Tour de France, but he was castigated as a freak on account of his dietary habits. Boyer was described by Jean-Marie Leblanc as 'an unusual sort of professional who lives to a strict regime (no red meat, plenty of green vegetables and dried fruit) and he avoids any products with colourants and chemical additives. In short, an authentic ecologist who is convinced of the physical and psychological advantages of living as close to nature as possible.' If vegetarians were perceived as hippies and 'authentic ecologists'– as they clearly were – then Millar was at pains to contradict that perception. Whenever he spoke about his vegetarianism he always stressed that it wasn't for ethical reasons; he didn't seem to want people to think he was an animal lover. Perhaps his thinking was that vegetarianism might equate to loving animals which would equate to 'softness' or some weakness or other.

To some, including Roche, Millar's vegetarianism was interpreted as further evidence of his desire to be different, to set himself apart. 'When you sit there in a restaurant with the team and everyone asks for meat, and he asks for salad . . . You're sitting there thinking, "Why can't you have the same as everyone else?"'

At least, that was what Roche thought then. Now he thinks a little differently. 'He had his ways of doing things and you had to respect him, because he did what no one else did. Everyone else followed in a line. But Robert would come to the dinner table with these little bags of nuts, oils, raisins, hazelnuts, then he'd add them to his salad and food. He had to have his own stuff. If he didn't have those little bags, it wasn't Robert. You have to respect him, because he had the courage to say what he wanted, and he did what he wanted no matter what anyone else said or thought.' Inevitably it led to Millar being singled out by the older professionals, and teased. 'He got slagged, of course,' Roche confirms. 'But even then, he never explained himself, he just did it.' Roche wonders if there might have been something calculating about Millar. 'Maybe he thought, "I've got something you don't have, something that makes me different, and you don't know why I'm doing it." He was mysterious, he knew that.'

Both Roche and Graham Jones recall Millar's catchphrase at the dinner table – '*sans* sauce'. 'Everyone used to take the piss out of him for that,' says Jones, 'but he was very particular about it.' Yet both acknowledge that he was, in many respects, a visionary. 'Regarding nutrition, diet, training, Robert was way ahead of his time,' says Roche. 'Robert would know how many calories he'd had that day; he knew everything. And you look over at the dinner table on a race now and all the French riders have these little bags . . .' Roche can remember the exasperation all too well, though. As he describes a typical mealtime experience, he seems almost to feel it, too. 'When there are sixteen of you sitting down, and the girl comes along with a salad, puts it down, and Robert says, "Can I have mine *sans* sauce?" and hands it back; and then the girl comes back having taken the sauce off, or thinking she's taken the sauce off, and Robert looks at it, and says, "I told you without sauce," and hands it back, and all the time he's not looking at anyone, he's got his head down, but he knows that everyone's looking at him, and there's silence because he's created this terrible atmosphere at the table . . . and everyone's thinking,

"Who *is* this guy?" But it didn't stop him. Being in a world that's not your own, doing your thing, and thinking, "To hell with what you think, I'm doing what I think is right" – that was very courageous.'

Unsurprisingly, such displays of individuality didn't seem to endear him to the difficult-to-please Maurice de Muer. Things didn't improve following another incident on that pre-season training camp on the Côte d'Azure in February 1981, when Madame de Muer put in an appearance in the company of her beloved dog Scotty.

As Scotty yapped at the heels of de Muer's riders, the story goes that the dog was surreptitiously slipped a piece of bread wrapped around an amphetamine tablet – though some witnesses claim it was a sleeping tablet. Whatever it was, Scotty gobbled it up and had some kind of hyperactive fit – just as depicted, following an uncannily similar incident, in the Farrelly brothers' film *There's Something About Mary*. But, unlike in the film, Scotty keeled over and died. A heart attack was the verdict.

1981 was, if anything, worse for Millar than 1980. While expectations – his own and those of the team – might have been relatively low in his first year as a pro, it was understood that by his second year he should step up to the plate. And what made things worse was that both Stephen Roche and Phil Anderson were making waves and being hailed as the future stars of the sport.

Having missed Paris-Nice, Millar finished nineteenth in the Criterium National – not bad, but not as good as the previous year. In early May he was twenty-first in the Tour d'Indre-et-Loire, won by Roche – his third stage race win of the year. Then came a more impressive performance: seventh in the five-day Tour de Romandie, after taking fourth in the 180km Busigny to Anzère stage, won by Italian star Giuseppe Saronni. In June, in the Dauphiné Libéré, the traditional Tour de France warm-up race, Bernard Hinault won the last four stages, 'pulverized' the opposition, and then said, 'I thought the race would be harder.' But *Cycling* reported that Millar was finding his feet. 'On both of the last two tough mountain stages, Britain's Robert Millar and American Greg LeMond shone ... Millar showed a welcome return to form with fine performances on the Ventoux and the previous day's five climbs, which must have boosted his confidence for the Tour de France.'

Perversely, Millar's prospects might also have been boosted by Roche falling abruptly out of favour with de Muer, who severely reprimanded the young Irishman for taking a holiday on the French coast. He called him a 'tourist' and demanded that he take his racing more seriously. In *Cycling*, it was also reported that de Muer was suspicious that his riders were over-indulging between the sheets: 'Too much sex can be tiring for the riders and he accuses them of having too much if they're not going well.' For his part, Roche believes that his performances indirectly helped Millar. 'Here was I coming in, a guy who'd done the same thing as him ... I think he thought, "If he can do it, why can't I?"'

However, Millar's sterling performance in the Dauphiné, followed by fifth in the Tour de l'Aude, wasn't enough to gain him a first ride in the Tour. Jean-Marie Leblanc commented on the selection, 'Millar, not short of talent as a climber, was a good prospect for the Tour but the Peugeot team is not short of talented riders, and Millar [like Roche and LeMond] waits for another year'. Leblanc referred to the emergence of the English-speaking riders as 'one of the most significant developments this year ... the presence of riders of Anglo-Saxon origins, Jones, Sherwen, [Sean] Kelly, Anderson and Boyer, not to mention two who have played very active roles this season, LeMond and Roche ... It is an important phenomenon'. And de Muer, beneath that gruff exterior, also appeared to think highly of his English-speaking contingent, telling Leblanc, 'You realize that because they have left their own countries to seek their fortunes elsewhere they have a greater sense of responsibility and are more battle-hardened than our young French riders. We usually find they have few complaints about such matters as equipment, accommodation, etc. It's true that when they arrive they have a certain individualistic amateur attitude which doesn't fit in with pro racing. But once installed they learn quickly.'

Anderson, in particular, earned de Muer's praise, and in early July he repaid his faith spectacularly. Following stage 6 of the Tour de France, in the Pyrenees, Anderson became the first Australian ever to wear the leader's yellow jersey. 'Unbelievable,' said Anderson. 'A dream come true. A dream I never thought I would reach. I never thought I'd be riding in Europe, let alone the Tour de France.' Anderson, nicknamed Skippy, went on to finish tenth overall in his debut Tour.

For Millar, just as in the previous year, his focus turned to the world championship, in Prague. He and Jones travelled together in the latter's car, stopping in Germany en route, then puncturing on the motorway in the middle of the night, queuing for six hours to cross the border, and finally arriving in the capital of Czechoslovakia after travelling for a day and a half. Arthur Campbell was there as chairman of the UCI Technical Commission. On the morning of the race he was inspecting the cars, checking for illegal advertising, when he saw an open door and a pair of legs protruding from the vehicle. 'Here was Robert,' says Campbell, 'so I went round and said, "Are you hiding?" He smiled. I said, "You all right?" I'd heard they were stuck at the border, as a lot of them were. We chatted. But I always asked him the same question: "How's your mum; how's your dad?" And he said, "She's dead."' Campbell was stunned. He asked Millar why he hadn't come to see him when he was home. 'I wasn't at the funeral,' replied Millar. 'I didn't know – they couldn't get in touch with me.' Campbell continued, '"Robert – communication," I said. I couldn't say any more. He held his hands up, and that was it.'

Millar's mother, Mary, who had been suffering from carcinomatosis, died on 30 July 1981. She was 47.

Despite the circumstances, the Prague world championship, on a course that wasn't as testing as Sallanches the previous year, saw another outstanding performance from Millar, even if ultimately he placed 'only' fourteenth. It might have been a different story. As the 280km race entered the final two kilometres, near to the summit of the modest climb on the circuit, and with twenty-eight riders in the leading group, Millar launched an attack, instantly opening a gap of 150 metres. Freddy Maertens, the Belgian who went on to win the race, believes that Millar's attempt was foiled only by the presence of so many Italians in the lead group. 'The entire national team of Italy was there – nine riders,' says Maertens. 'They brought him back, but it was a good attack. I knew Millar, I'd seen him in other races. He was a rider to take care of.'

Millar was being taken care of in Prague, by his former Scotland team manager, Ian Thomson, who looked after Millar during the race, making sure he got his water bottles and musettes (small bags of food) in the feeding zone. 'Everyone else looked to the manager and mechanic to do things for him,' says Thomson, 'but Robert arrived, went to his room and prepared everything himself. He had his musettes laid out, with the food he needed, and he told me, "Hand this one to me lap ten, this one on lap fifteen . . . these are the bottles I need." I've never met someone so professional and organized in my life. He knew exactly what he needed.'

From the world championship, Millar went to the ten-day Tour de l'Avenir, the 'Tour de France of the future', with a strong Peugeot squad including Jones and Roche and led by a young Frenchman, Pascal Simon. For Peugeot the race was a triumph, strong teamwork helping Simon to the overall victory. Roche placed sixth with Millar eleventh, including fourth in the final mountain time trial, from Morzine to Avoriaz. He earned praise for his work on Simon's behalf.

The year ended with Roche declared Man of the Year by *Cycling*. Looking ahead to 1982, he said, 'Maurice de Muer says it is the best team he has had for years. There is a good atmosphere. Our two Belgian *soigneurs* [masseurs] look after us [the English speakers] better than they do the French because they know we are clean. We get better treatment and are accepted better.' On Millar, Roche commented, 'He has not been having a lot of luck . . . A lot of the younger French pros sit on the back and are reluctant to have a go. [But] Robert is inclined to keep himself to himself. He's too polite at times . . . yet he's not afraid of having a go.'

6

The Little Cockerel

The only private life I have is in my head.

Jack Andre greets me on the outskirts of Troyes, standing proudly beside an estate car busily plastered with the branding of various local sponsors, and, in big, bold lettering, the name of the amateur team he runs: UVC Aube.

Millar moved to Troyes early in his professional career, initially staying with Andre and his wife while he looked for lodgings. There are Andre equivalents throughout France: racing cyclist turned coach, svengali, motivator and manager, but most of all perennial enthusiast and supporter. Andre was a decent rider himself: he finished twelfth in the 1958 world amateur road race championship, only to be posted to the French war in Algeria, from which he returned with malaria. 'I needed a year to get back into racing and I wasn't the same,' he explains. 'I made a choice: I had learned hairdressing before I went away so I studied for my diplomas.' There was, he adds, another reason for his opting not to pursue a professional career: 'I realized the other riders were taking stuff. I had my liver done in by malaria so I didn't take stuff. But I still won 230 races in my career.'

These days Andre is retired but '90 per cent' of his time is still devoted to cycling – or, more accurately, to helping racing cyclists. The enjoyment is the same, even if the sport has changed, though 'enjoyment' is perhaps the wrong word: it is a vocation, virtually a lifelong commitment to helping *coureurs*, among them an astonishing number of Britons. He reels off a list that features the names of virtually every good British cyclist of the last fifty years; it seems he has had a hand in helping them all. Perhaps the affinity comes from the fact that his name is the British 'Jack' rather than the French 'Jacques', though he has helped plenty of French riders, too. He is small in height, but lean and stocky, with thick, muscular forearms, and bushy salt-and-pepper eyebrows that match his coiffured thatch of hair. He seems eager to help me in my 'search' for Millar, though he is keen in the first instance to establish an important point. 'I was Robert's confidant,' he points out.

Andre was a confidant to others, too, such as Pascal Simon, the French rider befriended by Millar at Peugeot, who encouraged the Scot to move to Troyes. 'I was like a father for all the riders I helped,' says Andre, refusing to discriminate. 'They could confide in me and trust me. I was there for them when the chips were down.' He describes professional cycling as a business, and just as ruthless, as well as sometimes cold and unfeeling, with no room for sentiment. 'When things go well there are always lots of people around; but there's no one around when the chips are down.'

Andre takes me to his house, on the outer fringes of Troyes, about ten kilometres from the centre, and opens the garage – a treasure trove of cycling equipment and memorabilia. There's a large picture of 1950s Italian icon Fausto Coppi, and an even larger card-backed poster of Millar, attacking a climb with a determined look on his face and wearing a white-and-red polka-dot King of the Mountains jersey. Andre pulls out the fading, slightly dog-eared portrait and stands alongside it, inspecting it once more and beaming with pride. In the corner, inscribed in felt-tip pen, is the message 'To Jack Andre, a friend for life'. Beneath that is the squiggly autograph of Robert Millar.

Andre has not seen Millar for more than ten years. Not that he's too surprised at his disappearance. He remembers Millar accompanying him to a mass-participation 'cyclo-tourist' event in 1984, just when his career was taking off. He was beginning to attract considerable attention. 'But Robert wanted to be anonymous,' says Andre. 'It's complicated. With all the big champions' – and it's clear that Millar, as far as Andre is concerned, deserves such a description – 'there is always something in their personality that's a bit strange and a bit different. Robert was like a little cockerel. He liked to stand out, but he hated people chasing him.'

Andre is more effusive than Billy Bilsland, but there are similarities between the two. Both would have supported Millar and encouraged him; they wouldn't have pushed him or fussed over him. And Andre says that he could be frank with Millar. With a creased brow and vigorously flapping hands, he explains, 'When his ways got too much for people – when his attitude would annoy them – I was able to tell him, and he respected me. But I respected him, also.' I ask Andre whether he thinks Millar, apparently so self-contained and self-reliant, needed someone to help and guide him. He pauses a moment. 'Most of all, he needed someone to trust.'

For Millar, 1982 was all about the Tour de France. Apart from the great race representing the pinnacle of the sport, he had been told that it would offer him the chance to double his salary. Finally he hoped to get his chance, and he made his ambitions clear when he was 'threatened' with a racing trip to Florida and California in the early part of the season. He feared these races would be too much, too soon. 'They talk about them as training races, but there's no such thing as a training race as a professional,' he said.

In the end it wasn't America but Colombia, and the 1,300km national tour, where Millar was sent, but further into the season, in May, with Pascal Simon and Graham Jones among his team-mates. But the earlier interview, in which Millar complained about racing in the cold of the early season, sparked a mini row on the letters page of *Cycling* magazine. 'With a negative attitude like Millar's, why doesn't he let someone take his place who would dearly love to do what he does?' asked one correspondent, a Mr R. Gair. 'R. Gair hasn't a clue what he's talking about,' came the angry response from a member of Millar's first club, the Glenmarnock Wheelers. 'Robert has one of the most positive attitudes towards cycling, and has been totally dedicated to the extent that he used to train every night, usually all night, on dark country roads, in all weather, as an amateur. Robert is a glutton for punishment, and certainly does not love it. He is only motivated by his personal dreams to be a good professional and ultimately ride the Tour de France.' It's revealing to note that although Millar relished the punishment of training, the correspondent felt it necessary to clarify that he certainly did not love it. Perish the thought!

Having again been overlooked for Paris-Nice, Millar had a quiet start to the season, but he showed that he had his climbing legs in the hilly Tour of Romandie, where he finished seventh, just before leaving for Colombia for a race which, because it was held at altitude, was considered useful preparation for the Tour de France. For Millar, the signs were promising for the Tour. By the end of June Maurice de Muer had selected nine of his ten riders, with the tenth place left open; it would go either to Millar or to an older Frenchman, Andre Chalmel. Enhancing Millar's prospects was the fact that Chalmel had had a dismal spring; going against them was Chalmel's status as a respected professional: he was president of the Union Nationale des Cyclistes Professionels, the French professionals' trade union. Yet the team leader, Jean-René Bernaudeau, made it clear that he favoured Millar, and as the Tour approached Millar himself was so confident that he would get the nod that he missed the British championship, anticipating that he would be called to attend a pre-Tour Peugeot rendezvous in Paris. Later, Millar revealed that he had been told he was a 'probable' for the Tour. But with depressing predictability de Muer elected to send Chalmel, in circumstances that left Millar seething. 'As it turned out, I only found out through a friend that I wasn't in the Tour team after all,' he said. 'He read about it in *L'Equipe*. No one bothered to tell me.' Even reflecting on the saga two years later, Millar remained bitter. 'What they did to me you wouldn't do to a dog,' he told Robin Magowan of *Cyclist Monthly*. (Presumably he wasn't thinking here of Madame de Muer's unfortunate Scotty.)

Not surprisingly, it was rumoured that Millar was looking to leave the Peugeot team, but two things changed that. First, Maurice de Muer announced his retirement, and his replacement was a younger man, Roland Berland. Second, Millar salvaged his season, and considerably increased his marketability, by finishing runner-up to a dominant Greg LeMond in September's 'Tour of the Future', the Tour de l'Avenir. His performance highlighted to Peugeot, and to Berland, that they would be crazy to let him go elsewhere. He re-signed with the French squad for a substantially improved contract.

At that time a veil of secrecy was thrown over what cyclists were paid; suffice to say it was considerably less than footballers or tennis players. Although the sport's showcase event, the Tour de France, generated somewhere between twenty-three and thirty million francs (around £2.7 million), the riders saw little of that, with only two million francs (£182,000) distributed in prize money. In the Peugeot team in 1982, 6,000F was the basic monthly pay, with some riders – specialist sprinters or climbers,

Millar in Glasgow Wheelers colours in 1977, limping across the line after crashing in the Leyland GP.

Above Racing for France's top amateur club, ACBB of Paris, on the way to third in the 1979 Tour de Haut Languedoc.

Right The 18-year-old Millar grimaces after a British road race.

Below British team-mate John Herety (no.2) leads Millar (no.4) in the 1979 Sealink International.

Above Millar leads Peugeot team-mate and close friend Pascal Simon in the 1982 Dauphiné Libéré.

Below Ahead of the 1984 world championship in Barcelona, Millar chats with his former mentor Arthur Campbell.

Right Clothing adjustments on the move during Millar's debut Tour de France, 1983.

Left With Patricio Jimenez of Colombia on stage ten of the 1983 Tour, en route to his first professional victory.

Below At a pre-season Peugeot presentation, Millar poses somewhat awkwardly with team-mates Allan Peiper (left) and Sean Yates.

Above Climbing through the crowds in the polka-dot jersey in a time trial stage of the 1984 Tour.

Left Crowning glory: the first and only English-speaking King of the Mountains in the Tour de France of 1984.

Above Entering the velodrome on the final time trial of the 1985 Vuelta, with victory seemingly assured.

Above Defending yellow in the 1986 Vuelta, with 1985 victor Pedro Delgado on the far right.

Right The second of his three Tour de France stage wins at Guzet-Neige in 1984.

Left Former coach and mentor Billy Bilsland with Millar in his cycle shop in Glasgow.

Being introduced to the crowd in his home city of Glasgow before the Kellogg's criterium, 1985 (Graham Jones is behind, looking down).

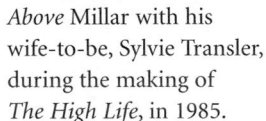

Above Millar with his wife-to-be, Sylvie Transler, during the making of *The High Life*, in 1985.

Left With his two-year-old son, Edward, at home in Bercenay-en-Othe.

Left Relaxing after a training ride in his renovated farmhouse, by the 'walk-in' fire-place, 1991.

who were capable of winning classics and stages – on 10,000F, and the team leader, Bernaudeau, reportedly on 30,000F (£2,750). It is likely that Millar's improved contract was worth somewhere between 6,000F and 10,000F per month, though prize money, traditionally pooled and shared among the team, would boost this. But it wasn't until 1990, when LeMond signed a three-year deal worth $5.7 million with Z (the company that took over as title sponsors of the Peugeot team) that cyclists' salaries began to move into the public domain, and also into the premier league of earnings. Eventually Lance Armstrong – admittedly an exceptional case – would be earning in the region of $18 million a year, even if 'only' around 20 per cent of that constituted the salary from his team.

For Millar, money was – it hardly needs stating – of huge importance. Lurking at the back of his mind was the idea of returning to work in a factory in Glasgow, a prospect that terrified him. He had lofty sporting ambitions, clearly, but his mission, his *raison d'être*, was more complicated than that. Coupled to his dream of becoming a world-class cyclist was his dream of escape, permanent escape, from where he had come. 'I remember one of his goals was to make a million pounds,' says Ronan Pensec, a team-mate of Millar's in three different teams between 1985 and 1995. 'He did everything towards that. He wanted to be successful in cycling so that he could put his feet up afterwards. I thought that was a great idea!' Of course, Millar was acutely aware of the limited timespan of a professional career; he knew that, at best, he was likely to have a decade to earn enough money to set himself up for life, which is certainly what he intended to do. After all, what else could an individualist dream of than of being absolutely self-reliant? But it meant two things: he had to earn as much as he could, and he couldn't go crazy with what he had.

Which brings us, metaphorically at least, back to *péage* barriers on French toll roads. As Stephen Roche witnessed first hand, Millar had ingenious methods of saving, or not spending, money. But carrying a set of bolt cutters in the boot of the car wasn't his only ruse. Just as renowned was his trick of leaving his car at the airport car park, sometimes for weeks, then driving it out without paying the full fee, or, in some cases, anything at all. By retrieving a buggy from the airport and driving it up to the entrance of the car park he could activate the barrier and collect a new ticket, which he'd then use to leave the car park. 'I learned a few tricks from Robert,' says Roche with a smile. Then he adds wistfully, 'You can't get away with that one any more.'

Patrick Valcke, the mechanic at Peugeot, recalls that when the airport car park ticket scam didn't work, Millar would put a back-up plan into operation. By driving so close to the car in front that the bumpers were touching, he could trick the barrier into allowing two cars out for the price of one. This could be a risky business, however. On one occasion Millar misjudged the manoeuvre and strayed too far from Valcke's rear bumper, with one inevitable consequence: the barrier came down and smashed his windscreen. 'He made an arse of it,' says Valcke, laughing and shaking his head. 'He got a real kick out of screwing the taxman, screwing the road tolls. It was almost orgasmic for him to screw the road toll for five francs! But I tell you, he took as much pleasure screwing someone out of five francs as he did for screwing them out of ten thousand. It was the same level of pleasure.'

Even later in his career, when his salary put him in the sport's top bracket of earners, Millar persisted with his extreme, and eccentric, money-saving scams. Dag Otto Lauritzen, another team-mate, recalls one journey to Nice for a pre-season training camp. 'Every time there was a gate open on the freeway he turned off, to save money on the tolls. I saw him use the bolt cutters, too. He would save maybe twenty francs but we would drive for an hour because we'd get lost on the small roads.

We were always late. It was terrible to drive with him.'
Interestingly, Lauritzen isn't convinced that his behaviour should
simply be put down to Scottish stinginess. 'I don't think it was
about money; it was more of a sport for Robert,' says the
Norwegian. Others agree with this, and Valcke points out that he
wasn't unique in this regard. 'You think, "Shit, this guy's earning
a huge wage and he doesn't want to pay five francs for the *péage*."
But he wasn't alone. A lot of riders who made a decent wage did
the same. And for Robert it was the principle. Robert was huge
on principle when it came to not paying money.'

As far as Graham Jones is concerned, it was just another act
of rebellion. Certainly Millar seemed always to enjoy getting
one over on the 'establishment' or the authorities, whether
that meant wearing a denim jacket to school, sleeping in the
toilets at Weir's, avoiding tolls on French roads, or, as he
allegedly did while at the ACBB, sewing up a sleeve in his
jacket and filling it with food as he wandered around the
supermarket. Though 'enjoy' is perhaps not strong enough:
he seemed to need to get one up on the authorities, to thumb
his nose at the establishment.

Less well known is Millar's generous side. On visits home to
Glasgow, although he sold off much of his racing kit, he kept
the most prized garments – his personal kit – to give to the
young cyclist he'd later help set up at the ACBB. Millar was
friendly with Brian Smith's father Don, a well-respected figure
on the west of Scotland cycling scene. Smith junior was 13 and
just getting into cycling when Millar visited the family home.
'Every year after that he'd give me his personal kit,' says Smith.
'The stuff he sold was the team kit, but this stuff had his name
on it. He gave me the shirts he'd raced in. I used to wear them
all the time.' Smith claims he has no idea why he was singled
out by Millar for special treatment. 'I think it was because he
liked my dad.' Regarding his reputation as a spendthrift, Smith
offers this line of defence: 'He was thinking of the future, that's

what he was always doing. He didn't like paying money to the authorities – who does? – but he wouldn't screw other people out of money.'

His excellent ride in the Tour de l'Avenir – the best ever performance in this race by a Briton – didn't necessarily mean any extra money for the Millar coffers. In 1982 Millar hardly raced – only fifty-five days, he reckoned, 'less than half that of most professionals . . . It also means that I have made less money than the others. Coming second in the Tour de l'Avenir doesn't mean any extra: the team has only made about £800 during the race.' But, he conceded, for a man who had recently been dubbed 'the forgotten man of British cycling' by one journalist it certainly 'means a lot for my career'. It rankled, however, that in three years as a professional he had yet to win a race. If he stood out in the peloton, it was as much for the small pearl-white stud that now adorned his left ear as for his modest *palmares* (effectively, his cycling CV).

A largely disappointing season – summed up by Millar's decision to give up his place in the world championship, held at Goodwood in Britain, citing poor form – was followed in December by the most fascinating interview yet. As he would sometimes do, Millar revealed more of himself than he perhaps intended, in this instance to the *Cycling* reporter Dennis Donovan.

Was he, as his reputation suggested, difficult to get on with?

'Basically, I'm shy,' replied Millar. 'It's the way I was brought up. I was taught that my opinions don't count for much.' He also feared failure: 'When you arrive at a certain level and say what you are going to do, you can fall flat on your face.' But, he continued, 'I would say that I'm self-motivated and very independent. Not selfish. If I can do something myself I will do it, I don't like to ask. It's the environment I was brought up in. I'm more independent than the rest of my family. Sometimes I don't need people at all.'

Is it a handicap being a Scot?

'Why do you ask? No, it's more an advantage being a Scot. You have to work harder because, being a Scot, you are reckoned to be inferior.' But he added that his country wasn't foremost in his thoughts when he raced. 'In my mind, I'm doing it for Robert Millar. If Peugeot are paying, then I'm doing it for Peugeot. If the BCF [British Cycling Federation] were to pay, then I'd be doing it for them. If I thought anything it would be for British cycling, not Scottish, because that's too limited. Politically, I think differently . . .'

Finally, he was asked whether he felt he was following in the footsteps of Ian Steel, the Scotsman who won the world's hardest amateur race, the Peace Race, and his mentor, Billy Bilsland. Again Millar's response is as intriguing as it is defiant and uncompromising. 'At no time am I in the shadow of Ian Steel or Billy Bilsland,' he said. 'I'm more in the shadow of Tom Simpson. Comparisons have been made between myself and Billy, but it's best not to compare. It's no good making the same mistakes twice.' It isn't clear what he meant by this; perhaps simply that he hoped to become more than just a good *domestique*, or team helper – a star in his own right, possibly.

Millar also described riding the Tour as his 'burning ambition', yet he seemed to be at pains to paint a fairly bleak picture of cycling on the continent, which hardly sounded more appealing than growing up in Glasgow and going to work in Weir's factory. 'Racing on the continent is a jungle,' he said. 'You have to consider when you turn up for a race that if you don't win it, then you may not eat next week [he's referring here to amateur racing]. When people first go to the continent to race from Britain they think it's glamorous. It's not.' However, he did concede that he did it 'because I like doing it. At the level I'm at I have to earn my money. Now and again I have to do something that I don't want to do, but I have to improve my commercial prospects.'

When asked to look ahead to the future, and life beyond cycling, there was a degree of uncertainty. 'I don't know. I didn't finish my engineering studies. If I'd stayed to finish them I would have been too old to come to France. I will race until I am 32 and will stay on the continent. Nothing interests me at the moment, and I don't see myself as an official. I'll be a masseur, a mechanic, or something. I couldn't get into the political side.'

As well as the departure of Maurice de Muer and the promotion of Roland Berland to the position of *directeur sportif*, there were other changes at Peugeot for the 1983 season. Through the revolving door came another young British rider, Sean Yates, and an Australian, Allan Peiper, both via the ACBB. Heading in the other direction was Graham Jones, who left to join the Wolber team, where he would serve the now former Peugeot leader Jean-René Bernaudeau. The departure of Bernaudeau meant that Millar's friend Pascal Simon was expected to step up to the rôle of co-leader, alongside Phil Anderson. All of which, on paper at least, seemed to augur rather well for Millar.

A packed racing programme – Tour of the Mediterranean, the Haut-Var, Tour of Corsica, Criterium National, Tour of America (where Millar blamed illness on being 'not thin enough yet'), Liège-Bastogne-Liège, Flèche Wallonne, Circuit de la Sarthe, Tour of Romandie, Tour de l'Oise, Dauphiné Libéré, Midi Libre, Tour de l'Aude – took Millar up to July and, finally, surely, his Tour de France debut. Managing third behind Simon and LeMond in the Dauphiné, the prestigious mini Tour de France that acts as a precursor to the main event, meant his selection was a fait accompli. A week after the Dauphiné had apparently concluded Millar found himself promoted to second, Simon having been relegated for testing positive following the final stage. For Simon it meant a slap on the wrist and a token fine, no more (he maintained that the positive reading came from taking a hayfever treatment, micorene, administered by the team doctor). It changed nothing as far as the Tour was concerned: Simon started as Peugeot's de facto leader, with support from Millar and another Tour debutant, Stephen Roche. In a prescient development, it was also the first Tour de France to be shown live on British television: ITV's flagship sports programme *World of Sport* was due to broadcast coverage of stages on three consecutive Saturdays, following a preview show on the opening day of the race.

For any Tour debutant, particularly one with his eye on the mountain stages, the first week of the race can be a fraught, nervous ordeal. A large peloton containing 140 of the world's best riders, many of them in peak condition and all of them eager to shine, means that the pace is fast and, given the fighting that goes on to maintain a good position in the bunch, crashes are relatively common. For Millar, hoping merely to survive the first week unscathed and remain relatively fresh for the mountains, the opening to the 1983 Tour was a disaster.

After a good team time trial in which Peugeot placed second – though Anderson complained that Roche and Millar were the only team-mates who worked with him – stage 3 took the riders to Roubaix and over the infamous cobbles that feature in Paris-Roubaix, the one-day classic also known – and here's the giveaway – as the Hell of the North. 'A day of heat, punctures and crashes,' reported *Cycling*. Millar did not fall once, nor twice, but three times in the course of the 152km stage from Valenciennes, finally limping in more than fourteen minutes behind the peloton. Any hopes he had of making an impression on the overall standings had disappeared in the clouds of dust blown up by the *pavé*. 'I was brought down on the very first section of *pavé*,' explained Millar. 'I got up, but someone fell off right in front of me fifty metres later. I went right over the top of him.' He remounted again, got himself into a chasing group that was within three hundred metres of regaining contact with the peloton, then hit another rider who crashed in front of him. 'That was the end for me.' The next day's stage didn't feature cobbles, but at 300km it didn't offer much chance for recovery from his injuries, either. 'It was so hot I got through fifteen *bidons* [bottles] of water, perhaps more,' said Millar. 'But I didn't feel hungry, as my breakfast kept coming up.'

Welcome, Robert, to the Tour de France. Only seventeen days to go.

Just as the race entered the mountains, a doping controversy hit after it was revealed that Joop Zoetemelk, the 1980 winner, had tested positive for a synthetic hormone after the team time trial. What is most striking, considering this with the benefit of hindsight, and with today's much-changed perspective on doping, is how open and frank riders were on the subject; and also how hard done by they felt to have been snared. 'It's a medicine I took before the season to help build up my system,' explained Zoetemelk with a shrug. 'The test leaves me puzzled. I haven't taken the hormone for over three months.' The bigger scandal was that Zoetemelk threatened to abandon the race in protest, though in the end he was persuaded to stay by his wife and the president of the Dutch federation. He received a one-month suspended ban, a 1,000 Swiss franc fine, relegation to last on the stage, and a ten-minute forfeit overall. By the end of the Tour another five riders had tested positive. One of them, Patric Clerc, also held up his hands. 'I plead guilty, but I had to look after myself after riding the Dauphiné Libéré and Bordeaux-Paris, which left me exhausted. If I hadn't done so, I would not have ridden the Tour.'

Ironically, Millar's crashes on stage 3 proved to be a blessing. Had the rough and broken roads to Roubaix not cost him so much time then it is likely, as Millar himself acknowledged, that the events of 11 July – Millar's dramatic entry on to cycling's world stage – would never have unfolded.

Stage 10 of the 1983 Tour de France took the riders on a classic Pyrenean stage from Pau to Luchon over a distance of 198km with the typically rugged and uneven profile of a mountain stage, its four peaks jutting skywards like sharks' teeth. This was the toughest stage of the 1983 Tour, with the passes of the Col de l'Aubisque at 55km, Col du Tourmalet at 120km, Col d'Aspin at 152km and the Col de Peyrosourde at 183km, followed by a fast 15km descent into the spa town. On the 18km Aubisque, ranked 'hors catégorie' (so steep that it is deemed to be beyond classification), the ace Dutch climber Lucien Van Impe – the only cyclist Millar ever described as a hero – jumped clear of a dwindling group of front-runners to lead over the summit, and thus take maximum points towards the King of the Mountains competition. Millar was in the group, comprising twenty-one riders, just behind the 36-year-old Dutchman, riding a record fourteenth Tour and gunning for his sixth King of the Mountains title. Behind them, and in major trouble, was the Irishman Sean Kelly, wearing the race leader's yellow jersey.

Millar was vigilant throughout, joining a nine-man counter-attack and then responding to an acceleration by a member of the Colombian team, Patrocinio Jimenez, on the lower slopes of the Tourmalet. It hadn't been an attack, Millar said later, simply a case of Jimenez setting a pace that those behind – with the exception of Millar – couldn't match. Jimenez was first over the 2,113-metre summit of the Tourmalet, the highest point of the 1983 Tour; behind the Colombian and the Scot, Laurent Fignon and Pedro Delgado were chasing, but more than four minutes further back. Still, there remained two first-category climbs and 60km before the finish; it was asking a lot of two Tour novices to hold their advantage. On the 26km descent of the Tourmalet their lead began to tumble alarmingly, prompting Millar to have words, in the little Spanish he knew, with his companion. The Colombian nodded. They seemed to have an agreement, but what did it involve?

There was perhaps a clue when Jimenez led up the penultimate climb, the Col d'Aspin, taking maximum points at the
top, but by the final ascent, the Peyrosourde, Millar looked
fresher; he seemed to have more in reserve than the
Colombian. And as they neared the summit, with Delgado now
closing on them, Millar made his move, just five hundred
metres from the top, where an excitable crowd thickened to
such an extent that there remained only a narrow corridor of
road. With Jimenez leading, but labouring, his body betraying
signs of almost total exhaustion, Millar launched a decisive and
devastating attack, sprinting around the Colombian's right
shoulder. Jimenez's head dropped; he had no response. Millar,
meanwhile, raced through the corridor of cheering fans and
gave it everything on the descent, his small frame perched on
the nose of the saddle, pedalling furiously, mouth open, nose
almost touching the centre of his handlebars, eyes wide open
and betraying an almost maniacal desire to win, while the
Peugeot team car, with Roland Berland at the wheel, pulled
alongside, telling him to give it everything, because Delgado
was getting dangerously close.

It was just as well Millar did ride so hard: when he arrived in
Luchon he was only six seconds ahead of his Spanish pursuer.
Jimenez, who lost a minute and a half in the final 15km, was
overhauled by both Delgado and another chaser, Pascal Simon,
who took over the race lead. It was a day of carnage. Sean Kelly,
in his yellow jersey, conceded more than ten minutes to Millar.
Roche was another three behind Kelly.

Ever the professional, Millar managed to slip his white
Peugeot racing cap onto his head before he crossed the line.
Then came what would become his familiar salute: both arms
in the air, clenched fists falling down behind his head, then
pumped back into the air, palms open. And he was smiling. 'I
knew when I got up in the morning I was going to win that day,'
Millar remarked later. 'I just felt it. I just felt that nobody was

going to beat me that day. I was very confident all day.' What had he said to the Colombian? 'I can speak a little bit of Spanish and he can speak a little bit of French, so we could communicate a bit. He was worried that I was going to leave him earlier, eh. And I was worried that he was going to go up the hills faster. I attacked him at the end; I could see he was very tired. But I knew even if it came down to the sprint I'd have beaten him, eh.' In another interview, Millar said that the 'deal' he cut with the Colombian was designed to ensure that he wasn't dropped. 'I said to Jimenez he could win the mountain so he wouldn't go too hard . . . I just told him, "Montana." He said, "Sí, sí. Primero, you segundo." So I said, "OK." . . . I said to him if he went easy up the hills I would go easy on the descent, eh.' Nearing the finish in Luchon, Millar said that he 'looked round at three kilometres to go and I could see the guy [Delgado] coming. So I put myself on the rivet again . . . And then at 500 metres I took the hat out for publicity, put the hat on nice. And put the arms up, eh. Always have to remember that.'

Millar's victory was widely acclaimed as Britain's greatest stage win in any of the major tours. It was the first in the mountains. He became the first Scot to win a stage, of course, and only the fourth Briton, joining Barry Hoban, Brian Robinson and Michael Wright, who, despite his name and passport, was brought up in Belgium and could barely speak English. Even more surprisingly, and although he managed to finish sixth overall in 1962, a stage win in the Tour eluded the late, great Tom Simpson. But what was so impressive, and so inspiring, about Millar's stage win was the style with which he won it, and the terrain on which he won it. At the time, a Danish journalist turned to John Wilcockson, a British colleague, and said, 'What a beautiful sight. Your Millar is simply tremendous.' Wilcockson, in turn, compared Millar's climbing ability to Fausto Coppi, Federico Bahamontes and Charly Gaul – arguably the three greatest mountain goats of all time.

And yet, as Millar himself conceded, he might never have been allowed to escape with Jimenez had he not lost those fourteen minutes on stage 3. He had reason, in the end, to be grateful for the *pavé*.

Back in Glasgow, in Billy Bilsland's bike shop, the phone rang. It was *Cycling* magazine, and Arthur Campbell, who was visiting the shop at the time, answered.

'Hello, Arthur. Good news for you. Robert's won today's stage.'

'No. You're joking. Are you serious?'

'Yes, it's true.'

The line fell silent.

'We don't produce many,' Campbell said eventually, 'but when we do, they're good.'

Pascal Simon can recall vividly the evening of 11 July 1983, when Millar, his team-mate, room-mate and friend, won the Pau-Luchon stage of the Tour and Simon himself took over the race leader's yellow jersey. The memory prompts a smile from the lanky, still lean Simon, sitting at home in Troyes on his fiftieth birthday. 'The whole team were knocking on the door, going "Ding, ding, ding, can we come in?" We had the yellow jersey, the stage win, the money from the stage . . .'

One of those team-mates was Allan Peiper, who that same evening asked Millar a teasing but good-natured question: 'How come you win nothing as a professional for four years then come along and win the biggest stage of the Tour de France?' Millar either did not pick up on the gentle humour, or he did but considered that the question deserved a serious response regardless. His reply is highly revealing: 'Because for those four years I have worked hard, I have always worked hard, and what happened today is a reward for those years of effort.'

The bespectacled Simon sits back in his chair, allowing his long limbs to relax, and he chuckles, looking inordinately content. But then he frowns. Because Simon didn't just take over the yellow jersey that day more than two decades earlier, he also became the outstanding favourite to keep it all the way to the finish in Paris. With a lead of more than four minutes on the unproven Laurent Fignon, he could hardly have been in a stronger position. Just as importantly, he had a strong team to support him, with Millar emerging as one of the strongest climbers in the race.

But the next day, disaster struck. After 46km, Simon fell in a crash near the front of the bunch, where he was sitting, defending his yellow jersey. Simon's team waited for him to remount and they paced him back to the peloton, but he was in pain. He dropped back again, and was helped only by Anderson, Millar, and then Roche, who was ordered by Berland to drop back. At the end of the stage Millar and Roche were credited with keeping Simon in yellow. But Simon was in desperate trouble: he had broken his left shoulder blade. Remarkably, he struggled on for another six days, until the race reached the Alps. He abandoned on the 223km stage to Alpe d'Huez, becoming the ninth rider to quit while wearing the yellow jersey. By then his advantage had been trimmed to just fifty-two seconds over the eventual winner, Fignon, but even today many refer to the 1983 Tour as the race that Simon lost rather than the race that Fignon won.

The Peugeot team and Berland, its *directeur sportif*, made a dreadful mistake in effectively sacrificing Millar, Roche and Anderson to the futile defence of Simon's yellow jersey over those six days. It was obvious to everyone that Simon would be doomed as soon as they reached the Alps, and so it proved. Millar even made it into a potentially decisive break with Van Impe that raced to a lead of ten minutes on one stage, but he was ordered not to work by Berland. The break was caught with seven miles to go.

Millar had devoted himself to nursing Simon through that second week, but with his team leader gone he was at least free to pursue his own ambitions, which meant trying to win the King of the Mountains competition. He'd worn the polka-dot jersey for one day, and remained in contention as they entered the Alps. In the end, Van Impe was imperious, matching the record of Federico Bahamontes, the 'Eagle of Toledo', with his sixth King of the Mountains title. But Millar, who eventually placed third in the mountains classification, continued his ascent of the overall classification and eventually finished fourteenth in Paris, despite suffering stomach trouble in the Alpine stages. It was the best British performance since Tom Simpson managed the same placing in 1964. It was also far and away the best ever Tour for English speakers, with Anderson ninth, Kelly seventh, Boyer twelfth and Roche thirteenth. Roche maintains that this Tour provided him with the first evidence that he could live with the best in the high mountains, and he says he has Millar to thank for that. 'I modelled myself on Robert for climbing. I wasn't a climber. But on the stage to Morzine [stage 18, which included six major climbs] Robert and I sat second and third on the Col de Joux Plane. I followed him all the way up. When he was pedalling he had a rhythm. I had a tempo.' It is a subtle but important distinction between the natural, instinctive climber and the strong all-rounder, as Roche would become.

There was another clear difference between Roche and Millar. While Roche tended to greet reporters and fans with a smile, Millar typically did not. 'The autograph hunter thrust a grubby piece of paper under the nose of Robert Millar but he was wasting his time,' reported Cycling's Martin Ayres, who followed Millar around the Dijon time trial, the Tour's penultimate stage, and then observed him waving the autograph hunter away. Ayres reported that a substantial convoy had followed Millar around the time trial, which was testament to the impact he'd made on the race. Not only that, but in one of the cars sat none other than Jacques Goddet, the man who directed the Tour for more than half a century, and who, as Ayres observed, 'probably never dreamed he would see a Scot, an Irishman, an American and an Australian in the first twenty'. It wasn't a stage that was suited to Millar's talents, the only incident of note being when a camera-wielding supporter stepped out into the road, moving aside at the last minute. 'That fool of a photographer' as Millar referred to him.

Another smaller setback for Millar had come on the first Alpine stage, which had seen Simon's withdrawal. On visiting the Peugeot mechanics he'd learned that they hadn't prepared his 'special bike' for the stage to Alpe d'Huez. He was, reported *Cyclist Monthly*, 'violently angry, cursing his mechanics'. Millar later complained that being denied his lightweight carbon-fibre machine meant he was 'so tensed up about it that I didn't ride well'. Patrick Valcke says that Millar could be quite obsessive in his attention to apparently small details, though he described him as 'demanding but fair'. 'He always had strange little habits on the bike,' he adds. 'We worked out his ways. When he didn't ask us mechanics for anything special it meant he was going to have an average day. When he came to ask us for something – say, new tyres for the next day – then you knew he was going to do something special. It was a sign. With me, he was never nasty. He was quite able to lose the plot with the *soigneurs* if his musette didn't have the right stuff in it. But then again, who wouldn't? The thing about Robert was, he never spoke down to you. He could speak to the team mechanic and the team manager exactly the same way. For him there was no difference, and no compromise.'

In August, Millar found himself in demand on the lucrative post-Tour criterium circuit. It is in such races that riders who have made a name for themselves in the Tour can cash in. They are typically held on relatively short, spectator-friendly circuits, and are invariably won by a local 'hero', which usually owes as much to an arrangement with said hero's fellow riders as it does to his strength and tactical nous. But such arrangements do not compromise the crowd's enjoyment, and it ensures that the financial rewards tend to be split fairly evenly among the big-name riders.

Millar based himself in St Niklaas in Belgium after the Tour, to enable him to race in Belgium and Holland, and to make regular visits to Britain to ride in two of the new Kellogg's events, which were modelled on the continental criterium circuit. In total, Millar rode twenty events in August. Even allowing for their status as little more than exhibition events, it is incredible to contemplate that he went straight from the three weeks of the Tour to racing on a virtual daily basis for the next month.

The Kellogg's races, held in cities throughout the UK, represented an intriguing development, and they provided more evidence that seismic change was afoot in the world of professional cycling. After the English speakers' emergence as genuine contenders in the Tour de France, the revolution was now taking place on British soil too, in the shape of lucrative and well-attended events backed by a big sponsor and featuring some of the biggest names in the sport. Anderson, Roche, Kelly, Sherwen, Peiper and Jones were all regulars, and even the Italian star Francesco Moser managed an appearance in Bristol. Millar rode in Manchester and Birmingham, but missed what would surely have been a triumphant homecoming in Glasgow – which is perhaps why he opted not to go. Nevertheless, a crowd of some twenty-six thousand materialized on the streets of Glasgow for the evening race.

It was the start of a golden period for the sport in Britain. Alan Rushton, the man behind the Kellogg's criteriums, which later evolved into the Kellogg's Tour of Britain, says that 1983 was the breakthrough year, after 'a lot of effort to crack TV'. It was also a consequence of a new television channel, Channel 4. 'At that time cycling was the thirty-first most popular television sport in Britain,' Rushton continues. 'There were twenty registered professionals in Britain in 1983, and it was dwindling. But in 1984 there were forty, then fifty, sixty, and seventy in 1987.' The city-centre events were televised at peak time, from 8 p.m. to 9 p.m., drawing up to 2.8 million viewers. By 1987 cycling had become the fifth most popular TV sport in the UK, outperforming rugby union and Formula One. 'Millar, Anderson, Kelly, Roche, Peiper and Sherwen were vital to the whole thing,' says Rushton.

Come December and Millar was a shoo-in for Cycling's Man of the Year. 'I'll be going for the mountains prize and a place in the top six overall,' he said of his ambitions for the 1984 Tour. It was in this interview that he confessed to idolizing Lucien Van Impe. 'He was always a hero of mine. It was strange having to fight with him, but I learnt a lot. I'm not afraid of him and next year he'll be a year older.'

In the event, Van Impe didn't ride in the 1984 Tour. But in the little Belgian climber's place there was someone there who bore more than a passing resemblance to him: Millar. They had a similarly slight build anyway, and both stood at five feet six inches, but now Millar's hair had been transformed from a short back and sides to a curly mop, just like Van Impe. Noticing this, the Irish journalist David Walsh described the Scot as 'quiet, self-effacing, one thinks of Robert Millar as impish – Van Impish'. Indeed. All Millar had to do now was inherit the diminutive Belgian climber's polka-dot jersey.

7

The Shirt in the Shop

I enjoy climbing. I enjoy seeing people disappear behind me . . .
You get a sadistic pleasure out of it.

Billy Bilsland Cycles sits on a busy main road in the east end of
Glasgow, wedged between a video store and a shop selling school-
wear, opposite a hairdresser's and a beauty salon, a few doors
along from a pawn shop. It is a typical and ordinary British bike
shop, modest in size and unostentatious. But amid the clutter of
tightly stacked new bikes, the colourful rails of clothing, and the
gleaming glass cabinets of components, this shop is home to an
historic and very special piece of cycling memorabilia.

Thousands pass Bilsland's shop every day, yet few would
know, and fewer still would care, that the item of clothing displayed high up on the wall, pressed flat in a glass case as if it
were a rare butterfly, happens to be one of the most prized
items in world sport. If this were in any town or city in France,
Belgium, Holland, Italy or Spain, it might be considered a cult
tourist attraction. As it is, you could visit Billy Bilsland Cycles
and miss it entirely. Most do.

So, open the door, take one step inside, glance up to your
left . . . a little higher . . . there it is: Robert Millar's polka-dot

jersey, his reward for being crowned King of the Mountains in the 1984 Tour de France. Its red spots might be a little faded, but otherwise it is perfectly preserved. To its right hangs a jersey belonging to the greatest cyclist of them all, the Belgian Eddy Merckx, with the message 'To Billy Bilsland Cycles, Best regards, Eddy Merckx'. But pride of place still belongs to Millar's jersey.

It has been there since 1984, when, following the Tour, Millar visited his old mentor. The shop was often his first port of call on trips home, and on this occasion Bilsland's protégé wandered in and tossed him the jersey. Actually, it's more than a jersey: it's the one-piece ensemble of shirt and black shorts that Millar wore in the final time trial. Had Bilsland been expecting such a gift? 'No,' he says with a shrug. Was he surprised? 'Yes,' he says with another shrug. But he went out and got it framed, and it has hung in the shop ever since.

It is a grey, nondescript afternoon in early summer, or late spring, when I call in to see the jersey. Amid the busy, bustling Saltmarket, five minutes from Glasgow city centre and the River Clyde, with the Gorbals on the other side of the water, it is an incongruous garment, a piece of exotica as well as memorabilia. 'L'Equipe' is spelled out in black lettering on the right breast, with 'Poulain' (a make of chocolate) on the left. The shorts are plain black apart from a small Le Coq Sportif logo.

Today, Billy has retired to his racing pigeons, leaving his son, Neil, to run the shop. I ask Neil whether anyone ever comes in to see it, or asks about it. 'Occasionally,' he replies, shrugging like his father.

Then I fulfil the purpose of my visit: I study the jersey, struggling to reconcile it with the deed, trying to recall how it was won. After all, it was this Tour de France that provided me with my first sighting of the Tour, and of Millar, on his way to winning the stage that proved a springboard to the King of the Mountains title. By virtue of winning that title, Millar became the first, and so far only, British rider ever to stand on the Tour's final podium in Paris. Staggeringly, he also remains the only English-speaking cyclist ever to be crowned King of the Mountains. Even the trio of English-speaking Tour winners, Greg LeMond, Stephen Roche and Lance Armstrong, never managed that. So the outfit that hangs in Billy Bilsland Cycles is pretty special. Very special. Though, again, I suspect that the neighbouring pawn shop wouldn't be particularly interested.

But as I try to block out the noise of buses and lorries thundering past on the road outside and sending minor tremors around the shop, and while I attempt to conjure in my mind the snow-capped Pyrenean peaks where this polka-dot jersey was won, I realize that there is something utterly appropriate, something very Millaresque, about the fact that the jersey is now so out of situ, so dislocated, that it can so easily be overlooked and ignored. It seems only right, somehow, that the symbol of Millar's greatest achievement hangs in a small shop on a busy thoroughfare in the east end of Glasgow, its owner having vanished.

Had Millar, like Eddy Merckx, thought to scrawl a message on it, it might have read 'Been there, done that, got the T-shirt'.

For the 1984 season, Millar moved from Troyes to Lille in northern France. His new apartment was modest but, later that year, in an interview with Glasgow's *Evening Times*, Millar demonstrated that his skills of diplomacy and tact were as polished as ever when he claimed that the standard of living was superior to that of his home city. 'Lille, where I live now, is much the same [as Glasgow] but at least I don't live in a tenement. I have a one bedroom flat but by Glasgow standards it's posh. It's not that I'm ashamed of being a Glaswegian, I most certainly am not, but abroad you find out what you have been missing.'

Millar's move to Lille was for purely pragmatic reasons, and it demonstrated that his work ethic remained intact: even after

winning a stage of the Tour he was not going to become com-
placent. Back in Troyes he had a girlfriend, Sylvie, but Lille
would be better, he reasoned, for travelling to races, in particular for popping across the border into nearby Belgium to ride
the flat, fast races held there virtually on a daily basis. Not
Millar's favourite kind of racing, far from it, but if he was going
to fulfil his potential then he needed to improve in those areas
he wasn't so good at, namely riding fast on the flat roads and
holding his position in a fast-moving bunch. If he could learn
to do so in a flying peloton of big, muscular Belgians, not afraid
to use their bulk and their elbows, then his prospects in the
major tours, of France, Spain and Italy, would rise sharply. Just
as he had turned himself from, in his excessively modest
opinion, average climber to great climber, he intended to
become a decent *rouleur*, too.

Moving to Lille meant that he became a neighbour to several
other professionals, including Graham Jones, Paul Sherwen
and Millar's Norwegian Peugeot team-mate Dag Otto
Lauritzen. It didn't mean that Millar had fallen out with his
Troyes neighbour and team-mate Pascal Simon. In fact, Sylvie,
who worked behind the counter of a canteen in a local factory,
was the sister-in-law of Simon's brother, Jerome, also a professional cyclist. As Stephen Roche only half joked, 'We don't meet
girls so we just end up going out with each other's sisters.'

Pascal was one of the few French riders with whom Millar
seemed to get along, and today Simon confesses that he isn't
quite sure how their friendship started, or on what it was based.
'We shared rooms with each other on races for years, but you
could never say we were best friends,' he says. 'He was discreet,
but I was like that too – a bit reserved. After a race we would go
to the room, each of us would have a shower, and then we
would lie down with a book. More often than not I went to the
rooms of some team-mates and left him on his own. I wouldn't
say today that he was one of my best friends. When he talked it

was mainly about training or the race. He didn't say much about his private life. We were quite capable of going out training together for two or three hours and not saying a word to each other.' Not that they trained together every day: Simon preferred to leave early, about 8.30 a.m.; Millar, on the other hand, would typically remain in bed until ten or eleven in the morning, because he rarely went to bed before two in the morning. As he put it to a friend, '"What am I going to do early in the morning?" He didn't see the point of getting up early if he didn't have to.'

Aside from his relaxed approach to getting up in the mornings, Simon admired Millar's dedication. 'Whatever Robert achieved, he did it through hard work. He punished himself on the climbs around here. Robert was one of the first guys to ride with ankle weights on.' He contemplates this for a moment, then adds, 'I think he was the only rider to do that.' Ronan Pensec was another colleague who spoke of Millar approaching training with an almost religious zeal. In fact, just about every former team-mate I met expressed admiration and even wonderment at his commitment – and they weren't exactly lacking in dedication themselves.

When, in 1988, *Cycling* magazine conducted a survey of the top riders' training methods, Millar was the first to respond, and he did so in the most detail. He listed the miles he'd ridden (1,860 between his last race on 17 October and resuming proper training again in early December), the hours he put in (fifteen a week in the winter rising to twenty from March to mid-April, then a minimum of twenty-five a week for the rest of the season), the gears he used, the food he ate, the frequency with which he had massages (twice a week), and also that he did thirty to forty minutes of weight training every day. Even in the off-season 'I don't like to stop, for then you get lazy. After two or three days doing nothing I want to ride again. The same goes for dieting. I might relax my diet just a little, but only for a month, then I keep it fairly strict again.' His sleep require-ments remained the same in summer and winter, 'about ten hours if possible'. 'I seek medical advice before the season starts, and every six weeks or so I have a blood test to check all the levels. It is very important to know exactly where you stand, then you know how to train as a result ... it is very important to have medical supervision throughout the year and not just at the start of the year. I don't really have a coach as such, but my doctor advises me following the tests done on my condi-tion, and advises me on the follow-up required.'

As for targets for each season, Millar said that he keeps this a secret. 'I can only deceive myself then if I fail.' Not that there is any reason to fail. 'You have to want to do it. It is no good only liking to do something. You will not get anything that way, but if you really want something, you will succeed sooner or later. Being an athlete calls for sacrifices, but what you get far outweighs the "losses" sustained. If you pay attention to what you eat – which has a lot more importance than you first think – and to how you train, and how much rest you get, then nothing is impossible.'

Apart from Pascal Simon, another rider who befriended Millar, in so far as this appears to have been possible, was Allan Peiper, the Australian who had joined Peugeot in 1983. Peiper is a fascinating character and something of a rarity in professional cycling. He had a tough upbringing, much of it on the move, some of it spent in a small town with an unmis-takably Scottish name – Bannockburn, in Victoria. But a tough childhood, in his case involving an abusive alcoholic father, is not what sets Peiper apart. Rather, it is his talent for observation and character analysis. He was, and is, possessed of a sense of curiosity and an interest in others that profes-sional athletes tend not to have – or at least not while they are professional athletes, since they are so absorbed, necessarily so, in themselves and in what they are doing. Yet even when he was competing as a young rider, learning the rules of this curious, complicated game, and just doing his best to survive in the 'jungle' of professional cycling, Peiper took a keen interest in his team-mates. He was certainly one of the few to look beyond Millar's tough and uncompromising exterior, and to wonder whether it might be 'a front', as he writes in his autobiography, 'a safety net, just in case he wasn't accepted, [and] a way of protecting himself from not getting hurt'.

Peiper confessed to me that he always had a soft spot for Millar, and he thinks there were perhaps abstract clues to his team-mate's 'softer', more vulnerable side in the way he padded around the room they sometimes shared on races. Millar walked everywhere, claims Peiper, on the tips of his toes, with the grace and poise of a ballet dancer rather than a cyclist. 'Rob wasn't a man's man, which I don't mean in a demeaning way. He wasn't one of the gang; he wasn't one of the boys. He might have given the impression that he didn't care what people thought about him, but the fact is that we all have ways of attracting attention, or wanting to be the centre of attention. If we're not able to do that with our personality, then we develop ways of covering up the fact. And the thing is that Robert was never going to be liked. He was never going to be Mr Popular. That's just a fact.'

Nevertheless, in Peiper and another 1983 Peugeot recruit, Sean Yates, Millar at least had two allies. Perhaps it was only the fact that all three spoke English, but there was a bond between them, an unspoken sense of loyalty that Peiper and Yates, both big, strong riders on the flat, felt towards the comparatively tiny, almost fragile-looking, but hugely talented man for the mountains.

Peiper and Yates, who remain firm friends, formed something of an unlikely double act. The languid Yates, a master of the understatement, could hardly be more different to the Australian – a fact to which he immediately alludes when I meet him in his native Sussex. Rolling his eyes, he says, 'I'm not a guy like Allan who thinks about everything, and is all philosophy and this and that. I was like, fuck it, turn up in France, ride the bike, see what happens, you know?' It was an approach that took Yates to the ACBB, to Peugeot and, in 1984, to the Tour de France.

Yates first encountered Millar at the 1979 national road race championship. At the time, Yates was determinedly building up his strength, and his bulk, believing that would make him a better, tougher cyclist. 'He was so bloody tiny I couldn't believe it, but so strong,' says Yates of Millar. 'I was doing all these press-ups and here was Robert Millar, who was like two foot two, and he was dropping me on the flat. I thought, "If Robert Millar can drop me on the flat then there's no need to be doing five hundred press-ups a day." So I stopped that.' Yates, who admits he didn't 'knuckle down' to the life of a dedicated professional until the late 1980s – and with spectacular results, such as a time trial stage win in the 1988 Tour de France, and a stint in the yellow jersey in 1994 – couldn't have been more at odds with Millar in his attitude and approach in their early years together. 'He must have had someone close to him in Glasgow who told him what to do,' Yates remarks. 'Nobody knows you're supposed to eat nothing, rest up every moment and train like a dog.' It took Yates years of watching people like Peiper and Millar to appreciate that. Another impression Yates formed of Millar at the time was that 'he could be a right grumpy little sod'.

There is a photograph of Peiper, Yates and Millar at the 1984 Peugeot team presentation which is worth a thousand words. Dressed in team-issue blazers, V-neck jerseys, shirts and ties, they look like schoolboys kitted out in their new uniforms. Peiper, tanned and healthy-looking, is smiling and appears relaxed and engaging; Millar, in the middle, looks malnourished and pale-skinned, lost in his own thoughts and looking like he'd rather be anywhere else; the comparatively chubby Yates is the only one staring directly into the camera, albeit with something of a dazed and confused expression. Studying the picture, it is impossible not to conclude that Millar resembles the kid who'd be bullied if he didn't happen to be flanked by his bigger mates; the popular, charismatic one, and the one who looks like he could be a rugby player.

For 1984, Millar, Peiper and Yates were the only English speakers left at Peugeot, Phil Anderson having made a big-money move to the Dutch Panasonic team, and Stephen Roche having effected a controversial exit to rival French outfit La Redoute. Millar's start to the season had him in the headlines early, when he took the lead halfway through the Paris-Nice eight-day stage race, ahead of Bernard 'the Badger' Hinault – the playground bully of professional cycling. Millar took the white leader's jersey at the summit of Mont Ventoux, the mountain that claimed the life of his predecessor as Britain's great hope, Tom Simpson.

But this was a race remembered not so much for Millar's performance on Ventoux as for the antics of Hinault. Stage 5, to Seyne-sur-Mer, was disrupted when three hundred striking dockyard workers blockaded the road, bringing the race to a halt. Hinault flew into a rage. He refused to accept that the race could be hijacked by striking workers – although, this being France, it wasn't without precedent – and was especially peeved because of the circumstances at the time, Millar having been dropped and Hinault poised to inherit the leader's jersey. According to Roche, Hinault's response was to ride at speed directly into the strikers. 'He came past me doing about 40mph, tightened his toe straps and went straight in on the top sprocket.' Other witnesses report that when he rode into the strikers he knocked several over, fell off himself, then got up and began throwing punches at those who still had the gall to be standing. Hinault was joined by another rider, Andre Chappius, who is said to have felled four of them, while the rest of the field kept a safe distance. In the end, Millar's sixth overall was a footnote. Hinault, despite having suffered a broken rib in the mêlée, managed third overall, behind Sean Kelly and Roche.

For Millar, the build-up to the Tour de France included another trip to Colombia, which was dominated by local riders, and the Tour of Romandie, where he won a stage at Crans-Montana and placed fifth overall. That was followed, in June, by a rare racing outing on British soil, where he was joined by Yates and Peiper for the Isle of Wight Classic. For Peiper, this trip provided an insight to a side of Millar's personality he hadn't previously seen. Going through airport security at Heathrow, the riders afraid that they were going to miss their flight back to France, a female member of staff asked to have a look in Millar's bag. 'Rob said, "What the fuck do you want to have a look in my bag for? There's fucking nothing in there." She got really pissed, you know. But he was really abusive towards her, really irate. Afterwards, I said to him, "Look, Rob, if you ever speak to anybody like that again in my presence I'll fucking knuckle you."' Peiper thinks his warning had the desired effect. He certainly never saw Millar lose his temper so violently again. Yates watched the exchange with bemusement. 'Allan tore a strip off him. I didn't take much notice. I was like, whatever. But I think it took Robert by surprise. He'd get arrested if he carried on like that today.'

Millar started the Tour as 'number two' in the Peugeot team, with Pascal Simon the designated leader. But the team's manager, Roland Berland, might have suspected that the roles would be reversed. 'A small car with a big engine' was Berland's description of Millar, which contained more than a hint of affection. Sean Kelly, one of the favourites for the 1984 Tour, was also quoted saying that Millar was 'special, but only on his day'. At the GP du Midi Libre, another prestigious stage race, Millar won the final stage, 186km from Castelnaudary to Saint

Esteve, outpacing Hinault, who placed third. His plans for the Tour, he said, were 'to wait until Bordeaux, then I'll see. I'm number two in the team. We [he and Simon] don't have to do anything before the mountains. But then it's up to us.'

Hinault won the prologue time trial and made a declaration: 'The Tour is just waiting to explode and you can be certain that Bernard Hinault won't be the last to light the fuse.' Equally, you can be certain that anyone who refers to themselves in such a way harbours a healthy conceit. The 1984 race was shaping up to be a battle between Le Blaireau, a four-time winner, and the Professor – the previous year's winner, Laurent Fignon.

A fourth place for the Peugeots in the team time trial kept Millar in contention, and, unlike the previous year, there were no cobbles to upset him in the opening week. The first real test, a week into the race, was a 67km time trial at Le Mans, where he slumped to forty-sixth, almost four minutes behind Fignon, the winner. Stage 9, two days later, took the peloton to Bordeaux from Nantes – an inhuman 338km. So bored were the riders that they amused themselves by stealing hats from roadside spectators.

Bordeaux, as Millar had pointed out, formed the gateway to the Pyrenees, and two days later he fulfilled his first ambition in the race by winning his second mountain stage, the 228km haul from Pau to Guzet Neige. The difference this time was that he was not an unknown who had been allowed to slip away by the leading contenders. It was an epic ride, on an epic stage, in intense heat, and judged to perfection by Millar, with echoes of his win the previous year, when he jumped clear of his two remaining breakaway companions on the final climb, just as a couple of pursuers – Pedro Delgado again, with the Colombian Luis Herrera – were eating into their lead. Among those who watched and marvelled at Millar's win was the Hollywood actor Dustin Hoffman, at the Tour to research a planned film. Hoffman, according to *Cycling*, 'looked no more a superstar than the fragile-looking Scot looks capable of hammering the best in the world of bikes'. After following him up the final climb, Felix Levithan, the Tour director, patted Millar on the back as he wheeled across the line, offering his congratulations with a hearty 'Bravo Meeyaaahh!'

With the victory, Millar climbed to seventh overall, while Simon languished in sixteenth. But Millar insisted that the status quo remain: Simon was the leader, not him. 'I am not a Tour winner. My friend and team-mate Pascal Simon has more chance of winning the Tour than I will ever have. I want to help him as much as possible.' The polka-dot jersey for King of the Mountains was another matter, though after the stage it remained on the shoulders of one of the riders who'd been in the breakaway with him on the road to Guzet Neige, Jean-René Bernaudeau. 'I'll let Bernaudeau look after it for now,' said Millar. 'I know the Alpine climbs, and that is where I hope to take it from him.'

It came on the most famous of the Tour's mountain stages, finishing with the twenty-one hairpins of Alpe d'Huez, on a stage that ended in victory for the tiny Colombian climber Herrera. It was a day on which Millar had promised to 'light the fuse', and he was as good as his word, leading over the first climb, the Col du la Placette. He remained in the thick of it all day, though it was his performance on the Alpe itself that gave Millar most satisfaction, and which proved so memorable to those watching at home. With Herrera dancing away up the climb, sending an estimated Colombian radio audience of twenty million into raptures, the battle raged between Hinault and Fignon. In a typically heroic/crazy move, Hinault had attacked on the approach to the Alpe, but he was overhauled as the road reared skywards, first by Herrera, then by Fignon and the Spaniard Angel Arroyo. Then, further up the climb, as the camera lingered on Hinault, a small figure appeared behind him. Millar had snared the Badger.

What happened next was possibly the cycling equivalent of the boy who's had sand kicked in his face rising up and getting his own back on the beach bully. Hinault, now being shadowed by Millar, and his face set in the familiar angry snarl, appears to flick his arm, signalling for Millar to come through and take his turn setting the pace. Hinault swings to the left and Millar passes him, but he goes wide, then injects some pace. Not a lot, but enough. A small gap opens. Hinault climbs out of the saddle, heaving his bike from side to side in a bid to keep up with Millar. The gap stretches. Hinault is ragged, toiling. He searches in the rear pocket of his jersey for something, pulls his hand back out and stuffs it into his mouth. The invisible elastic snaps; the proud Breton is dropped and the small Scot forges on alone, crossing the line fourth on the stage, moving up to fourth overall, and taking over the King of the Mountains jersey. Once again the TV commentator Phil Liggett is pinching himself. 'And the more I see it the more I find it difficult to believe that here is a man from Scotland leading the Tour de France up the slopes.'

That performance ensured that Millar became the first British rider to win one of the three main jerseys in the Tour. In the event he was declared best climber of the 1984 Tour de France, ahead of Fignon, Arroyo and Herrera, his closest rival and future nemesis Pedro Delgado having crashed out with only days to go. When asked about his triumph, Millar, in typically understated style, said, 'I'm really happy; it was my main objective for the year.' There was the added bonus of being the best ever British finisher. 'I think it's really good that I'll be the best British finisher in the Tour de France ever, in front of Tommy Simpson, who was the world champion. It's more than I could have hoped for at the start of the year.' Maybe he would go for the yellow jersey the following year? 'Yeah, maybe next year, or in a couple of years, for a day or two.'

For his high overall position in the Tour, Millar owed much to Peiper and Yates, who were constantly by his side on the flat stages. 'Sean and I were his two lieutenants,' says Peiper. 'That team was maybe the best environment for Rob. Pascal was his friend, and Michel Decock [the team's *soigneur*] was fond of Rob. A lot of things were in place that were beneficial to him.' But there were occasions when Peiper, though he was younger than Millar, had to act like an older brother. 'I remember we were looking after Rob on one of the long, flat early stages. I was in the white jersey [for best young rider on overall classification], we were flat out, doing 68kph, and Rob stopped for a piss! Roger [Legeay, assistant *directeur sportif*] came up and said, "Wait for Robert, he's stopped for a piss." I was so angry with him! "Don't you *ever* fucking do that again, you fucking idiot!" Back then Rob had a knack for pulling the shit all the time. On the flat stages he was never really concentrated on what he was doing; he would sort of float out of trouble halfway down the peloton, but he'd often be in the wrong part of the race.' It is not uncommon for climbers to struggle to hold their place at the front of the peloton, on account of their size if nothing else. Peiper insists that his and Yates's efforts on Millar's behalf owed more to their friendship than team orders. 'Sean and I were good mates – Siamese twins. Rob was just a misfit, but we were kind of thrown together. It was like the three of us pulled together. With Rob, we didn't have it on a personal level, but we connected in another way. And during that Tour we looked after him not because he was in the polka-dot jersey, but because we were mates. I doubt we'd even been told to by the team directors; and Robert wouldn't have shouted orders. But we would ride in the wind for him, look after him, make sure he wasn't getting dropped.'

In Paris, Millar held on to fourth, behind Fignon, Hinault and Greg LeMond; he finished ahead of Kelly, Angel Arroyo and his team leader, Simon. And, by virtue of winning a jersey, he stood on the podium in the French capital. 'No, I could not win it,' he continued to insist, regarding his chances of reaching

Paris in yellow. 'But I could go two or three places better.' Expanding on why he believed he could never win the Tour, he told Jean-Marie Leblanc, 'When I see Fignon in action I tell myself that I am on a lower level than him. I'm not only below Fignon, but Kelly, Hinault, LeMond and Anderson. I have a lot of admiration for Fignon's power and Hinault's pride, which forced him to attack and attack again.'

Millar then confirmed to Leblanc that he would stay with Peugeot in 1985, when, he said, he would again put himself at the service of Pascal Simon. This seems to have had as much to do with Millar's reluctance to accept the responsibility of team leadership as any confidence he had in Simon's ability to win the Tour. 'I don't want that responsibility [of leadership],' he told Leblanc. 'I want my freedom: that's how one finds openings to get away. If I'm favourite [then] I wouldn't be able to break away as I did in the Pyrenees to win at Guzet Neige.' It is this mindset, suggested Leblanc, that has given Millar a reputation as an individualist. 'Yes, I am an individualist,' Millar replied. 'What do you expect? I've had to make my own way in life. That's why you end up thinking of yourself first. Phil Anderson is the same. We had it hard to start with; we had to fight for success. That said, being an individual doesn't mean I'm selfish. When it's necessary, I work for others.' Leblanc persisted with the subject, saying that he'd been speaking to Berland, who said he didn't mix too well with the rest of the team. 'It's true that I have my own character and personality,' Millar responded. 'For example, I'm a vegetarian. I never eat meat, just a little fish. I have the impression that I bore everyone with my cornflakes, wheatgerm, my honey, my pollen . . . but it isn't serious. If I wear a small gold star in my left ear or have my hair permed, and it pleases me, who is going to moan at me?

'I have a much better life now,' he added. 'I like comfort. I have my television, my hi-fi, everything I need.' He likes cars, too, he said, and admitted that he'd like, one day, to buy a

Porsche. Not that he is indulgent or profligate. 'I have never taken a holiday. In the winter I stay at home reading books and listening to music. If I did take a holiday it would be to the coast for some sunshine, to do nothing.' Millar noted that his success had led to some interest from the British press, *Cycling* magazine (obviously) and *The Guardian* calling him on a regular basis. 'As for Scotland, I had one phone call from the *Daily Record* in Glasgow.'

Perhaps this was his perception, perhaps he was being disingenuous, because it is a fact that Millar's success in the Tour did raise his profile considerably back in Britain, and especially in Scotland. And it did bring him a measure of fame. Yet there was a curious ambivalence in some quarters. Bizarrely, two months went by before Millar's historic performance in the 1984 Tour was raised on the letters pages of *Cycling*, for example. Millar, who followed his ride in the Tour with a career-best sixth place in the world championship in Barcelona, was blazing a trail in this most continental of sports, yet the sport's diehard fans seemed more concerned with the British (amateur) team's dire showing at the Los Angeles Olympics. At last a letter appeared in *Cycling* paying tribute to Millar's spirit, and in particular his determination to improve at time trialling, which, perhaps even more than his ability in the mountains, was what had allowed him to claim such a high overall placing in the Tour. All that racing in Belgium was paying off, which was testament to Millar's commitment to self-improvement, and to addressing his weaknesses.

There may have been two other reasons for the relatively underwhelming response to Millar's success from aficionados. One was that with Kelly, Roche and LeMond also emerging as potential Tour winners, there was a plethora of English-speaking riders to support, a relative embarrassment of riches, making Millar seem one of many rather than a standout in his own right. The second was that Millar hadn't made many friends, among fellow riders but especially in the media, as he climbed the greasy pole. Within the sport, therefore, there was no short-age of people reluctant to proclaim him a hero, or to shower him in adulation. However, for those just discovering the sport, and Millar, it was a different story. They – we; I – had no such baggage. To us, Millar was Scotland's, Britain's, hero.

On 17 September, Millar raced in his home city of Glasgow in one of the Kellogg's criteriums. It was his first competitive appearance in Scotland as a professional, and here, at least, as *Cycling* confirmed, he was given a hero's welcome. 'Suddenly a roar went up from the huge crowd as their own Robert Millar, wearing the polka-dot jersey from the Tour de France [the one that was destined for Billy Bilsland's shop], was out on his own with the bunch chasing hard', though in the end he was denied the win when some of the home professionals chased him down. As Alan Rushton, the promoter of the Kellogg's events, notes, 'When Millar went up the road a lot more of the British domestic riders would chase him. Even in Glasgow, they wouldn't give him an inch.' While other riders were sometimes allowed favours, Millar, it seems, was not. But then, he never tried to hide his disdain for the British-based professionals, whom he accused of being unprofessional and second-rate. 'He didn't suffer fools at all,' says Rushton. 'He would take time to get to know people, but if he felt someone had done him down then he would take . . . a very strong position.'

Even if Millar's achievements weren't being fully acknowl-edged by the cycling community, the army of recent converts were only too ready and willing to hail this unconventional, aloof star of a sport that was baffling but also glamorous. Millar was so popular in Scotland, in fact, that he was voted BBC Scotland Sports Personality of the Year for 1984 – the first cyclist ever to be honoured. He was due to attend the awards ceremony in Glasgow early in January 1985, but he crashed his car near Toulouse en route to the airport after skidding on black ice. Instead, Neil Storey, who worked with Rushton, collected the Caithness Crystal trophy from Formula One legend Jackie Stewart. The crash left Millar with bruising around his eyes and ribs, but a week later, with a sore neck the only legacy of the incident, he was back training.

Quite apart from the sports personality award, that same winter saw Millar's profile rise even higher when he took over from the runner Steve Cram as the face of Kellogg's Start breakfast cereal. A thirty-second commercial was filmed in the Alps, and it began showing on TV screens and cinemas in spring 1985. 'He probably earned as much for that as he did in a whole season with Peugeot,' claims Rushton. The fee was rumoured to be around £20,000. The keys to the Porsche were almost dangling in front of him.

And the Kellogg's TV commercial was only the start (no pun intended) since the marketing department at the breakfast cereal company weren't the only people clocking cycling's increasing popularity, and noting that the British public were enjoying, in ever larger numbers, ITV's coverage of the Tour de France. It helped immeasurably, of course, that the sport no longer appeared to be dominated by Johnny European. The potential of cycling's showcase event to appeal to a yet bigger audience was identified by Channel 4, who were so impressed by the success of its evening broadcasts of the Kellogg's city-centre criteriums that they decided to begin broadcasting the Tour de France on a daily basis. In fact, the BBC had unsuccessfully attempted to wrest the rights to TV coverage from ITV in time for the 1984 Tour. In 1985, with the race to be broadcast by two terrestrial TV channels, the audience and interest in the UK was set to soar.

There was also interest in Millar from Granada TV in Manchester. After seeing the lengthy profile of Millar in the fashion and music magazine *The Face*, plans were developed to make an hour-long documentary film of the Scot who looked like he might become the first English speaker, and the first rider from a country outside the European mainland, to win the Tour de France. Neil Storey, a record company executive whose previous gig had been to work on U2's American tour, and who had only recently picked up the BBC Scotland Sports Personality of the Year trophy on behalf of Millar, was the man to liaise with Millar on the film project, to be produced by Rod Caird and directed by Peter Carr.

Storey's involvement came about through Alan Rushton and his company, Sport for Television, which had taken on a 'quasi management' role with Millar and some of the other top English-speaking riders. Storey, a cycling enthusiast, took an unusual sideways career step, going from head of publicity at Island Records to the same role at Sport for Television. He thus went from working with Marianne Faithfull, Bob Marley, the Eurythmics, Aretha Franklin, Frankie Goes to Hollywood, Talking Heads and Whitney Houston to working with professional cyclists. But he was struck more by the similarities than the differences, and actually compares Millar to a rock star. 'Robert was the Liam Gallacher of cycling,' he opines.

'I operated in pretty much the same way as I had within Island on the basis that cyclists were, to a certain extent, just the same as high-flying musicians,' Storey continues. 'It was just that their "stage" was slightly different. With Millar, as one of that year's Tour favourites, I worked a strategy of trying to turn the corner of perception for a low-level sport into one that had characters . . .' The publicity campaign, targeting newspapers and 'taste-making' magazines, featured a series of stepping stones towards what Storey regarded as 'the holy grail – a TV film'. The *Face* piece was, says Storey, 'a pivotal moment. It was the style bible, and I don't think Nick Logan [the magazine's founder and editor] had ever profiled a sports personality before, so it was a real coup. I learned later that it was very nearly the cover feature.

I think it missed out only because they didn't have their own studio pictures of Robert.' Eventually, the plan was for Millar, Roche, Anderson et al to be seen as 'stars as opposed to people who shaved their legs and pedalled fast uphill'. And to an extent, the strategy succeeded. 'It was a genuine thrill to be a part of it,' Storey adds. 'The continental stranglehold was weakening and the English-speaking riders were becoming the dominant force ... I was able to tap into all of that. It was a good time to attack the English-speaking media across the board. And if you trace it back, it was also a time when the broadsheets started to devote acres of space to the Tour.'

The documentary's director, Peter Carr, who confesses to not being particularly interested in sport, had previously directed a film about Manchester City, the making of which coincided – fortuitously for Carr, not so fortuitously for City boss Malcolm Allison – with the sacking of their manager. The film was highly acclaimed, and Carr was asked to make another one about sport. A pilot project on cricket failed to materialize. And then, thanks to *The Face*, Robert Millar flickered across the radar. *The High Life* was thus conceived. Rod Caird is credited with the idea.

Carr says he went into making *The High Life* 'in complete ignorance' both of Millar and the sport of cycling. 'But it wasn't the sport of cycling that was interesting,' he stresses, 'it was Robert himself. He was just so enigmatic.' But he could also be frustratingly obstinate, which led Carr to seriously question the project. 'I got halfway through making the film, I was in a little town somewhere in France, and I was making no headway with it at all,' he recalls. 'I rang back to base and said, "It's not working; I can't do this." I'd met Stephen Roche and found him pleasant and engaging, and far more accessible, so I suggested that we make a film about Roche instead. But Rod said, "No, absolutely not. We want the dark, mysterious film rather than the bright, breezy film. We want the film about Robert."'

Carr found Millar to be 'very articulate and intelligent' and was astounded by his language skills. 'He spoke fantastic French – not just good French, but perfect French.' He also has an interesting theory about the pressure on Millar from the British cycling community, which might offer another explanation for some of the apparent ambivalence towards him. Depending on where they stood in the great Tom Simpson debate, people were reluctant to give their unconditional affection and support to Britain's latest star either because they believed Millar was no match for Simpson or because they were afraid that he, like Simpson, whose death was so strongly linked to the use of drugs, would disappoint or let them down. 'I think there has always been a strong interest in cycling in Britain,' says Carr, 'but the thing about Robert was that he was lifting the burden of Simpson. There was a sense of national shame, almost, about Simpson. Millar was the one lifting the burden of guilt.'

It was a big responsibility, and to illustrate the point, the debate was continuing in the chatrooms of cycling websites even in late 2006, on the eve of the fortieth anniversary of Simpson's death. 'Simpson was BBC Sports Personality of the Year in 1965,' wrote one correspondent. 'Contrast that with now, where the sport hardly gets a mention. It wasn't just the fact that he was a great rider, he was also a very charismatic figure with a great personality. I believe that if he had lived, the sport would have gone on from there, with sponsors willing to properly fund a British trade team . . . and maybe a British Tour de France winner, which is the Holy Grail. My view is that the sport has never recovered from his death.' Another contribution noted that 'There was a lot of optimism about the future of British cycling at that time, and it died with [Simpson].' Of Simpson and Millar, this correspondent said, 'Difficult to say who would be best. On victories alone, Simpson; on presence in the big tour stages . . . maybe just Millar. Do we have another Millar coming up to take their place? Sadly, I don't think so.'

Storey's job on *The High Life*, which was to liaise with Millar, sounds, on the face of it, like it might have been the job from hell. But Storey insists that wasn't the case, though he does point out that he was used to dealing with rock stars. 'In the music world, you don't interrupt an artist or musician before they go on stage.' Millar, he discovered, was the same, and as long as you understood that, and followed his rules, you were OK. 'Everyone encountered the stubborn Robert, but all that meant was that he said, "This is when I train, this is when I sleep, this is when I eat; if you want to do interviews, this is the time I'm available." I understood that, and I thought it was reasonable. I thought it was normal!'

It seems remarkable, given his attitude towards the media, that Millar even agreed to the film, yet Storey says that 'in his own way he was up for doing it. I think he was a bit bemused that anyone would want to make a film about him.' Possibly because Storey played the game according to Millar's rules, the two got on famously. 'He was genial, charming and wonderful,' Storey enthuses. 'The public image of him was that he was taciturn, stubborn, and that he couldn't be bothered talking to people. I found him to be very talkative on a range of subjects, especially the goings-on within the professional peloton.' At that time – less so now – professional cyclists, even the biggest names, were perhaps the most accessible and approachable of athletes. As Storey points out, it wasn't uncommon for cyclists to be approached by journalists thirty seconds before the flag dropped, and they would all – or the majority of them at least – willingly offer a comment or two. 'But I think Robert was one who needed that time before the race for himself. He needed to focus.'

Storey has now returned to working in the music business, but he retains 'very, very fond memories of working with Robert. He should be a national hero. Think about how he must have felt: you do something that all over Europe is recognized as one of the great sporting achievements and you go

back to your own country, to a grey and dismal Glasgow –
though he was very fond of Glasgow, for what it's worth – and
it's like, "Fuck, what am I doing here?" Mentally it must have
been very debilitating.'

Two decades on, *The High Life*, with its exclusive soundtrack
by Steve Winwood (arranged by Storey), remains an outstanding sporting documentary. Carr's lack of expert knowledge is a
distinct advantage, since he asks Millar about his background
and his motivation rather than his race tactics, training or
equipment. With a clear and unbiased perspective, the film
explores the dichotomous nature of the sport – the glamour of
its stars and the dark underbelly of unofficial agreements and
combines between supposed rivals – with clarity and humour.
Rod Caird was absolutely right: Millar, as the film's protagonist,
proves a compelling subject, but it is the mundane, trivial
details that add humour and humanity.

'Ooh la la!' shouts Peiper, wolf-whistling as he and Millar pedal
past a couple of girls while out training. 'The girls down here
don't wear bras,' he explains to Millar. 'Tits all over the place.' I
didn't really appreciate Peiper's observation at the time. Aged 13
and watching *The High Life* with my parents, I was – officially at
least – into cycling, not girls. My face therefore resembled one of
the red dots on Millar's King of the Mountains jersey.

8

Cry No Tears

The Spanish destroyed their own race. There's no honour in
some guy winning because everyone wanted him to win.
Robert Millar, 1985

In early May 1985, Neil Storey travelled with a British journalist,
Charlie Burgess, to Barcelona, and then on to Tremp in the
Pyrenees where they were due to meet Millar, who was competing in the Vuelta a España. Football fan Burgess insisted first on a
visit to the Camp Nou – which was closed, so they let themselves
in – and they didn't arrive in Tremp until 4 a.m., identifying the
Peugeot team hotel by the rows of team jerseys hanging, drying,
off the riders' balconies. Then they demolished a bottle of whisky
before crashing out on the beds in the only room they'd found to
be unoccupied by cyclists. It was a 'primitive' hotel, says Storey,
with three riders to most rooms. Next morning the pair got up
early and wandered outside, where they saw – or, rather, were seen
by – Millar, who was standing on the hotel balcony.

'So, the Brits have arrived,' he said. 'You missed dinner. Did
you get lost?'

Storey had rarely seen Millar so relaxed and good-
humoured. In the café across the road, before the day's stage to

Andorra started, he gave Burgess an excellent interview, with some memorable lines, dripping with black humour, and then he cheerfully relieved his visitors of their car and music magazines. But Millar had every reason to be upbeat, even happy: with just over a week to go he was poised to become the first British cyclist, indeed the first English speaker, indeed the first non-continental European, ever to win one of cycling's three major tours.

There could be another explanation for his enthusiastic greeting of Storey and Burgess, however. It must have owed something to his sense of isolation in Spain. Hostility was being directed at him from all quarters, including the Spanish teams and the media, who didn't appreciate his terse responses to their questions, but especially by spectators. By the roadside, the fans made clear their antipathy towards the reticent foreigner with the unconventional appearance. One banner read 'Españoles, valientes, Que no gane El Pendientes' (Brave Spaniards, don't let the one with the earring win). 'The crowds throw things at you and spit at you because they want a Spaniard to win,' Millar told Burgess. In addition to the venom on the roadside, he also had reason to be suspicious of the tactics of the Spanish teams, who already had seemed prepared to join forces to work against him. Still, he couldn't have foreseen what was going to happen. Nobody could have foreseen it. In the end, the unfolding of an extraordinary set of circumstances meant that a week after his encounter with Storey and Burgess, instead of laughing, Millar would be crying tears of disgust and anger.

Later, Millar denied this. He was adamant that, contrary to reports at the time, he didn't cry. He seemed anxious to convey this point to the American journalist Sam Abt in his Lille apartment just a few days after the conclusion to the Vuelta. 'I was disgusted, I was really angry,' explained Millar. 'I'm still angry.' But, whatever the witnesses had said, he did not cry. 'Gorbals boys don't cry,' wrote Abt. 'Or, if they do, they don't admit it.' It was left to others, then, to shed tears on Millar's behalf on the evening of Saturday, 11 May 1985.

In scale and in atmosphere, the Vuelta differed from the other two big stage races, the Tour de France and the Giro d'Italia. To some extent this remains true today, but it was certainly the case in the early eighties, with Spain still emerging, blinking, from the Franco era. With great fanfare and razzmatazz, Spain hosted the football World Cup in 1982, but the sport of cycling seemed to be stuck in an earlier era, inward- rather than outward-looking, traditional and conservative as opposed to modern and vibrant. It didn't help that the country's flagship event, the Vuelta, had been in poor health. Through the 1970s it clung on to life in the face of diminishing fields, dwindling interest, and the humiliating domination of a succession of foreign riders, in part because of the home riders' unwilling-ness or inability to cooperate with one another.

The early 1980s began to see the emergence of some prom-ising Spaniards, at least, but still the national tour seemed to be susceptible to successful foreign invasions, even to wounds inflicted by Spanish hands. In 1982, Angel Arroyo supplied a welcome home win, only to then be penalized for failing a dope test. The title went instead to another Spaniard, Marino Lejarreta, but at considerable cost to the integrity and credibil-ity of the event. A year later the formidable Hinault came calling, beating the home riders into submission and, as was the Badger's wont, inflicting a few psychological scars in the process. After Hinault, another Frenchman, the unheralded and unglamorous Eric Caritoux, came and conquered the Vuelta, leaving the home riders looking rather hapless. A com-parison might be made with British tennis players at Wimbledon in the years before the emergence of Tim Henman, who finally guaranteed a home presence in the second round.

By 1985, the Vuelta still had a certain rustic quality, but there was some evidence of resurgence. A young rider from Segovia, Pedro Delgado, was proving to be a real talent: he was adventurous, exciting, and had the boyish good looks and charisma of a footballer rather than a cyclist. Delgado had also just signed the most lucrative contract in the history of Spanish cycling, with the Orbea-Seat team, thereby fuelling public expectation, but also heaping pressure onto his young shoulders. There were other pressures to produce a home winner. A deal with Spanish TV to broadcast the race on a daily basis apparently involved the organizers paying the broadcasters, rather than the other way around. According to Arthur Campbell, who was a leading figure in the UCI at the time, Spanish TV let it be known that this arrangement might be reviewed if the viewing figures were good. A home win would supply good viewing figures, which in turn could help safeguard the future of the race.

The slightly chaotic, less controlled nature of the Vuelta was highlighted early in the 1985 race when a dog scampered into the peloton as the 170 riders raced flat out towards the finish of stage 4. In truth, such an incident could happen in any race, but it seemed somehow more likely at the Vuelta. The resulting pile-up saw Ludo Loos of Belgium taken to hospital with a cerebral haemorrhage that left him paralysed down his left side. The Spaniard Jaime Slava suffered a fractured skull. A day earlier, Millar and his team-mate, Pascal Simon, had also fallen in the finale to the stage, losing a few valuable seconds. Otherwise, the opening few days were notable mainly for the fact that a 20-year-old Spaniard became the youngest rider ever to wear the race leader's yellow jersey: Miguel Indurain, who a decade later would become the first rider to win the Tour de France five times in succession.

Millar signalled his intent on stage 6, from Oviedo to Lagos de Covadonga, blowing the race apart on the 10km climb to the finish. Only five riders managed to live with him, and with a kilometre to go Delgado sprinted clear to take the stage, twelve seconds ahead of Millar. That put Delgado into the yellow jersey and moved Millar up to second, just thirteen seconds down. The next day saw the Scot attack again, and finish second again. He was edging closer to the jersey. As a bonus, it was an attack earlier on that stage by his team-mate, Simon, that had seen to Delgado, allowing Millar to close to within six seconds of the lead, which passed to Delgado's team-mate, Pello Ruiz Cabestany. 'I'm wearing the opposition down,' said Millar at the stage finish. 'I'm very confident.' Delgado, on the other hand, was distraught: he had lost almost four minutes, enough to all but extinguish his hopes of winning.

Millar's march towards the overall lead was steady and assured. He took over the yellow jersey after almost two weeks of racing in the Pyrenees, on Friday, 3 May. The timing looked perfect. Overall, he led Pacho Rodriguez, of Colombia, by thirteen seconds, and Cabestany by more than a minute with nine days of racing left. It was not a big cushion by any means, yet Millar's confidence that he could maintain his advantage was supreme, and it was shared by others. With a week to go 'he had only one rival left who could realistically stop him becoming the first Briton ever to win one of the world's big three', reported Burgess, who, with Storey, had been in the car that followed Millar earlier in the day, as he climbed to second in the 16km mountain time trial from Andorra, winding three thousand feet up to Pal ski station, where the cold wind whipped snowflakes into his face. Rodriguez won the time trial, and he seemed to be the only man Millar now had to watch. His other rivals, with the exception of Cabestany, were minutes rather than seconds behind.

The big test came on Friday, 10 May, on stage 17, a 42km time trial which Millar started with his lead over Rodriguez intact. Time trialling was not Millar's forte, but his move to

Lille, and regular forays into Belgium, paid off on the undulating circuit around Alcala de Henares. He finished third, forty seconds behind the winner, Cabestany, and three seconds slower than Rodriguez; he had punctured in the stage and been forced to change bikes twice, otherwise, he said later, he might have won the time trial. As it was, his lead had been cut to ten seconds but with just two stages to go. As soon as Millar rolled to a halt, Roland Berland, his *directeur sportif*, told him, 'You've done it, Robert.' According to one reporter there were 'tears of joy welling behind [Millar's] smiling, sunburnt face'.

Then came Saturday, 11 May and the penultimate stage: 200km from Alcala to Segovia, over the climbs of Morcuera, Cotos and Leones. Nothing to unduly worry Millar, who had been the strongest climber – the strongest rider – in a race that Sean Kelly claimed was 'harder than the Tour de France', and which the Spanish newspaper *El País* said was so fast that it 'seemed more like a motorbike race than a cycle race'. Millar was leading on merit, nobody doubted that. Yet Rodriguez had not conceded defeat, and he tested the water with an early attack on the slopes of the Morcuera. Millar countered easily. But he had a problem at the foot of the second climb, Cotos, as the sky darkened, the temperature plummeted, and dollops of rain, and then hailstones, began to pelt the riders: he punctured. No disaster. Pascal Simon and Ronan Pensec helped to pace him through the stragglers and back to the leaders.

Both of Millar's team-mates were tired, though, having ridden hard in defence of Millar's jersey for the past week. Simon, who hated racing in cold weather, admits now that he'd been able to offer Millar only limited help when his team-mate needed it. 'Normally I would have stopped immediately and waited with him when he punctured,' he says, 'but knowing he would soon be back and overtaking me, I continued. It was misty, with about four or five kilometres to the summit, and then it was raining on the way down. Berland came by me on the climb in the car shouting, "Wait for Robert! Wait for Robert!" I said, "No, I'll wait for him after the hill – at the bottom," because it was cold, and I was tired. He said if I didn't wait he'd sack me on the spot. That was Berland, panicking. So I waited, but I couldn't help him much; he was too strong. The tactics weren't good. If I had ridden conservatively and waited for Robert to catch me, I could have ridden hard in the valley [before the third climb].' Pensec, riding his first major tour, was similarly exhausted, and by this stage the team had already lost another valuable *domestique* in Sean Yates, who, 'completely shattered', had abandoned earlier in the stage.

With the limited help of Simon and Pensec, Millar rejoined the front group just before the summit of the climb; and as he did so, his exhausted team-mates dropped back. Millar then realized that Rodriguez and Cabestany had attacked, and were a little ahead, and the Scot, according to *L'Equipe*, produced 'another acceleration . . . that brought Rodriguez and Cabestany under control. If nothing else, [this] showed just how fresh Millar was.' Rodriguez and Cabestany's move was in contravention of cycling's unwritten rule that the race leader should not be attacked in the event of a puncture or crash. Not that the attacks would have surprised Millar: he didn't need to be paranoid to suspect that the supposedly rival Spanish teams would combine against him. In fact, he had initially tried to conceal the fact that he had punctured, thinking that he could stop, get a quick wheel change, and be back in the group before anyone noticed. As he explained later, 'I tried to drift back without anyone seeing, but the Spaniards saw and attacked.' Still, the panic was soon over: by the top of the climb Millar was back in the group and able to keep an eye on Rodriguez and Cabestany.

But, adding still to the intrigue and mystery that surrounds the 1985 Vuelta, accounts as to how events then unfolded vary. In an effort to research the story thoroughly, at one point, spread in front of me on my desk, I had five lengthy reports on the race, chapters from books, and transcripts of interviews with some of the main protagonists. I had hoped that by cross-referencing I could discover the truth, perhaps even provide the definitive account of what happened, but there are myriad inconsistencies. This tells its own story. It also vindicates Millar: if the reporters didn't know what was going on, how could he be expected to?

Thanks in part to the unexpected toughness of the stage, which was greatly exacerbated by the weather, the stage became chaotic, with the field stretched like elastic. Team cars, caught behind small groups of chasers, struggled to convey information or instructions to their riders. In any case, much of the information coming over the race radio was garbled or indecipherable. Berland later claimed that he didn't know what was going on as a consequence of this. But the major reason for the confusion was the weather: as it deteriorated, many riders donned waterproof rain capes, obscuring their numbers and effectively rendering them invisible.

A Spaniard, José Recio, had broken clear before Cotos, and he was joined on the descent by a rider all but camouflaged in his rain cape – Delgado. Cabestany, who was sitting third overall, reckoned by this stage of the race that Millar had the measure of him and Rodriguez, so he had encouraged his young team-mate to try to win the stage in his home town of Segovia. Delgado, who began the stage a hefty six minutes and thirteen seconds behind Millar, quickly bridged the thirty-second gap to Recio, joining him with 69km left to race. It is not clear whether Delgado escaped before Millar rejoined the front group, or if Millar simply didn't see him shoot off the front. But he was certainly there when another small group disappeared up the road, this one containing Kelly. 'But I wasn't worried about Kelly,' said Millar later. 'He was no danger.'

If Millar was concerned at all, it was with the progress of Simon and Pensec, who, having paced Millar back to the front group, had dropped back again. Both were on their last legs, but they were still determined to help Millar. On the approach to the third and final climb, Leones, they were in a twenty-man group around a minute behind their leader's group, frantically chasing to try to regain contact with him. Without team-mates for support Millar was isolated, vulnerable, his lead suddenly looking very fragile.

Meanwhile, the gap to the leading pair was increasing steadily, though Millar still had no idea that Delgado was one of the escapees. On the approach to Leones the pair had a lead of two minutes and seventeen seconds on Kelly's group. They also had two minutes and fifty-six seconds on Millar's group. The crowds were ten-deep on a road that climbed to five thousand feet, and they screamed encouragement at Delgado, who in the course of the climb increased his lead over Millar to three minutes and fifteen seconds. By now he had halved his overall deficit. There remained 43km to race.

And still Millar was oblivious. There were no time checks from the organization, the motorcycle provided for this purpose having seemingly gone AWOL, and Berland was either unaware or unable to convey any information to Millar. At the top of Leones, the final climb of the 1985 Vuelta, Cabestany rode alongside Millar and shook his hand. 'This is your race,' he told him. TV footage also shows Millar addressing Cabestany and Rodriguez. According to Cabestany, Millar offered his commiserations: 'It wasn't to be. I'm sorry. You tried, but it wasn't to be.' Cabestany, who knew full well what might transpire if Millar continued to ride in blissful ignorance, might not have rubbed his hands in glee, but he surely allowed himself a quiet chuckle.

Finally, with just 26km remaining of the stage, Millar discovered what was happening. Berland drove up to him and dropped the bombshell: Pedro Delgado was one of the men in front, with an advantage of nearly four minutes on Millar's

group. That was worrying enough, but over the next three kilometres the gap to the leading pair shot up, improbably, by
almost another minute, to four minutes and fifty-four seconds.
Now the alarm bells were clanging. And still, to Millar's
increasing consternation, there was no sign of Simon and
Pensec. Instead of his own team-mates he was surrounded by
ten riders, seven of whom were Spanish. Of the other three
riders, Dutchman Gerard Veldscholten of the Panasonic team
and Frenchman Eric Guyot of Sean Kelly's Skil team initially
assisted Millar, taking their turn at the front and helping to pull
the group along. The final rider in the group was the
Colombian Rodriguez. Millar tried to cajole him, telling him
his second place was at stake. 'He said he wasn't working
because he would rather see Delgado win,' Millar told
L'Equipe's Philippe Bouvet at the finish. Bouvet added his own
interpretation: 'Rodriguez had just been given an official order
by his [Spanish] Zor team to scuttle his own ambitions.'

Millar's problems deepened when first Guyot and then
Veldscholten stopped helping him, the latter complaining that
he didn't see why he alone should help. Bouvet reported that
this was the point at which 'things started to go sour. Millar was
totally alone, and those who would normally be allies began to
retract in brutal fashion.' Millar found himself ensnared in a
catch-22 scenario. He could ride flat out on the front to limit
his losses to Delgado, but this would give the riders behind
him, including Rodriguez, an easy ride to the finish. It would
also give Rodriguez a platform to attack him nearer the end
and reclaim the ten seconds. Millar therefore had to try to keep
the pace high while also keeping something in reserve in the
event of a late Rodriguez attack.

With 17km to go Delgado's advantage over Millar was five
minutes and twelve seconds. Now the Spaniard had only just
over a minute to claw back. Millar was chasing, but his effort
was being disrupted by the Spaniards in his group, who took it

in turns to sprint clear, forcing him to sprint after them, then sitting up and freewheeling as he made contact. An analysis by *Winning* magazine of their respective speeds over the final 10km had Millar averaging 41kph and the leading pair of Delgado and Recio recording 45kph.

On the outskirts of Segovia, at the gates of the sponsoring whisky distillery (prompting the Spanish newspapers to joke the next day that Spanish whisky was superior to Scotch whisky), Recio won the stage – a gift from Delgado for his efforts during the pair's great escape – and then all eyes turned towards the clock. When it got to six minutes the crowd began chanting Delgado's nickname: 'Perico, Perico!' Millar appeared just as it reached six minutes and thirteen seconds, but the cheers that erupted were not for him. He still had four hundred metres to race. In the thirty-six seconds it took him to do so, he lost the Vuelta.

Millar crossed the line still oblivious to the full, horrible reality. When he was told that the jersey had gone he 'swore loudly, with shock and anger'. Bouvet's description of what happened next, beneath the headline 'Millar Sacrificed in the Arena', is poetic and moving: 'He unclipped his feet from his pedals, stared at the ground and appeared oblivious both to the noise of a crowd that was delirious in his defeat and to the children crowding around him with their thumbs turned downward, aping his defeat. It became unbearable. Millar turned round and tramped off towards the Peugeot team car. He shut the door, and his eyes reddened. As a crowd gathered round the car to bathe in his distress Millar's only option was to bury his head in his hands and to collapse on the seat. The tears probably came next, but if they did they were ones of dignity.' His only words, reported Bouvet, were 'Every one of them was against me.' Berland added, 'It's rotten: the whole peloton was against us. It seems a Spaniard had to win at all costs.' Millar, said Bouvet, had been 'the victim of a formidable coalition', the main beneficiary of which was 'the newly crowned King of Spain, Pedro Delgado'.

Rubbing salt into Millar's wounds was Delgado's effusiveness in thanking the other Spanish teams – supposedly his rivals just as much as Millar's. 'I want to thank all the Spanish [teams], especially Javier Minguez, the team manager of Zor, who deprived Rodriguez [of] an attractive finish in the GC [general classification] to help boost the chances of a victory for a Spanish rider,' he told *L'Equipe*. 'Honestly, I swear that I didn't attack in the hope of winning the Vuelta. I attacked just to put Millar to the test and to help boost the chances of my friend, Cabestany. When Recio and I managed to build a three-minute lead the only thing going through my mind was that I could win the stage, but only the stage!' *L'Equipe* also reported Delgado's claim that he was oblivious to the fact that he might inherit the yellow jersey until a few kilometres from the finish. 'Recio's team manager shouted at me, telling us that if we managed to take a few seconds more off the peloton I could win the Vuelta. It was only at that moment that I asked what my deficit on Millar was in the GC. Up until then I didn't even know what it was.'

Speaking to Colombian journalists at the finish in Segovia, Javier Minguez did not apologise for sacrificing his rider, Rodriguez, in order to help Delgado to win. Quite the opposite. 'As things stood,' explained Minguez, 'Pacho [Rodriguez] was destined for second place and Millar for the title. Anything was preferable to allowing Millar the victory . . . it pained me to hold Pacho back during the last kilometres, but it was necessary to prevent Millar from reaching the pantheon of champions. Have no doubt: I was the artificer of Delgado's victory, and I don't regret my decision.'

The next day's final stage to Salamanca, witnessed by an enormous crowd of euphoric Spaniards, was the traditional showcase finale to a major tour: a flat 175km that ended in a mass sprint. It offered no chance for Millar to recoup his losses, but the inquest into the events of the previous day was only just beginning.

What, for example, had happened to Simon and Pensec? Their twenty-man group had seemed to be closing on Millar's group, but it transpired that on the road between the second and third climbs they had been forced to stop when the barriers of a level crossing came down. 'We were stopped for two minutes,' Pensec said. 'But no train went by before the barriers were raised.' It is not idle speculation to suggest that had Simon and Pensec joined Millar and been able to help him in the chase, it is almost certain that he would have held on to the jersey.

As intriguing as the story of the 'train that never came' is, most of the conspiracy theories concern the Spanish teams. Unofficial combines and alliances between rival teams were and are commonplace in cycling, sometimes formed because of national loyalties, but more often because deals have been done, involving money. Millar appears to have been undone by a deadly combination of both. But even the deals are not always as straightforward as they might appear. It is alleged, for example, that a favourite ploy of the Dutch Panasonic team – Veldscholten's team – was to help in chases not with any intention of catching whichever riders were being pursued, but to provoke another team into offering them payment not to work. It was reported at the time that Veldscholten's decision to stop helping Millar came just after an approach by the car of Delgado's Orbea-Seat team.

As for the Spanish alliance, the question is whether it was formed on the road, as events unfolded, or planned in advance. Theo de Rooy, the only other surviving Panasonic rider by that stage of the race, suggests the former scenario is more likely. 'I think it was an organized Spanish coalition,' he says, 'but it was not a coalition that was organized before the race; it happened on the day. Delgado was gone, and when something like that happens you have to be alert and you have to take action or you will be caught by the Spanish Armada . . .' Without taking 'action' – i.e. enlisting the help of other teams – there was no way that Millar could expect the assistance of non-Peugeot riders, be they Dutch, French, Colombian, but especially Spanish. 'If you have a choice about whether to ride or not, then it's easier not to ride, of course,' de Rooy continues. 'If you don't have a reason to ride, either tactically or for money, then why would you ride?' There was nothing sinister or personal about the coalition against Millar, he suggests. Yet de Rooy, with more than twenty years' experience as a rider and *directeur sportif*, admits that the 1985 Vuelta stands as a unique example of so many teams combining to prevent one rider winning. 'I've never seen anything like that happen, before or since,' he says

Even if the events of 11 May were not premeditated, there were certainly orchestrated efforts to unseat Millar earlier in the race. Stage 16, for example, saw the riders tackle 252km from Albecate to Alcala de Henares. In Albecate the previous evening, Millar sat down to dinner with his Peugeot team. They waited over an hour to be served, and when the food arrived it was, according to Millar, 'food you wouldn't give your dog'. Consequently, Millar 'blew his top' and left the hotel. 'The others couldn't believe it when I stormed out,' he admitted later. 'I went down to the cake shop and stuffed myself.'

Word seems to have spread among the other teams that Millar had missed his dinner. So the Fagor team, directed by Spanish legend Luis Ocana, hatched a plan: they would launch a surprise attack as soon as the race reached the feeding zone, where the team *soigneurs* hand the riders their food-filled musettes and drinking bottles, even though it's another unwritten rule that no one attacks at the feed. Sean Yates remembers it well. 'As we approached the feeding zone Ocana got his team to the front; he had told Cabestany and Delgado they were going to attack. Next thing there are eight Fagor guys up the road, with Delgado and Cabestany, and we had to kill ourselves for about eighty kilometres to bring them back. It was balls to the wall, and it was just us Peugeots on the front. That was the end of me.' Yates believes there was 'friction' between Ocana and Berland, as well as widespread Spanish antipathy towards Millar. 'It was a national tour and it had a real national feel to it in those days,' he says. 'I just remember the crowds on that tour were insane. They were thirty deep, shouting for the Spanish riders – it was incredible. It could be quite intimidating.'

More foul play was suspected regarding the lead Delgado and Recio were able to build, even as they were being pursued by Sean Kelly's group and, behind him, by Millar. 'From the start it was obvious that the race was receiving greater media coverage this year than in any previous year,' Kelly told the Irish journalist David Walsh some weeks later. 'This meant that there were more TV cameras and more photographers riding on motorcycles at the front of the peloton. If a rider or small group of riders made a break near the finish they were given a sheltered escort to the finish . . . When Delgado and Recio had a lead of one minute and forty seconds on the group I was in with fifty kilometres to go, I felt sure we would recapture them . . . we worked very hard, all the time believing that a stage win was possible. But what happened? The two leaders almost doubled their advantage. That for us was impossible to understand.' Kelly is reluctant to say it directly, but today he thinks it at least feasible that the two breakaways might have gained shelter from the motorcycles at the head of the race. He also feels that inaccurate time checks were a major contributory factor to Millar's defeat. 'I don't know if it was a mistake or deliberate, but later on I learned that we were getting wrong time checks when Delgado and Recio first went away. The weather may have been a factor in that, I don't know.' Kelly also reveals that his team, Sem, was asked to help Millar. 'But it was too late. It was with about 20km to go that we were asked to ride. I had a number of team-mates at that point and we could have helped, but by the time we were asked it was too late.' A few days after the event, Millar himself raised the possibility that Delgado and Recio might have been assisted in their great escape by the motorcycles. 'I don't know if he was really flying or riding a motorbike's slipstream,' he told Samuel Abt. 'That's what it's like in Spain when you're Spanish and behind a motorbike. . .'

Even if there was no 'help' from the motorcycles – and it would be impossible to prove – there was disappointment from some quarters that Spanish TV was so partisan in its coverage of the race. While the British media was largely indifferent to the fate that had befallen their leading rider, there was justifiable anger in France that one of their teams, Peugeot, had fallen victim to the Spanish coalition, and that 'the entire peloton [had been] in league for their downfall', as *L'Equipe* claimed. 'One of the most unnerving things was the way the partisan Spanish TV guys commentated on the whole episode,' wrote Bouvet. 'One of them even managed, live on television, to suddenly transform himself into the PR officer for Domingo Perurena [Delgado's team *directeur sportif*], saying, "In the name of Perurena I want to thank all of the other team managers for their help." Millar didn't deserve that, but it has to be said that the Spanish coalition was not entirely to blame.'

'Level crossing or not, if you ask me it was the tactics of Berland which lost it for Robert,' states Pascal Simon. 'We could have raced it differently. But, also, I think there were teams who were paid not to ride with Robert . . .' Yates also blames Berland. 'Berland was a fucking idiot. To be a manager and to be confronted by that situation . . . he should have been aware that there was more than one scenario that could happen that day and he should have got something sorted. It was a fiasco.' Theo de Rooy, too, reckons that 'Peugeot were sleeping'. The main criticism of Berland is that he had no 'arrangements' set up with rival teams in the event of a crisis, which is certainly what the stage to Segovia became. Reflecting on it later, Millar admitted, 'I was naive and new to being leader in the race . . . If I'd known then what I do now I would have reached some agreements.' But he and others conceded, too, that it was Berland's job, not Millar's, to do such deals.

Millar told Peter Carr, for *The High Life*, that he too blamed Berland. 'It was Berland's fault. Everyone who was there knew I should have won. Berland knows I should have won it.' Later, Millar explains, 'It's kind of common knowledge in Europe that other teams can be bought to give you help in certain races if your team gets into trouble. It's up to the *directeur sportif* to deal with these kinds of matters because it would be a bit hard for me to go and talk to [other teams'] *directeurs sportifs* to try to get their team to ride, because it's not my level. It's between the managers. And it's up to him to realize what the right time is to do his job.'

When Carr put Millar's accusation to Berland, he claimed he had been let down by unnamed people. 'Above all, we were let down by people who betrayed us. That's all. I blame them.' Who are they? asks Carr. 'I'm not saying who they are. Robert Millar knows, and I know myself. It certainly wasn't a team failure, or any fault of mine. Because we took every precaution. We knew it would be difficult, very difficult, but everything was arranged so that Robert could win, and there were people who didn't behave properly.' Berland is initially vague on the question of whether he actually did any deals to enlist the help of other teams. 'We didn't want to seem like people who waste our money . . .' But, says Carr, if you want help from members of other teams then you have to pay, don't you? 'If you want, yes, arrangements can be made. But that wasn't a problem, because it was done.' Cabestany shed more light on this when speaking to Alasdair Fotheringham in *Cycle Sport* in 1997: 'When Berland tried to start making deals, twenty kilometres from the finish, everything had been agreed on. And you don't go back on deals.'

For Berland, the 1985 Vuelta seems to have effectively spelled the end of his career in professional cycling. He left the Peugeot team at the end of the season and now, with his wife, runs a caravan park in the west of France. But the events in Spain continue to hang over him, and form an indelible stain on his reputation as a *directeur sportif*. It is clear, too, that he remains bitter, not so much because the race was lost, more because he feels he *was* let down; that he, as much as Millar, was the victim of betrayal and double dealing. He reiterated to me much of what he told Carr. 'I had already taken some precautionary measures the night before [Saturday's fateful stage] with a team that no longer had anything to race for. For sure, it wasn't a Spanish team – there was no way they were going to help us. And we knew fine well that they might try something. We'd virtually won the race, having controlled it for most of the way. But we knew we weren't yet in the clear.

'Robert punctured at the bottom of the second col and while we were delayed they [Recio and Delgado] attacked.' Then Berland makes an intriguing new claim, suggesting that he, at least, did know that Delgado was one of the escapees, and that Millar's refusal to chase on his own was a tactical decision rather than because he was scared of a counter-attack by Rodriguez or Cabestany. 'At one point Robert was only fifty metres behind the front two but I told him to stop chasing. The plan was to sit back and wait for the team-mates [Simon and Pensec] who'd been dropped.' Berland reckons the race was lost 'in the last five kilometres, but we were in a trap. Delgado shouldn't have won the Vuelta, he was only going out to try to win the stage. Our main concern was watching Cabestany.' In the event, 'We ended up playing a little bit of poker.' And losing spectacularly.

More than two decades on Berland has nothing to lose any more, so he does name the team with which he'd made the 'precautionary' arrangement the previous evening. It was Panasonic, the team of Veldscholten, who initially helped Millar and then dropped back, allegedly after an approach by Delgado's team car. 'After the attack of Delgado and Recio had got to a certain stage I called upon the help that I thought I'd been assured the night before,' Berland claims. 'But when I went to the team car of Panasonic I got "no" for an answer. They didn't keep to their word. Millar would have won if he hadn't been double-crossed. After telling us they would help they were bought off by the Spanish during the stage.' Berland insists he was clear about what happened, and – slightly contradicting his earlier claims – suggests that it was nothing against Peugeot, Millar or himself. 'It was a widespread anti-sporting practice in Spain at the time, even when Hinault was in his prime – although it was a lot harder to get away with stuff like that when Hinault was a main player in a race. I think today they have understood that racing shouldn't be like that.'

Berland does reproach himself – almost. 'In retrospect I almost regret not telling Robert to persist with his chase. If he had then I'm sure it would have turned out differently. But I wanted Robert to sit back and wait for the others to come back so we could launch a chase together as a team. I think the turning point was Robert puncturing. That incident was like a signal to the rest. He only lost around twenty seconds but it was enough to send his rivals into a frenzy. There are other factors, too, that didn't help us. It was raining, there was fog. But my biggest disappointment was the fact that people promised things and didn't deliver. If we'd known that was going to happen our tactics would have been totally different. Personally, I don't feel I'm to blame.'

Perhaps adding to his sense of regret – quite apart from the fact that the fiasco seems to have cost him his job – is that

Berland believes he enjoyed a good relationship with Millar. 'I think we worked well together, which I believe wasn't the case with his other team managers. He was a little bit strange, but you couldn't argue with his results. He was truly professional, and thanks to that, and his results, I had a lot of satisfaction. Sometimes he did things that made you wonder, then wouldn't do things that you thought might have helped him, but that was just his way. I had quite a good relationship with Robert, though it was sometimes complicated. He was definitely very individual, but at the same time, man to man, I could understand why he was like that.'

Curiously, although he seemed to lose respect for Berland as a consequence of what happened at the Vuelta, Millar seemed to have no problem with the rider who won, and whose path he would cross on so many occasions in the future. In 1997, he said, 'Delgado didn't win, I lost . . . I didn't begrudge Delgado at all because he wasn't to blame, but the other Spaniards didn't get gold stars in my notebook.' As for Delgado, he has always maintained that his first major tour win – he went on to win the 1988 Tour de France and another Vuelta in 1989 – was above board. In his autobiography, *A Golpe de Pedal* (*With a Stroke of the Pedal*), he admitted, 'Robert Millar has never done any damage to me, I've done more damage to him, [but] the fact is, we get on quite well.' Of the day when he achieved the seemingly impossible by clawing back a deficit of more than six minutes, Delgado offers thanks once again to the *directeurs* of the other Spanish teams, who 'sacrificed their chances for me', then appears to contradict himself by insisting that all was fair on the road to Segovia. 'We all know the Armada wasn't re-armed that day . . . I thought it was over for me [but] I was wanting to do a good ride in my home town. There are lots of questions: what on earth were Peugeot doing?' At the time, he'd told reporters, 'I didn't win this Vuelta, the Peugeot team lost it. I can understand how disappointed Millar feels but it wasn't my fault that he was left isolated by his team. When all the row has died down I hope I'll be able to talk to Millar about it.' Delgado's first major tour victory came about, he explained, through a combination of extraordinary circumstances. Ironically, in the previous year's Vuelta Delgado had been foiled in his bid to win the stage into Segovia when he was chased down by riders who were, very obviously, working on behalf of other teams. 'That day I found out about alliances in cycling and I felt cheated,' writes Delgado, without irony, in his autobiography.

Some months after this book was published I received an email, apparently out of the blue. The sender? 'Pedro Delgado.' I had tried to contact Delgado during my initial research, but without success. Here, though, was a lengthy account of his rivalry with Millar, towards whom the Spaniard clearly feels great respect. By far the biggest chunk of the correspondence, however, was reserved for his own version of events at the 1985 Vuelta, recalled in detail and at length, almost 23 years on. 'I was facing the [penultimate] day with excitement at the prospect of arriving in my home town,' Delgado writes. 'As a tactic I tried to attack from far out, to force the leading team to work hard, and to isolate Millar as much as possible during the final. Then I would always have the option of winning the stage. It was a really fast start; everybody is always in a rush at these starts, and the *peloton* began to split on the mountain pass of the Morcuera. On the second mountain pass [Cotos] I tried to attack again, but if it's not Millar who keeps me from attacking it's someone else. While Recio was allowed to get away, I couldn't find the moment to leave them behind. Then the weather became bad – a lot of fog and hail – and I decide to take the risk on the descent, and finally get away.

'A few kilometres later I catch [Recio] and go to the front, and I pull him with me. He wants to win the stage but he doesn't want to do any work because we still have to ascend the

Leones, 45km from the finish. The gap is growing. I realize how hard it is going to be to win the stage, so I reach an agreement with Recio: he will help me increase the gap between me and the leader. Millar couldn't relax and would have to push hard to reduce the gap. And this time the fortune Goddess was on my side. The director of the Peugeot team does not inform his cyclist how big the gap is. And the other team, Zor, decided to pass responsibility to the Scot, trying to make him nervous.

'Pello [Ruiz Cabestany] told me at the end of the stage that when they reached the summit of Los Leones, Millar congratulated both Pacho and him for having fought in such a sporting way. What could I do? I thought, it will be his turn next time. At the end, when [Millar] started to realize the situation, it was late, and he didn't have any team-mates to help him; he was by himself trying to close the gap, with the handicap of having on his wheel his two closest rivals . . . he was forced to keep some energy for the possible attacks. Six minutes, 13 seconds seemed insurmountable, but it became 6' 49" on a stage I consider historic.

'Outside Spain you could hear rumours about a coalition of Spanish teams, but that was not the case. As I said, the director made the mistake of not telling him how the gap was increasing, and the Zor team never defended the second position of their Colombian cyclist . . . these two circumstances permitted a race that I had all but lost to change on the penultimate day.'

Just four hours after losing the Vuelta, Millar spoke to John Wilcockson in his room, in a residential and sports complex by the banks of the River Moros. 'Millar was in the bathroom washing his shorts,' wrote Wilcockson in *Winning*. 'His eyes were red. He was depressed.' Finally, he spoke. 'I haven't said more than three words since we arrived here. I will try to sleep tonight, but I guess I won't be able to . . . I am completely disgusted with it all.' He spoke of revenge against the Spanish riders, reserving particular animosity for the Fagor team, which he considered had ridden against him throughout the race, with nothing to gain themselves. 'I haven't lost this race because I cracked up,' said Millar. 'You can't compete against the whole peloton.' Then he added, 'I feel betrayed. After all my efforts it's sickening to lose like this. I hope that one day I will get my own back on all those who combined against me today.'

For Millar, the 1985 Vuelta was a steep learning curve. He now appreciated that there was more to racing, and to leading a team in a major race, than strength and ability. Tactical nous and guile, even cunning, also featured in a complex equation. In his article in *The Face*, which appeared not long after the Vuelta, Burgess described cycle racing as combining 'heroism, selflessness and selfishness, heartbreak and skulduggery. It is a glamorous, sweaty, strength-sapping and sometimes even dirty business.' And for Millar the lessons were as profound as they were demoralizing. When he spoke to Samuel Abt in his Lille apartment a few days after returning home, he admitted that 'all I felt was sad. The guys in the pack, they acted sympathetic, but I felt they were laughing behind my back.' He seemed, talking to Abt, to be forcing himself to be philosophical, trying not to take the nature of his defeat too personally: 'What's done is done, it's history now. It's the kind of thing that happens. Well, maybe not very often – it was so blatant, so scandalous. But you have to be calm because I'll be racing with them for the next ten years.' He admitted, though, that he was finding it difficult to be calm. How could he remain angry at so many people? asked Abt. 'Easy,' replied Millar.

Much later, Millar would admit to another journalist, William Fotheringham, that his 'cynicism gradually grew', but many of the seeds were surely sown at the 1985 Vuelta. 'As you know, it's very much a jungle mentality,' Millar wrote in an email to Fotheringham, 'and there are more people who will show themselves to be untrustworthy than those you can trust.

After a few bad moments you learnt that trust was something that others earned and certainly not a foregone conclusion.'

Jack Andre, Millar's friend and confidant in Troyes, watched the extraordinary events of the Vuelta from a distance and drew his own conclusions. 'I have a feeling that he was happier sticking to his principles [of the best man winning] than sacrificing those in order to win at all costs,' suggests Andre.

The *Face* feature on Millar acted as a preview to the 1985 Tour de France, with Millar, 'the frail kid' or 'scrawny Bowie fan from the back streets of Glasgow . . . on course to become the first Briton ever to win'. He shared top billing on the cover with Sting, the actor Rupert Everett, and the singer Lloyd Cole. 'The only private life I have is in my head,' said Millar, aping the previous month's cover star, Morrissey, who might have used such a line as a lyric.

For the fashionistas and music fans of *The Face*, Millar was suitably enigmatic and interesting (a letter in the next month's issue lavished praise on the feature, the correspondent noting that 'I've always thought that continental cycling was too subtle and elegant to have much of a following in Britain'.). 'Millar can go for days without speaking to anyone and not mind,' wrote Burgess. 'He likes to go out on the streets "just to look at ordinary people living ordinary lives" but gets bored after more than a week in his swank Lille apartment with its simple Euro furniture, marble floor, concierge and, outside, a free Peugeot 505 from his sponsor.' Millar tells Burgess he is upgrading to a Peugeot 205GTi: 'Every cyclist drives fast because their reactions are quicker than a normal person's.' His hero is David Bowie. 'As a person, through his music and style, Bowie chooses what everybody else will choose six months later. He comes out with the right thing at the right time.' But he has never seen Bowie perform. 'I don't have time for concerts.' Burgess is intrigued by his vegetarianism, though Millar stresses that it isn't for ethical reasons, but because of the 'shit' – the chemicals and toxins – that gets fed to animals. He likes apple tart and ice cream at the Lido on the Champs Elysées and has considered the possibility of starting a health food shop when he retires. 'Oddly,' notes Burgess, 'he has looked into the idea of a McDonald's franchise in France, where their market share is low. He had [a McDonald's burger] once and thought it was muck.'

Every month, Millar tells Burgess, he sends a blood sample to a specialist sports doctor in Bordeaux for analysis. Regarding his sport, he enjoys climbing, enjoys 'seeing people disappear behind me. If you are good at climbing you know you are not suffering as much as the others. You get a sadistic pleasure out of it.' He adds that the will to win is in the stomach or not there at all. 'There are people who have the talent but they just want to grab it and end up scratching the surface. You have to have it inside, and that makes the difference. The hint of victory gets the adrenalin going. You feel that maybe ten million people are watching. It makes you feel you are making history. You know you are going to win before the finish and already you are thinking about what to say and whether your hat is in the right position.'

Burgess, with Storey, had left the Tour of Spain before its disastrous denouement, but even in the café in Tremp Millar had spoken of a 'mutual mistrust' between Peugeot and the Spanish teams. Burgess, however, picked up no sense of foreboding. Millar was confident that he could and would win the race, and that he would continue as a professional for the next decade, though he seemed reluctant to look too far into the future.

'Where will you be in ten years?' asked Burgess.

'Maybe in a hotel room somewhere,' Millar replied.

9

He Loves Being a Star

I like it around here. It's so ugly it makes the rest of the world look really beautiful.

In June, on the eve of the Tour de France, Millar moved back to Troyes from Lille, and in mid-December he married his girl-friend, Sylvie Transler, in a modest civic ceremony in Troyes Town Hall. No one from Millar's family was in attendance, nor were any of his team-mates. Jack Andre was a witness, Sylvie's parents were there, and also present was Peter Carr, still working on his documentary.

Neil Storey had observed Millar's relationship with Sylvie from close quarters when they travelled to the Isle of Man for the British championship a couple of weeks after the Vuelta defeat, and some six months before they were married. In those days it was unusual for girlfriends or wives to travel to races, but Sylvie was with Millar on the Isle of Man where, according to Storey, 'it pissed with rain the whole time'. Millar, he adds, 'hated being there: he was made to ride that race. But he was with his young lady and they walked around holding hands, going shopping all the time. He was being trailed by Pete [Carr] and his crew and he knew he had to give time to the film.' As for Sylvie, she was, according to Storey, 'very quiet, very shy, and she spoke absolutely no English. Any communication was via Robert. But she was there or thereabouts the whole time. They were very affectionate towards each other. She seemed like a very sweet, very ordinary provincial French girl. He seemed to be head over heels in love with her.'

The wedding, says Carr, was a curious affair. This confirms appearances, since the ceremony does feature in *The High Life*, and it does look unconventional, to say the least. Millar is dressed in what appear to be white robes and he is standing frozen nervously to the spot. So is Sylvie, who is pretty but mousy and shy-looking, her dark-brown bobbed hair framing as well as partially hiding her face. Both spend much of the time staring at the ground. Carr recalls that when the ceremony finished Millar suggested they all go to a neighbouring bar for a drink. 'So I said, "Let me buy you all a drink, Robert," and he said, "No, I'll buy – it's my wedding, eh." I had a glass of wine; her parents, who were peasantfolk as far as I could tell, also had a glass of wine. And then, after about fifteen minutes, Robert stood up and said, "I'd better be going now." And Sylvie got up and followed him out.'

Carr then witnessed a disagreement between the newly-weds. They were due to move to Wielsbeke in Belgium the day after the wedding, but there was a problem. Sylvie was determined to take her pet cat, but Millar was reluctant to pay to have the animal immunized, which was compulsory if it was to enter Belgium. Carr thinks the cost was in the region of seventy francs. 'This led to a furious row,' says Carr. 'Robert refused to pay it, but eventually he came up with a proposition: they'd wrap the cat up in a bit of carpet, and if they got caught trying to smuggle it across the border, they'd just let it go.' Jack Andre, always ready with a rational explanation for Millar's idiosyncratic 'ways', nodded knowingly when the anecdote of Sylvie's cat was related to him. 'Robert didn't like cats,' he commented.

Millar's team-mates had no idea he was getting married. Most didn't even know that he had a girlfriend. 'It was a shock' for Allan Peiper. 'I don't think I even had any knowledge that he was interested in women, now I think about it. There'd been no women on the scene, and then all of a sudden he was married. He never said anything about it. I never got an invitation . . .' Later, Peiper did meet Sylvie. 'She was very quiet. That's all I can remember.' Phil Anderson's analysis is even more uncompromising: 'He didn't seem to have the skills for getting on with men, let alone women.' Stephen Roche got to know the couple a little bit better. 'Sylvie was very strange, very strange,' he says. 'She was like Robert. Put them together and they were terrible. Normally [in a relationship] you need a bit of one and the other. But they were identical. They were like two little children.' Andre, whose wife later befriended Sylvie, was another who was surprised when Millar and Sylvie got together. Though Millar confided in him regularly, he neglected to mention that he had a girlfriend. 'I just went to the house one night and she was there,' shrugs Andre.

The attention of 'taste-making' publications such as *The Face* and the new daily broadcasts on Channel 4 might have augured well for Millar at the 1985 Tour de France, but the Tour of Spain had sapped his strength as well as his spirit. A week after the Vuelta finished in Salamanca he sent a letter to the offices of *Cycling* informing them of his move back to Troyes. 'I've still got some morale after the Tour of Spain,' he wrote. He also issued a mild reprimand for their coverage of the race: 'I think you were a little hard on Peugeot.' On the calamitous events in Spain he was pragmatic, philosophical. Or that was how he was determined to appear, anyway.

It wasn't just Millar's strength that deserted him later in the summer, at the Tour de France, for it was here that the Peugeot team, still under the management of Roland Berland, finally imploded. 'Bad morale is like an infection,' said Allan Peiper halfway through the race. Millar confirmed this to Peter Carr for *The High Life*, saying that he had been going well the first week, when 'everything seemed OK, then in the second week I was tired, and just worn out inside . . . there was no real kind of spirit in the team any more. They were all fighting for their life every day when they got to the hills and nobody could do their job any more . . . There was one day when everything went really badly and I told them all [that] it kind of wasn't the way to do it, eh. And they didn't appreciate the idea of me telling them what they should be doing, because I was younger than most of them, they'd been doing it longer than me, and I wasn't French.' Millar conceded that 'it was difficult for me to say they were all useless, eh. Because they were saying the same about me behind my back.'

Peiper had tried at the start of the Tour to instil a positive attitude in a team where the cracks seem never to have been too far beneath the surface. 'At the start of the Tour I got everyone in a room and said, "Listen, we've got to start working as a team because we've got two guys who could win: [Pascal] Simon and Millar." We spoke well for three or four days, had team meetings, then it was finished – back to fisticuffs. A lot of them don't like that we speak English. But I can't talk to Robert or Sean in French. That would be ridiculous.' Berland, claimed Peiper, had no respect from the riders. 'He's a nice bloke because every time I ask for something he does it for me, but that's not what being a team leader's about. A team leader is someone who comes in when you've got bad form and shakes you by the throat and says, "What's going on? Haven't you been training or looking after yourself?" A team leader, after twenty days [of not winning], doesn't say, "Listen, I'll give you more money if you win a stage." He says, "If you don't win the stage you'll go home tonight."' In a sign that the Australian remembered the lessons he'd been taught at the ACBB, Peiper added, 'It's got to be [about] winning, not money. The money comes after the winning.'

Carr then asked Peiper if he thought Millar had the killer instinct necessary to win a race like the Tour de France. 'Yeah, Robert's got it,' Peiper replied with a smile. 'Robert likes money, but he loves winning. He loves being a star.'

But for Millar, the 1985 Tour did not enhance his star status; instead it provided 'a lesson', the lesson being that he 'definitely rode too many races' in the early season. In an interview towards the end of the Tour that he agreed to give only after Carr's researcher, Don Jones, had spent more than an hour trying to persuade him, he appeared particularly downbeat, speaking quietly and slowly. 'I don't know how to perform any more. I'm tired. Inside. I've lost all ambition. There's no kind of team spirit. Just two halves in the team.'

If that interview was strained – and the bleakness of the scene is enhanced by Millar's emaciated appearance more than two weeks into the Tour: he looks half the size of a normal adult – then it was nothing compared to his toe-curling exchange with *Cycling* reporter Keith Bingham at the end of stage 17, which finished, after 210km, at a cold, misty Luz Ardiden, high in the Pyrenees. This interview, punctuated by awkward silences, was captured in its excruciating entirety in *The High Life*. It begins with Bingham, tape-recorder in hand, approaching Millar as he sits on the tailgate of the team car, with a towel hanging off his shoulders, which look no more meaty than a wire coathanger. 'Even the British journalists accompanying the Tour get a cold response,' notes the film's narrator, unnecessarily.

> Keith Bingham: The race seemed to go well for you until what point?
> Robert Millar: Till the Tourmalet.
> KB: The Tourmalet. And what was that like for you?
> RM: I kind of blew in the middle.

KB: In the middle, yeah? Did you recover at all?

RM: No.

KB: No ...

RM: Nobody would ride on the front with Phil [Anderson], eh.

KB: Yeah, why not?

RM: I dunno.

KB: So, how would you sum up today?

RM: Eh?

KB: So, I mean, how would you sum up your effort today?

RM: Not too good, eh.

KB: On Saturday you gave the impression that you might topple, or you might get Herrera [a few days earlier Millar had told Bingham he could still beat the Colombian to the King of the Mountains title, saying, 'All is not lost – I've got more life in me than the rest of the team put together']. Now do you not think that's possible?

RM: Nah, I don't think so.

KB: Is a stage win possible?

RM: I doubt it.

KB: You doubt it?

RM: Nuh.

KB: OK, Robert, cheers.

Adding to the confrontational atmosphere of the interview is Millar's body language. He doesn't make eye contact with Bingham, staring instead at the ground and into a polystyrene cup containing hot, dark liquid, and stirring it with such vigour, if not violence, that at any moment you expect the liquid to pour into his lap from the hole he seems to be drilling. Then there would have been trouble.

Bingham, a genial Merseysider and one of the most approachable of reporters, says that such interviews were typical, but admits today that 'perhaps it was our fault, as reporters, for not getting to the real Robert Millar, through to the person'. Not that Bingham was alone in finding Millar hard work. And this created a dilemma for reporters. With the other English-speaking cyclists, most notably Stephen Roche and Greg LeMond, proving so acquiescent, you can understand their reluctance to persist with the taciturn Scot. Another English-speaking journalist, the Australian Rupert Guinness, wrote in his book *The Foreign Legion* that his first exchange with Millar, in 1987, ended with a 'rude expletive' after Guinness had attempted politely to introduce himself. 'I was wounded by his indifference, and decided to adopt the same policy, even if he went on to win the race. Luckily he didn't and my foolish conviction went unchallenged.'

Even Phil Liggett admits that he resolutely failed to establish any kind of rapport with Millar. 'I didn't have too many bad experiences with Robert because I really didn't bother to contact him,' he says. 'He annoyed me.' It is a testament, then, to Liggett's professionalism that he was able to deliver the impassioned, and inspiring, commentaries that form the soundtrack to so many of Millar's best performances. But it is also mildly disappointing, like discovering that David Coleman was no great fan of Sebastian Coe, or that the hairs on the back of Bill McLaren's neck didn't stand up when Scotland beat England at rugby. 'For a while we never actually spoke,' Liggett continues. 'He was very difficult to approach. Rupert [Guinness] was right. Our attitude was, if he doesn't want to speak to me, I won't speak to him, fuck him. He had a sense of humour, a wry sense of humour, though sometimes you weren't sure if he was being funny.' The problem for Liggett was that he, ITV, and later Channel 4 were desperately keen to champion a British rider. On one occasion Liggett invited Millar to join him in the commentary box after a Tour time trial stage. Millar said yes but then reneged on the agreement. 'He did a shit ride, told a kid to fuck off, knocked his pen and paper out of his hand, and just rode off,' says Liggett. 'He never bothered to come and see me. I mean, we were desperate for some English-speaking riders on *World of Sport*, before the Channel 4 coverage started. To watch him climb was a dream. He was such a talented boy up the mountains. He was perfect in his preparation, he looked good, and he was a professional bike rider through and through. But there were these violent mood swings. You never knew if you went to speak to him whether he'd just ride off.'

It is tempting to wonder whether things might have been different today, when there is a preoccupation with personality. Ironically, Millar might have had a more positive public image, his maverick approach and eccentricities considered highly marketable rather than simply odd, his reluctance to engage with the media tantalizing and intriguing for journalists rather than off-putting. Curiously, Millar seemed to offer more of himself to journalists such as Burgess and Carr – who as non-cycling specialists would be likely to ask more general, sometimes off-the-wall questions – than he did to the specialist media. Then again, he would typically be more open when speaking to journalists away from the racing environment where, as Neil Storey observed, he seemed to need to enter a zone that excluded outsiders and discouraged intrusions. These days even the specialist cycling publications resemble more general titles, with an emphasis on personality and lifestyle over technical details and equipment. 'Perhaps today more effort would be made to ferret information out of someone like Millar,' Liggett suggests.

As a counterpoint to some of these experiences – other journalists, such as Robin Magowan, claimed that it wasn't uncommon for Millar to simply pretend that he had never previously met them when they made an approach – it should be noted that Millar could, on occasions, be more obliging than the vast majority of riders. In November 1984 the then *Cycling* editor,

Martin Ayres, travelled to his apartment in Lille with a postbag full of readers' questions. Millar spent four hours reading and answering these queries; the resulting feature ran to six pages. Again, though, this reinforces the point made by Storey, that Millar in pre-race mode, or mood, could provide a stark contrast to the relaxed, out of competition Millar.

Channel 4 struck gold in choosing to begin their daily broadcasts of the Tour de France in 1985. I know because I was glued to it, even though it did bounce around the schedules, between 5 p.m. and 11.50 p.m. But at least it was on. And it was an epic race, won for a record-equalling fifth time by Bernard Hinault despite a crash in St Etienne that left him with a broken nose and four stitches in his head. The Badger never looked more formidable than in that final week. The swollen nose and two black eyes kind of suited him, complementing the angry snarl. In the *Observer*, Julian Barnes, then a TV critic, was also impressed. 'There are few more thrilling sights than a helicopter shot of a 100-man peloton in full arrowhead cry through the French countryside . . .'

Millar finished a disappointed and disillusioned eleventh overall. He also managed to wind up Hinault. 'There was one stage when I attacked to try to win the stage and Hinault didn't appreciate the fact that this meant an acceleration in the bunch. When they caught me he gave me a bit of a bollocking because it gave him sore legs and he wasn't very happy about it. I'm impressed by Hinault, but I'm not impressed by his personality. I do what I want to do.' Some months later, Millar was more candid: 'Hinault hates me. He does not hide his feelings, and though I don't mind that, I dislike him for thinking himself so superior.'

On the Tour's final stage to Paris, Millar also suffered what *Cycling* called a 'final humiliation' when he was relegated from second to third overall in the King of the Mountains competition.

'The Peugeot rider arrived seething and suffering,' reported the magazine. In a stage that is traditionally a promenade, the third-placed rider in the mountains competition decided to attack the small climbs on the way into Paris to try to dislodge Millar from second place, and snatch the prize money that went with it. To make matters worse, it was Pedro Delgado.

After the Tour, Millar rode the Kellogg's criterium in Glasgow in front of a huge crowd and a TV audience of 2.2 million. But the star of the show was unimpressed with the antics of the British-based professionals, whom he accused of using roughhouse tactics – pulling jerseys, using their elbows, and cutting him up on the corners. 'They are dangerous,' complained Millar after the race. 'The guys have no respect for each other.' In August he again excelled in the world championship road race, placing tenth, and in September he returned to Spain to win the Tour of Catalonia ahead of Sean Kelly. He was asked if that counted as revenge for his Vuelta defeat. 'Not really,' he replied. 'I had to beat Sean, not the Spanish, to win this time.'

By now he had already decided to leave Peugeot, his first and so far only professional team. Later, he would explain that 'I got tired of all the crap with the French guys, like them expecting us to speak French all the time, even when I wanted to say something to Peiper or Yatesy. They were becoming paranoid about us talking about them or something.' Millar signed instead for one of the richest and most formidable outfits in cycling, the Dutch Panasonic squad. It was the team Berland claimed had 'betrayed' him in the Vuelta, but Millar was either oblivious to that or he didn't care. On the plus side, the move would take him into a new earnings bracket – estimates of his salary at Panasonic range from £60,000 to £90,000 a year – and it would also guarantee him the kind of team support he'd lacked during the 1985 Tour. Moreover, with Peter Post as *directeur sportif* the one thing everyone could be assured of was strong leadership and organization. Allan Peiper, who had

complained so bitterly during the Tour of Berland's ineffective-
ness, was another Panasonic recruit for the 1986 season.

In the team's earlier guise as Raleigh, Post had also been Billy
Bilsland's *directeur sportif.* 'I got on the wrong side of Post from
day one, which was a mistake,' says Bilsland with some understatement. 'He came to see me at the start of [the one-day
classic] Kuurne-Brussels-Kuurne. Two of the other British
riders had gone home, and he said, "Where are they?" So I said,
"Should you no' know that? You bein' the manager . . .' He didn't
like that.' But Bilsland had no qualms about Millar joining Post.
'Post is a winner. If you ride well, you're fine.' Arthur Campbell,
on the other hand, had one reservation. 'I was at a UCI congress
and Peter Post was there. He came up and said, "I've signed
Robert Millar." I said, "Well, I'll tell you something: he can't ride
two major [three-week] tours in a season." And Post said, "I'll
remember that." But it was the first thing he forgot . . .'

Known as 'the Emperor' in Holland, Post belonged to the
Alex Ferguson school of management, with an emphasis on
discipline. 'One of his principles was never to be satisfied, even
when we won,' recalls Theo de Rooy, who rode – or survived –
under Post for eight years. Peiper adds, 'Post ruled Panasonic
with an iron rod. He had a very powerful character and most of
us were frightened of him.' He was in his mid-fifties when
Millar joined his squad, his stature and presence enhanced by
his height ('his shoulders permanently high, like a great bear',
as Les Woodland once wrote). He had been a top rider himself
from the 1950s to the early 1970s, when his career was ended
by an horrific crash. When he went into management he initially worked with a number of British riders – hardly surprising, since the squad, though based in Holland, was sponsored
by Raleigh. Bilsland did well to survive more than a season with
him, because Post's verdict on the British was pretty damning.
'You get these really tough riders from Ireland – Kelly, Roche,
and now [Martin] Earley,' he said in 1987. 'They are like hungry

boxers. I think maybe the English [*sic*] riders have too comfortable a life back home and they are not so ready to accept the hard – and it is hard – life of the international man.'

For 1986, Post had not only Millar and Peiper but also Phil Anderson on his books. Anderson had been with the team since 1984 and had flourished under Post. Indeed, until they fell out in 1988, the hard-as-nails Australian and the tough Dutchman formed something of a mutual appreciation society. 'He listens to what I say to him; he is a thinking rider and we have a good working relationship,' said Post in 1987. By then, a year into working with Millar, he was also positive about the Scotsman – or as positive as Post was inclined to be. 'Robert Millar – not perhaps as tough as Phil, but I have big hopes for him in the Tours.' At the 1986 Panasonic team presentation, in The Hague, Millar had another well-qualified supporter in the great Eddy Merckx, who had replaced Raleigh as the team's bike supplier. 'Peter Post wanted to strengthen his team for the Tour de France and I believe he has made the right choice in taking Millar on,' said the world's most famous Belgian.

Now living in Belgium himself, and married to Sylvie, Millar prepared for the 1986 season with renewed enthusiasm. But the change of team and circumstances obviously were not enough to instil him with unbridled confidence. His superstitious side was revealed in the pages of *Cycling*, the magazine reporting that when he applied to the British Cycling Federation for his 1986 racing licence he asked to be allocated the number two – his lucky number. Another irreverent item of news was that a little-known English group, The Johnny Seven Band, had written and recorded a song entitled 'Can Robert Millar Win the Tour de France?' The band's vocalist, John Martin, explained, 'I was inspired by Millar's efforts so I wrote the song.' A recording of the song, he added, had been dispatched to Peter Post. Had the musician been John Martyn, of Millar's old school Shawlands Academy, then perhaps the song might have achieved some airplay – as it is, 'Can Robert Millar Win the Tour de France?' seems to have sunk without trace.

Millar had a slow start to the season, since Post had dictated – contrary to Campbell's counsel – that he would contest two major tours, those of Spain and France. On his return to Spain he showed no signs of anxiety, far less fear, winning stage 6, the 191km mountainous leg from Santander to Lagos de Covadonga, and in the process taking over the race leader's yellow jersey. For the next six stages he wore that jersey with, reported *Cycling*, 'some arrogance, in defiance of the whistles and boos that greeted him everywhere'. As the race settled into a pattern the Spaniard Alvaro Pino claimed the lead from Millar. Stage 17, to Sierra Nevada, was the one where Millar fancied wresting it back, but he couldn't shake Pino. 'I did all I could,' said Millar after the race. Eventually he finished the Vuelta second once again, one minute and sixteen seconds down on Pino. 'Everyone is always upset with a second place,' he commented, 'but I am not as disappointed as last year. This time I have been beaten fair and square, while last time I fell into a trap.' Millar followed this with another strong stage-race performance, placing second to the American Andy Hampsten in the Tour of Switzerland, on the eve of the Tour de France.

Hampsten provides an interesting perspective on the Panasonic set-up and the mentality instilled by Post. He rode for 7-Eleven, the first American team ever to ride the Giro d'Italia (in 1985) and Tour de France (1986). This squad was the forerunner of the Motorola team, but in its early days it had a very strong American flavour, in terms of attitude and approach. In this sense it was in stark contrast to many of the traditional European teams, especially one like the Peter Post-led Panasonic. 'For some reason 7-Eleven and Panasonic were together a lot, usually at training camps in Italy between the races in spring,' Hampsten recalls. 'And we had a lot of fun – well, it wasn't a lot of fun, but we made it fun. We'd go out for training, riding somewhere for coffees and pastries, and then back. But the Panasonic riders had to do the coffee and pastry rides on the sly. For them it was a twenty-four-hour-a-day job. They were hardcore; it was a nasty world they were in, where your team-mates would rat on you if you had too much fun. I don't know if they were showing off to each other, or for our benefit, but they were really mean off the bike, and also on it. At 7-Eleven we laughed a lot, mainly at how much more serious they were than us. It reinforced our ideas about the European pro scene. But I think Robert enjoyed our company. I had a lot of fun with him.'

In *Cycling*'s Tour preview edition the headline said it all: 'Millar Gets His Orders – Win Tour de France'. The order came from Post, of course, but Millar appeared almost as bullish as his boss. He also seemed to be relishing life with Panasonic: 'The team has such a reputation to uphold that the riders get up to the front, [they're] not messing about in the middle or the back of the bunch.' In Panasonic, he added, 'You don't give up your place in the line without a battle. I fight a lot harder now. They say Post is hard, but as long as you deliver he's OK. He asks a lot of his riders and if you don't come up to scratch you can expect a bollocking in front of the rest of the team.' As for his prospects in the Tour, Millar's main goal was to win the King of the Mountains jersey again. 'I can go for it in the Pyrenees, then see how the other contenders are going for the overall.'

This interview was conducted while Millar was in London for a preview screening of *The High Life*, so he was also asked about some of the contents of the film, including Peiper's suggestion that he wasn't suited to the role of team leader because he didn't have 'the strength as a human being to control other people'. To that, Millar responded, 'I can't go round shouting at guys, it's not in my nature. But the point is that now I have someone to do the shouting for me – Henk Lubberding. He's the team captain and he stimulates everyone in the team,

including me.' The other aspect of the film that 'raised eyebrows' during the preview screening was the discussion of the
seedier side of cycling – the 'buying' of rival teams and riders.
'I think people will realize that it is a professional sport and in
any professional sport you will find people prepared to pay for
help,' explained Millar.

There was one other remark made by Millar in that interview that, with the benefit of hindsight, is both revealing and
also a little poignant: 'I don't want to be remembered as
someone who won the King of the Mountains one year and
nothing else.'

If anything, the 1986 Tour de France bettered the 1985 race.
There was also an improvement for British viewers: Channel
4's daily coverage went out at peak time, 6.30 p.m. Bernard
Hinault was back for the final time, but he had vowed to help
his young American team-mate Greg LeMond, to pay him back
for his assistance the previous year. This supposed vow,
coupled with LeMond's understandable suspicion of the crafty
old bugger, made for a very entertaining Tour indeed, particularly when Hinault took the yellow jersey at the halfway point.

LeMond's fightback coincided with Millar's emergence as
one of the strong men. He had ridden a good time trial, placing
ninth, but had also crashed twice on stage 10. 'That was no
problem,' Post informed reporters. 'A little graze. Nothing. We
are waiting now to see how he goes in the mountains.' Millar
also downplayed the seriousness of his accidents, but it's worth
dwelling on this: falling off a bike at 30mph, onto tarmac, while
protected only by lycra, can never be dismissed as 'nothing'. It is
bloody painful; and it isn't just part of the job of being a cyclist,
it is a routine part of the job. When it happens, cyclists don't stay
down until the referee blows for a foul; they bounce back up
and inspect the damage much later, when the blood has con-
gealed and glued clothing to skin with more effectiveness than

Araldite. Arguably it is not the falling off that's the most painful aspect of crashing, it's taking off your clothes later. Cyclists' hips, elbows and knees all look as if they've been attacked by a blowtorch, dotted as they are with translucent white blobs. As Millar told Alan Fraser of the *Daily Mail* in 1994, 'You have to be afraid. Either you realize the danger of hurting yourself or you are stupid. Is it sore? Try it some time. Go down a hill at 30mph, jump off, and see what it feels like.'

It was in the Pyrenees, as stage 13 took the riders from Pau to Luchon – scene of Millar's stage win in 1983 – that LeMond made his move, while Hinault 'fought back like a tiger in a cage'. Between the battling team-mates, Millar climbed to second on the stage, just over a minute behind LeMond. He also ascended to fourth overall and inherited the polka-dot jersey. But could he win the Tour? 'No, I don't think I can. But LeMond can. He will be the first English-speaking rider to win the Tour de France and he will do it in the Alps. I think I'll be in the first three in Paris. My wife is coming to the race at Alpe d'Huez and I hope to win there.'

This was the stage witnessed not only by Sylvie but also by his old flatmate from his year at the ACBB, John Parker. But on the morning of the big Alpe d'Huez rendezvous Millar awoke with his heart pounding at sixty-five beats a minute. Normally, even on the Tour, it was forty-two. He had suffered the previous day, admitting that he was 'smashed' on the final climb, the Col du Granon. And now, on stage 18, from Briançon to Alpe d'Huez, came another day of murderous climbs. On the first, the Col du Galibier, Millar had to be pushed by a team-mate, Eric Vanderaerden. It was a similar story on the Col de la Croix de Fer, and then on the twenty-one hairpins of the Alpe, where Parker was, you will recall, on hand to give him a push. Quite apart from the private hell he was in, it helps explain why Millar didn't recognize his former colleague, as does the fact that there was some abuse being directed at him and his colleagues in the 'grupetto' – the backmarkers on a mountain stage. Among the others in the group was Millar's team-mate Vanderaerden, wearing the green jersey of points leader. Much later, Millar speculated that it was the presence of the polka-dot and green jerseys together that angered sections of the crowd. 'The sight of the polka jersey and the green jersey suffering at the back of the race didn't please parts of the crowd . . . some made the usual lazy, overpaid comments, the usual laughing at those in distress; typical scenes of those who jeer because they think you'll be affected or put off by it, but in reality most of the time it never really bothered me too deeply. I remember Eric exchanging insults with a few of the Dutch [fans] but I was too ill to take any notice.'

Yet, in contrast to the small minority of yobs, Parker must have been one of dozens, if not hundreds, who in contravention of the rules, but in accordance with tradition and human decency, pushed those who appeared to be in the greatest agony. Twenty minutes ahead of Millar, LeMond and Hinault crossed the line arm in arm, though the psychological warfare would continue. In a scenario with echoes of the 1985 Vuelta, LeMond stated that 'eighty per cent of the peloton are racing against me'. He also said he was aware of rumoured threats that he would be 'taken out' mid-race. 'If I don't win because of an accident and Bernard wins because I've been knocked out by some rider in the peloton, I just say it will be his worst victory and that's a bad way to go down in history.'

The day after Alpe d'Huez was a rest day, which gave Millar an opportunity to recover. It emerged that he had been suffering from stomach pain, which prevented him eating during the stage preceding the Alpe. By the rest day he had been diagnosed with a throat infection, and he spent the day in bed. Next day he struggled on, losing six more minutes. 'I've drunk five litres of water today, I was sweating so much after the antibiotics,' he said. 'Of course I will finish. I will get to Paris. I just feel so bad that I should be captain of this great team who have done everything they could for me, only for me to lose everything. That's life, eh?'

His resolve couldn't last. On stage 21, the penultimate day of the Tour, as Hinault, now in the polka-dot jersey, led the field over the day's first climb, Millar was dropped. He struggled on but abandoned, reportedly in tears, 30km from the finish. The climb that did for Millar was the Col Croix de l'Homme Mort – Dead Man's Cross. 'It's all over,' he said as he climbed into the car of his *soigneur*, Piet Boot. 'I've nothing left, no more power.' Later, he told *Cycling*, 'I should have stopped on the Alpe d'Huez stage because I knew my reserves were nil then. But I couldn't do it. Not when the team had done so much for me.'

In the autumn, Millar's contract with Panasonic was renewed for 1987, after rumours that the Japanese electronics giant was to withdraw its sponsorship. One of Millar's final races of the season was the Nissan Classic in Ireland, where he spent much of the race fulfilling what for him had become an unfamiliar role, as a *domestique*, putting himself at the service of other riders. 'It's good to work for the others for a change and sit on the front instead of in the middle of the bunch,' he said. 'It's easier on the brain as well.'

In their New Year issue, *Cycling* published a major interview with Millar. Nick Sanders travelled to Wielsbeke for a training ride in his company, but he was held up when bad weather led to the cancellation of his ferry. This could have spelled trouble. But no. 'I had never thought of Millar as a man of warm, spontaneous emotions, able to laugh off a morning's delay,' wrote Sanders. When he did eventually arrive at Millar's house – a modern semi-detached brick house rented to the Millars by a local carpet factory owner who also gave Sylvie a job – Sanders expected a 'frosty greeting' but instead found someone who 'talked quickly, nervously even'. 'I had been led to believe he was dour and uncooperative [but] he could not have been more giving.'

Millar tells Sanders that he has few friends in Belgium. 'Pascal Simon and I got on well when I lived in Troyes, but here people keep themselves to themselves.' Sanders says he'd imagined that Millar would be 'a man of few words, laconic in his observations', but instead finds that he has a 'curious self-deprecating sense of irony', and that he talks incessantly, 'drawing breath only to laugh'. But 'you do not need to be too attentive to note his shyness'. Millar gives his stock response to a question about the sport: 'It's a jungle.' With his career having followed a steadily rising trajectory up until now, Millar also shows an astonishing level of self-awareness and offers a calm, rational analysis of his place in that 'jungle'. While many riders at this stage of their careers – having just turned 28 and having already had three top-four finishes in the major tours, Millar was on the cusp of his peak years – might still be unashamedly aiming for immortality, Millar seems almost resigned to falling short of that: 'I feel stronger [but] I now know my limits and I must make the most of what I have.' The implication being that this might not be enough for him to win the Tour de France.

'He has a survivor's view of life,' notes Sanders as the pair of them set out on a training ride that takes them over roads spattered with mud and cow shit. 'It's so dirty here with half the fields on the road that you become completely unrecognizable after 200 yards,' says Millar. His opinion of Belgium is bleak but witty: 'I like it around here. It's so ugly it makes the rest of the world look really beautiful.'

Does Millar ever visit Scotland? asks Sanders. 'Hardly ever. My home is over here.' Does he not wish to see his family? 'Yes, but we are not a close family. Once or at most twice a year, that is enough.' He becomes more effusive as they stare into the window of a cake shop in Courtrai. 'I love cakes. Sylvie stops me eating too many. It brings me out in spots.'

On his train journey home, Sanders considers that Millar is 'a breed apart . . . as I flicked through my notes there was a sentence heavily underlined. "I don't want to become Scotland's best cyclist," he had said. "I want to become the best British rider ever."'

'Giro Course Just Right for Millar' read the headline in *Cycling* on the eve of the 1987 Tour of Italy. The race was unusually hilly, with no fewer than five mountain-top finishes, and Millar was in good form as he prepared to make his debut in the world's second-biggest stage race, the highlight of the spring being fifth in arguably the toughest of the 'classics', Liège-Bastogne-Liège. Stephen Roche, second at Liège, was also back to his best form after a season blighted by injury. In this respect the Dubliner appeared jinxed: so far in his professional career he had ridden well in years that ended in an odd number and then spent the following season fighting a running battle with injury.

The Giro d'Italia started on 21 May in San Remo with a prologue time trial won by the country's pin-up and defending champion, Roberto Visentini. But the opening weekend was notable mainly for a remarkable display of strength by Millar's Panasonic team. On an unusual 31km stage that finished at the top of the San Romolo, they placed four riders in the first five: Eric Breukink was first, Phil Anderson second, Millar third, and Peter Winnen fifth. Roche split them, finishing fourth. The Irishman then won the day's second stage, a kamikaze downhill time trial, but he was not amused. 'Three riders have been killed this year,' he said, '[and] it seems they are looking for a fourth.'

Things were about to turn a lot nastier for Roche. Just before the Giro began he'd given Nick Sanders an interview in which he'd said, 'It is a hard sport and to get where we have we have all been two-faced – you know, knives in the back. If you do not use other riders or a given situation to your advantage [then] they will use you.' Prophetic words, as it turned out, with Roche finding himself at loggerheads with his team-mate and co-leader, Visentini, cast as a hate figure in Italy, and with no shortage of blades scratching at his back. If anything, Roche's ordeal in Italy made Millar's experiences in Spain during the 1985 Vuelta appear tame.

Riding for the Italian Carrera team, Roche took over the race leader's pink jersey at the beginning of the Giro, then surrendered it to Visentini, before – much to the annoyance of his team – claiming it back as the race hit the mountains. It was here, too, that Millar began to make his presence felt, slowly climbing up the overall classification, from seventh to fifth to fourth as the race entered its third and final week. He also had a firm grip on the King of the Mountains jersey. But Roche, though still leading the race, had a major problem. Although Visentini was not in the form he'd been in twelve months earlier, he was still the man favoured by his team. He was Italian, after all. The anti-Roche campaign went deeper still, and became more pernicious. Going into the last week, only one of his team-mates, the Belgian Eddy Schepers, was even speaking to him, far less helping him. On top of that, there was unprecedented hostility from the crowds, which Roche will never forget. 'The tifosi [Italian fans] wanted me out the race,' he says. 'They wanted to kill me. They were spitting at me, hitting me. Looking back on it now, if you'd said to me before that Giro that this scenario would arise, that I would become the most hated guy in Italy for three weeks, with people spitting at me, a police guard outside the door of my room, a mechanic looking after my bike exclusively, a *soigneur* preparing my food exclusively for fear that someone would poison me . . . I'd have said that's not sport, I'll not bother. Looking back now, I must have had character to come through that. Because there was no way I was going home, no way. They could hit me, spit at me, do what they want, but I wasn't going home.'

Quite apart from the daily exposure to the ugliness of a rabid tifosi, Roche faced the practical problem of how to win the race with only one team-mate. He needed help; he needed allies. Visentini, with all but one member of the Carrera team at his service, had the gall to accuse others of collusion with Roche, urging Carrera to take action against the Irishman and Schepers. 'The Fagor team is working for Roche,' he complained, 'in collusion with Millar.'

It seemed at the time far-fetched to suggest that Millar would jeopardize his own high placing in the race, his status as Panasonic team leader, not to mention his relationship with the fearsome Peter Post, to work on behalf of a rider on a rival team. On the face of it, his position improved further when he won stage 21, the mountainous 248km from Como to Pila; it saw him leapfrog his team-mate Breukink to second overall, behind Roche. He also had two other Panasonic team-mates, Winnen and Anderson, in the top ten. There seemed no way that Millar could risk putting the interests of Roche before those of his own team, which still, on paper at least, had much to race for.

Yet Roche confirms that Millar did indeed help him; that by the end of the race he was, effectively, a team-mate. 'Yeah, yeah. Robert understood that I was under pressure, that I wasn't getting help from my own team and I was isolated. I realized he could help me, and I knew that if I needed help he'd be there. I had a weak team in the mountains and I knew Robert would be there to help me if I needed him. Knowing he was there gave me confidence.' Roche, in other words, made the sort of 'arrangement' with Millar that Millar should have made during the 1985 Vuelta. 'Yeah,' Roche agrees, 'but everything happened so fast in the Vuelta. I think the manager was at fault too.' But it is the fact that Roche took responsibility for this himself that sets him apart from Millar; and it goes some way to explaining his two major tour wins to Millar's none. Roche relished the responsibility of leadership, and the wheeling and dealing, the deal making and tactical decision making, inherent in the role. 'There was a buzz there, looking around, seeing what was going to happen, talking to guys. When you were there you had to read the race, to feel things. Yeah, Robert was looking for his *directeur sportif* to do things, make decisions – which is right, that was his job. But when Robert realized what was going on he should have done something straightaway. He should have talked to someone. But that was Robert, he was shy, he didn't have the personality. Even in the Tour of Italy, I'm sure Robert was dying to ask if I needed a hand, but I had to ask him. He wouldn't come to me. It was towards the end when I did speak to him, when things started getting very difficult.'

Patrick Valcke, the former Peugeot team mechanic who had followed Roche to La Redoute and then on to the Carrera team, also remembers enlisting Millar's help. 'We were in the shit,' he says. 'We had only Eddy Schepers helping Stephen, and the Italians wanted Visentini to win. We had to go looking for someone who would help Stephen in the mountains. So we went to see Bob. His answer? "OK." That was always his answer – "OK."' As Valcke says this his face creases into a smile. 'I remember on that Giro we had a tactic in the mountains: we kept Stephen in the middle of the road with Eddy Schepers and Robert Millar on either side. We had to because with the tifosi going mad for Visentini it was too dangerous. We were scared they would force Stephen off his bike. It was extraordinary.'

Roche doesn't say that he 'gifted' Millar his stage win at Pila – which made him the first and only British rider to win stages in the three major tours – but he does say that 'another stage win was no use to me. Robert had helped me during the week.' On that stage, Roche, Millar and the Spaniard Marino Lejaretta bloke clear on the 15km climb to the finish. 'I might not have beaten him anyway, but Robert winning was good for me. It kept him happy, kept his team happy.' Surely Millar was taking a big risk helping Roche? 'Yeah, yeah,' acknowledges Roche. 'Breukink was well placed, too. But Robert did it intelligently. He rode for me but he won the King of the Mountains, he won a stage; and of course, when you speak to your boss at the end of the day, he'll understand. You might have helped Roche but you won the stage, you won the King of the Mountains, so everyone's happy.'

To Theo de Rooy, who also rode that Giro and was a frequent room-mate of Millar's, it was obvious, even if it remained unsaid, that Millar was helping Roche, and he recalls that 'Peter Post was not satisfied, he was angry. It was an extremely hard Giro; I worked my balls off as a *domestique*. For the team it was a successful Giro [Millar finished second, three minutes and forty seconds behind Roche, with his team-mate Breukink third, a further thirty-seven seconds back], but Post was not satisfied because we didn't win it! Sometimes he would shout at dinner time, but that was not a very tactical approach in the case of Robert, because he was not a guy who was impressed by such behaviour. He wouldn't respond to that, which I can understand.'

Still, de Rooy goes on to suggest, even if Millar did risk incurring the Emperor's wrath by putting Roche's interests before those of his own team, Post might have implicitly understood his reasons. 'Stephen was a very well-accepted rider among our team. He was Irish, but the mentality of British and Irish riders fits well to the mentality of the Dutch. We also had problems with the French, Spanish and Italian riders, mainly because of the language barrier. Of course, you can be certain that if you have Post as a team director then you must try and win for yourself and the team; but if you cannot win for yourself, and you're in a situation to decide for someone else . . . if you have to make that choice, then of course you should help the guys you like the most. Stephen was a guy we liked.'

10

Domestique De Luxe

I just wanted to show I'm not finished, as a lot of people seem to think.

'Today I am 47 years old,' says Patrick Valcke, 'and I can honestly say that Fagor was the worst experience of my life.'

He is sitting in a pizzeria in Rennes, where he now works for the town's football club. He is friendly, talkative, full of energy, excitable, and he is wearing a black bomber jacket and black jeans. He has dark, slightly thinning hair, but he doesn't look 47. It's hard to believe that he first worked with Millar, as a mechanic with Peugeot, as long ago as 1981. Harder still to comprehend that at the end of 1987, when he was still only 28, he was appointed *directeur sportif* of Fagor, a new 'super team' (with an old Spanish sponsor) to be led by Stephen Roche, with the cream of the English-speaking talent in support. Robert Millar, Sean Yates and the Sheffield sprinter Malcolm Elliott were all signed by Fagor, on generous salaries, for 1988. For Millar it was payback for the help he had given Roche during the 1987 Giro. But what it turned into, says Valcke, was 'a black period for all of us'. He pauses for a moment, takes a bite of his pizza, then adds, 'Hellish.'

Valcke suffered a heart attack in the middle of 1988 – a direct consequence, he believes, of what happened with Fagor. It was therefore good to see him looking so well on the day I met him. And not only well, but happy. Happy because, apart from the Fagor episode, he is reminiscing about some good times, many of them involving Robert Millar. 'I would love to see Robert again,' he says. 'I don't care about the rumours that surround him; he can come and see me any time. My door is wide open to him. He's someone who was a big part of my life for fifteen years. When you called and said you wanted to talk about Robert Millar I was happy, really happy.'

Tears are welling up in Valcke's eyes as he speaks, though he is still smiling. 'I get really emotional because it makes me think about the good old days when I was younger, but it also makes me realize how extraordinary Bob was.' Valcke alternates between the familiar, friendly 'Bob' – which he says with urgency, almost spitting it out – and the more respectful, almost reverential 'Robert'. 'Bob went against the grain in everything he did. When I talk about Robert my mind is flooded with images and memories. But it's a bit strange. I almost have a feeling of regret. I was so close to Stephen [Roche], we used to call each other every day, and we'd eat at each other's houses. But now, when I think about Robert, I think, how could we have drifted apart? What happened? It's strange.'

Then Valcke laughs again. 'He was funny to watch. We used to laugh at him for sitting sideways on the saddle. He would have his hands on the bars, and it seemed he was riding beside his bike. We would say to each other in the car, "Look at the toad go!"'

Millar was still a Panasonic rider, and he still had a working relationship with Peter Post, when the 1987 Tour de France began in Berlin. It was the first time the great race had started behind the old Iron Curtain, prompting a million photo opportunities of garishly costumed professional cyclists – especially exiles from Eastern Europe – alongside the crumbling Berlin Wall. After Greg LeMond's win the previous year, this – Roche's year – was an even bigger hit in Britain. The Channel 4 coverage, having started three years earlier with a daily audience of around two hundred thousand, had climbed to an average of 1.2 million. 'On exceptional days,' says Phil Liggett, bristling with pride, 'it went up to one and a half million.' These were 'huge figures for Channel 4. We were rivalling *Coronation Street.*' The final stage of the 1987 Tour, which saw Roche's coronation in Paris, was watched by 3.2 million in the UK. 'There were stories of people running into television shops and pubs to see if he'd won the Tour,' Liggett recalls. 'It was huge.'

But it was another disastrous Tour for Millar, adding credence to his and Arthur Campbell's conviction that he was not up to two three-week stage races in the same season. The 1987 Tour also sounded the death knell as far as his relationship with Post was concerned.

Millar reckoned that he rode much of the Tour at only 'seventy per cent' capacity. He was suffering from the ailment that is the curse of the stage-race rider: diarrhoea. Given the relentless routine of stage races, the fact that the body's immune system is depressed, and the sheer volume of fluids and food (up to eight litres and seven thousand calories) that need to be taken on board on a daily basis, a cyclist's stomach has a lot to contend with. Yet Post, angry at the Giro, was incandescent at the Tour. He had no time for a rider suffering from diarrhoea. 'Post gave me a lot of stick,' Millar said after the race. 'You have no force [and] you can do nothing about it. It was no use complaining to the other guys in the team because I couldn't follow the bunch anyway. Post was going crazy, but if I could have been [with the leaders], I would have been.' The stomach trouble passed, but Millar struggled to Paris, finishing nineteenth overall – respectable for most riders, poor by his standards.

He had been signed by Post to win the Tour de France but it was beginning to look like this was beyond him. Jacques Anquetil, the first five-time winner of the Tour, was another to recognize Millar's limitations. He told Jean-Marie Leblanc that the Scotsman did not have the physique to support two big stage races in one season. 'If he wants to shine in the Tour de France he should cut all the other long stage races.'

Quite apart from this vexing question of one tour or two, it was surely inevitable that his relationship with the dictatorial Post would eventually turn sour. Later, Millar revealed that after the 1987 Tour he spoke to his *directeur sportif* on only two occasions, which might explain why Post declined to be interviewed for this book. 'He's like a big kid and thinks he's in the army,' said Millar of Post in December 1987, having signed his six-figure contract with Fagor for 1988. 'If you argue with him the rest of the riders won't talk to you. They keep their distance. I never did really like the way that Panasonic ran things, or Post's domination.'

Much later, Millar revealed more about the circumstances that led to his departure. 'Post used to wear my ears out,' he wrote in *Cycle Sport* in 1997. 'During my second season with him he did something so unbelievable that I began to question his sanity. We were at the GP of Zurich, the team didn't have any wins from the classics campaign – Post's big thing – so he was hyper-stressed to get some kind of a result in Switzerland. He put us up in the Hilton which was very expensive, as he reminded us, but then we had no excuses if we didn't get results as he, Post, had done his best.

'Everyone except him had to eat in the snack bar because it cost too much for us to eat in the restaurant. So the evening before the race we were eating in the snack bar when Post popped in to check on us. It was near the end of the meal and they brought out the dessert, which was crème caramel. Now, I don't like crème caramel so I got up and was making to leave when Post asked me where I was going. I told him I had finished eating and was off to my room. He said that I hadn't eaten my crème caramel and that I'd better come back and eat it! But, I told him, I didn't like crème caramel and I'd had enough, then turned and started to leave. He began shouting – and by now everyone in the place was listening – to come back and eat the crème caramel because he had already paid for it and I, as a rider, had to eat it! As I left the snack bar I could still hear him shouting [for me] to come back . . . As the lift went up I heard him fading into the distance: "Come back! Come back!" He didn't speak to me for three days afterwards and the others told me he'd never forgive me. I was convinced he was going crazy. It was time to move on again.'

In his appraisal of his time with Panasonic, Millar did, of course, gloss over some of his more eccentric behaviour – especially, funnily enough, at meal times. 'It wouldn't have been him leaving the crème caramel that annoyed Peter,' notes Millar's old Panasonic team-mate Allan Peiper, 'it would have been standing up and leaving before dinner. Peter wanted to put across the idea that you had to be sociable. To be a team leader, you had to motivate and gather your troops around you. And that's the one thing Rob failed on. He wasn't able to be a Lance Armstrong or Bernard Hinault type of leader, gathering his troops around him.' It was while at Panasonic, and during the 1987 Tour, that Millar, upon being served a plate of pasta, took one look at it and threw it away. 'It was either too hard or too soft,' says Phil Anderson. 'We were in France, so it was probably too soft, and he just picked it up and threw it straight down on the floor. It had sauce on it, too. He said something like, "This is not al dente!" I was sat across the table at the time and I was surprised. I thought, "There's obviously fire in there somewhere."' On another occasion Sean Yates recalls Millar sampling the vegetarian offering, scowling, calling over the waiter, and saying, 'Excuse me, is it possible to bring some taste for this?' And on yet another occasion, later in his career, the Australian Scott Sunderland tells of Millar being served up a plate of overcooked spaghetti, 'like glue,' and telling the waiter 'this would stick on anything.' Upon which, to prove the point, he threw it at the ceiling.

Eventually, Millar was able to look back on his time with Panasonic with a detached perspective that allowed him to give Post credit where he felt it was due. 'Good riders, good presentation, a big sponsor,' he said. 'You got the impression that other riders were impressed when Panasonic showed up at a race.' And as every professional athlete knows, the devil is in the detail. 'Even the clothing fitted just right, which, amazingly enough, I hadn't been used to . . . I learned more about how to race here in six months than I had in six years at Peugeot.'

On paper, Fagor and Roche was a marriage made in heaven. Stephen Roche, his historic treble making him the world's most marketable cyclist – only Eddy Merckx had won the world championship, the Giro and the Tour in the same year before – was able to write his own cheque. And Fagor, a Spanish manufacturer of household equipment, had the budget to indulge him. Patrick Valcke says that it was actually Fagor who made the initial approach to Roche. 'You are going to have a scoop here,' he tells me with a smile, 'but we received an offer from Fagor of seven million francs for Stephen. A two-year deal, so fourteen million francs for Stephen. Tax free. That made us sit up and think.'

'It was my dream team,' says Roche. 'Me and Patrick, we were in it together. We went there with our own conditions. We put the team together – a lot of English-speaking riders – a brilliant team. It was the first time we'd all been together and capable of winning in the sprints [with Malcolm Elliott], mountains [Millar], time trials [Yates] and overall [Roche himself]. Everyone was on good money; I negotiated all the salaries. We'd have cleaned up.'

Unfortunately for Roche, the even-years injury jinx continued: after his glorious 1987, 1988 was a disaster. The portents were there before the season even started, for he had to have an operation on his left knee over the winter. It meant three months off training, and Fagor, having invested so much, hit the panic button as early as 4 January, when the team convened in San Sebastian. It was here that the riders discovered that the Fagor boss, Augustin Mondragon, had decided to sack the management team selected by Roche of Valcke and Philippe Crepel, who had been in charge of one of Roche's previous teams, La Redoute. In protest, the riders walked out of the team photo session.

Roche entered into eight hours of crisis talks with Mondragon, with the outcome that both men were reinstated, Valcke as *directeur sportif*, Crepel as manager. 'There was no actual aggro between myself and Fagor,' claimed Roche at the time, 'just a misunderstanding over some important aspects of team management. But the roles have now been decided satisfactorily and all is well . . . I wanted Philippe Crepel and Patrick Valcke to be in charge of the team's arrangements, but the bosses Mondragon and [Miguel] Gomez obviously felt they were not right for the job and dismissed them.' With the pair reinstated, Roche was confident that matters had been resolved. '[Crepel and Valcke] are both very important to the team. I felt it is my team and that is accepted by the bosses. They want me to deal with them directly if there are any problems. I will be spokesman for all members of the team and this suits me. There are no changes in the squad of eighteen.'

In Roche's absence, Millar became de facto leader. He rose to the challenge at the Criterium International, finishing third overall, and at the hilly classic Liège-Bastogne-Liège, where he achieved his best ever classic placing of third. His performance impressed the winner, Adrie Van Der Poel, who admitted that he was 'most worried about Millar. He was looking very

Millar in 1985, his final year with Peugeot, flat out in the Tour de France prologue.

Above Climbing in his first Tour in 1983; a first, brief appearance in the polka-dot jersey.

Above The perm and pierced ear are new touches for the 1982 season, his third as a professional.

Above On the 1984 Tour, Millar, with Allan Peiper on his left, awaits the start of the team time trial.

Left About to attack breakaway companions to win his second Pyrenean stage of the 1984 Tour.

Right A smiling, relaxed Millar in yellow at the 1985 Vuelta, before being ambushed by the 'Spanish Armada'.

Left Defending yellow in the 1985 Vuelta, alongside 1986 winner Alvaro Pino.

Above Millar sprints towards the finish of a time trial stage during the fateful Vuelta.

Right On the podium during the 1985 Vuelta, with third-placed Pello Ruiz Cabestany on his right.

Above In the polka-dot jersey at the 1986 Vuelta.

Left Suffering in the heat after a post-Tour criterium in 1985.

Above Leading Greg LeMond in the 1986 Tour de France.

Right In the 'best foreigner' jersey in the Vuelta.

Left Stephen Roche silences the hostile tifosi at the 1987 Tour of Italy, with Millar in the King of the Mountains jersey.

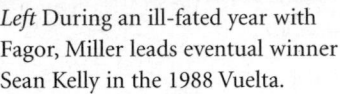

Right Looking like he's fallen from an aircraft, Millar hits the tarmac in TVM colours.

Left During an ill-fated year with Fagor, Miller leads eventual winner Sean Kelly in the 1988 Vuelta.

Below Reunited at Panasonic in 1986 with his old ACBB and Peugeot team-mate, Australian Phil Anderson.

Left Nursing teammate and yellow jersey holder Ronan Pensec on the slopes of Alpe d'Huez, 1990 Tour de France.

Above Millar inspects his wounds after another spill in 'Z' colours.

Above In British colours at the world championships in Utsunomiya, Japan, 1990.

Above Surrounded by the world's best climbers – from left to right, Andy Hampsten, the late Thierry Claveyrolat and Tony Rominger (behind).

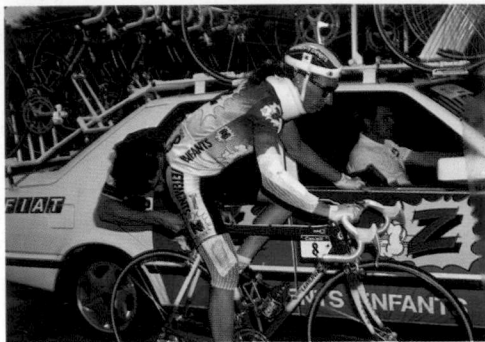

Left Surviving the 1991 Tour de France with the worst crash injuries of his career.

Right Millar leads his old rival Pedro Delgado, in the twilight of their careers, to the summit of Europe's highest pass, the Col de la Bonette, on the 1993 Tour.

Above Winning the 1995 British road race championship on the Isle of Man, Millar's final professional race.

Right At home in Daventry in 2000; the picture that accompanied the 'sex change' story.

comfortable, especially on the climbs.' But Roche, still hopeful
of being back to defend his Tour de France title, wasn't overly
confident in his team-mate and friend's abilities to lead the
team into the summer. 'You must know how to handle Bob,' he
told *Cycling*. 'If things are right he's capable of anything. We
know we can rely on each other completely. He can't be the
leader, the pressure from the media gets to him and he cracks,
but I think he's going to make a great contribution to the team.'

Yet despite Millar's great ride at Liège-Bastogne-Liège, and
Roche's assurances that all was well, serious trouble was
brewing at Fagor. On 9 April, just six days before Liège-
Bastogne-Liège, Valcke was sacked (again) by Mondragon, and
Pierre Bazon appointed in his place. Then, contrary to an
earlier promise that Millar would not be required to ride both
the Vuelta and Tour de France, in late April he found himself in
Spain for the big race. While Elliott and Yates both won stages,
Millar rode into sixth, but he was underwhelmed . . . by just
about everything. His form 'wasn't too good', he said. 'I had a
lot of problems at the wrong time. I finished where I finished.
It was a disaster; things went from worse to worse.'

In fact, Millar had performed an important job at the Vuelta,
not for Fagor or Roche, but for the other great Irishman, Sean
Kelly. In an echo of the 1987 Giro, Millar played a key role in
helping a rival to win a major stage race, in this case Kelly,
helping him to control the race in the mountains and ensuring
that he, unlike Millar in 1985, didn't fall victim to the Spanish
Armada. Frank Quinn, the Dubliner who by now was acting as
business manager to both Kelly and Millar, thinks that it wasn't
the only time one helped the other. 'They co-operated a lot in
races,' reveals Quinn, 'more than anyone will ever find out
about.' But Kelly admits that 'Millar helped me on the road' in
the 1988 Vuelta. 'I spoke to him, asked him to help, and he was
willing to do so. He rode on the front for me and was very valuable to me in the mountains, when I was without team-mates.'

On Fagor, Millar's comments after the Vuelta were unambiguous: 'Let's just say that riding for Peugeot and Panasonic was paradise in comparison as regards organization. And when our manager Patrick Valcke was sacked it didn't do much for team morale. Morale has been low too because of Roche's injuries.'

Reflecting on the Fagor fiasco today, Sean Yates is even more scathing. 'Fagor was a fucking joke. The managers didn't know jack – they were useless. This guy Gomez was appointed general manager, and he just used to turn up at races and scream at us from the car, saying he wanted us to attack in the feed zone, do this, do that. He was a lunatic. You would not believe that team. I rang my dad during the Vuelta and said, "You've got to get me out of here!" Every time we went to a race start we got lost. Every time we went from the finish to our hotel we got lost. Not. A. Fucking. Clue. I remember Malcolm [Elliott] and I found these cans of beer on the bus – they treated it like some kind of boys' club and entertained guests during races, giving them lunch and everything. So we gave the cans of beer a good shake every morning. Give them a nice surprise when they opened them.'

However, the nadir for Millar came not at the Vuelta but at the Tour de France, in an incident that is still widely recalled, and which has featured, probably more than once, in *A Question of Sport*'s 'What happened next?' round. Stage 14, from Blagnac to Guzet Neige, where Millar had won his stage four years earlier, took the riders 163km, with the three major climbs stacked towards the end. Millar escaped in the Pyrenean foothills, with 90km still to race, in the company of thirteen riders, who remained together until the Col d'Agne, an 18km beast with a final three kilometres at an average gradient of one in twelve. The lush, wooded Pyrenees was Millar's domain: he crossed the summit alone, five seconds clear. There was a regrouping on the descent, but on the smaller Col de Latrappe

Millar forced the pace again, reducing the break to just four riders: a Frenchman, Philippe Bouvatier, and two Italians, Massimo Ghirotto and Ennio Vanotti. On the final climb, to the Guzet Neige ski station, Vanotti was dropped, and Ghirotto also began to struggle. Bouvatier led, with Millar on his wheel, looking as if he was struggling, allowing a little gap to open only to then recover and claw his way back to the wheel of his opponent. They were into the last five hundred metres. This pair would fight out the finish.

Then, as *Cycling* reported, 'came the living nightmare'. As Bouvatier led Millar around the final corner, just three hundred metres from the line, he followed the directions of the gendarme at the side of the road – or thought he did. In fact, the gendarme was signalling to the vehicles directly behind the leading pair to take the diversion before the finish. Bouvatier misread the instruction and went off course; Millar, his eyes trained on his companion's back wheel, followed him. Behind them, Ghirotto did not make the same mistake, remaining on course to take the stage win. Millar was quicker than Bouvatier to realize the error and turn around, and crossed the line second.

This was followed by perhaps the most excruciating Millar interview yet. For Channel 4 he was quizzed by Paul Sherwen, by now Phil Liggett's colleague in the commentary box. Millar communicated in a series of grunts. For *Cycling* he was able, apparently, to take a 'philosophical view of the fiasco', though he did say, 'I would have won, I'm a hundred per cent certain of it.' In *L'Equipe* Millar blamed the gendarme for misdirecting him, though Liggett is keen to defend the policeman. 'He wasn't sent off course,' he insists. 'I remember it was the famous gendarme with the moustache; he'd done thirty tours. The next day Robert was in the papers saying the gendarme had sent him off course; so this gendarme went up to him and said, "Robert, why did you say that about me? You're telling everyone I sent you off course." He didn't, he [just] did what he did every day

– he was pointing to the cars to leave the course, not the riders.' Meanwhile, Ghirotto obviously didn't share Millar's belief that, had the leading pair stayed on course, the Scotsman would have come around Bouvatier in the final few hundred metres. In acknowledgement of his victory by default he gifted one of the main prizes, a Peugeot car, to the Frenchman. But in the record books stage 14 of the 1988 Tour remains Ghirotto's.

Millar's bitterness was only exacerbated that evening when his *bête noire* at Fagor, Miguel Gomez, 'didn't say bad luck or anything like that, they just opened a bottle of champagne and got drunk instead'.

Mentally, possibly physically as well, this 1988 Tour was perhaps the low point of Millar's professional career. On the stage to Guzet Neige Paul Sherwen, in the commentary box, remarked that the Scot's head 'looks like a skull at the moment – he's lost so much weight during the Tour de France'. Even as the race got underway in western France the *Cycling* reporter noted that he looked 'thin to the extreme of gauntness'. At times during the race he was 'curt to the point of rudeness', and before a time trial stage he waved away a reporter, explaining simply that he had 'caught me on a bad day'.

It was a bad month. The team was a shambles; its leader was missing, with the responsibility of leadership thus falling onto Millar's reluctant shoulders; and, on the day when Millar sought to rescue his season, he was sent off course. Four stages later, as controversy erupted when the race leader and eventual winner, Pedro Delgado, tested positive for a substance on the IOC's banned list (but not yet on the UCI's list), Millar abandoned. For the third Tour in a row he had been plagued by stomach trouble.

Valcke's health problems were of a different magnitude. 'I had been a bit apprehensive about working with Fagor,' he admits now. 'They'd sacked Luis Ocana, who wasn't exactly a nobody. They had money, but they were dangerous with it.

When I started to prepare the race programme in January, Miguel Gomez stuck his nose in. He was working with Fagor – he was the paymaster – but you could also class him as a danger to the public. He wanted to do everything.' The Fagor management had 'spies' in the team, Valcke alleges, including a couple of Spanish riders and mechanics. 'After just a few weeks they began telling me which riders to pick for certain races, and I had to remind them, "Hey, who's the team manager here?" Obviously word got back and so Fagor sacked Crepel. That left me on my own. And to top it all, Stephen wasn't riding well – he had a knee problem. Even after the operation, and going to see specialists, we didn't know what the problem was. Then Gomez steps into the breach, saying, "What is your world champion doing now? Just shut your mouth and listen to team orders. You're suspended on full pay." I was stunned. Robert couldn't believe what was happening. I was paid, and paid well too, but I had to sit at home and watch the races I was supposed to be working at on the television.' Valcke spent much of the year house-bound, and it was during the 1988 Tour that his health deteriorated. 'I had a heart attack, although that's not important now,' he remarks, with forced casualness. 'But it was because of that whole episode.' The only bright spot was Yates's outstanding Tour time trial victory in Wasquehal, in Valcke's home region, even if the deposed *directeur sportif* could only enjoy it on television.

For Roche, some of the bitterness of the Fagor fiasco remains, as well as regret that his 'dream team' never really saw daylight. 'I think that Robert, even today, maybe holds it a little against me,' he says. 'We spoke about it once. Sometimes I think he thinks I did it purposefully – that I wasn't performing and it was all in my mind; that I was world champion and going off to all the parties and everything else. But I had a problem with my knee and I spent a fortune trying to get it right in Germany. Why would I have done that if it wasn't a genuine injury?'

Roche certainly harbours no resentment towards Millar. 'Robert was one of the guys who saved the team that year,' he says, highlighting his strong rides in Liège-Bastogne-Liège, and the fact that, amid so much confusion and uncertainty, he managed to be one of the leading riders at the Vuelta. 'The problem was that, at the end of the day, the main person wasn't there. If I'd ridden that year we'd have had a super two years, but I was the key element, and I was missing. If I'd been there the Fagor management would have stayed out of things; as it was, they were paying a world champion, he wasn't performing, and they were paying Millar, Yates and Elliott the money I'd recommended.'

By October Millar had almost found sanctuary in a new team – or, rather, an old one. His former Peugeot team, now known as Z (it was sponsored by Roger Zannier, who ran the Z chain of children's clothing shops and was, according to Millar, 'actually a nice person, considering he was a successful businessman'), wanted him back. 'I want him and I have the money,' said the team's *directeur sportif*, who happened to be Millar's short-lived (smoking) room-mate from his first Côte d'Azure training camp, Roger Legeay. Z wanted Millar, and he wanted them. Or, rather, he didn't want Fagor. 'I like a stable situation,' he said in mid-October. 'I don't need another year like this one. I have had no motivation. All the talk and uncertainty has played on my mind and caused me sleepless nights.'

The problems associated with Fagor do not seem to have ended with Millar signing for Z. Midway through the following season, on a trip to Edinburgh to ride the McEwan's LA city-centre criterium, he told Doug Gillon of the *Glasgow Herald* that he was still being pursued by Fagor for compensation. In their view, he had broken the two-year contract. 'My lawyer is settling it,' Millar said, adding that he was just 'glad to be away'.

Arthur Campbell believes that the financial fallout from Fagor continued to dog Millar. A few years later, when the

Dutchman Hein Verbruggen had been appointed president of the UCI, he called Campbell and asked him to relay a message to Millar. 'Hein phoned me and asked, "Are you still in touch with Millar?"' Campbell recalls. 'He said, "Give him a word of advice . . . He arranged for his money from Fagor to go into some account on Jersey or Guernsey. It's a bit complicated . . ."' Campbell gently advised Millar to make sure that his financial affairs were above board and in order.

When, in 1997, he guest-edited the edition of *Cycle Sport* devoted to his career, Millar penned articles on all his professional teams, each one accompanied by a picture of him in action. The exception was Fagor, where instead of a picture there was a purple box containing a message: 'There was supposed to be a Fagor picture here, but they don't deserve one, and there won't be one of P. Munoz either. Ed's decision.' Munoz was the Spanish rider favoured by the Fagor management. 'Although not a bad rider, [he] was a complete plonker,' was Millar's blunt assessment. 'To this day I'll never autograph anything to do with Fagor. They wasted my time and everyone else's too.'

It was a reinvigorated Millar who appeared in Stirling in mid-January 1989 for the second of the two Robert Millar Training Camps. This one – for which Millar again waived any fee, asking only for travelling expenses – was even more hotly anticipated than the first, because this time Millar wasn't recovering from an operation on his backside. He would thus join us on training rides. Given that it was out of season, he was relaxed. Talkative even. And happy to dispense golden nuggets of advice, including the immortal 'a wet hat's better than no hat' and 'don't ask me about the Tour de France – you're not riding it'.

In the midst of Millar's worst year as a professional, he and Sylvie had become parents. He was asked about fatherhood in Stirling, specifically whether he would encourage his son, Edward, to take up cycling. He considered the question. 'I'm not going to force it upon him,' he replied. 'I have seen fathers who push their sons, and by the time they have reached 12 or 13 they have had enough. If he didn't want to take part in any sport then I wouldn't object.'

In Stirling, I remember being struck by how thin Millar was. His hair was long and lank – the perm was growing out – and his cheekbones were sharp, as if his cheeks had been gouged out. On the training rides he wore a colourfully emblazoned purple and yellow Z team jacket, complete with hood (which he didn't use, naturally). Off the bike he wore a brown leather jacket that looked too big for him, and which also looked suspiciously like the jacket he'd worn in *The High Life*, recorded four years earlier. In every way he appeared more comfortable, more at ease, on the bike.

All the top Scottish riders of the day were in Stirling for the weekend, and I, aged 15 and having just completed my first year of racing, looked up to them. But they, in turn, looked up to Millar. He inhabited a different world. He breathed the rarefied air of continental cycling, though had the uninitiated seen him out on the roads around Stirling they would never have been able to tell. Somehow this added to the mystique.

There was certainly an aura about Millar. In some respects, he was so uncool that he was cool. Dennis Donovan was the *Cycling* reporter who travelled north to report on the weekend, and he noted the 'two sides to Robert Millar's personality – one, the non-communicative introvert who is likely to tell the press to go to hell – or worse'. The other side was the 'smiling, wise-cracking Millar with a wicked humour that kept his audience enthralled'. Millar told Donovan that he would not return to live in Scotland when he retired. To do so 'would be like community service'. Now 30, he thought he'd race for another six years. 'At the moment there is no one coming through who is better than me,' he said. When he retired he might do something 'possibly connected with cycling', but 'with a bit of luck I might be able to make enough money so that I won't have to work any more'. He also claimed he'd have emigrated to Canada or Australia if he hadn't been a cyclist. 'I would have travelled. I only spend a third of the year at home as it is, and my wife has now got used to me not being there.' Donovan asked him whether he had any regrets. 'There are things I would still like to do, but they are personal. Regrets, of course, but who hasn't? I have regrets when I have hesitated in certain races and knowing that I shouldn't have done . . . There have been situations which I didn't exploit, and I just fell apart.' The Fagor experience had scarred him. 'One by one they destroyed each individual.' And as Roche suspected, Millar did hold him at least partly responsible. 'Yes, I do feel that Stephen Roche let the team down. I was very disappointed with him.'

In this interview there is another indication that Millar had realized and accepted his place in the pecking order, and the limits of his ability. 'I think [Peter Post] saw more in me than there was,' he said. At Z, Millar would gradually turn into a different kind of rider, one capable of leading the team in races other than the major tours, where he was happy to hand that responsibility over, and to work in the service of other riders. Eventually he would become what might be called a '*domestique* de luxe', though he still had a personal ambition at the 1989 Tour de France: 'to win the mountains competition'.

During the question-and-answer session that followed the morning training ride, Millar's instruction that we shouldn't ask him about the Tour de France was rooted in common sense. As he told us, 'You have to have personal goals that are not unobtainable, and until you achieve them then you don't tell anyone, in case you fail and they laugh at you.' He didn't specify who 'they' were. 'Progress should always be in steps –

like a ladder. If you do two steps at a time then you are likely to fall on your face. Progress from level to level. If you reach your maximum then you should be happy.' Whether Millar was 'happy' is a moot point. 'Each year your training must be harder than the year before or else you will stay the same as the year before. Curiosity means I must always try something else. I'm always disappointed with my achievements. Winning is important, but it doesn't count as much as participation and the pleasure you get from your own performance. If you knock yourself out in your training it is possible that you can be happier than winning a race.'

Millar's visit to Stirling coincided with the first signs of the dawning of a new era in training and preparation. The old and trusted methods of training – miles, miles and more miles – were starting to be questioned. Millar, of course, had never subscribed fully to this school of thought – witness the interval training as a teenager in Glasgow, the weight training with Billy Bilsland, the riding with ankle weights when he was a professional. As he indicated in Stirling, he was an innovator, driven to try new things by his own curiosity, but this made him pretty unusual in the conservative and stuffily traditional world of cycling.

Another guest in Stirling was somebody nobody had really heard of. It was Peter Keen, one of the new breed of sports scientists, who spoke with certainty about new methods of training using pulse-rate monitors, and riding shorter distances at a higher intensity, and about revolutionary methods of 'refuelling'. Keen, who went on to great success as coach to Chris Boardman, seemed to have stepped straight from the laboratory. In Stirling he went head to head with Millar, who was 'from the field', so to speak. It was an intriguing match, or mismatch. How would the theories of the boffin in the white coat – though Keen didn't actually wear a white coat – play with the continental pro? Another of the Millar paradoxes, of course,

was that his willingness to innovate and experiment sat sometimes uneasily alongside his natural cynicism.

Keen gave a presentation on a new product called 'Maxim', a
glucose-polymer powder mix that, he told us, would transform
the way we 'fuelled' during training and racing. At the end of
his talk, the chair of the session turned to Millar, who was
sitting impassively at the other end of the top table. 'Do you use
Maxim, Robert?' he asked. Whether he intended it or not,
Millar's reply was a masterful put-down: 'No. I use water.' He
also seemed inclined to be dismissive of the new vogue for
testing riders' physical capabilities in the laboratory, at the
expense of gauging their abilities in actual races, against real
people. 'The results of these tests are not always the results that
you can get on the bike. There was one rider who was told to
give up racing after some tests. He finished fourth in the world
championship.' As for pulse monitors, 'You don't need a pulse
monitor to train well, but I use one as a guide occasionally.

'I train my own way and keep it to myself,' he continued.
'Competitors won't tell you how they train because they know
that if you are smart you could take their place. They have
learnt through trial and error themselves, and it is not in their
interests to tell you. They will tell you less and less as you get
better, and in my case if the top pros read my training methods
then they are going to try them. I normally train on my own.
Sometimes I meet Wayne Bennington [an English professional
based in Troyes]. It is not deliberate, we just train on the same
roads. He tends to go one way, and I tend to go in the other
direction, but sometimes one of us will turn round in the road
and we'll ride along together. We talk half in French and the
other half we spend teaching each other English.'

I don't remember 'getting' all Millar's humour at the time. I
don't think it was just that I was too young, and not yet fully
attuned to such a cynical world view, though this might have had
something to do with it. It was Millar's manner that was discon-

certing. Nothing in the tone of his voice, or the expression on his face, indicated that he was joking. Reading now what he said then, and being more familiar now with what I recognize was his distinctive brand of wry humour, it is difficult to suppress a smile. But at the time I suspect that most of us just looked puzzled. The lines were funny. The delivery was terrible.

What I do remember is being in awe of some of the training methods he did divulge: interval training up the same hill as many as twenty-five times; going flat out, and in the biggest gear, at the end of a five-hour training ride, and doing this 'three or four times a week', in most types of weather. 'It doesn't matter if it is a headwind, I just keep it in the biggest gear and if I'm lucky my knees don't break. After this type of training then racing should be easier.' On the day before a race, 'I do just enough to remind the legs that I am still a racing cyclist.'

But the other memorable aspect of Stirling in mid-January 1989 was that it was cold, wet and windy. What, we asked, should you do when the weather is so bad? 'Don't go out,' Millar replied.

'Back to the Glory Days for Millar' read the headline in *Cycling*, above a report on stage 10 of the 1989 Tour de France. Tuesday, 11 July was the day in question, 136km from Cauterets to Superbagneres, climbing four major mountains in – where else? – the Pyrenees. Millar, who escaped early on the 20km ascent of the Col du Tourmalet with Frenchman Charly Mottet, led over the top of the climb, but they were being pursued by the Scotsman's old adversary, Pedro Delgado, the defending Tour champion. Delgado had selected this day as the platform for his epic attempt to recover the two minutes and forty seconds he'd conceded on the first day of the race, when he inexplicably missed the start of the prologue time trial. He attacked the field as they dropped down the other side of the Tourmalet, vividly described in *Cycling* by

Keith Bingham as 'a dangerous 1-in-8 descent which spirals from the splintered rocky crags to the green valley floor, 17km below the summit'.

By the Col d'Aspin Delgado had bridged the gap to the leading pair, with Millar once again leading over the top of the 13km climb. He was also first up the Peyresourde, but the trio were together as they began the climb to the finish at Superbagneres. Bizarrely, Delgado stopped for a pee at the bottom, though he quickly regained his companions. And when he did, Mottet began to struggle, his shoulders rocking, his face set in an anguished expression; at one point, the Frenchman asked Millar why he was going so fast. Then a spectator ran alongside the three riders, bellowing in the leader Delgado's ear, and irritating the Spaniard so much that he reached down, grabbed his drinking bottle, and threw it angrily at the spectator. Delgado then took his frustration out on the pedals, stamping down with more force. Mottet couldn't cope and was dropped. Millar, too, looked in trouble. But he continued at a steady pace while Delgado's rage subsided, and his tempo slowed.

Inside the last kilometre, Millar rejoined him; but not for long. Delgado raised the pace once more, and again there was daylight between his back wheel and Millar's front. But yet again Millar recovered, and as they rounded the final corner he had moved up to Delgado's shoulder. He shifted out of the saddle and stood on the pedals, just enough to inject the speed needed to come around Delgado in the final metres. He crossed the line a length clear but without the time, on this occasion, to don the cotton racing cap, or even to pump his arms in the air in celebration. Instead, Millar flashed across the line with his mouth gaping wide open, gasping for air.

This effort moved him up to second in the race for the King of the Mountains polka-dot jersey, and to eighth in the overall standings. It was, he said, the hardest of his three stage wins in the Tour. 'My first win was in the Pyrenees so every time I come back I'm motivated,' he told Bingham. 'And I was very angry about the delay the day before, when I fell and had to wait for service. I was OK on the early climbs, but in the end Delgado had both me and Mottet hanging on. He was accelerating five hundred metres at a time . . . I had to grit my teeth to hang on. I'd done a lot of work and was fairly tired. But I knew that Delgado wanted to get rid of Mottet [who was third overall]. And I knew that if I could hang on until Mottet was dropped I'd be OK.'

Millar reached Paris in tenth overall – his second-best Tour finish – and fourth in the mountains competition. He rued his crash on stage 9, but overall it had been a good Tour for him. Significantly, it was also the first year since 1984 that he had tackled one rather than two major tours.

In fact, 1989 was one of Millar's best. Before the Tour he'd finished second overall in the Dauphiné Libéré, winning the mountain time trial stage and the climbers' prize. Then, in late August, he returned to ride the third Kellogg's Tour of Britain and, to widespread astonishment, won it. It was Millar's first victory on home soil since his 1979 amateur road race title. It was also hailed as the best Kellogg's Tour yet, thanks mainly to Millar's aggressive riding on the mammoth 141-mile stage from Birmingham to Cardiff. This stage, reported *Cycling*, 'gave British fans a rare chance to see Millar at his mighty best'.

During the race, a rumour emerged that Millar's Z team was being merged with – wait for it – Fagor. The other rumour was that the Tour de France winner, Greg LeMond, was to be signed as team leader. The uncertainty may explain Millar's strange behaviour during the Kellogg's Tour. Apart from riding outstandingly well to win it, he gave a series of enigmatic interviews to the TV and press in most of which he appeared utterly miserable. He even threatened to abandon mid-race. Had it been a problem with the organization, or was he unhappy with his form?' 'No, none of those,' he replied. 'I was just generally fed up. We all get depressed now and again. I haven't been home for three weeks and have had only seven days at home since the Tour de France.' In TV interviews he alluded to 'personal issues' which he was keen to attend to, and which might cause him to abandon the race. Certainly the rumours about the team couldn't have helped Millar's mood. Roger Legeay flew to Britain mid-race to assuage any fears. 'You could say I'm happier,' said Millar after speaking to Legeay. 'I'll know what's happening by the end of the week. I've got two or three options, but I won't play them off against each other, just go for the best offer.'

In the end, the Z and Fagor marriage never happened. Z remained, but with a significant change: with an increased annual budget of £3 million it became the wealthiest squad in the peloton. In its new recruit, it also had the world's first million-pound rider – Greg LeMond, who signed a three-year contract worth in excess of a million a year.

LeMond, though more gregarious – more American – than Millar, was not dissimilar to the Scot in some respects. Like Millar, he seemed to view the sport from a different angle, questioning some of its traditions and challenging 'the knowledge'. LeMond had his own eccentricities, which Millar seems to have appreciated and enjoyed. Writing in 1997, Millar recalled that LeMond 'would sit and read a book in the restaurant when the service was slow, which appalled the French, who regarded eating as some kind of social event. One time we got a table directly in the sun and it was sweltering hot behind the glass windows, so Greg just took his shirt off and got on with reading his book.' An equipment junkie, LeMond usually had three pairs of shoes in the team car and would sometimes change them mid-race. 'He always seemed to go back to his favourite black pair,' wrote Millar, 'which were seriously knackered, but then so were his feet.'

Another example of LeMond's unconventionality was – shock, horror – that he brought his wife to races. In an interview with Doug Gillon of the *Glasgow Herald*, Millar explained, 'Greg brings his wife to races. That's unheard of, against the code. The managers hate it. [Cycling is] a bit like the [football] World Cup. The managers allow the wives in, let the players have a little bit, then send them home. Then he goes to the cinema in the evening after a stage. The continentals can't believe it. Sylvie never comes to races. Not the done thing. It's frowned on – part of the mystique. Besides, you are too knackered. We are not glamorous. We don't get many groupies grovelling after us. After a day in the saddle, our faces look ten years older.'

Millar liked LeMond. He told Gillon on the eve of the 1990 Tour de France that he was looking forward to helping the American defend his title. 'He is no prima donna. He is one of the guys. Everyone will ride for him until he falls apart. I am being held back, but if I'm needed, I will ride for him, too . . . the first day I will be going to work is stage nine, the first climb.'

His hair by now approaching mullet proportions – long at the back, with a short fringe, and frequently worn in a pony tail – Millar enjoyed an exceptional build-up to that 1990 Tour. This despite a blood-curdling crash during Paris-Nice in March. On a 'never-ending series of tight hairpins' down into Mandelieu, Millar misjudged a corner and went down, sliding to a halt with a team car, belonging to the Spanish Banesto team, finally stopping only inches from his head. Millar 'just escaped death', according to *Cycling*. 'Yes, I was aware,' Millar confirmed. 'I could smell the car's disc brakes.' He got up, carried on, and finished fourteenth in Nice.

In May he won a mountainous stage in the Tour of Romandie and finished second overall, and in June, after many years of trying, he finally won the Dauphiné Libéré stage race – a significant addition to his *palmares*, and arguably his career-best victory. He emerged triumphant from a two-man duel with the Frenchman Thierry Claveyrolat, a climbing specialist with a similar build and style to Millar. It was the first British victory in the week-long stage race dubbed the 'mini Tour de France' since Brian Robinson's success in 1961.

Second to Andy Hampsten in the Tour of Switzerland completed Millar's impeccable build-up to the Tour, in which his job was to support LeMond. Millar seemed perfectly happy about this, appearing content that it was 'Greg's neck on the line, not mine'. Prior to that 1990 race there was also a suggestion from Millar that the size, and the pressure, of the Tour was getting to him. 'You get a lot more hassle,' he told William Fotheringham. 'It's like the Derby – people get invitations to come to the Tour de France and watch guys sweating up mountains. There's a lot of people taking the mickey out of you and it just isn't funny any more.' The increasing media interest in the Tour was also making the racing more dangerous, and more stressful. 'The last forty ks are desperate. If you're riding in the middle [of the peloton] you're always listening for the crash to come . . . You have no trouble getting to sleep because you've no nerves left at the end of the day . . . you have two hundred guys all trying to be in the first twenty. You learn to swear in seven different languages.'

In the event, although LeMond did run out the winner in Paris, it wasn't Millar's work for the American that stood out. In his new role as *domestique* de luxe, Millar, after crashing on stage 4 and losing nine minutes, put in an extraordinary performance on the showcase stage to Alpe d'Huez when another team-mate, Ronan Pensec, was in the leader's yellow jersey. On the slopes of the Alpe, Pensec was isolated and potentially in trouble. It was touch and go whether he'd keep the jersey, until Millar, gesturing to Pensec to position himself on his back wheel, rode to the front of the group and almost literally towed his French team-mate up the mountain. In doing so, Millar sacrificed his own chances. Yet it was one of his finest and most memorable performances, leading Pensec for around 15km, and with wonderful efficiency and effectiveness limiting the advantage gained by a group that contained Pedro Delgado and the Italian Gianni Bugno. Alpe d'Huez, where Millar had mixed memories – catching and dropping Bernard Hinault in 1984, ill and toiling in 1986 – is an epic arena, its twenty-one hairpin bends providing the spectators with an awesome perspective on the race. And it was up its steep steps that Millar carried out his metronomic pursuit of the leaders on Pensec's behalf, all the while checking that the yellow jersey was still in his shadow. It did the trick: Pensec kept the yellow. Afterwards, Millar admitted that he had sacrificed his own chances. 'I was capable of winning if I'd wanted to, we could have pulled the group back if I'd wanted, but then Ronan would have had to respond to all the attacks. It was important that I stayed beside him. It's what I'm here for. I can win another day.'

For any Frenchman to lead the Tour is a career-defining moment. For the two days that he was in yellow, Pensec was the most famous man in the country. But it was solely down to Millar that his tenure had been extended for another day. 'Of course you could say that it was his job,' says Pensec now, 'but the way he stayed with me that day showed something more than that. It showed that he was close to me, and not just as team-mates.'

Pensec's warmth towards Millar comes as a bit of a surprise. Known principally for his spiky black hair, Pensec had a peripatetic career – drifting around teams in Spain, Belgium and France after leaving Z – and it is not a shock to hear him expressing gratitude towards Millar for what he did for him on the slopes of Alpe d'Huez in 1990. But in appearance and personality, the two hardly appeared to be kindred spirits, Pensec as friendly and extrovert as Millar was shy and introverted. 'I don't have one bad thing to say about him,' Pensec continues with evident sincerity. 'He was an example for me throughout my career. I tried to model myself on him. We had the same physique – we were small climbers. He was different from other people, and I respected that he wasn't afraid to stand out from the crowd. He was reserved, but it's better to be cold than to be arrogant.'

Pensec launches into an impassioned paean to his old team-mate. 'You have to understand that cycling can be a very individualistic sport. And that corresponded perfectly to Robert's personality. On the other hand, Robert was happy to drive himself into the ground to help me or to help someone else in the team when it was his job to. He was a true professional. And it's not because he didn't want to come and have a drink [with the guys] after dinner that you can call him an idiot. I could see the bigger picture . . . Listen, no one's got the right to say a guy is this or that just because he's got a strong character. In any case, I've got nothing but the utmost respect for Robert, for what he did for me, for what he helped me become.'

Millar's promise after that stage to 'win another day' wasn't realized, illness once again forcing him out. With LeMond the winner, it was yet another missed opportunity: Millar never did savour the experience of riding past the Eiffel Tower and into Paris as a member of a Tour-winning team. He admitted later that his abandonment of the 1990 Tour was a source of regret for this very reason.

In the autumn he performed well once again in the Kellogg's Tour of Britain, finishing second after crashing heavily on the final stage into Manchester, half a mile from the finish. He and the man in yellow, Michel Dernies, came down together. They were equal on time so the win would go to whoever could get back up first. It was Dernies. It was Millar's second crash of the day. On the podium, Millar – demonstrating that his mood was much improved on the previous year – plucked two roses from his bouquet of flowers and handed one to each of the 'Kellogg's girls'. 'I can laugh about [the crash at the finish],' he said. 'But it's not funny.'

Cycling's coverage of the race attracted criticism from one correspondent, who objected to the fact that Millar's 'quotes seem to be arranged to make him out as some kind of "deep" and wacky character. Personally, I now turn the sound off when he and [Sean] Kelly are interviewed. Perhaps both should have the services of a spokesman within their teams, as they set no acceptable interview standard as far as I can see.' Another letter, some months later, requested that no more paper be wasted on Millar. 'Why we have so many pictures of him and interviews, muttering and unsmiling, I cannot understand. There are so many more pleasant and interesting characters in the peloton.'

The first letter prompted a defence of Millar from 'Linda Luxerre and co.' of Woodford Art College. 'We don't really follow cycling as a sport,' the letter read, 'but we were all glued to the television during the Kellogg's Tour. Why, you may ask, do five (hard-working) art students take such an interest? Well, the most exhilarating part of the Tour was watching Robert Millar being interviewed. We all just love his wit, cute accent and coy smile – so please print this letter and let Mr Millar know he is well appreciated.'

11

You Don't Put Ordinary Fuel in a Sports Car

I am still angry at being stigmatized.

'If you get in the car,' says Jack Andre, 'I will take you to Robert's house.'

He is referring to the house in the village of Berceney-en-Othe to which Millar and Sylvie moved from Wielsbeke in early 1988, just before the birth of their son Edward. From Andre's house in the Troyes suburbs we drive east, leaving the city behind and heading across gently undulating Champagne countryside, a succession of yellow cornfields, dark beetroot fields, and lush green forest. It seems vast, mainly because it's so uniform: no sign of sea or mountains, just rippled landscape, as if an enormous patchwork carpet has been thrown down, without its wrinkles shaken out. The villages we pass through are small and quiet. The roads are virtually empty. There are as many bikes as cars, possibly more.

We approach a group of three cyclists, and it is immediately obvious that they are racing cyclists: upper bodies motionless, legs tapping out a fluid, easy rhythm. Andre brakes and the rider at the back lifts himself out of the saddle, swivels round, recognizes the UVC Aube team car. He is wearing the rainbow jersey of world champion – we subsequently learn that he is the 2005 world firemen's champion – and he drops back. He and Andre begin chatting. 'We've been talking about Robert Millar,' Andre tells him, and the rider snorts a laugh – 'Ha!' – and shakes his head. 'I used to train with Robert Millar. He would ride two hundred kilometres just so he could eat a salad!' There are some good riders in the area, Andre tells us as we accelerate past the three cyclists, but none in the same class as Millar. For the umpteenth time, it is noted that Millar was 'special'.

After fifteen miles we crest a hill and are greeted by an extraordinary sight. Nestling in the dip below is the pretty, peaceful village of Berceney-en-Othe, home to a cluster of fifty or so houses and a church whose spire reaches high into the sky; but a little further beyond the village, dwarfing it, is a satellite station of such vastness that it looks utterly surreal. It's more bizarre than ugly, a big white blot on the landscape that must present estate agents with a formidable challenge. Then again, from the village none of the big white dishes, so prominent from the top of the hill, are even visible.

We drive into the village. On our right is the church, with a side street just past it, into which we turn and immediately stop. Opposite us is a primary school, a farm, and a nineteenth-century farmhouse, a '3' painted on its high walls, next to its large gates. Behind the walls, a big, handsome, box-shaped home stands side-on to the road. Over a period of several months Millar oversaw the renovation of this old farmhouse, customizing it for the racing cyclist – walk-in shower room on the ground floor, a bike room, a weights room. But its position makes it difficult to see inside: there are no windows looking out on to the street. Through the railings of the gate we can see the front garden, with a small gravel driveway in front of the house and children's toys scattered across the lawn. At the far end there's a large Tudor-style barn, the loft of which once included a 'jersey room' housing a collection of Samsonite suitcases containing hundreds of neatly folded cycling shirts – the yellow, polka-dot and team jerseys that Millar had worn and won in his career, even the national champion's jersey altered by his mother, dating from 1979. When Millar lived here, there were also a couple of vehicles in the drive: a Citroën rally car and the Porsche he'd always promised himself.

Maybe I'm reading too much into it, but it seems significant that Millar's dream house is side-on to, rather than facing, the public road.

Millar's 1990 concluded with a good fourth in the season-ending 'Race of the Falling Leaves', the Tour of Lombardy. He returned home to Berceney-en-Othe, to spend much of the winter supervising work on the house and mountain biking in the nearby forests. It had been his best ever season, with the exception of 1984. The big disappointment had been missing out on reaching Paris with his Z team in the company of the yellow-jerseyed Greg LeMond, though he did not lose out financially. It is the tradition in cycling that prize money is split among the team. Still, Millar said that LeMond's win had been worth 'nothing great – middle five figures', and by late November he was still waiting for the money. 'It comes from the French federation at the end of the year,' he said. 'They keep it as long as they can to get the interest. You can get tax difficulties from that.'

Disrupting the picture of domestic bliss in Berceney-en-Othe was Millar's admission, to *Cycling* journalist William Fotheringham, that he planned to return to the UK within the next year or two. 'At first I thought I would stay [in France],' he said, 'but now I know I won't. I understand the French mentality, and there are some things I can never accept. I always gave the impression I didn't like Britain, but that was from the experience I had of the country before . . . Now I realize if you're brought up somewhere it's difficult not to want to go back.' He ruled out Scotland, however – 'It rains too much.' Instead, he fancied 'somewhere in the Midlands, the Cotswolds, or the South West'. He added that though Berceney-en-Othe was 'ideal for training', with the bonus that 'no one comes to annoy you', it wasn't where he wanted to live, or die. 'At the weekend when it was drizzly and dark I could see my life ticking away as the clock went round,' he told Fotheringham. 'I don't want to die here. I like a bit of action.' He also found family life in France claustrophobic. 'Families in Britain are all split up. Here they live in the same street and all eat together on Sunday. It gets to me.'

It was November 1990 when Fotheringham first went to visit Millar at home. The journalist and cyclist had established a good rapport since an awkward first meeting at the 1989 Nissan Classic in Ireland. There, the 24-year-old Fotheringham, on his first journalistic assignment, had asked Millar a question at the end of a stage and received 'a classic sarcastic put-down'. But he didn't retreat or take offence. Instead he rephrased the question, making it clear that he would appreciate an answer; and Millar obliged with a 'very good explanation, explaining the rationale behind what had happened in the race'. Fotheringham admits he was determined to forge a good relationship with Millar. 'To be perfectly honest, I thought it would be good for my career,' he says. 'I suppose I was quite cold-blooded about it, though I did like the guy a lot. I also realized that if you made the effort with Robert then you actually got far more out of him than from anyone else: he was so analytical. As he explained to me later on, his guardedness, or unfriendliness if you like, was a defence he used to filter out the time wasters and idiots. It was a defensive carapace. I think if you got through that, you were fine.' Certainly Fotheringham and photographer Graham Watson found Millar friendly, open and warm. 'He was very welcoming. And at the end of it all he escorted Graham and me back to the motorway – quite unprecedented for a bike rider.'

According to Fotheringham, Millar appeared proud of the house, by then more or less finished to his satisfaction. Its features included 'big fireplaces, and colossal beams running across each room'. 'It was OK when I bought it,' Millar said, 'but it wasn't spick and span like this.' During the interview Millar picked up a flip-flop and threatened to throw it at a fluffy grey cat – it is unclear whether this is the same cat that was smuggled into (and back out of?) Belgium. Two-year-old Edward entered the room at one point and swiped a car magazine from the table. The other incident Fotheringham can recall is Sylvie's brief appearance. She was 'incredibly nervous. She came into the room, looked at us, and ran away. It was incredible.' He was also taken into the 'jersey room'. 'Millar's whole career was in that room,' Fotheringham says.

'The thing about the house was that it was very practical,' he continues. 'There were not many frills to it, it wasn't flash or lavish, but it was well thought out and properly done. When he came in from training he could power-wash his bike then put it in the bike room; he could do his weights and rowing in the weights room; and then he could walk into the shower. I'd say he'd spent the *right* amount of money on it. It was large but not too big. And it had a huge fireplace – you could walk into it.'

Fotheringham, who reported on many of the big races in Europe, began contacting Millar in advance of his trips to ask if he wanted him to bring anything. And usually he did: 'always chocolate, always Dairy Milk and Cadbury's creme eggs – he was really into them; car magazines; paint on one occasion to touch up a car; and Royal Jelly once – he wanted it for the vitamin content'. So regular did Millar's orders become that it got to the point 'where he'd actually fax me with an order – it was like, "Please bring the following to Flèche Wallonne . . ."'

Millar even agreed to start writing a diary for *Cycling Weekly* (the magazine had by now been renamed) during the 1991 Tour de France – a major breakthrough for someone who'd had so little time for the media. During the Tour he met Fotheringham every morning in the Village Départ – the large tented and cordoned-off area restricted to riders, press and VIPs – to talk about the previous day's stage. There was no payment for doing it. 'He was brilliant, brilliant at analysing the race and observing things, and he loved telling the stories of life inside the peloton, which were fascinating,' says Fotheringham. 'I think he was quite flattered to be asked to do the diary and he was well up for it. We'd meet every day and have a coffee; it was a nice routine. He was very committed to it.'

Apart from the diary, Millar's 1991 Tour was notable for one of the worst crashes of his career. It happened in the first week, on stage 6, and it was described in his diary thus: 'I am wrecked – big cuts on my thigh and elbow and twisted vertebrae in my neck. I don't know what caused the crash. I think it was a Colombian. He came back, I never had time to hit the brakes and lost the front wheel. I was the first down in the road and everybody hit me. I wasn't really conscious of where I was for a while. Five or six guys came down with me, but when I got up they were all away.' The crash happened towards the end of the stage, and enormous crowds spilled onto the road, swarming around the fallen riders, with the convoy of team cars backed up behind, trying to squeeze through, blasting their horns and poisoning the air with their exhaust fumes. It was a chaotic scene, and Millar was in the middle of it, dazed, confused, and in considerable pain. He eventually remounted and finished in a small group some minutes behind the peloton.

In the evening an osteopath tended to him, 'but the muscles are too stiff to work – at the finish my head was stuck to the right'. The next day saw Millar take the start wearing a neck brace. He was involved in another crash during the stage, and in the evening the osteopath 'put the vertebrae back – two in my back which were stopping me breathing decently. One in my neck, at the top where the nerve centres are. I can't sleep because I can't lie on my back or face. Normally I lie on the right, but that is where the wounds are, and I can't lie on the left because of my neck. I have been lying on my face, which means I will suffocate. Much as I wish I could not wake in the morning, I did, and I am still here. A dream is to wake up and be out of the Tour de France. A nightmare is to wake up and be going up hills.'

For several days Millar rode with large gauze bandages covering his right arm and thigh, and a neck brace, which seemed only to emphasize his diminutive stature. Despite the injuries and the handicap of wearing a neck brace, which he wryly described as 'warm', he finished the Tour. He also continued his diary to the end, recording that he 'needed earplugs to get up Alpe d'Huez', such was the noise from the spectators; and that he managed to acquire, for Sylvie, one of the fleet of official Fiat cars, which were sold off (with a third knocked off the price) at the end of the race. He seemed particularly tickled by this, though in fact it was a ruse he carried out on more than one occasion.

He admitted to having pancakes and chocolate 'for morale', but a regular theme in the diary is the sheer suffering involved in riding the Tour – it is as if he is seriously questioning this for the first time. He also displayed a gift for insightful observation and unerringly accurate description. On the Champs Elysées, where kamikaze sprinter Djamolidine Abduzhaparov provided one of the most spectacular and horrific crashes ever seen, hitting the barriers at full pelt and being tossed like a rag doll onto the road where he remained stricken for several minutes, Millar's diary reads: 'Went past Abduzhaparov on the Champs Elysées, lying there looking like he'd fallen out of an aircraft.' Which was exactly how he did look. Inevitably, Millar reserved his scorn for 'all the vultures falling over each other to take his photograph'.

Other than the crash, it was a largely uneventful Tour for Millar. LeMond, still the Z team leader, failed to make it three in a row as 1991 witnessed the dawn of the Miguel Indurain era. Battered and bruised, Millar finished seventy-second, and followed that with fourth in the Kellogg's Tour of Britain and fifth in the GP of the Americas. His most notable and impressive performance of 1991 had come in June, when he won the mountain time trial in the Tour of Switzerland, beating Andy Hampsten into second, though he also managed second to Tony Rominger at the Tour of Romandie, second to Charly Mottet at the Classique des Alpes, and fourth in the Dauphiné Libéré.

At the end of the season Millar left Z, having not been offered a new contract. He signed instead for his second Dutch team, TVM. This was an interesting set-up, to say the least, but it perhaps reflected the 33-year-old Millar's more relaxed outlook. 'I think he had a sense that he wasn't going to go any further, that he'd done what he was going to do,' suggests Fotheringham. 'He could afford to relax a little.' Andy Hampsten also found his climbing rival more relaxed at this time: 'I think he enjoyed being in a team with such a crazy bunch of characters.'

But at times TVM, under the eccentric management of Cees Priem, could be too relaxed. As with Fagor, navigation was a problem. 'There were never any maps in the team cars so they always got lost,' said Millar later, 'something always went wrong. They even got lost in Holland.' But this was consistent with the eclectic collection of personalities involved. Apart from Priem, who chuckles today about his 'theatrical, spectac-ular' pre-season team presentations – which seem to have been as much of a priority to him as the racing – there were what might euphemistically be called 'characters' in the team. As Millar explained, 'There were two guys in the team fighting for the craziest person award, [Denmark's] Jesper Skibby and [the laidback Russian] Dimi Konyshev. Jesper* was like a hyperactive kid on speed . . . I'm sure if he'd saved some of that energy he'd have won a lot more races, but then I suppose Konyshev was saving that energy for him.' Another maverick was the leader, Gert-Jan Theunisse – a climber like Millar, and also a man with his own peculiar eating habits. He would eat in his room rather than with the rest of the team.

Millar's regular room-mate at TVM was the Australian Scott Sunderland, who introduced Millar – who by now had a motorbike to add to his car collection – to the world of Harley Davidson motorcycles. 'You only got to read his *Easy Rider* magazine when he'd finished, and then you had to put it back in the plastic cover before you put it down,' Millar recalled. 'More importantly, it was never to leave the room without his approval.' Sunderland also introduced Millar to 'the delights of *Beavis and Butthead*, without which my education would have been incomplete'. Indeed, for a while Millar seemed obsessed with the MTV cartoon characters – and, given their cynical, subversive, black-as-coal brand of humour, you can perhaps see why. So inspired was Millar by *Beavis and Butthead* that he proposed a cartoon strip to *Cycle Sport* magazine. *Sleeveless and Short Legs* ran for several months.

Priem insists it was his intention to cultivate an unconventional atmosphere. 'We had a lot of unusual characters, but I like that – when people are a bit different you always have good morale. Robert was quiet, but he had fun, I think. He was not the guy who made the fun, we had other guys who did that, but Robert was always smiling. I got on well with him. He was a good professional, a good worker, and never someone

---

* In 2006 Skibby published his autobiography, *Skibby – Don't Get Me Wrong*, in which he admitted to doping during his fifteen-year career, which included nine years at TVM (1989–97). The products he confessed to using, starting in 1991, included EPO, steroids and growth hormone.

who caused a problem. If he had a problem he'd try first to fix it himself.'

But against the backdrop of all this apparent fun and frivolity, Millar was to experience the darkest, most depressing moment of his career. On 14 May 1992, after the 218km stage 18 from Salamanca to Avila of the Tour of Spain, in which he finished third, he attended dope control. His urine sample was sent away for analysis to Madrid, where the lab determined that it contained an excess of testosterone. Millar had tested positive.

'You don't put ordinary fuel in a sports car,' said Billy Bilsland cryptically, or not so cryptically, when I asked him about Millar and drugs. For years it was the subject that dared not speak its name. There was a tacit acceptance, as explained earlier, that top-level cycling and 'medical assistance' – a term that includes legal as well as illegal treatments, and also a large and shifting grey area – went hand in hand. Everybody knew it; there were countless stories. But nobody really talked about it. Truth be told, nobody really cared. The sport was in a state of collective denial.

Millar's positive test was one of four during the three-week Vuelta, which led to conjecture that the laboratory in question – the Central Testing Laboratory in Madrid – was being more stringent and using more advanced methods of detection ahead of the Barcelona Olympics, to be held later that summer. 'It is a natural development,' said Dr Cecilia Rodriguez of the Madrid lab. 'The system [of detection] gets better all the time.' When news of Millar's positive test was leaked – against protocol, the Spanish newspapers knew before he did; Millar learned his fate from his fellow riders – he requested that the second analysis be carried out in a different laboratory. 'Millar is devastated by the information and cannot believe that it is happening to him,' said Frank Quinn, the Irishman who was by now acting as Millar's business manager, and who also looked after Sean Kelly, Stephen Roche and Malcolm Elliott. 'During his professional career Robert has given hundreds of samples in all the major tours and classics,' Quinn continued. 'This is his first positive.'

'It's impossible,' Cees Priem said. 'Millar is a vegetarian. For years he's only used natural food. He never takes any chemicals.'

In Stirling three years earlier, during his question-and-answer session, Millar had been asked about drugs. Doping had been in the headlines after Pedro Delgado's 'false positive' – he tested positive for Probenicid, a masking agent banned by the IOC but not, yet, by the UCI – during the previous year's Tour. 'Riders will sometimes get injections for tendinitis, which means an injection of cortisone, and it is a painkiller, of course,' explained Millar. 'It is not a good thing to have done. It can look bad on TV if the cameras pick it up, and [it's] not the image that we want to show. However, if it happens outside sport, at someone's normal place of work, then no one thinks anything about it; it enables the person to get on with their work.' I have a vague memory of Millar highlighting the discrepancy between the cyclist who uses cortisone and is branded a cheat, and the footballer who uses cortisone to 'play through the pain barrier' and is hailed a hero. Somebody said it, and I'm sure it was Millar. Whoever did say it, the point seems reasonable, although one doctor did point out to me that there is a big difference between using cortisone as a 'therapeutic' aid and in a 'large doping dose'. 'There is always someone looking for an easy way to success,' Millar said in Stirling. 'Ben Johnson's disqualification at the Olympic Games [also in 1988] was the best thing to happen in sport. There is so much at stake at the top level and there will always be someone willing to take the risk, but drugs do not make the athlete. The people who make the drugs are always one step ahead of the doping controls. Cycling is one of the cleanest sports compared to tennis, athletics and football.'

Two weeks after the Vuelta, Millar's B-sample was confirmed as positive. His punishment was a fine of £1,100, the loss of his third place on the stage, and a ten-minute penalty, which dropped him from eleventh to twentieth in the overall standings. He was also given a three-month suspended ban. Now, such a penalty seems hardly a punishment at all, let alone a disincentive. In any case, nobody batted an eyelid; not really. Ben Johnson's positive test at the Seoul Olympics might have sent shockwaves around the sporting world, but his capture, hailed as such a milestone in the 'war on doping', merely masked the problem, as subsequent revelations concerning other competitors in that 100-metre final have indicated.

And in cycling, despite Millar's assertion in Stirling, the malaise went much deeper, arguably because of a general and long-held acceptance that the sport was so demanding that doping was inevitable almost to the point of being justifiable, in a way it could never be for a 100-metre sprint. Cycling's governing body, the UCI, also stands accused of complacency towards doping. In fact, in the trial that followed the 1998 Festina drugs scandal – when the world's number one ranked team was discovered to operate a sophisticated doping programme – the French judge went further, accusing the UCI of making 'a deliberate and long-term decision to restrict its action to [being against the] excessive [use of doping products],' rather than against doping products *per se*. This, suggested the judge, amounted not merely to complacency, but to 'quasi-tolerance' of doping.

In the Tour de France, so one argument went, the products used were performance-enabling rather than -enhancing – though there are obvious difficulties in claiming such a distinction. Whatever the nuances of the argument, the fact was that among professional cyclists positive tests seemed to be more an occupational hazard than a potentially career-ending transgression. Those who tested positive made a few noises of protest and declarations of innocence before carrying on as normal.

But Millar did care. He was angry and confused. 'I'm really fed up with the whole affair,' he told Fotheringham a few weeks later. 'Before, I thought the guys who tested positive were the ones who played and lost. Now I've seen how it happens and I think it's a lot of rubbish. They give you the feeling they can do what they want. They say, "You have too much testosterone." I think you ought to be able to say, "OK, do a blood test and let's see the level."' Millar later told Doug Gillon of the *Glasgow Herald* that he asked the UCI to carry out blood tests at his own expense, but was refused. 'If you're caught drink driving and [you] blow in the bag you can request a blood test,' Millar continued. 'I didn't really expect the second test to be negative: it's in the same lab, with the same sample. I would have preferred the second test to be in Paris or Brussels – it seems more objective, but in the rules it says it has to be the same. I would have liked to have gone to the Classique des Alpes [originally on Millar's race schedule, to follow the Vuelta] to get a placing and pee in the bottle, and make them look like idiots when I test negative. I can't take the risk of getting six months [to test positive again would have meant a six-month ban].' Millar appeared puzzled by the fact that he hadn't been riding particularly well at the Vuelta. 'When you have too much testosterone you're supposed to be as strong as a horse,' he pointed out. He was annoyed, too, at the way things had been reported by the British press. 'They made me sound like Ben Johnson,' he said, before adding, 'I just want to find out what is happening inside me . . . I have a test which I did before I went and I can compare it. Before the Tour of Spain I had less than average testosterone.'

A couple of years later, Millar spoke again to Gillon about the positive test, in the light of the similar case of the British runner Diane Modahl, who was eventually exonerated, though her levels of testosterone were reportedly much higher than

Millar's. 'I've been watching the Modahl case with interest,' said Millar. 'I don't think sports science knows nearly enough about the relationship between hormones in humans under the pressure of pushing their body to the limit and beyond. The day before I tested positive I had come off, landing on my head. I was all but knocked out. The doctors admitted they had no idea what happened to hormone production under such circumstances. They told me, "Next time you come off, stay on the ground."' He then echoed Priem's argument: 'I won't eat chemically processed food, just natural things. I am a vegetarian, not on moral grounds, but because I refuse to ingest the chemicals which livestock are fed. I simply could never use drugs.'

The level of testosterone recorded by Millar – which is measured not by volume of the hormone, but by its ratio to the non-muscle-enhancing epitestosterone – was not publicly disclosed, but he told Gillon that he was only marginally over the limit, which at that time was 6:1 (testosterone to epitestosterone). Though testosterone had been banned since 1980 (following the Moscow Olympics, where retrospective testing reportedly suggested that 80 per cent of the medallists registered excess levels of the hormone), there still appeared to be some confusion among the sporting authorities as they sought to determine at what point the ratio became suspiciously high, suggesting the use of synthetic testosterone. After Millar's positive test the UCI changed the rules, deciding that when the ratio was as high as 10:1, cases would be 'investigated' rather than automatically declared a case of doping and punished. Millar claimed that had this rule applied in 1992 he would not have failed. In 2005 the level was reduced again, to 4:1.

As for the more general question of drugs in cycling, it is still an awkward subject. Comparisons have been made to speeding on the motorway: driving fast is not the problem, getting caught is. For many years there were also widely accepted practices which, though legal, might attract suspicion, such as injecting vitamins and iron. It is a subject that Allan Peiper addresses, as honestly and directly as any former cyclist, in his book, *A Peiper's Tale*. Speaking to me, he explains that there were doctors who worked with the Peugeot team in his and Millar's day, but they didn't tend to be involved for long. 'I wasn't really open to these doctors,' he says. 'I went to the hospital in Paris where they did give us testosterone injections, but they were playing around with it. There was another doctor in 1984 who came to the Tour of the Mediterranean [at the start of the season] and never came back. For that [1984] Tour we had nobody, no medical support, no vitamins or anything. I did it purely on bread and water. I think in the last week of that Tour I had one, maybe two vitamin injections, but [not having medical support] really killed my body. When I think that Robert finished fourth in that Tour in a team like that, where nothing was organized, and there was no medical support, that's incredible.' In his book, Peiper also reveals that at his first training camp with Peugeot, in early 1983, 'the first thing I learned was how to use a needle. Not for doping, but for vitamin injections, because if you need vitamins it is more effective to inject them. The whole thing was treated as a sort of initiation rite. Everyone would be in the *soigneur*'s room and you had to inject yourself in the backside while they all watched you. And you couldn't throw the needle in, you had to push it in slowly so that you could feel it going through each layer of fibres.' Peiper adds that 'the outside world thinks that medical support means drugs, that anything to do with a needle is drugs, but that's not how it is'.

Today, Peiper says he didn't know Millar's views on doping – or anyone else's, for that matter. 'It wasn't a question you really discussed. I mean, for professional bike riders, drugs are the bogeyman. In those days it was laughable. In the 1970s they took amphetamines to have a laugh, now you go to jail for it. Guys were maybe dabbling with a bit of cortisone. But I rode three years with Peugeot and there was no professionalism there, none at all. Medically, I mean, there was no back-up. Maybe some of the older guys were still dabbling in the amphetamine days, but that was the French scene. All the French guys used to love to go and race back in France where they could charge up.' In his book, Peiper claims that 'back in the early 1980s, when I turned pro, there was a saying in the bunch that if you had never been positive you were never any good ... doping and amphetamines were a joke, no more serious than truancy or drinking from your dad's whisky bottle'. He also compares the professional scene to the school playground: 'you weren't allowed to have lollies at school, but you had them in your pocket and you ate them anyway when the teacher wasn't looking'.

Millar, however, did have medical back-up. But it wasn't organized by the team. As he openly told Charlie Burgess and William Fotheringham, among others, he had blood tests every four to six weeks; one of these, as he said at the time, had informed him that he had 'less than average testosterone' prior to the Vuelta. He even told Fotheringham how much he paid for the blood tests: roughly £100 a time, and out of his own pocket. They involved a trip to a local laboratory to have a blood sample taken, which he then sent away to be analysed – but where? If it wasn't anyone connected to his teams, then who conducted these tests?

In 1980, Millar's first year as a professional, he was introduced by Pascal Simon to Dr François Bellocq, a Bordeaux-based sports doctor. Bellocq had started working with the Peugeot team in 1973, but he left in 1979 to open a clinic in Bordeaux. Among his clients were a number of leading professional cyclists, as well as athletes (including Patrick Abada, the French pole vaulter, and the man known as 'Monsieur Pole Vaulter', Jean-Claude Perrin) and several footballers from Bordeaux FC, including François Bracci, Daniel Jeandupeux and René Girard. Before the 1978

World Cup in Argentina he was contacted by Michel Hidalgo, the French football coach, to help the squad prepare.

In 1991 Bellocq authored a book, *Sport et Dopage – La Grande Hypocrisie*, with a preface contributed by another high-profile sportsman and patient of the doctor's, the Formula One driver Alain Prost. As the title suggests, Bellocq considered the subject of doping to be riddled with inconsistencies, falsehoods and hypocrisy. It was also the case that his practices had been, in his view, mistakenly confused with doping. In the book Bellocq explains his philosophy and modus operandi. He describes many other sports doctors as 'charlatans' and defines doping as 'adding to the body a product which it does not already possess in its natural state. It could also be classed as giving the body something it already possesses in its natural state but in doses which go beyond all understanding.' To do so, claims Bellocq, 'carries no advantages'. In a puzzling analogy, which possibly loses something in translation, he likens it to 'wanting to fart higher than your arse will allow'.

'Since the start of my career,' he writes, 'I've always wanted to help the professional athlete, but never would I ask or take pleasure from someone transforming themselves into a laboratory beast either for his profit or for mine. You can never make a thoroughbred out of a shire horse. That's why I believe that the limits of sports medicine amount to stopping an athlete from digging into his body's resources, and replenishing a body from which professional sport demands so much.' Later, he explains, 'Just as a car needs water, oil and fuel to run, a body needs electrolytic, metabolic and hormonal balancing to perform to its potential. In professional sport, the accumulation of competition, training and stress destroys this balance.' Hence, according to Bellocq, the balance needs to be restored, to be 'fixed during periods of rest'.

It is the mention of 'hormonal balancing' that will raise eyebrows. As Bellocq goes on to explain, this is a 'process that doesn't happen on its own. It needs biological intervention, which is allowed in numerous countries but in France is usually regarded as doping. Worse still, we seem to have put hormonal rebalancing and doping into the same basket.' This, claims Bellocq, amounts to 'heresy'. He had already rehearsed the point in an earlier interview, in 1988: 'In France one confuses doping with the re-establishment of the hormonal equilibrium. Doping is an excess of the re-establishment. It is the same difference as between the love for a good wine and alcoholism.' 'Hormonal Rebalancing' is the title of chapter 3 of *Sport et Dopage*, and in it Bellocq expands on his thesis 'Effects of prolonged muscular efforts on the surrenal (suprarenal) metabolism in the case of professional cyclists', which, he points out, had gained him a grading of 'très honorable' at medical school. At the heart of it, and central to his philosophy, is a concern with the health of the athletes in his care. Health is his buzzword, which shouldn't be a surprise: he is a doctor, as he reminds the reader.

When appointed by Peugeot, Bellocq says he 'had an idea of how top-level athletes needed to be treated if they wanted to look forward to a life after retirement'. And he explains how he applied the necessary treatments during the Tour de France: 'During the three-week Tour de France we proposed a treatment based on small quantities of suprarenal (surrenal) hormones after twelve days of competition. In our opinion, the use of the corticoids helps delay fatigue in professional riders. It's up to us [as doctors] to help these riders, who in effect are putting their health at risk. We believe that administering small doses of corticoids orally can help riders avoid serious accidents.' He continues, 'Our aim is not to start a debate on whether or not this is doping,' only to then state that 'giving back to the body that which is completely natural to it, but which has been lost during physical exercise, does not amount to doping'. Indeed, in Bellocq's book it seems to amount to much the same as feasting on a plate of pasta to replenish depleted carbohydrate stores.

Bellocq's arguments remain highly pertinent to the drugs-in-sport debate. Some of his claims can appear shocking, but they cut to the heart of the matter in the context of professional cycling. 'The repetitive and intensive efforts that are demanded of cyclists prompt them to use certain medicines,' writes Bellocq, rehashing the decades-old argument, and justification, for doping. 'It's clear that the problem of ethics in sport is a false problem because we are in the presence of athletes for whom sport is not a distraction but a real job. It's not physiological[ly possible] to compete for four consecutive days at over 200km including three or four cols at over 1,500 metres in altitude. At this level, cycling is no longer a pleasurable pastime but a very dangerous sport as far as health is concerned.' Specifically, Bellocq believes that an event over several days, such as a stage race, causes a depletion of magnesium, potassium and vitamins. And after six to seventeen days, there is a drop in the secretion of suprarenal hormones, including testosterone. 'It is impossible for these glands to recharge their stocks in less than 24 hours,' he writes. 'The suprarenal glands need 48–72 hours to recuperate, and that has been demonstrated biologically.'

In 1989 Bellocq attended the Tour to conduct tests on some riders (it is unclear whether Millar was one of them). 'Not one rider, after eight days of racing, had a level of cortisol at the normal level,' he notes. 'It's outrageous, given that there is still another two weeks of racing left.' In such circumstances, 'not doing anything' to remedy the situation 'could be deemed dangerous. And I remind you that all imbalances, except hormonal imbalances, can be medically treated in complete legality.' It was an aberration, as far as Bellocq was concerned, that the administration, or 'rebalancing', of naturally occurring substances such as hormones was deemed illegal.

'So,' he asks, 'what are the solutions?

1. Rest.
2. Doping – I am formally opposed to this as it invites
    hormones into a body without any biological proof
    and the doses are anarchic, dangerous and repetitive.
3. Rebalancing – still a taboo subject but it is punctual,
    short-term (around three days) and uses small doses.'

While with 'doping' Bellocq said that the doses were often
'wildly calculated', with his preferred method of hormonal
rebalancing the dosage was the key factor. He adds, 'Personally,
I have never advised more than three or four "cures" of HR
[hormonal rebalancing] in a year. On average, we usually aim
for one or two.'

Bellocq reserves most of his ire for the inconsistencies and,
as he sees it, the hypocrisy of the doping question. He claims
that while many cold cures 'give the user a hit of 80–100mg' of
cortisone, he would prescribe a similar dose – three treatments
of 30mg – to 'a rider who is racing all three national Tours' in
Spain, Italy and France. 'Let's not forget,' he adds, 'that cortisone is prescribed at least once or twice a year by most doctors
in France to treat asthma attacks, hay fever and other allergies.
Does that mean that all of those who have taken it should be
called dopers? . . . In all honesty, is it better to die at 22 years old
having tested positive, or live until 70 having been hormonally
rebalanced between the ages of 20 and 30?'

One of Bellocq's highest-profile patients was Bernard
Hinault, and in an interview with French medical magazine
Tonus in 1988, the five-time Tour de France winner agreed with
his former doctor's views. 'There should be systematic check-
ups [of professional riders] every month,' said Hinault. 'That
way the products that are forbidden now would be allowed,
albeit in reasonable quantities. There are some hormones that

could be used, no problem, as long as their use was in conjunction with a monthly medical check-up. I agree with Dr François Bellocq, who was my doctor, when it comes to these kinds of treatments.'

Similar views were expressed in early 1993 by Pedro Delgado and Miguel Indurain, when the UCI threatened to stiffen the penalties for doping offenders. 'A repressive policy is not the best way of fighting doping,' said Indurain, who had by then won two of his five Tours de France. 'There must be a campaign of education, explaining the health problems and convincing cyclists not to dope themselves.' Delgado was more frank: 'We are not asking for special favours for riders, but cycling is a special sport. It is society that has created the problem of doping – asking for more spectacle and more of a battle – and it doesn't know how to solve it.' Given the drugs scandals to hit the sport since 1998, Delgado's warning carries an eerie ring. But the Spaniard had a novel solution: 'The ideal would be for us to control ourselves; that the riders themselves should work out the norms, and make sure we follow them. But it's very difficult to follow through.'

In his book, Bellocq summarizes his theory with an argument that, on the face of it, sounds compelling:

I know that the idea of HR scares everybody. Why? Because as soon as you mention cortisone, you think about its negative side. Let's not forget that skin grafts are treated with cortisone, and so are a lot of other conditions. Some critics say, 'Well, an athlete isn't sick.' I disagree. And if I decide to show other doctors the biological results (mostly for cortisol and testosterone) for an anonymous rider from the Tour de France who has been racing for five, six hours a day, what medicine will they prescribe him? There's a good chance they'll say to me, 'Let's wait a couple of days and see if his levels go back up.'

But that's the problem! You just can't do that with
professional athletes. The next day they're up and away
racing. That's why I believe that HR is not dangerous. All
it requires is nine or ten days of intervention a year, while
doctors are going around giving out more than that to treat
mid- to long-term conditions like asthma, colds and other
infectious diseases . . . I'm on the Tour de France and after ten
days I analyse the riders, and see that they need to be treated. If
I'd given the results [of these tests] to any other doctor, they
would have prescribed exactly the same thing, except for one
slight difference – their doses would be a lot bigger than mine.
Some of those same doctors would probably end up asking
for them [the riders] to be hospitalized!

So, because they're sportsmen they're not allowed the right
to be treated. Which moral, which philosophy, which ideology,
excludes them from such a right?

Finally, and forcibly, Bellocq argues, 'It's a question of life or
death. The day I took my doctor's oath, I promised to aid
anyone in a situation of danger.' Professional cycling, according
to Bellocq, poses such a risk.

There seems an irresistible logic to Bellocq's arguments, even
if they are in the modern era about as fashionable as commu-
nism. Indeed, when I suggested to a medical professional, an
authority on drugs in sport, that Bellocq's theories contained
an 'irresistible logic' his eyebrows shot up at such a speed that I
thought they would have to be scraped off the ceiling. Suffice
to say, he didn't agree, calling some of Bellocq's arguments
'disingenuous – enhancing a natural body substance is still
doping; there are so many natural chemicals that could "be
restored" to give an advantage. When does replenishing a lost
component become adding extra?' Bellocq's proposals, said this
doping expert, might be 'superficially attractive,' but 'they do
not stand up to close examination.'

Yet even in the midst of the biggest doping scandal ever to befall cycling, in the aftermath of the 2006 Tour de France – when Tour favourites Jan Ullrich and Ivan Basso were excluded from the race after being implicated in blood doping; and the winner, Floyd Landis, tested positive for testosterone – there was an echo of Dr Bellocq's argument in an interview with Dr Daniel De Neve, the doctor to Belgium's top professional team, Davitamon-Lotto. De Neve told *Cycle Sport* magazine that, given that a rider's ability to assimilate vitamins and minerals can diminish in a long stage race, he might, perfectly legally, administer an injection to redress that situation. He was then asked whether a rider's testosterone level might also fall during a stage race, making recuperation more difficult. 'Yes, that can happen,' replied De Neve. So, would he administer testosterone to redress that situation? 'If you were asking me if it would be better for him medically, better for his health for me to do that, then I'd say, probably yes. But I don't do it because it's against the rules.'

Another cautious advocate of Bellocq's proposals appears to be Dr Michele Ferrari, who is most famous for his work with seven-time Tour de France winner Lance Armstrong. In March 1995, Ferrari, speaking about hormonal rebalancing, seemed to be reading directly from the Bellocq script when he said, 'Maybe in ethical terms this is a bit dubious but there are some rules to follow and these rules are clearly stated. For me, everything that bike riders do to help themselves within these rules is not something you can blame them for. These are professionals, this is the way they earn their living. Anything that helps is OK – as long as you stay within the rules. It's true that the margin of error is narrow and so riders are taking a risk – but not in terms of their health, that's strictly for the newspapers looking for scandal.'

There are solid arguments against Bellocq's proposed re-drawing of the anti-doping rules to allow hormonal rebalancing. One is cost: to take such treatments would be expensive, prohibitively so for many. But even if HR was permitted, a bigger issue is surely that it places enormous faith and trust in doctors. While there is no evidence to suggest that Bellocq was not sincerely concerned primarily with the health of his athletes, who is to say that less reputable doctors would not seek to create 'laboratory beasts', whatever the health – never mind the sporting – implications? Ironically, Bellocq himself, in mistrusting and directing so much scorn towards his fellow doctors, seemed to undermine the very system he proposed.

Pascal Simon, who says that 'Bellocq was taking care of most of the peloton at the time' including Hinault, Delgado and LeMond, has 'nothing bad to say about the doctor. He never gave me miraculous products that enhanced my performance . . . he asked us to trust him, and we did. We didn't know what was in the pills he gave us, but we didn't suspect there was anything illicit. He told us there was nothing dangerous in them. But look at me – I'm fit and healthy at 50. I always had a fear of doping, and what we took cost us a fair bit of money. It's true, we didn't know what was in the pills . . .' Simon repeats, trailing off. 'But half the time I wouldn't take them. And most of the time I wouldn't notice any difference whether I took it or not.'

The rotund, friendly Bellocq was, adds Simon, 'someone who we respected, but he also had a heart. His door was always open for us, and not just when we went there to be treated. We could spend four days at his house and come and go as we liked. Bellocq was someone who would do anything to help athletes, and cyclists in particular. He wasn't the kind to go around saying, "I helped Delgado win . . ." He truly loved the sport and he regarded the pros who came to him as his kids. When you got to know Bellocq, he was a gem. Really a nice, simple guy. What he was doing was helping to fix the damage that had been done to the body, because it was his philosophy that top-level sport is damaging to your health. What he was doing was relieving the body of the dangers, such as ageing too quickly. For me, it wasn't doping. Not at all.'

François Bellocq died on 5 June 1993, and in his monthly column in the August issue of *Cycle Sport* Robert Millar penned an appreciation:

> *François Bellocq was one of the few real friends I had in cycling. He didn't make the distinction between the good rider and the guy with less talent. His friends were always important even when they were riding badly and he would still talk to you even if you couldn't scratch yourself in a race. There are not many people you can say that about. I first met him in 1980 when my room-mate at Peugeot, Pascal Simon, suggested letting François look after my health. I had tried a couple of sports doctors in Paris, but they seemed more interested in taking my money than keeping me alive, so I thought why not try Bellocq? The other guys seemed happy with him.*
>
> *My faith in François was well placed. He wasn't your typical doctor, he didn't want just to cure you, but he tried to prevent the problems. He didn't try to make you any better than you were, he tried to keep you healthy so you could use your potential to the full. I suppose that's why so many of his riders enjoyed long careers.*
>
> *Sure, some of his theories didn't meet with the approval of his so-called peers, but they seem like common sense to me: prevention is always better than cure, he would say. Yes, he would get involved in controversy involving drugs in cycling, but he was one of the rare people defending the rider's right to survive, and he cared that we were treated as human beings. Read his book and you will see what I mean.*
>
> *June the fifth won't be the only day I remember him: to his family and friends I say, your loss is our loss.*

By the time of Bellocq's death the sport of cycling was undergoing fundamental change. While Bellocq complained in *Sport et Dopage* that some of the 'medical research' on athletes conducted by doctors in the USA, the Soviet Union and East Germany 'overstepped the limits of what is acceptable', he would doubtless have been even more horrified by some of the developments in cycling in the early 1990s, specifically the prevalent and unfettered use of products which posed very real health risks. By then, the drug of choice was not amphetamines but EPO, a product that increased the red blood cell count, thus increasing a rider's capacity for transporting oxygen. 'You can never make a thoroughbred out of a shire horse,' said Bellocq, but EPO perhaps comes closer than any other substance to making this possible. And because it also thickens the blood, it could cause cardiac arrest when the heart slows down during sleep. It has been estimated that there are as many as eighteen unexplained deaths of cyclists from around this period.

Pascal Simon retired at the end of 1992, and he remembers Millar visiting him at his home on the outskirts of Troyes. 'We didn't see each other a lot after I gave up cycling,' says Simon, 'but I do remember Robert coming by the house and telling me, "Pascal, you've stopped at the right time. EPO is widespread and there are guys climbing the mountains with calf muscles like bodybuilders. They ride with their mouths shut because they don't even have to breathe, and they're riding twice as fast as us."'

This could have been a major reason for Millar's increasingly cynical attitude towards his sport. At the end of the 1992 season, even after finishing a respectable eighteenth overall in the Tour de France, he claimed that 'the Tour of Spain wiped me out, physically and mentally, with the things that happened'. For him, the positive test effectively marked 'the end of the year. It took something away that they don't have the right to take away and there was nothing I could do about it. It made me realize I'm not going to ride a bike forever . . . it made me put a date on it.'

In the period immediately following his positive test Millar sought refuge in the home of someone who by now had become a good friend. Wayne Bennington, the English professional who also lived in Troyes, had actually been a friend since 1983, when Millar shared a flat with him after lodging with Jack Andre. But their friendship really developed when Millar moved back to Troyes in 1988. He even arranged for Bennington to join him on the Z team in 1990. Bennington remembers vividly how Millar responded to, as he saw it, the shame and stigma of testing positive. 'He was round my house every night that week after testing positive. He was really pissed off. I think it was the only week in his entire career that he didn't go out on his bike. He just felt so angry about it.'

Again, the question is, why? At that time, cyclists who tested positive were hardly cast into the wilderness, as Ben Johnson was. The lenient punishments handed down then were indicative of how such transgressions were viewed – as an occupational hazard rather than a career-ending offence. So, why? Frank Quinn thinks it was because it tarnished a hitherto unblemished record. 'He'd been a pro so long with no positive tests that it hit him very hard,' recalls Millar's former manager. 'Though the sanctions in those days were limited it was a serious blow; he was very put out. The fact his name was up in lights, or in the headlights, for something like this, he hated that. Guys who liked the limelight, they accepted the highs and lows. But Robert never matured in that respect. He never embraced fame.' Bennington suggests that it was because Millar 'was somebody who cared about his image and he didn't like people making assumptions. He knew what was happening with his body, and why it happened, and he was angry. I've never known anybody like Robert, so in control and organized . . .' The implication being that it was the loss of control, the sense of powerlessness, that angered him.

Bennington and I meet in the bar of a cheap hotel on the outskirts of Troyes, where he still lives, driving a taxi for a living. It is immediately obvious that Bennington is different to Millar's other acquaintances – and by now I have met more than 30 of these, from school, work, cycling. Tall and lanky, with dark hair greying at the edges and combed into something almost resembling a teddy boy style, he bounds into the bar, eager and a little awkward. The awkwardness, I come to realize, derives partly from the fact that he has been living in France for so long that English has effectively become his second language. He struggles to express himself and searches for words and phrases. At one point he asks, 'Eccentric – do you use that word?' (So perhaps Millar hadn't been joking in Stirling when he said that on training rides he and Bennington would 'teach each other English'.) What is most different about Bennington is that he speaks about Millar with the affection of a friend. Others had spoken with admiration and fondness, but usually tinged with nostalgia or regret – that they didn't make an effort to get to know him better, that they judged him unfairly at the time. But with Bennington, who comes across as being a little vulnerable and on edge, there is none of that. 'We were good friends,' he confirms. 'I still am. I just don't hear from him.'

The fact that it was to Bennington that Millar turned in the aftermath of his positive test indicates that the friendship was mutual. Though perhaps not entirely equal. 'Robert's the sort of person I'd have liked to have as my big brother,' says Bennington warmly and with real feeling. 'I was a bit younger and he taught me a lot about life, not just cycling, but life, my personal life. He was knowledgeable about other things. When I split up my first marriage, he said, "Why did you do this? Why did you do that?" It was all logical – he was very logical. He was very smart.' He could also be generous. 'I remember when we went to races,' continues Bennington, 'or somewhere on our motorbikes, Robert would always arrange to pay the most expensive bill and me to pay the cheaper one'. When Bennington suffered a broken leg in a motorbike accident, which meant that he couldn't work, Millar lent him a 'substantial' sum of money 'to see me through a difficult time. I didn't find him to be tight with money, just careful, and his family had everything they wanted.'

Bennington originally travelled to Troyes to ride for Jack Andre's club, the UVC Aube, and his first residence was the team flat, which he shared with Millar and two amateurs. The amateurs were untidy, Bennington recalls, and when Millar got in late one evening and discovered the flat in a mess he woke them up and gave them a 'bollocking'. If it wasn't clean by the morning, they'd be out. He also remembers 'Robert driving me to the station at the end of the season and I was thinking, "Shit, he's a Tour de France stage winner." He was, like, my idol. But I got friendly with him straightaway. I would stay up chatting to him, just trying to learn. He was someone who never went to bed before two in the morning. That was his way of living. He'd get up at ten, eleven in the morning. He'd say, "What am I gonna get up early for? I'm not going to do anything early in the morning." That was his logic.'

When Bennington says that Millar taught him about life, he really means it. His conversation is peppered with pearls of Millar wisdom that have clearly embedded themselves in his brain – Millarisms, you might call them.

'He used to say to me, "The best thing in life is not having to get up to go and work in a factory." His dream was to never have to get up in the morning to go to work.'

'He used to say, "It's your legs, your career, your life, you have to do what you can with it. Everyone has the same chances."'

'He used to say, "It's the way you fell out the hole: you've got the legs and the lungs you fell out the hole with. You can make yourself a bit better, but you've got what you fell out the hole with."'

'I remember another one: people told him that if he ate meat he'd be big and strong, and he'd say, "I don't eat meat because I don't *want* to be big and strong."'

'He used to say, "What do they give animals? They give them shit. So if you eat animals, you eat shit."'

'Cycling was a job for him. He used to say, "I'm going to work." He was paid to do a job.'

'I've seen him say to journalists, "I'm here to ride my bike, fuck off."'

'The first thing he said to me was that it's a jungle and I'd need to be tough to survive.'

'People who came over [to France] and missed their family, missed their friends, they didn't make it. He taught me that.'

'Robert's a man with a capital M. My father-in-law, he used to shake his hand and say that you could tell he was very strong – very, very strong. Training with him almost destroyed me.'

'He was just legs. He had the upper body of a 14-year-old boy.'

'Robert's ambition was to be world champion. I think he wanted to be Robert Millar, world champion. And it would have been for himself, not for others.'

'Robert didn't need friends, he didn't need other people. But he didn't hurt other people.'

'He would never buy a new car. It would have to be six months or a year old. He was happy like that.'

'I don't think Robert could coach anybody; he would expect people to give 100 per cent, and no one could do that, except Robert.'

'One thing I never understood: you'd see him sitting down before a race and eat next to nothing, then next day he'd be up there. He wouldn't eat. He went out training without any food. Literally, he could ride 200km a day without any food.'

'He was misunderstood by a lot of people.'

'I realized that he wanted to hide. I don't really know why, but I guess it was just to be Robert Millar. He didn't want to answer to anyone.'

'One thing I don't understand is, why didn't Robert get an OBE or something? Look at what he's done in all three tours. Knowing him, I think he would have liked it, not to show people, just for himself.'

'Is there a square or a street in Scotland named after him? Why isn't there? There should be.'

Bennington reels them off, these Millar maxims and observations, punctuating them with warmly recalled memories. And then he says, 'There are a lot of things I know about Robert but I will never say them. You can write that if you want, so he can read it.'

12

Life in the Fast Lane

We don't have team meetings, we have séances.

In June 1993 a relatively unknown cyclist from Scotland, Graeme Obree, was in the Isle of Man for one of the biggest events on the domestic calendar: Manx cycling week. Just two weeks later, Obree travelled to Hamar in Norway and, on a homemade bike that included parts from a washing machine, upset the cycling hierarchy by beating one of the sport's most prestigious records – the World Hour Record, set by the Italian Francesco Moser in Mexico in 1984. It was a feat that knocked the Tour de France off the front page of *L'Equipe*, a triumph that catapulted Obree to international fame, and a story that captured the imagination of a public well beyond cycling, eventually becoming a feature film. But in the Isle of Man, before all that, Obree was virtually anonymous outside the slightly obscure British time trialling scene.

He and Millar were put up in the same hotel on the Isle of Man. 'It had a big staircase,' Obree recalls, 'and I was at the foot of it, about to make a phone call.' When he spotted Millar coming down the stairs, dressed in his cycling gear to go out training, Obree put the phone back on the hook and turned to face the staircase and the approaching figure, keen to introduce himself to the country's greatest ever cyclist. 'I stuck my hand out and said, "Robert, pleased to meet you – I'm Graeme Obree." But he didn't even look at me.' Obree's eyes widen like saucers as he recalls this. 'He just walked straight past me and out the door.'

Six months later, Obree was invited to attend the BBC Scotland Sports Personality of the Year ceremony in Glasgow. Nine years after Millar became the first cyclist to win the honour, Obree was poised to become the second. And to mark the occasion, Millar – who missed the 1984 dinner after crashing his car en route to the airport – was invited as a special guest. Predictably, he was seated between Obree and his wife, Anne. Obree had warned Anne that Millar was rude and unfriendly so they decided to give him the 'cold shoulder'. This went smoothly at first; the three of them sat in silence. Then Obree was asked, 'Graeme, have you met Robert?' 'So I said, "I've met Robert, but Robert hasn't met me." I explained what had happened in the Isle of Man and Robert's response was, "That's life in the fast lane." I said, "Really? I haven't actually found life in the fast lane to be like that."' For the remainder of the evening Obree found Millar to be quiet but civil. Millar even came over to say goodbye at the end, and extended his hand to shake Obree's. Obree reciprocated, extending his hand then withdrawing, putting his thumb to his nose and waving his fingers in the classic 'Got ya!' style. 'That's us even then,' he told him. Obree thinks Millar might have smiled. But he isn't sure.

Almost a year later, when Obree was in Sicily for the world championship, he received a phone call in his hotel room from Millar. It was the first time the pair had communicated since that dinner in Glasgow. 'He asked me if I'd be interested in riding in a pro team,' says Obree, 'and I said, "Yes – absolutely!" So he told me he could get me into this new French team, Le Groupement. I was very interested. I'd been talking to other teams about the possibility, and with Frank Quinn, who was my manager as well as Robert's. I knew I wouldn't really be an integral part of a continental team, because I had no real road-racing experience, but I had a good chance of getting the yellow jersey in prologue time trials and winning the world championship. Robert was very friendly when he phoned, very chatty. And, thanks to him, I signed for the team.'

There are several contenders for the *annus horribilis* of Millar's career. Take your pick of the three between 1980 and 1982, when Maurice de Muer wouldn't select him for the Tour de France; or 1985, when the Tour of Spain was swiped from his hands; or 1988, and the Fagor fiasco. A strong contender for the most frustrating year in his professional career is 1992, when, apart from the positive drugs test, he found himself embroiled in a dispute with the British Cycling Federation over his refusal to ride the national road race championship. (The contenders don't end there either, which is where Obree and Le Groupement come in.)

The end-of-June British championship was in Kilmarnock, only twenty miles from where Millar grew up, and the BCF declared that participation was compulsory for riders who wished to be selected for the world championship. Millar was in no state to ride, mentally or physically, and he was a no-show. Possibly he also resented being told what to do, and he contested the BCF's right to exclude him from the national team for the world championship. Later, he claimed he'd been suffering from tendinitis. But the BCF stuck to its guns and wouldn't budge on their non-selection policy for the world championship. Millar responded by threatening to sue.

The season petered out, though in August Millar had returned to the Kellogg's Tour of Britain, which also started in Scotland. I travelled from Edinburgh to Dundee to witness the start, but I was one of many to catch only the briefest glimpse of the local hero. He sneaked onto the signing-on podium, cleverly and very deliberately eluding the MC, and disappeared before he could be spotted and introduced to the crowd. At the start of the next day's stage in Edinburgh he went even further to avoid attention, failing to sign on at all – a transgression for which he was fined a hundred Swiss francs. He was also spotted having a heated exchange with Alan Rushton, the Kellogg's Tour organizer. 'The discussion was a matter of money,' Millar revealed some time later. 'It boiled down to Alan and I disagreeing about the start fee. Not the first time we had disagreed, and there was no way I was going to accept his stories.' The contretemps with Rushton explained Millar's reluctance to participate in the razzmatazz of the pre-stage presentations.

March 1993 saw the 34-year-old Millar, now one of the grand old men of the peloton, line up at Paris-Nice alongside one of the bright young things, a 21-year-old Texan named Lance Armstrong. Indeed, it was in the company of Armstrong that Millar bridged the gap to a leading group of ten as the bunch was whittled down on the slopes of Mont Ventoux. After that he managed another consistent ride at the Vuelta, finishing fifteenth overall. And then it was the Tour de France – Millar's eleventh start, putting him just one behind the British record holder, Barry Hoban.

There were two Tour highlights for Millar. One was securing another Fiat car, this time with 40 per cent off and only 11,000km on the clock. And, in a race that announced the arrival of Armstrong as a major new talent – he won stage 8 to Verdun – the highest pass in Europe gave Millar an opportunity to demonstrate that he was still one of the world's best climbers. His performance that day is still talked about in reverential tones. There was already something about stage 11 of the 1993 Tour, from Serre Chevalier to Isola 2000, that appealed to the imagination; but it might also have appealed to Millar's sense of history. It was an Alpine stage of 180km that included the ascent of the Col de la Bonette, 22km long and climbing to 2,800 metres (9,000ft). Remarkably, Europe's highest pass had been visited only once before by the Tour, in 1964, and on that occasion the first rider over the top was Spain's Federico Bahamontes, the 'Eagle of Toledo', one of the sport's great climbers and a five-time winner of the King of the Mountains title.

Millar started the mountain in a leading group of five, but in its foothills he moved clear – just by riding tempo, he explained later, rather than attacking. Only one rider managed to stay with him, another rider in the twilight of his career: Pedro Delgado. So often rivals in the past, the Scot and the Spaniard now worked together in tandem; but as the road steepened, still 14km from the top, the pace set by Millar proved too much. Delgado was dropped, and Millar reached the summit alone and in front, visibly straining on the final slopes, where the gradient reared up again – 'I blew my brain out at the top,' he said later. There were still 50km to race, but leading the Tour over the Col de la Bonette, with Miguel Indurain in hot pursuit, filled Millar with satisfaction. 'That's the kind of thing which motivates me now I'm getting older,' he admitted.

But there was still a stage to win. For 50km Millar forged on alone at the head of the race as, behind him, the chase gathered momentum. There was one climb left, to the finish at Isola 2000, and at its foot Millar's capture seemed inevitable. Anticipating this, French television declared him the 'moral winner', whatever happened. Six kilometres from the summit he was indeed caught, by a small and select group comprising the men who were challenging for the overall win, led by Indurain and the Swiss rider Tony Rominger. 'I needed two minutes at the bottom of the [final] climb,' Millar would admit later. As it was he had only forty seconds, and at the fourth hairpin he was caught and immediately dropped. That was Millar done for, then, his epic escape ultimately proving a worthy but futile effort. As Stephen Bierley noted in *The Guardian*, when Millar was caught 'he was finally and completely done'. Having climbed with such grace and style, 'Now he appeared hunched, small and frail.'

The TV cameras remained focused on the metronomic Indurain and Rominger; until, remarkably, a small figure reappeared in the picture. It was Robert Millar. He had dropped back, recovered, and then dug deep to make one final effort. He sprinted past the Indurain-led group just four kilometres from the finish, in time to race, alone and in front, past Scotland's national flag, the saltire, fluttering from the hands of a gaggle of Millar supporters by the side of the road. For two kilometres he persisted, but Indurain, sniffing the finish, led the chase – you could almost see his nostrils flaring. As Millar reflected at the finish, 'Indurain rode, so what more can you say? I saw him riding and persisted a bit, then saw the gap was closing so I put it in the little ring. He was winding it up, so I let it go because I'd tried my best and was going to finish sixth or seventh.' He was seventh, a minute behind the stage winner Rominger, but he had, as Bierley noted, 'ridden a colossal stage, with such panache and daring that his name will be forever associated with the Col de la Bonette'.

Another Millar curiosity: the wheels on his bike that day were not the team-issue models. Rather, they were super-light, super-expensive wheels with fewer spokes than standard wheels and state-of-the-art titanium hubs. They were the work of renowned Liverpudlian wheel builder Pete Matthews, bought by Millar out of his own pocket – virtually unprecedented for a professional cyclist – and delivered by William Fotheringham along with a titanium bottom bracket (also paid for by Millar) and the usual consignment of Cadbury's Dairy Milk and creme eggs.

In his diary, Millar reflected on his great escape over Europe's highest pass in characteristically wry, understated style: 'I thought I was going to win a week's holiday or 100 bottles of wine or something . . . but instead I got sore legs.' In the Pyrenees he was in the thick of it again on a long slog of a sixteenth stage, 230km from Andorra to San-Lary-Soulain, which included five major mountains. Millar was up with the leaders all day and placed fifth at the finish, but in different circumstances he might have been going for a fourth stage win in the Tour. On the slopes of the final climb, Pla d'Adet, he was alone pursuing the strongmen, Indurain and Rominger. 'If there had been a hairpin or a slight easing of the gradient I would have made it up to them,' Millar reflected at the start in Tarbes the next morning. 'It would have looked good, just those two and me in front. I had to get to their wheels and I just couldn't get there – I would have got there if they hadn't attacked again. I was at my maximum.'

In Tarbes on the morning of the final day in the mountains Millar told Fotheringham, 'I've got my little plan.' He put it into action on the slopes of the Tourmalet, where once again he was the main aggressor, only to again be foiled by Indurain and Rominger, whose dominance meant there was little for the other riders to fight over. Millar at least tried. When he reached Paris for the eighth time, in a final overall position of eighteenth – his sixth top-twenty placing – he could reflect with satisfaction and no little pride on his performance.

Which was just as well as it was to prove his final Tour de France. It shouldn't have been: he said in August 1993 that he wanted to beat Barry Hoban's record of twelve Tours, though it seemed to be an ambition thought up mid-conversation. 'How many has [Hoban] done?' asked Millar. 'Twelve? If he has, I want to do thirteen . . . I would like to have done more Tours by the time I stop than any other Brit.'

But in April 1994, during the Tour of Spain, Millar suffered a knee injury. It is interesting and revealing to note now how rare injuries were for Millar: in fifteen seasons as a professional, this seems to have been, if we discount the inevitable saddle sores, his first serious non-crash-related injury. It was a severe case of tendinitis, aggravated by racing in cold and wet weather at the Tour of the Basque Country in early April. During the Vuelta Millar had the knee treated on the move, dropping back to the TVM team car to be tended to by the doctor, who appeared to administer an injection. While this delicate operation was being carried out, motorcycle-mounted photographers buzzed like wasps around the scene. For Millar, that added insult and irritation to injury; but the driver of the TVM car was even angrier, with the photographer from *Marca* later alleging that he had tried to drive him off the road. Perhaps the reaction was because, as Millar had told us in Stirling, it wasn't the kind of image he wanted to present. The pictures in the next day's papers featured him holding on to a car while a doctor hung out of it and jabbed a needle into his knee, as well as Millar's angry reaction. In the end the injury defeated him. He abandoned on 30 April, on the stage to Sierra Nevada.

In typical Millar fashion he was able to rationalize the injury. He calculated that his knee had flexed to turn the pedal seventy million times in the course of his career; it could also be estimated that he'd ridden approximately three hundred thousand miles in his professional career; and that he had completed around two thousand days of racing. The figures suggested, to Millar, that a knee injury was simply the inevitable result of so much wear and tear.

Curiously, or perhaps not so curiously, he seemed to have a similar attitude towards life itself. He told several people in the course of his career that he considered that the efforts he made as an athlete, and the strain that put on his body, would curtail his life. 'Remember, professional athletes like cyclists don't live long,' he told Simon Pia of *The Scotsman* in 1998. 'The Chinese say you only have so many heart beats, and cycling uses up a lot of them.' He wasn't being glib. 'If I live beyond 60, any year's a bonus,' he said to Bennington. And going further back, to when he was a teenager, he told Jamie McGahan that he feared for his long-term health. 'His mother wasn't very well, and with his dad having a limp because of polio, I think he was combining the two of them,' McGahan reasons. 'I remember him talking about it. He felt that, genetically, he was predisposed to having bad health in the future.'

Several years into his retirement, he candidly and rationally explained this thinking, telling Fotheringham in an email, 'Being as good a bike rider as I could be was always very important to me, but there were times when it wasn't healthy to chase that idea . . . being so focused on something isn't always good for you. I think I raced too much probably because I liked racing. There were times I over-trained looking for the extra percentages. As you know I could be very intense [but] I accepted that the energy I was expending as a pro bike rider would probably mean that I wouldn't live as long a life later.' Such thinking is received wisdom in professional cycling. To paraphrase the writer Geoff Dyer, who was talking about jazz musicians, it isn't that they die young, they just get older quicker. In an article he wrote in the *Guardian* in 1998, Millar stated, 'The riders reckon that a good Tour takes one year off your life, and when you finish in a bad state, they reckon three years. I've ridden eleven Tours, [and] finished or got close to the end of four in a bad state, so you work it out.' Another casual comment made by Millar, this time to Graeme Obree, also invites conjecture that his fears relating to life expectancy were serious. He told Obree that he had financial provision only up to the age of 55, which could be interpreted as a bleak prediction given that he didn't appear keen to work beyond cycling.

It is also a little puzzling, because there is little doubt that Millar should comfortably have fulfilled his ambition of earning a million pounds during his career. 'Robert was in the six-figure bracket all the time,' claims Frank Quinn, his business manager. 'His ability to win stages in the major tours guaranteed that. From at least 1988 [when Quinn began representing him] he was in six figures.' However, he rejects the suggestion that Millar's salary was ever as high as £400,000, as has been reported in the past. It seems unlikely that it ever climbed beyond £200,000, but that could be topped up by endorsements, arranged for him by Quinn. While the English-speaking riders were at a slight disadvantage – according to Quinn, 'very rarely did they get sponsorship in their own countries' – the Dublin-based manager could tie up deals with international shoe, sunglass and helmet manufacturers. By the late 1980s, a top rider like Millar could command at least £10,000 a year for wearing a certain brand of shoe. Personal appearances could be worth £1,000 a time. But in pursuing such opportunities Quinn faced a major challenge with Millar, whose attitude towards journalists and other people he didn't know – and didn't trust – could be 'a bit iffy'. Quinn explains, 'I had serious chats with him about that. "Try to be more courteous," I said, "no more than that." But I heard him use very extreme language. The thing was, that didn't reflect the Robert I knew – not at all. We had a good rapport. He was very honourable; he treated me very well, paid me well. I couldn't say anything bad about him.'

Millar made the disclosure to Obree that he had financial provision only to the age of 55 as they drove from Paris to a Le Groupement get-together in Lille on 21 December 1994. Both had signed two-year contracts with the new French team, which for Millar offered a welcome escape from the consistently chaotic and anarchic TVM.

Following his abandonment of the Vuelta, Millar had returned to racing at the Tour of the Mining Valleys in June, after eventually finding a French physiotherapist who diagnosed his injury as crystals forming on the ligaments, and cured it in a matter of days. Having appeared destined to miss the Tour for the first time since 1982, Millar's prospects suddenly brightened. Cees Priem asked him if he was willing to start his twelfth Tour, and Millar said yes. But in the event it was another rider returning from injury, Gert-Jan Theunisse – who spent much of his career either injured or serving doping bans – who took Millar's place, having allegedly threatened TVM with legal action if he wasn't selected. Millar was reported to be 'seething'. Theunisse abandoned on stage 12.

Despite worrying that he might be 'flogging a dead horse', Millar confirmed in the autumn, on signing with Le Groupement, that he intended to ride for two more seasons, though there was a caveat: 'I'll see how bad next year is.' Another tongue-in-cheek comment – though, as things turned out, it was prophetic.

From the outset, Le Groupement was an unusual set-up. The sponsor was new to cycling, but in Patrick Valcke it had a *directeur sportif* whom Millar knew well, first from Valcke's days as a mechanic with Peugeot, then from the pair's ill-fated spell at Fagor, and whom he liked. The reunion had come about with a phone call in the autumn. 'I called him after months of not seeing him,' says Valcke. 'I told him I was building a team and I wanted him on board. By the end of the call he had practically signed, and we hadn't even talked money yet. I told him, "Robert, don't worry, you'll be paid what you're worth." He said, "OK, I'm interested – but who'll be in the team?" I said, "Listen, Robert, trust me and you'll be paid OK, and it won't be a team full of clowns. It will be a real team."' Valcke was true to his word about the riders: as well as Obree, the team also included another of Millar's old team-mates, Ronan Pensec, and two more big names: France's world champion and Tour contender Luc Leblanc and the veteran Dutch sprinter Jean-Paul Van Poppel.

But it was the identity of the sponsor, and the nature of its business, that intrigued people, right from the beginning. Le Groupement Européen des Professionnels du Marketing was a pyramid sales company selling everyday products: clothes, toys, domestic goods and cosmetics. Its chairman was the company founder and a self-made man, Jean Godzich, who employed five hundred staff at the company headquarters at Fleury-sur-Andelles, near Rouen. There were also 1,300 distributors, but the company depended most on its team of 50,000 independent salespeople – the base of the pyramid: in effect, private individuals who sold directly to their friends through the company catalogue. By 1995 Le Groupement had a turnover of £80 million, and Godzich confirmed a five-year £4 million-a-year commitment to the professional cycling team. Yet as soon as the company's sponsorship was announced, the negative headlines began. Rumours emerged that the company had close ties to a religious sect. Salespeople then came forward with terrible tales of woe, claiming their work for the company had led to various awful fates befalling them. Before the season had even started, the team was on the back foot. Companies sponsor cycling teams to raise their profile and increase positive publicity, so from day one Le Groupement found itself engaged in a serious PR battle.

None of this unduly concerned either Millar or Obree as they made their way from Paris to Lille for the team get-together. Obree had been on holiday in Arizona when he got a phone call from Frank Quinn telling him that he had to travel to France, but he misunderstood the instructions and flew to Paris instead of Lille. Millar saved the day by agreeing to pick him up at the airport. 'Robert was delayed,' Obree recalls, 'and it was a three- or four-hour drive to this chateau – a big, austere place with dark wood panelling. I was just waiting for Norman Bates to jump out.' But what struck Obree most forcibly was the welcome the pair received when they arrived, late – that is, the coldness of it. 'We arrived and the rest of the team were finishing their meal. We walked in and there were no hellos, or how are you[s] . . . no handshakes or anything. Robert said hello to a few people but as soon as I arrived I felt uncomfortable. I could see instantly see that it was a completely unfriendly, insincere environment. Guy Mollet [the team's general manager] made it clear to Robert that neither of us was getting any dinner because we were late.'

Valcke points out that Obree already had two black marks against his name: one for missing a first team rendezvous in Florida in early December (and then travelling to the US on holiday); the second for flying to Paris instead of Lille for the second get-together. His continental road career had therefore not got off to the best start. The 'punishment' of being sent to bed without dinner was intended to teach Obree a lesson, not the grizzled veteran Millar. But the team, equally, might be accused of insensitivity in its handling of Obree, whose brother had died in a road accident in October, and for whom the experience of being in a professional road team was an entirely new one. Nevertheless, it seemed that the three-strikes-and-you're-out rule applied: when he failed to attend the team's training camp in the Alps, beginning on New Year's Day 1995, Obree was sacked. Accused by Valcke of a 'lack of professionalism', his continental road career had lasted just two days, ending before he had even donned Le Groupement's garish, multi-coloured racing kit. Obree has no regrets. 'I was glad I was never part of it,' he says. 'It was horrendous. Within a matter of minutes of being there I developed a dislike and distrust of these people and I just wished I could be beamed back home again – it was just before Christmas Eve. And this was Robert's life.'

It wasn't all negative, though. Obree's first impressions of Millar were revised on the car journey. 'He talked a lot about Glasgow. He was like Billy Connolly – he reminded me a lot of Billy Connolly actually. He does a great jakey impression' –

a 'jakey' being one of the classic Glasgow characters, a drunken down-and-out, usually with an aggressive streak and a chip on his shoulder. Obree says that Millar's impersonation was uncannily accurate. 'He'd say, "Ah'm goin' tae chib you, big man . . ." He was really good at it, and funny. He was continually taking the piss out of Glasgow, but in a good-natured way. I don't know if he was just happy to have another Scot there, but we had a laugh . . . I mean, if you're around these French gits – sorry to call them gits, but they were gits – who wouldn't even get off their chair, wouldn't give you dinner, wouldn't even shake your hand or acknowledge you on your first day in a new team . . . I think he found me . . . interesting. I think he was comfortable with me once he realized I wasn't on an ego trip and I wasn't going to take anything from him.'

On that shared car journey Millar told Obree what to expect from the team. 'He was pretty matter of fact about it all. He said we would be treated like naughty school kids and be punished for being late, sent straight to bed without supper. Which was pretty much what happened. I took my luggage upstairs. I was sharing a room with Robert and a German, Marcel Wüst. He was all right, actually. But I'd come prepared for French hospitality: I had my cornflakes, skimmed milk, bowl and spoon. Robert shared my cornflakes with me. I think he was impressed that this rank amateur would come so prepared.'

The unfriendliness towards Obree continued the next day. 'The French riders spoke among themselves. Marcel told me they were insulting me in French. I said, "I know, I got that impression." I realized that Robert had a survival strategy – he must have needed one. His was: I'll reject you before you reject me. That's what he did with me, I'm sure, on the Isle of Man, when he walked straight past me. I've analysed it. Robert's world was a world of insincere people who'd use you and get what they could from you. I think Robert was naturally suspicious of people and very protective of himself. That's why he'd be unfriendly to autograph hunters, or people wanting to have a photo taken with him. They wanted a piece of Robert Millar but they didn't give a shit about him. You're basically a public servant. And he didn't want to be a public servant.'

In Le Groupement's defence, Valcke argues that the team had good morale; that the riders bonded at the Alpine training camp in early January that Obree failed to attend. Had he appeared, he would have shared a room with Ronan Pensec, as Valcke mixed the nationalities up to encourage integration. But even after his brief time with Obree in Lille, Millar seemed to fear that his fellow Scot and Le Groupement – or, more to the point, a pro team environment – might be an ill-matched union. 'I told him that he should keep his head down and not cause any hassle,' Millar told *Cycling Weekly*. 'He was miffed that they wanted him to go [to Lille], but I told him it was a job, and you have to do it. He didn't seem to know where he was going.' What Millar didn't say, though it must have weighed on his mind, was that it was his name, as well as Obree's, that was at stake. He had, after all, recommended Obree to the team.

Twenty-two months after his dismissal, Obree dropped a bombshell in an interview for *L'Equipe*. He claimed that '99 per cent of elite riders are taking EPO or a similar drug'. In his autobiography, *The Flying Scotsman*, published in 2003, he suggested that his refusal to subscribe to an organized medical back-up programme had contributed to his dismissal from Le Groupement. He said that an English-speaking team-mate 'explained that there would be medical back-up in the team, and that £2,000 would come out of the contract to pay for it. He explained that the real cost would be £8,000 and the team was making up the difference. I said that I was happy to train and race the way I have always done, and that I would not need the medical back-up, and to pass it back to the director ... Later I wondered if it was my refusal of medical back-up, my non-appearance at the ski camp or the team's finances that caused the greatest problem.' All Obree will say now is, 'I was told that for £2,000 a year I'd be looked after, and that this was a bargain, because to buy all that stuff myself it would cost £8,000. I said no and decided to opt out of that programme. But I think that any discussion I had, with any rider, was sanctioned from the highest level. As far as the medical back-up went, you fitted in or you were thrown out. I feel now that my career was robbed.'

But for Valcke and Le Groupement the episode with Obree was the least of their worries. There was serious trouble brewing, and the warning signs were visible as early as March 1995, with the cycling season in its infancy. The company reported that sales had fallen by 35 per cent in the first two months of the year, a decline attributed to 'a campaign of denigration', according to a letter published in *L'Equipe* from a Le Groupement director in which he also railed against a 'lynching by the media'. Negative publicity had continued to dog the team – or, more specifically, the company, whose involvement with cycling had exposed it to a level of interest and scrutiny it would otherwise have avoided. Jokes such as Millar's 'we don't have team meetings, we have séances' might have been intended as humorous, but they hardly helped win the PR battle. 'One thing I want to clarify,' says Valcke today, 'is that Le Groupement wasn't a sect, as the journalists at the time would have you believe. One day it emerged that the boss of the team had been part of some Evangelist movement in the USA. It caused uproar in France. The media sent special teams of reporters to follow the team's moves. It was really heavy. In the US they were used to these kinds of religious [movements] but it was really foreign to the public in France. It became an obsession for the media for weeks on end. Every week there were journalists trying to bring out a scoop about the team. In the end it was journalists who destroyed us.'

That March, Millar found himself back in Colombia, riding the Classico RCN stage race, with a view to the world championship, being held there in September. It was a disastrous trip, not least because it exposed Millar to extended time in the company of Luc Leblanc, the world champion and Le Groupement team leader. Millar was unimpressed by Leblanc. In his column in *Cycle Sport* he referred to him only as 'Stuart' after the hapless nerd in *Beavis and Butthead*. In a later column he was uncompromising, even cruel, in his analysis of 'Stuart': 'A sad case of a boy in man's shoes; a strong-willed, weak-brained hypochondriac with bad feet; the author of 1,001 excuses; unbelievably strong, totally unpredictable. The eyes still see, the legs still turn, the brain is stillborn.'

Millar was due to lead the team at the Giro d'Italia before going to the Tour de France to support Leblanc – assuming the world champion's various injuries cleared up. A similar scenario to Fagor seemed to be unfolding, with Leblanc, like Stephen Roche in 1988, sidelined with a knee injury and Millar required to step reluctantly into his shoes – 'to put my neck on the line', as he saw it. But in early April it was announced that Le Groupement would not, as planned, contest the Giro. Valcke explained that the decision had nothing to do with any uncertainty over the team, it was simply that the riders were not going well enough.

Otherwise, it was business as usual. In May the team contested the Midi Libre, a traditional Tour de France warm-up event; it was won by Indurain, and Millar was nineteenth. Then came the Dauphiné Libéré, where Leblanc's injury woes continued but Millar demonstrated that he was coming into some form, attacking on the climb of the Col de la Croix de Fer, and placing thirty-first overall. In June he returned to the UK, spending a few days in the Midlands – he was spotted training in the country lanes around Northamptonshire and Leicestershire – before travelling to the Isle of Man to have another go at winning a title that had surprisingly eluded him – that of British professional champion. It was on a course familiar to him, the mountainous Manx TT circuit where, in 1978, at the age of 19, he had first shown what he might be capable of, even if on that occasion he lost the sprint to the only man who managed to stay with him on the climb, Steve Lawrence.

Seventeen years later came a performance acclaimed by all who witnessed it as phenomenal. On the second of three ascents of Snaefell mountain Millar made his move. When he launched his lone attack a group of six riders had a substantial lead of three minutes and forty seconds on the main bunch; but over the next lap Millar pursued them relentlessly. It was, reported *Cycling Weekly*, 'poetry in motion', one man against five (one of the leading break had been shed on the climb), yet Millar gobbled up the miles, eating into their advantage. He pulled back more than two minutes on the climb alone. Behind him, fifteen chasers – including Brian Smith – pursued Millar, but made no impression.

Following Millar was the magazine's experienced photographer Phil O'Connor, who later described what happened. 'When the first break of the day heard that Millar was chasing alone at three [minutes] forty [seconds] with fifty miles to go they probably feared what would happen, but they could never have guessed it would be so savage. He tore up the mountain for the second lap and in no time I had used a whole reel of film. This was Britain's finest ever climber doing what he does superbly, and there was no need to have a look at the lead group – he would be seeing them shortly anyway. His move towards the leaders was inexorable – he caught them at Creg Willys [near the bottom of Snaefell]. The leaders looked at him and knew, as night follows day, that the gold medal was gone. Millar could have waited until halfway up the mountain but he applied the pressure bit by bit until he was alone with

Chris Walker . . . But then Millar was gone. For the next ten minutes he entertained me and my motorbike driver to perhaps one of his final displays of his greatest gift . . . the king of the mountains.'

'It's always good to win a race and to get another jersey for the collection,' said Millar after being presented with the champion's white jersey, with its narrow blue and white bands. Another of the leading riders, Jonny Clay, described Millar's victory as inevitable; 'it was [just] a question of how long we could hang on to him'. Brian Smith, who finished fifth after twice winning the championship, was happy for Millar. 'I'm pleased Robert has won at this stage of his career. In my eyes he's always been the best in Britain, and he showed it today.'

Incredibly, it was his final professional race.

With just seven days to go until the Tour, Millar returned to France and on Monday, 26 June travelled to the Le Groupement headquarters in Rouen to pick up a new bike. It had been another troubling month for the team. On the 16th it was reported that Patrick Valcke and Guy Mollet were attempting to merge Le Groupement with another team, AKI, but it was made clear to them by Jean-Marie Leblanc, the director of the Tour de France, that a merged team would not be invited to his race. A week later – on 23 June, the day Millar won the British road title – there was a blow of a different kind for Mollet: he received a one-year suspended jail sentence for tax evasion.

When Millar arrived in Rouen, he met a flustered Valcke. 'Valcke was all red in the face,' reported Millar, 'because he had just come out of the meeting with the company where they had told him there was no money. He said, "You're not riding the Tour." I said, "Ah, that's OK, it would have been a month of suffering anyway." Then he said, "And you're not getting paid," and I realized it was serious . . .'

Valcke's crisis meeting had been sparked by the failure of Sport Competition – the holding company that ran the team – to pay its staff the previous month. The sales figures had continued to make depressing reading and the title sponsor had hit serious cashflow problems, as a result of which it had been forbidden by its bank from writing cheques. The management wanted the team to go to the Tour without revealing to them the extent of the problems, nor the very real possibility that they might not get paid; but when Valcke discovered this plan, he called the meeting. The result was not only that the team pulled out of the Tour, but that it ceased to exist. In an ironic twist, the squad invited to take its place at the Tour was AKI, the team with which Le Groupement had held merger talks.

Millar initially seemed philosophical. 'I was not shocked or surprised they had financial difficulties because they had met so much criticism,' he said. But there was regret: 'I was coming into good form, and I would have liked to have gone to the Tour and tried to win a stage. As it is, I'm now considering my future as a bike rider, because I don't know if I'll race again this season and I have a two-year contract with the team. I think financially something will be sorted out for the riders, as we have a lawyer acting for us . . . a lot of the guys were shocked, particularly the younger ones. When myself and Jean-Paul Van Poppel found out that we were probably going to get our money we tried to cheer up the others and make the best of the situation. The guys who came off worst were the mechanics and *soigneurs*.'

Valcke remains certain as to the cause of Le Groupement's untimely death. 'I can say that it was really the journalists who killed this team off,' he maintains. 'We could have gone on. We had really good riders, but in the end it became too much. I said, "It's time to stop." It was my decision. At the time the boss of the team said, "Monsieur Valcke, I pay you x million francs to give my company publicity. We've had too much negative publicity so I've decided you and the team will be getting paid at the end of the Tour." I said, "OK, if you're not paying [then] we won't ride the Tour de France. I'm not going to ask my riders to kill themselves on the bike for three weeks solid if they might not get paid at the end. So if you don't pay before the start of the Tour, bye-bye." I held a meeting with the riders, and all of them agreed I had made the right decision. I called all the riders in, one by one. I told them we have to speak man to man. They all came to the team's headquarters. There was a huge media presence, all the mechanics, all the backroom staff. And they all supported my decision. As regards Robert, he was at the end of his career so it wasn't as much of a blow as it was for a guy like Luc Leblanc, who was the reigning world champion. Robert knew it was the end of his career. And his reputation wasn't good. People used to say, "He's a shit-stirrer, he's a pain." But for me, Robert was one of the good guys. If he told you yes, then he meant yes. He was a man of his word. And for me, that means more than reputation.'

It was the last that Valcke saw of Millar.

By mid-July there were rumours of another sponsor coming in to take over the team. Millar appeared to be more open-minded about his future, even speculating that he might ride the Tour of Spain, which by then had been moved by the UCI from April to September. 'They threatened that if we didn't go well in the Tour de France then we'd go to the Tour of Spain,' Millar noted, tongue presumably embedded in cheek. 'We're not going well in the Tour de France, so all we need is another sponsor.' He had resumed training, just in case.

By the middle of August, he appeared more resigned. 'I don't think I'll race again this year,' he said. And there remained uncertainty over whether he and the others would be paid what they were owed by Le Groupement. The French federation had attempted to intervene, cashing in the guarantee given at the start of the season, but Le Groupement opposed it. Millar kept training, but only two hours a day. He was, he admitted, 'pretty bored'.

Quite apart from the outstanding salary from Le Groupement, Millar's money worries were mounting. The French tax man was apparently after him, though his manager Frank Quinn says this was not a new development. 'He was on the hit list of the income tax guys for a few years. The tax difficulties were ongoing; it went back for ever with Robert. Like all athletes, he didn't like paying tax.' This may sound a surprising statement, but it makes some kind of sense when you consider the limited timeframe of an athlete's ability to earn. 'There were also problems associated with the fact that Fagor was a Spanish team,' Quinn continues. 'Some of the payments from them wouldn't be public knowledge.'

Millar was caught in limbo: stay in France and hope to find a new team, or leave, since his unemployment was surely more likely to result in a knock on the door from the tax man. He had even joked to William Fotheringham of 'having his passport in his pocket, ready to go missing when the tax man came calling'.

It is unclear precisely when Millar left. Nor is it clear whether he intended his departure to be permanent – probably not, given that in January 1996 he was still talking about finding a team and racing. But what is certain is that in the autumn of 1995 Robert Millar packed his bags and left his home, and his family, in Berceney-en-Othe. Wayne Bennington remembers it well, even if he can't pinpoint the precise date. When asked if he knew that his friend was planning to leave, Bennington shrugs. 'Yeah. But I can't say why.' Was it because of his worries over an unpaid tax bill? Bennington shrugs again. 'The circumstances . . . it actually turned out what he wanted anyway. I knew he was leaving. It got to the point where he had to. His wife knew, too. He didn't just disappear from her. I think he waited until the last possible moment, but he had no choice in the end. And he was living at home [in Berceney-en-Othe] until the last moment. When he did go, I drove him to the station.'

Quinn suggests that his departure had long been planned, and that it owed something to an increasingly difficult relationship with Sylvie. 'It had been pretty fractious for a few years and he was trying to get out,' he says. 'The relationship with his wife had been going downhill in the later years – it happens when you're away from home six months a year. But I know he had planned to move back to the UK for some time. Things became quite difficult for him in France. The tax situation gave him problems. But I know he made arrangements with his wife before he left, sorting things out with the property and so on.'

Other than Bennington, no one else seems to have known Millar's plans. There were no goodbyes to Pascal Simon, for example, or his confidant and 'friend for life' Jack Andre. 'I didn't know he'd left until the next month,' says Andre. As for Sylvie, Andre's wife lost touch with her. He understands that she remarried, but says, 'I don't see her.' And then, waving his hands vigorously, he issues a strange warning: 'Don't try looking for Sylvie – that's as complicated as looking for Robert Millar.'

There is another intriguing dimension to Millar's departure, and the fact that he turned up in what seemed an unlikely place – Daventry, in the Midlands. There seemed to be a new lady in his life. Several team-mates claimed that she'd been spotted at or around races as early as 1992. Her name was Linda, and it has been suggested that she wrote one or two letters about Millar to *Cycling Weekly*. You will recall from chapter 10 the paean to Millar published by the magazine in autumn 1990 praising his 'wit, cute accent and coy smile' whose author was one Linda Luxerre of Woodford Art College. There is a Woodford near Daventry. Only a theory . . .

Dag Otto Lauritzen, a team-mate of Millar's at TVM from 1992 to 1994, remembers meeting her. 'I met that woman several times, a red-haired woman, but he was still married, so it was a bit spooky.' Sean Yates recalls Millar's personality changing slightly in this period, that as well as appearing to be more relaxed about racing he was 'lightening up' off the bike as well. 'He became more outgoing, he was cracking the jokes, being a bit of a wide boy, by the early nineties. I remember at the Nissan Tour [in Ireland in 1992] he'd be hanging out at the bar with some girls. And there was this red-haired girl at a lot of the races. Yeah, Robert was a bit different, and people took note of that. He was still a strange cat, though.' His manager at TVM, Cees Priem, also provides intriguing evidence that Millar had an eye for the ladies, chuckling, 'Yes, Robert, he would always look at the nice girls. He liked the ladies, yah?'

But, as I mentioned, in interviews, even as late as January 1996, Millar seemed to be holding on to the hope that his career wasn't over. Early in the new year he spoke to William Fotheringham from his new home in Daventry, having just completed a four-hour training ride. In many respects it was business as usual, and he was carrying on as normal, even though there was no team, no salary and, at 37, few prospects. Instead there was, unusually for Millar, only uncertainty. 'I don't know if I should pack it in because I'm not good enough or not motivated enough, or if I should try to ride some races up to the Olympics. I'm stuck between two chairs.'

The Atlanta Olympics was an unusual target for Millar to aim at. Although it was the first time the games had been open to professionals, and therefore Millar's first possible appearance in them – in 1980, you will recall, he turned professional and thus ruled himself out of the Moscow games without a second's thought – his motivation for wanting to go was unclear. To put himself back in the shop window? To give a sense of purpose to the training he was still putting himself through? To cling on to his identity, his sense of self, as a cyclist? Certainly Wayne Bennington feared for Millar in retirement.

'My wife and I were both quite worried about him in terms of when he stopped cycling,' he says. 'Even for me, when I stopped riding it took me a long time to adjust. When you get to the end of your career, especially if it just stops, it's quite hard. But with Robert, [cycling] was all he had.' But Bennington also suggested that perhaps Millar really did fancy he could win a major title. If not Robert Millar, world champion, why not Robert Millar, Olympic champion?

With the help of Quinn, Millar had been searching for a team. 'I don't see anything coming,' he admitted by January, six months after the collapse of Le Groupement. He had been linked with the US Postal Service team and his old Z team, by now sponsored by the insurance company Gan, and which included Britain's other top rider, Chris Boardman. Millar dismissed US Postal, saying 'they're living in a dream world' – a remark that might now haunt him, given that this was the squad with which Lance Armstrong went on to win seven Tours de France. As for Gan, Boardman suggested that he had pushed for his team director Roger Legeay to re-sign Millar. 'I wanted Robert to join as his knowledge and experience would be invaluable,' said Boardman. 'The first time I asked, Roger refused point blank. The second time it was, let's get off the subject.' For his part, Millar said at the time that 'I would have gone to Gan. They only had to make me an offer and I would have had no choice but to accept. Then again, maybe Legeay has other reasons.' Today, however, Legeay insists that he didn't reject the idea of Millar rejoining his team. 'I liked Bob a lot, he was a true professional,' he says. 'I don't remember Chris proposing him.'

Fotheringham asked Millar why he even wanted to continue to the Olympics, since it would surely mean paying his own way. Surely he could retire now and be content with what he had achieved during his career rather than bitter about how it had ended? 'In the long term it doesn't matter,' Millar agreed.

'I did reasonably well with what I had to play with, although you always think you could have done better. It doesn't matter how you finish [your career] because you are judged over the long term, but in terms of personal satisfaction it's good to plan when you are going to stop doing something. If I say I'm going to pack it in tomorrow, am I going to have a sore head for four years because I didn't force myself to do something for three months so I could finish on a decent note? It wouldn't be a failure, but it would be something like it. Is stopping on a low note going to make me into a miserable old bugger like you see at the seaside, with nothing to do? I don't know, because I'm not there, but it wouldn't surprise me.'

He admitted that it was an effort to force himself to continue training – 'I do ask myself why I'm doing it' – and also seemed to be increasingly resentful over the circumstances of Le Groupement's demise, especially the fact that he was still owed money. 'I've realized that the FICP [the professional federation] and UCI structure doesn't protect riders and team personnel. If [sponsors] want to come in and have a long-term commitment they should put money up at the start of the year . . . the present rules only say it has to be three months. If the Tour had been in June and we'd ridden for nothing then they could have pulled out after getting the publicity. There are rules to say that if I pull out of my team contract I have to pay it back, but if the other party pull out they can just walk away.'

If you do retire, Fotheringham asked, what will you do? 'I don't really have to do anything any more,' Millar replied, 'but that doesn't mean I'm not open to reasonable job offers. The trouble is, I don't know much about the real world – I know a lot about cycling, so I'm limited. I have no idea of what I would like to do. It's like when [Barry] Hoban stopped and there was talk about how they should have used his knowledge. It would be logical for me to work with the [British Cycling] Federation in some way if they want my image and my knowledge, but [if]

I'm not part of the plan there's not much I can do.' On the increasingly likely possibility that his winning ride in the British championship was his last ride as a professional, Millar admitted, 'It's a sorry story really.'

And so it dragged on for a couple more months, Millar apparently clinging on to the last vestiges of hope, or perhaps simply unsure as to what else he should, or could, do. In any case, it is another piece of received wisdom that professional riders should not simply stop training when they retire; that they should taper down, for the sake of their health, and allow the body, and perhaps the mind too, to readjust to a huge change in lifestyle. So Millar's training wasn't entirely in vain.

In early March he used his monthly column in *Cycle Sport* to formally announce his retirement. It hinted at the efforts to which he had been going to find a team.

> *After a lot of humming and hawing, postponed deadlines, unanswered faxes and unreturned phone calls, the reality of my situation has crept up on me. Even though I had started training again in mid-December [1995] I suppose that I was just trying to postpone the decision or even hide from the facts, but now I know: no more racing.*
>
> *It's funny how a few of those horribly miserable fog-laden days make you think straight and question just why you are out in such crap. I suppose when I had some kind of clear objective for the coming year I could handle it, but when I'm no longer in that position common sense prevails. It's kind of ironic that when you can't see very far you end up seeing straight. So it's change of direction time.*
>
> *It would have been nice to have done just one more year . . . but it's not a sport/business with a lot of sentiment, and just as it is hard to get into, so it's just as bad when it turfs you out unexpectedly. I don't look upon not finding another team for '96 as a failure, though when I was younger*

I would have. No, it comes more as a disappointment, more like having to leave before I felt I'd achieved everything I wanted to while I could still hold down a decent team spot. I suppose I wanted to retire from racing with some kind of honour, say goodbye to my friends, say thank you to the people I trusted, have one last laugh and then go with few regrets, knowing that it was what I'd chosen to do. But things don't always go according to plan and life is very rarely fair.

He went on to quote Laurent Fignon – 'it's not how you retire that matters but what you did beforehand that will be remembered' – and then had some fun with the stereotypical image of retirement: 'What do retired people do? If they're old they might read the newspaper all day, drink sherry, visit the garden centre, watch cricket, go on coach trips to Brighton, maybe pass some time just standing in queues, listen to Radio 4, drive a Volvo, put gnomes in the garden and wear cardigans . . . My problem, and I do wonder if "problem" is the right word, is that I'm not quite old enough yet to get away with any of these pastimes without people questioning my sanity or mental age, so I'm going to take a bit of time to figure out what is worth doing with myself.' He also seemed to be bringing down the curtain on his writing. 'I can't really justify doing this column,' he wrote. 'It's time to vacate this space.'

Millar's retirement marked the end of an era. In an earlier interview he had expressed a desire to be 'the last of the heroes', by which he meant the final member of the English-speaking 'Foreign Legion'. The pioneers, Paul Sherwen and Graham Jones, were the first to go, in 1987; they were followed by Allan Peiper in 1992, Stephen Roche in 1993, and Phil Anderson, Sean Kelly and Greg LeMond in 1994. In fact Sean Yates was the last man standing, holding on for one more season than Millar, before finally hanging up his wheels in 1996 having spent four years mentoring the young Lance Armstrong. Armstrong was one of a number of Americans who by then had infiltrated the sport, and there were just as many, if not more, Australians. But with British cyclists it was a different story. Behind Sherwen, Jones, Yates and Millar there was a vacuum. After a decade of promise and excitement, when it seemed that the sport in Britain was on the verge of moving into the big time, much of the optimism seemed to die with the bit-by-bit dismantling of the Foreign Legion.

There was more evidence that cycling was retreating into the margins. At the end of 1994 Kellogg's confirmed that their backing of the Tour of Britain was at an end. They had decided to sponsor the TV show *Gladiators* instead, which meant that in 1995 there was, for the first time in forty years, no Tour of Britain. Six years later, Channel 4, having purchased the broadcasting rights to international cricket, dropped its nightly Tour de France programme. For the legions of armchair fans this was a particularly hard blow to take, but with Roche, Millar, Kelly and Yates all gone, and Channel 4 repositioning itself as a mainstream broadcaster, it was perhaps inevitable. Still, it represented a hugely symbolic end to a golden era of British and Irish cycling.

13

A No-Pain Zone

Some people never let go when they retire. But I did. It's just the sort of person I am.

What happens to professional cyclists when they retire? How do they adjust from training five, six, seven hours a day, to doing nothing? After spending months of the year on the move, and the period between February and October hardly at home, what is it like to be at home, with no job, no purpose?

Some cope well. Sean Yates started a gardening business. With typical modesty, he reasons, 'I never considered myself a star so it didn't bother me to go from being a professional cyclist one day to digging holes the next.' Others don't cope so well. 'The rooster comes home,' says Allan Peiper. 'You're confronted with your demons. You release pressure and emotions by riding, but releasing them isn't the same as dealing with them. Once you stop riding you don't have that release any more, and then you have the black hole. It's especially hard for creative personalities: you ride, and you think you're someone, then you stop and you're nobody. All of a sudden you're standing in front of the mirror, looking at yourself and having to deal with the person you are in a new world. If you look around, a lot of us are divorced. We all had a partner when we were cycling, they fitted into a slot along-side the job we were doing, then we stop cycling and we're lost. Eddy Merckx said that you can spend the rest of your life looking for something that consumes you like cycling, but you never find it, because it's a one-off. Most people don't find that their whole life – something you can live twenty-four hours a day, that you can put your whole being into, that you can become.'

Phil Anderson likens the professional team environment to an institution, observing that riders can effectively be 'institu-tionalized'. Graeme Obree agrees but offers a characteristically extreme viewpoint. 'A lot of cyclists go from being loners to being institutionalized,' he says, 'and then suddenly that's it: your time in the institution is over, goodbye, no counselling, no workmates, no proper social circle – ditched. You'll be thawed out and put back in society, with no occupation or skill to fall back on. What does that do to you? It certainly leads to a lot of introspection. Do you even know what type of person you are if you've spent most of your adult life in that institution?'

Strangely, the cyclists who seem to cope least well when the curtain falls on their careers are climbers. I mean the *pure* climbers – the very few who, when the road soars upwards, are able to take flight, as if they are fleeing those whom Millar nick-named the 'animals' – all-rounders like Hinault, LeMond, Indurain, Armstrong. Necessarily, the climbing specialists are small, fragile and birdlike in build, power-to-weight ratio being all important in the mountains. And perhaps, in some cases, a rider's physical build is not so easily separated from his psycho-logical make-up.

A roll-call of the leading climbers of the last couple of decades would include Marco Pantani, Luis Herrera, Thierry Claveyrolat, José-María Jimenez, Richard Virenque and Robert Millar. Arguably Pedro Delgado too, though he may be ruled out on account of his all-round skills. A rare breed, then, and, yes, 'special'. 'I don't know if it's something about climbers,' Dag

Otto Lauritzen says, 'but Pantani, Claveyrolat, Jimenez and Robert, they were all special guys. When I say special, I mean freakish, extreme. They were extreme in everything – in eating, losing weight, training, suffering. Also, they spend a lot of time on their own.' Paul Sherwen suggests that climbers tend to have more introverted, introspective personalities. 'I've got a theory that, while sprinters are extrovert characters, who make this explosive effort at the end of a race, climbers, because they suffer in silence, tend to be quieter and more withdrawn.' Sherwen's theory has it that climbers are able to internalize their emotions and feelings. It is certainly an advantage to be able to do so, since an important part of their art is the ability to wear an inscrutable 'mask' of calm, concealing the physical pain and suffering. Hiding what they are feeling, in other words.

It is astonishing to count the number of casualties among those who, like Millar, specialized at suffering in silence on the tortuous 20km cols of the Alps and the Pyrenees. Two of the more obvious recent examples are Pantani, the Italian whose flamboyance masked a tortured soul, and Jimenez, a Spanish climber of dazzling brilliance and unpredictability. Both died within a little more than two months of each other, while the memories of their racing days remained shockingly vivid. Pantani was 34 when his heart failed in a hotel room in Rimini in February 2004; Jimenez was 32 when he died in December 2003, also from a heart attack, in a psychiatric hospital in Madrid – poignantly, he was giving a slide show presentation of his career at the time. In the cases of both Pantani and Jimenez, the fatal cocktail was depression and cocaine.

Another tragic figure is Thierry Claveyrolat, a regular adversary of Millar's: he finished second to Millar at the Dauphiné in 1990, won the King of the Mountains in the Tour that same year, then replaced him at Z in 1992. Claveyrolat was exciting to watch; he had the ability to change pace, and could yo-yo erratically and thrillingly on the steepest climbs. But in retirement he fell into a deep depression, the catalyst for which was his involvement in a car crash in August 1999, in which a family of four were seriously injured. On the eve of the trial, a month later, he shot himself. He was 40.

And there is Charly Gaul; less tragic, perhaps, but no less enigmatic. The 1958 Tour de France champion from Luxembourg so excelled in the high mountains of the major stage races that he was known as the 'Angel of the Mountains', and it is a tribute to him that the most gifted climber of each generation is often assigned a variation on the same nickname. Like other climbers, Gaul was a maverick, and a star. At the height of his fame his postbag bulged with sixty fan letters a day, most of them reputedly penned by female admirers. But shortly after his retirement in 1965, the rider known for his panache, daring and exuberance simply vanished. Initially he opened a bar beside the main railway station in Luxembourg City. But six months later he abandoned the bar and his wife, escaping deep into the Ardennes forest. And there, for nearly two decades, he lived as a hermit in a hut filled with Christian symbols and trinkets, without piped water or electricity. When journalists or fans did track Gaul down, he waved them away. With his long beard and thousand-yard stare he had grown, literally and figuratively, distant. In 1983 Gaul emerged from the forest, offering no explanation for his disappearance. It was something he never talked about publicly, though he remarried, had a daughter, and began to follow cycling again. Perhaps tellingly, he had a special affinity with Pantani, whose talent he admired – and whose demons he possibly recognized. He was particularly upset by Pantani's death. By this time Gaul had become, in the words of the Tour director Jean-Marie Leblanc, 'with his beard [and] his slightly rounded figure a sort of sage, a father figure' to the climbers of the modern era, though in many respects he remained distant, the thousand-yard stare still there. He died in December 2005, two days before his seventy-third birthday, after falling in his home in Itzig, Luxembourg.

It is to Gaul that Millar was compared by William Fotheringham in his book *Roule Britannia*, in a chapter on Millar entitled 'The Small Yin' – an acknowledgement of the similarities between him and the 'Big Yin', Billy Connolly.* On Millar, Fotheringham writes, 'If he is not exactly on a par with Lord Lucan, there is perhaps a parallel with another cyclist who conquered the Tour's highest peaks then dropped out of the public eye . . . the late Charly Gaul, who became a recluse in a forest in Luxembourg.'

When Millar did retire there were various and varied opportunities for him to continue working in the sport. He spent much of the winter of 1995 abroad, in Spain, Majorca and Lanzarote, as the star guest on a number of training camps for British cyclists, organized by Graham Baxter. Millar would lead the training rides, then take question-and-answer sessions in the evenings, specializing – as ever – in delivering disarmingly frank answers. 'He really shocked some people with his answers,' says Baxter. 'He wasn't very good at first, but the Q-and-As became really interesting. They were a real highlight of the camps.'

He also tried his hand as a pundit, joining David Duffield in the Eurosport commentary box at the San Sebastian Classic and the Tour of Spain. 'My trip to Paris [Eurosport HQ] for some commentating introduced a little excitement into my semi-retirement,' wrote Millar in a column. He predicted that the commentary 'could turn into a pretty cool hang-out, as you don't even need to be able to spell properly. Hopefully it'll turn out OK (ah! the butterflies) so write in and tell them it's great and I may get to go to the Vuelta too.' Duffield thought that Millar showed some promise. 'He wasn't the greatest raconteur,'

---

* In an interview in the May 1998 issue of *Bike* – a motorcycle magazine – Millar said, 'I met Billy Connolly and he's my hero. Jeez, he even knew who I was.'

he says, 'but what he said was very good, it was very interesting. But it just wasn't very much. He could be abrasive and he said some things that were a little bit shocking, such as when he passed an opinion on some of the riders. He was very precise on the racing and the terrain and not so good on the personalities. I didn't get the impression that commentating was something he really wanted to do.'

Millar's efforts to end his writing career had been thwarted, meanwhile, and in retirement he began a new column, pushed to the inside back page of *Cycle Sport*. He also contributed the occasional article, containing little nuggets of cold logic or mordant wit, or priceless advice, such as this, in his survival guide to the Tour de France: 'Learn to swear in different languages. Other riders will appreciate your efforts to communicate. They'll also know who you're talking to.' Other tips were equally practical, and they demonstrated that Millar hadn't spent fifteen years racing in Europe without thinking deeply about what he was doing, and coming up with ways of making it slightly easier, or more bearable. An especially memorable image conjured up by Millar related to the thousands of spectators who line the mountain passes awaiting the riders' arrival at the summit. He compared them to Red Indians, poised to ambush and 'pick off the stragglers'.

In a later email to Fotheringham, Millar explained how and why his mind conjured up such images. 'There is a lot of boredom time in a long bike race and in training. You might be active physically, but mentally it's not always very interesting [and] having a sense of humour helps in those moments. Often I'd see things during a race and it would trigger a thought process in my mind, like seeing people standing on the top of hills we were about to climb – that always reminded me of when the Indians were waiting to ambush the cowboys in an old Western movie . . . waiting ominously, silhouetted against the sky, arrows to the ready, waiting to pick off the stragglers.'

It is a vivid visual image, but it is more than that: it also invokes the anxiety the sportsman, even the elite sportsman, can feel. Very few athletes are able to articulate what it actually *feels* like to be competing at such a level, in such an arena, and many would not wish to, since it would involve an admission of vulnerability and fallibility – but Millar has this gift. Through his image of the Indians, you begin to understand something of how the rider feels as he approaches a 20km Alpine pass on a stage of the Tour de France. It takes you inside Millar's mind, which isn't super confident, but nervous, daunted and fearful – vulnerable. Not super-human, but normal – human.

Millar's gift for writing was encouraged by Fotheringham, but it isn't clear how important it was to Millar himself. Did he see it as a sideline, a diversion, or was it a passion? At school, says his old classmate Willie Gibb, he showed no interest in the written word – until he became keen on cycling and started to devour books on training, as well as *Cycling* magazine. Interestingly, most of his training methods and dietary habits seemed to come from these books. In his early years as a pro, as he told Charlie Burgess, he would happily go for days without speaking to people, sitting in his one-man apartment in Lille with his hi-fi and his books. Wayne Bennington says that Millar never discussed his articles, or even mentioned his writing to him. Fotheringham admits that he was initially reluctant to write, and that 'it took a great deal of hard work to make him do it'. While the Tour de France diaries had simply involved having a conversation, Millar's contributions to *Cycle Sport* meant actually putting pen to paper. 'He said, "How the fuck am I gonna write it, eh?"' Fotheringham recalls. But he was persuaded to do so, and his articles were always handwritten, always submitted by fax, and always on time.

In a column in 1996 he reflected on retirement. The training, the travelling, staying in a different room every night – he was glad all that was over. And while retirement could be a little boring, he suggested that 'life's not half as bad as some people would have you believe . . . You see, there's this great myth about having to get yourself a good, stimulating job when you stop racing, otherwise you'll end up half-crazy or depressed or something else sinister, but, hey, cycling isn't exactly an intellectual pastime. You won't get overwhelmed by MENSA members while getting dragged through France or Belgium at 45kph, and you don't need any academic qualifications to ride over the Tourmalet and go down the other side in the fog, so just what you would do with a mentally challenging job beats me. No thanks, I've had enough of that suffering lark to last a lifetime, so I've declared my body a no-pain zone. It needs a rest after fifteen years.'

Such defiance was a regular feature of Millar's post-retirement output. Did he protest too much? After all, he was by now competing in the occasional mountain bike race – not exactly the safest or most relaxing way to spend your retirement.

His work for the magazine reached its zenith in February 1997 when that month's issue was devoted to, and guest-edited by, Millar. It provides a fascinating overview of Millar's career, even if it isn't really the 'warts-and-all story' Millar promises in his introduction: 'You might be tempted to think that I'm going to cover my back and defend myself, make excuses and give deep explanations, and perhaps even make everything look rosy – but I'm not. This is the warts-and-all stuff and, even though sometimes people or events might not show me in a particularly good light, I'm not going to hide or say it wasn't me.' His sign-off is interesting: 'I haven't tried to do all this differently, the writing included, just to be different. I'm just being mc.' Complementing the text and pictures are Millar's career facts, though they're limited to top-three placings. As he explains, 'If you didn't stand on the podium then you didn't do anything worth remembering.'

The main feature is a compelling Millar retrospective, tracing his life from Glasgow to France. Written by Kenny Pryde, a fellow Glaswegian, it reveals more than you might think Millar would be comfortable with, including the story of him lighting his own fire on the Glasgow drum-ups, as well as various other tales that only reinforce the impression of Millar as a slightly strange and anti-social loner – a 'funny guy', as the article is headlined, though Pryde makes it clear that he means 'funny ha ha, not funny peculiar'. (It was Millar's Norwegian team-mate from Z, Atle Kvalsvoll, who was credited with the 'funny guy' remark. Incidentally, Kvalsvoll, a climber, is another who retains only good memories of Millar: 'He was very smart, very honest, and he taught me a lot.') Pryde's article also includes a remark by Jamie McGahan that McGahan subsequently regretted. 'I am full of admiration for Millar as a cyclist,' McGahan told Pryde, 'but as a human being he is a dead loss.' McGahan cringes at this now. 'I am ashamed of that comment,' he says. 'If I was to meet him now I'd be embarrassed, and I'd take it back.' Yet the remarkable thing is that Millar, who as editor had to approve the content, let such a comment pass.

Just as revealing is the four-page selection of Millar's favourite photographs from his career. It includes pictures of some of his best wins, but the first and biggest is a grainy black-and-white image of him heading out on a training ride in the depths of a grey Glasgow winter. It dates from January 1980 and it is, writes Millar, 'the only picture of cycling I've ever framed and put on my wall at home. I'm not into having reminders of racing when I'm trying to relax so you'll never find photos, trophies or medals lying around. This is art. Glasgow, a damp January morning. Time to go find some green bits.' The juxtaposition of this scene with the colour and the glamour of the Tour, Giro and Vuelta is intentionally striking, of course; but so, perhaps, is the fact that Millar has his back to the photographer, riding *away* from the prying eye of the lens and into the distance.

Another feature in the magazine is a round-table discussion involving Millar, John Herety and the retired Irish professional Martin Earley in which they reminisce and suggest ways to improve the standard of British cycling. 'I came back to this country through my own choice,' said Millar, 'and I thought the federation would be in touch with me, to do some training weekends or something, but I've never had a phone call.' This might suggest that he was reluctant to make the first move, though in fact he did. And a month later he accepted a major new challenge – and a proper job. Having applied for the position, in March 1997 he was appointed British national road coach. 'After I stopped racing I was in the happy position of being able to do anything I wanted,' explained Millar. 'This was a job I wanted to do.'

In describing what his approach would be, he echoed the lessons he had been taught, twenty years earlier, by Arthur Campbell and Billy Bilsland. 'We need to instil in our international riders the understanding that every title they win is just a step up to the next level,' he said. 'Once they've climbed that step they are at the bottom of the next one, and they need to keep climbing all the way up to the Tour de France and world championship. I will be teaching people how to race, not how to train.'

Many were surprised that Millar had accepted such a job, and some had reservations. Frank Quinn, who continued to act as Millar's business manager, discussed it with him. 'I was surprised he took it. I advised [Sean] Kelly to stay away from the [Irish] federation when he retired and I spoke to Robert in detail about that too. People like Robert and Kelly didn't fit into the bureaucracy of these organizations. They couldn't attend meetings and votes and all the shite that goes with it.' On balance, however, Quinn thought that the job might be good for Millar. 'I encouraged him to take it in the end, because I thought it might bring him out of himself. And I knew he had a lot to offer, there was no question of that. Robert had knowledge and experience that can't be bought. I did feel it would be difficult for him to hang in there; he'd need a lot of encouragement. And he was aware of the political side of it. But I felt that if he survived that then he could have stayed in the job for ever.'

By the end of April, Millar was beginning to apply his unusual methodology to the job of national coach. This saw him spurn the usual means of observing his riders – from a following car – and instead ride the races himself. He didn't ride to win, he stressed, but just to 'float around' the bunch in the country's top races, the Premier Calendar series. It was the best vantage point to assess the riders' ability, he reasoned. Now, as one of the riders who took part in those races, I can say that it was more than a little surreal to look up and see Robert Millar 'floating about' in front of you. And the very fact that he was able to float around so comfortably in the country's best events was of course something of an indictment on the standard of racing. 'I'm sure if most of these guys went to a French amateur classic they would get a kicking,' was Millar's frank assessment a month into the job.

He gave an interview to Fotheringham at the time, outlining his ideas and his motivation in going for the job, which he revealed was 'a personal ambition because I always thought I could do it'. Fotheringham asked whether, given his 'reputation as an abrasive character who doesn't suffer fools gladly', he had the necessary 'interpersonal skills' for such a job. 'It's up to me to learn that,' Millar replied. 'I'm not a perfect individual and I know it's up to me. I don't think it's a bad thing if I come with a repu-tation of "if you upset me, I'll tell you directly that you've upset me". People will approach me more carefully. People who expect me to grovel to them and don't merit it, and aren't influential in what I have to do, won't get any more respect than they deserve.' What is most striking about Millar's comments is his apparent obliviousness to his own talent. 'If I can do it with my physical ability then someone else can do it with theirs,' he suggested at one point. 'I look at the physical ability I had,' he added later. 'I never thought I was talented but I worked at it. That's what it comes down to – you don't get big legs from watching television.'

Millar went on to say that he wanted British riders to get away from the 'little pond' of domestic racing, otherwise, as he explained, 'when you go to Europe and get a kicking you might say "they're all on drugs" or "they're better than us because they're French or Belgian" – and neither is the case'. In five years, he would like to see 'five or six guys in the Tour de France'. In the shorter term, 'If the level hasn't improved after next winter, I'm responsible.'

Certainly 1997 was the best year I ever had. It's all relative, of course, but making it into the top ten in the Premier Calendar road races was a major breakthrough. In late April I even managed to win a stage of one, an eighty-mile race on the outskirts of Hull, and the following week the phone rang. It was Robert Millar. Although we had ridden a few of the same races – him 'floating', me grovelling – I hadn't spoken to him since the training camp in Stirling in 1989. And even then I hadn't spoken to him; I had mumbled and nodded before going to retrieve my wet hat. What I remember most about that phone call was that my heart seemed to be trying to escape from my chest, and combined with the racket of my brothers fighting in the hall, it wasn't easy to hear what he said. He spoke very quietly in short, staccato sentences; questions were easily mistaken for statements, because the tone of his voice didn't vary. But he was phoning to say that he had decided to select me to represent 'Britannia' – effectively the Great Britain B team – in the 1997 Manx International, the race Millar himself had won two years earlier. Subsequently, I had to phone him on a couple of occasions – after taking tranquillizers and locking my brothers in a soundproof booth – though I don't recall him answering. Famously, his answer machine informed the caller that he would return the call 'if it's necessary'.

Millar didn't have much longer in the post – which, I hasten to add, had nothing to do with any questionable selections for the 1997 Manx International. In the autumn he and the British team travelled to San Sebastian for the world championship.

In San Sebastian, the only riders who had any real chance of performing well were Chris Boardman and the Anglo-Italian Max Sciandri, who'd won a bronze medal in the previous year's Olympic road race. They – along with a young Scot, David Millar, who was only embarking on his professional career – were the only Brits in continental teams, the only riders who deserved to be described as 'elite', in Millar's opinion. He was, to put it politely, pragmatic about the chances of the others.

John Herety was also in San Sebastian, working for Boardman; so was Boardman's coach, Peter Keen. Herety isn't very comfortable discussing what happened in San Sebastian, for reasons that will become clear, but also because he is reluctant to criticize Millar. Yet he says Millar was 'terrible, but he wasn't . . . He could give riders information through his own experiences, but the problem was that the rider had to understand these experiences. Some just weren't able to take in what he told them; they were lost.

'His style of management was . . . quirky. He still wanted to ride with the riders; he believed that was the best way to teach them. I think he genuinely thought it was the best way, but for me that was someone trying to cling on to what he was . . . there was something going on there. Was it to let people know he was still good? Because he didn't have to do that – everyone knew he was a fantastic rider.

'My experience of him in San Sebastian was a little bit strange. I went there because I was working for Chris Boardman, but for the under-23s road race Robert didn't go to the start with them. He stayed in the hotel. So I asked the riders if he'd given them a team talk and they said no. I couldn't believe that the national coach hadn't given them a team talk. In fact, I think he had – but in his own style. I don't think they realized that *was* the team talk.

'Although he was national coach, he still seemed like a loner. He kept himself to himself. In the professional road race I drove the team car, which I was embarrassed to do. But I happened to be there and no one else was going to do it. Robert came down halfway through the race and I said, "Do you want to drive?" And he said, "Fuck off – I'm not doing that." I got on with him, so he didn't mean that as an insult. But he genuinely thought he had nothing to add by driving the team car behind the race. And you know what? He was probably right. He knew the pro scene better than I did; he knew the riders better than I did; he knew the only one who could do something was Max, and he knew he couldn't tell Max anything he didn't know. So he was right . . . but it didn't look good. And Peter Keen was there.'

Within a few weeks, Keen was the man appointed by British Cycling as the new performance director, charged with establishing an ambitious 'world-class' programme to be bankrolled by millions from lottery funds. Keen's job was to devise an all-new World Class Performance Plan, and one of his first acts was to dispense with the post of national road coach – Millar's job. Instead, the post of national road manager was created, with Herety appointed.

Today, Keen offers this explanation for Millar's departure: 'Frankly there is no story to tell other than that Robert failed to engage, communicate or evidence activity of any significance that led me to think he was suited to a formal professional coaching position. Competing and coaching in sport are two very different things, even though they clearly have many things in common. Professional coaching in a highly accountable publicly funded role is a task that requires very specific skill sets, attitudes and insights, that in my judgement Robert did not possess. There have been many things I did in my tenure at British Cycling that, on reflection, I regret or would have done differently. Letting Robert go was not one of them.

'I didn't know Robert personally and therefore had no insights into him other than a few brief meetings in the four months between my arrival and the end of his fixed-term contract (which I chose not to renew). But like every other cyclist

growing up in the early 1980s, I admired him as the outstanding British rider of his generation.'

Such was the success of the World Class Performance Plan
set up by Keen that, by the early 2000s, Britain had become the
world's pre-eminent track cycling nation. Road cycling proved
a more difficult nut to crack, however. In 2004, for the first time
in nearly thirty years, there were no British cyclists in the Tour
de France.

Was Millar bitter at losing his job with British Cycling? If he
was, he didn't say so publicly – at least not at the time. He continued to write and to spend the winter months in sunnier
climes, as the star guest at training camps. On one such camp
he shared a room with Brian Smith, the fellow Scot who as a
teenager had been the grateful recipient of Millar's old jerseys,
and who had then followed him to the ACBB and to a career as
a professional. Smith says that on the training rides Millar still
displayed incredible strength on the climbs. But the incident he
remembers most vividly is returning to their shared room to
find Millar spread-eagled by the window. 'The windows were
open and he was sitting there in his Oakleys [sunglasses] and
his cycling shorts,' says Smith. 'I said, "What the hell are you
doing?" And he said, "Trying to get a sun tan. I'm pale white."
He would never sit outside with other people, so he was sun-
bathing in the room.' Smith laughs. 'It was the same at dinner.
He'd go at the last minute, just before they stopped serving – it
was totally deliberate, so that he didn't have to make small talk
with people. But I got on really well with him; it was good
bonding.' Sean Yates also attended some of these training
camps in the late 1990s and is less sympathetic. 'He'd sneak in
ten minutes before breakfast closed and ten minutes before
dinner closed. He'd come out on the rides, he'd do the question-
and-answer sessions, but the rest of the time he must have been
hiding in his room. He seemed more eccentric.'

In early 1998 Smith took the opportunity to ask the now

out-of-work Millar whether he would be interested in managing the Scotland team in the revived Tour of Britain – sponsored by the Prudential and thus to be known as the Prutour. Millar agreed.

'Millar has Mountain to Climb to Lift Scots Riders' read the less than flattering headline in *The Scotsman* on the morning of Saturday, 23 May, the day of the start in Stirling of the Prutour, which included the world's number one ranked squad, Festina, as well as US Postal and Chris Boardman's Gan team. 'Brian Smith asked me to help so it was no problem,' Millar told *The Scotsman*'s Simon Pia. 'I'm here to drive the car.' Pia reported that Millar 'inspires awe' in the Scottish team, quoting one of them saying that it was 'a bit like Ruud Gullit coming as player-manager to Stranraer'. Which it was, for five of us at least, the sixth member of the team being Smith, who had been one of Britain's top professionals over the previous decade. 'This week I'll instruct them about the first three days,' Millar told Pia. 'That's the most important part. I will talk tactics with them. I have something to offer and believe that success comes from the top.'

Thinking back now to the experience of riding in a team managed by Robert Millar, I kick myself. When you are racing you are so focused on what you are doing – on yourself, fundamentally – that everything else fades into the background. This partly explains why I didn't get to know Millar better during the nine days of that race. But there were a couple of other reasons. Someone asked me after the Prutour what I thought of Millar – whether I liked him. 'I have no idea,' I replied. 'I was too busy trying to make sure that he liked me.' There was also something about Millar that implicitly discouraged any kind of interrogation. For one thing, it was obvious that he had a well-honed bullshit detector, which you didn't want to risk activating. Added to this is the fact that we Scots, as a rule, don't like to make a fuss or draw attention to ourselves. It was very important to be seen to be blasé, to act as if having Robert Millar as our manager was No

Big Deal. (Others on the race thought it was a huge deal – which was kind of the point.) I wasn't the only one who spent the week tongue-tied while trying to act as though being in a team managed by Robert Millar was a perfectly normal, run-of-the-mill experience. A team-mate, Gary Paterson, says, 'I remember thinking, "Wow, Robert Millar's our manager!" He was my boyhood hero, but it didn't seem right to make a fuss over him when we were the ones supposed to be racing. I also remember the first team talk being a bit of a let down. The gist of it was that we were way out of our depth and that we should just try to enjoy it . . . He was basically right, though.'

Following the first proper road stage, 120 miles from Edinburgh to Newcastle, there was a knock on the door of my hotel room. I was sitting on my bed, waiting for my bag to be delivered and, having had a hard time, feeling sorry for myself. I answered the door – it was Millar. He handed me my bag and walked into my room.

'How'd you feel today?' he asked.

'Not brilliant.'

'I expected you to be one of the guys up there,' said Millar, not really meaning that he thought I'd be 'up there', but that I might finish in the bunch rather than be dropped.

'Yeah, er, so did I,' I lied.

'The first stage is always hard in this kind of race. These guys like to show the amateurs how good they are so they don't get any ideas. But you'll be better tomorrow. Everyone has bad days.'

Indeed they do: I was to have six more – all in a row. But the point was that Millar, in this brief exchange, did what he could to lift my morale. He also offered some advice about using my size – I'm six feet three inches tall – to hold my position higher up the bunch. I was never very good at this, a fact that the five-foot-six-inch Millar must have struggled to comprehend.

But others suffered an even more inglorious fate. Stephen

Russell, a Scotland team mate, was disqualified on day one. He had been dropped relatively early in the stage with two members of the Dutch Rabobank team, both of whom, according to Russell, were suffering from 'the runs'. Their team car dropped back to cajole them. Sportingly, they cajoled Russell, too. In road racing 'cajoling' covers a multitude of sins. There are subtle ways to gaining assistance from a team car – sitting directly behind it, taking an extended time to let go of a drinking bottle as it is handed out of the car, or, rather more blatantly, just hanging on. On this occasion the trio weren't so subtle; they held on, were spotted by a race official, and disqualified. That evening, Millar defended Russell vigorously and the organisers relented – they offered Russell his place back in the race, but on the condition he paid a £300 fine. Russell, anticipating even tougher days ahead, didn't think that would be money well spent. Millar agreed and appeared a little downcast, though he had seemed to relish the confrontation – or the renewal of old conflicts – with officialdom. 'That bastard once fined me £50 for pissing by the side of the road,' he noted of one of the officials in question.

As the Prutour wound its way down towards the finish in London, Millar said less and less about the actual race – because we weren't really participating in the race, we were trying to survive. Only on one stage did the Scottish team figure, thanks to Smith, who made it into the winning break and placed eighth into Reading. Millar offered his congratulations at the finish. 'It's about time you did something,' he told Smith.

That Prutour came just weeks before the biggest drugs scandal ever to hit the sport of cycling, when a Festina team employee was stopped on the France–Belgium border with an enormous consignment of banned products, including EPO and growth hormone. It seemed to blow the lid off the can, exposing a highly sophisticated and organized doping programme within Festina. Millar's old team TVM was another squad implicated, having been monitored for several months after a team car was stopped earlier in the season with a similar stash of illegal products.

Millar was, not surprisingly, sought for comment. In the midst of the crisis he contributed an article to *The Guardian*, and one of his quotes was pulled out as a headline: 'I Can Understand Guys Being Tempted'. In the article, Millar explained, 'You can't describe to a normal person how tired you feel . . . In 1987, when I finished in a really bad way, it took me until the end of November to recover; by that I mean until I could wake up and not feel as if I had already done a day's work.' During the Tour itself, 'The best way of describing how you feel is that it's as if you were a normal person doing a hard day's work, you've got flu, and you can just about drive home and fall into bed.' Noting that you become so fatigued that you cannot sleep, Millar added, 'By the end of the Tour you need sleeping tablets.' As well as the physical pain, he described the mental torture: 'people yelling at you, the cars, the helicopters . . . you tend to let go mentally before you crack physically'. It wasn't until the final paragraph, after this lengthy description of the suffering involved, that Millar addressed the drugs question. 'I can understand guys being tempted to use drugs in the Tour. Given the real-life situation of drug use, I'd say it's no worse than in the real world where one million ecstasy tablets are sold every weekend. Why should sport be different from real life? I don't think it's an isolated cycling thing, people just expect sport to be cleaner than real life.'

The following year, Millar moved from *Cycle Sport* to a new magazine, *Procycling*, where he would act as 'technical consultant' – meaning bike reviewer. Mainly this involved riding bikes in exotic places, often in the company of top riders. The first issue saw Millar riding with Jan Ullrich, the 1997 Tour de France winner, and his Telekom team. 'Ullrich is a very quiet, focused character,' wrote Millar. He added that this 'can give the impression of coldness, but that's no bad thing in the pro cycling environment: it's something to hide behind when the bad times come'.

Millar was ideally suited to the role of bike reviewer. He proved to be a connoisseur of equipment and aesthetics, once lovingly describing, on an Italian-designed frame, 'the little hint of metallic blue on top of the celestial green which brought the whole bike up-to-date without being flashy or smacking of trying too hard to be modern'. Surprisingly, he also confessed to being in awe of one of his test-ride companions, the Italian star of the 1960s and early 1970s Felice Gimondi. 'It's an honour just to breathe the same air as the great man . . . Some people look perfect on a bicycle, and Gimondi is one, having a natural grace that escapes most of us mere mortals.' Millar's claim to be a 'mere mortal' does not smack of false modesty – he seems to mean it. His positive bike reviews were rich and exuberant, and they showed a different side to his personality; negative reviews, meanwhile, were typically candid and cutting. The reviews are also humorous and self-knowing – 'when you spot your reflection in a window the bike looks so classy that it's not really vanity, but just confirmation of your excellent choice'.

Another revealing bike test followed a visit to Tuscany, where Millar stayed with one of his old climbing rivals, the American Andy Hampsten. According to Millar, this was 'easily the most pleasant assignment so far for the magazine'. On Hampsten, he was effusive: 'It's great to be able to talk to someone who doesn't constantly talk about bike races or how many litres of fuel their car uses . . . The best thing about Andy is that he isn't a typical, short-sighted bike rider who is only interested in racing and training. Conversations with him range from skiing in Colorado, through to wines, architecture, Californians, trekking, olives, farming and his big love – Italy. He is definitely a cultured person; almost, you might say, arty.'

Praise indeed, and today Hampsten is keen to return the compliment. 'He was a great guy, a lot of fun,' he says of Millar.

'We went head to head in a lot of races and when we were racing it was serious, but I liked him a lot. He always had something very funny and incredibly cynical to say. He would see things so much darker than I would.' Hampsten says that he picked up on Millar's increasing cynicism towards the end of his career, especially with regard to the Tour de France, which he thought had become too big, too stressful, and too much of a circus. 'I remember riding the Tour of Romandie. I was having a pretty miserable time, so was he, but the sun came out and I tried to start a conversation with him. I said, "Oh well, if nothing else, this is good preparation for the Tour de France." And he bawled, "The Tour de France, the Tour de France! That's all people think about . . . there could be a Chernobyl in France and all people would talk about would be the Tour de France."'

On the visit to Tuscany, Hampsten recalls, 'It was spring, and my impression was that he was just having fun. He seemed to be enjoying himself. But I do remember one journalist who was there asked him a very direct question about drugs, to which Robert replied, "I've got a son in high school and I'm much more worried about the drugs he'll have to contend with there. A cyclist isn't going to mug him, is he? In all our cities drugs are a serious problem, so why focus on professional cyclists?" He always had a very different perspective, that's for sure.'

Hampsten's lasting impression of Millar might surprise some people: 'Robert was, is, a really nice guy in a nasty sport.'

Millar's comments on Hampsten, and his championing of his varied interests, seemed to indicate a broadening of his own horizons. He mentioned in *Procycling* that he had a new hobby, tae kwon do, which now 'forms the basis of my current, medium and long-term goals. Medium term being a blue belt by October and long term a black belt about two years after that.' His cycling had been reduced to no more than ninety minutes at a time as a consequence, since he discovered that cycling affected his flexibility. To improve his tae kwon do, he also revealed that he had been trying to put on weight. 'After so many years of being lean I find it difficult to gain any weight, and as a result any kick or punch in the ribs at tae kwon do has no cushion of fat to penetrate before touching the nerves.'

Millar's appearance began to change. He did put on weight in the upper body; this was apparent in some of the pictures that accompanied bike tests in *Procycling*. He also grew his hair longer, wearing it in plaits or braids. Someone who saw a lot of Millar at this time was Sandy Gilchrist, his old Scottish teammate, who now worked as a mechanic and was sometimes on duty at the Graham Baxter training camps. 'I wouldn't say he was trying to shock, but I think he was trying to be different with the hairstyle,' says Gilchrist. 'But I didn't think much of it: he'd always done his own thing. He was just being Robert.'

Millar would often be with his partner, Linda, and she accompanied him to some of the camps; they would socialize with Gilchrist and his partner. The couple by now had a daughter, but they didn't live together, instead having their own houses in Daventry, albeit on the same street. And according to Brian Smith, the relationship wasn't plain sailing. 'He and Linda went through rough patches,' he says. 'They always seemed to be going through rough patches.'

In May 2000, Millar accompanied another exiled Scot, Jimmy Rutherford, to the Pinarello Gran Fondo, a mass-participation ride in Treviso, Italy. He and Rutherford had become good friends and Millar coached Rutherford's son, a promising junior cyclist. Prior to that summer's Tour de France, Millar also gave an interview to Natasha Woods of the *Sunday Times* which provided more evidence of an increasing distance from the sport. He claimed to watch the Tour de France these days with only 'a certain amount of interest'. Millar, noted Woods, offered an 'enigmatic answer' when asked what he does now: he mentioned the bike tests, but 'otherwise I do nothing'. He enjoyed living in

England, but added that 'If I lived in Scotland I'd be voting SNP [Scottish National Party] . . . when you live in England all you hear is that Scottish people are just like peasants.'

He also spoke about retirement – 'Some people can never let go when they retire, but I did. It is just the sort of person I am' – and, for the first time, his dismissal as national coach. 'I didn't fit into their political world,' he said. 'Being a coach should be about giving advice to athletes, not rubbing noses with the latest minister for sport or deciding what colour the team tie should be. But there is a lot of that in cycling. There are lots of guys who want to go to this Commonwealth Games or that games because they can add to their set of blazers. It is sad.

'Coaching was something I could have done, but the British Cycling Federation judged I wasn't apt to do it. I found that pretty amazing. I reapplied for the job once, but they said they had people more qualified than me. I don't need these put-downs. So I walked away. I am going to forget more about cycling than these guys are ever going to learn.'

It seems safe to say, then, that Millar was hurt, and that he was still hurting more than two years on.

A month after that *Sunday Times* article, another Millar story appeared in the national press, this time in a Scottish tabloid, the *Sunday Mail*. An investigative reporter, Charles Lavery, had followed up a rumour that had been circulating in the cycling world, though its origins remain unclear. Some claim that it began with a throwaway comment by a cyclist in Glasgow, others that it was spread by a retired cyclist with a grudge against Millar. The story was that the country's top cyclist was rumoured to be having a sex change. Together with a photographer, Lavery travelled to Daventry and set up camp outside Millar's house, staying there for five days. On 27 August 2000, the following story appeared in the tabloid underneath the headline 'Cycle Ace Millar in Health Riddle':

Scots cycling legend Robert Millar was last night at the centre of a health scare. The former King of the Mountains has grown his hair long, wears it in pigtails and seems to be showing signs of hormone treatment. Friends of Millar, who became the pride of Scotland at the 1984 Tour de France, last night voiced concerns for him. One close pal said: 'He looks terrible. You would think he was in the middle of a sex change. Every time we meet him, he seems to have a bigger chest. He looks like Martina Navratilova, for God's sake, but he won't talk about it to anybody. Everyone is concerned for his welfare, but he has always been quite independent, so he doesn't feel the need to share his feelings or talk about what he's going through.'

Millar, 41, claimed victory on the tortuous mountain section of the Tour de France 16 years ago and ever since has been afforded god-like status by younger cyclists. He now lives in a £130,000 semi-detached mews house in Daventry, Northamptonshire. He has retired from the sport, but still keeps two cycles in his garage, a top-of-the-range racing cycle and a mountain bike.

But neighbours have noticed the physical changes in the man who was named BBC [Scotland] Sports Personality of the Year for 1984. One said: 'He has always kept himself private and seems nice enough, but just recently we have noticed some changes in the way he looks and dresses. He seems to have developed some breasts. He seems a nice chap and he doesn't bother anybody around here. I suppose it's a case of each to their own.'

Robert was born in Glasgow's tough Gorbals district in 1958. The tae kwon do expert was a competitive cyclist for 15 years, earning a place in history when he made his tremendous impact in the Tour de France. He captured the imagination of the nation back in 1984 as he tackled some of the toughest peaks in the world in his bid to be crowned King of the Mountains in the world's toughest cycle challenge. He was the first Briton to

*win the mountain stages of the gruelling contest, and his
prowess earned him riches. In his last year of competitive
racing, he is believed to have netted more than £400,000.*

*Until recently, Millar was involved in the British Cycling
Association [sic], but left under a cloud, complaining that
people running the sport were too interested in politics and not
enough in young cyclists coming through the ranks.*

*Now neighbours don't even recognize Millar, who looks
gaunt and unwell.*

*Yesterday, he answered his door wearing a three-quarter-
length, white night-shirt and sporting long, beaded pigtails.*

*He said: 'This has nothing to do with anybody else. I have
been answering questions from people like you for 20 years.'*

*We asked Millar three times whether he was going through a
sex change.*

*He said: 'I don't have to answer to you or anyone else. It's my
business.'*

Charles Lavery says that what most surprised him about the
story was that there was no response from Millar after it was
published. For those five days there was no sign of Millar, and no
sign of life inside the house. He was about to give up and return
to Glasgow when, on the fifth day, the garage door opened and
Millar appeared inside. He tried to speak to him while the photographer took pictures, but they returned to their hotel room
feeling that they lacked any real 'evidence' and that their story –
which had been based on nothing more substantial than gossip
in the first place – was a non-story. When they developed the pictures, though, they discovered that the wind had blown Millar's
night-shirt against his chest, revealing, according to Lavery, 'what
looked like breasts'. He will not say who the 'close pal' was.

When the story appeared, Millar phoned William
Fotheringham. 'It was very rare that he phoned, but I really,
really remember that phone call,' Fotheringham says. 'It was

forty minutes. He wanted to know what to do, how to deal with it, should he take them to court and do them for libel. I said to him I didn't think it was worth it. I said the grief it would cause him, not to mention the expense and the profile it would give him, would be counter-productive. I said, "Keep your head down and don't wind them up." He was very disturbed by it. They were camping out on his lawn, looking in the windows, interviewing his girlfriend, his neighbours. He thought they went to France to try to find his son, and I think that's what he really took exception to. He did address the issue, he said, "They asked my girlfriend . . . she knows I'm not a woman!"'

The next month there was no Millar bike test in *Procycling*. He returned in December, but there were no pictures. But in January 2001 he was back, and there were more reviews and sporadic 'Robert reckons' columns until September, some months with pictures, some months without. He reappeared in January and February 2002 and then disappeared again. By October, his name was no longer appearing in the magazine's credits.

James Poole, the magazine's commercial director and Millar's main point of contact, says there was nothing sinister in the fact that Millar's picture didn't always appear alongside his bike reviews. 'It was a matter of logistics and timing rather than anything else,' he says. When the *Sunday Mail* story appeared, Millar broached the subject himself. 'I didn't ask, he brought it up,' Poole continues. 'He said something like, "You're obviously aware there are a few rumours flying around." He said someone had it in for him. That's all he said about it. But I think being door-stepped put him under some stress. We respected his decision to stop doing the bike tests. We said, "In your own time." But his bike tests were very powerful; he didn't bow to anyone. He's a loss to the magazine.'

Then Millar stopped working on the Graham Baxter training camps, and Baxter lost touch with him. 'I'd have him back tomorrow,' he says.

In the meantime, the sex change story spread like wildfire, partly because it was undeniably salacious, but more because it went unchecked by Millar. He simply ignored it. Allan Peiper ('No one would really care if it is true – the world's moved on'), Phil Anderson ('So, is it true Robert's a Sheila?'), Sean Yates ('I got a text telling me about it when I was in Australia'), Ronan Pensec ('If the rumours are true it doesn't matter to me, maybe he didn't feel right'), Patrick Valcke ('It's not a rumour – it's true, everyone in cycling thinks so'), Wayne Bennington ('I don't think it's true but even if it was he'd still be Robert Millar – still my friend'), even Billy Bilsland ('If he's in touch with his feminine side, so what?') – all are familiar with the rumour, and only Bennington has heard from Millar since the story broke. To all intents and purposes Millar does seem to have disappeared, and the assumption most make is that the catalyst was the sex change story. Yet his continued employment at *Procycling*, up to eighteen months after the *Sunday Mail* story was printed, suggests that it wasn't. He also continued doing the training camps for some months after the story appeared.

Then in August 2002, a full two years after the publication of the story, Millar appeared at the Commonwealth Games in Manchester; he was there to help the Scottish team, at Jimmy Rutherford's invitation. While there, he rode around the road race circuit with the team. 'And he took his shirt off in front of the team,' says Rutherford pointedly. 'He drove up to Manchester at his own expense and didn't ask for anything,' Rutherford continues. 'He rode around the road race circuit with the team and pointed out the bits on the circuit where they should watch out, telling them to be careful in the pits area, because he could see it was dangerous. And everything he said was spot on. I didn't feel, though, that he really got the respect he deserved from some of the guys. That was sad.'

A month after that he appeared in the north of England again, this time at one of the country's top road races, the Tour of the Peak – a race Millar won back in 1978. This time he joined Graeme Herd, the Scottish coach, in the Scotland team car. 'For the whole race he sat there in the car telling us what would happen,' Herd recalls. 'His patter was brilliant. We were behind the bunch and with unerring accuracy he'd pick the guys who'd get dropped next. I'd say, "Nah, that guy looks OK," and then it would be boom!, and he'd be gone. It was a riot. He had a black, black sense of humour. It's possibly the funniest few hours I've ever spent in a team car.' At the finish Millar was asked to make the presentation to the winners, but he declined.

Rutherford is the only person connected to the world of cycling who seems to have been in regular contact with Millar in 2002 and into early 2003. Did he ask him about the sex change rumour? 'I asked him, but he just said, "People can make their own judgement."'

In 2003, Millar and Linda left Daventry to move to a new house in Dorset. It meant an end to the tae kwon do classes he'd attended in Daventry for three years. I tracked down one of his instructors, Jackson White. 'He worked up to black tag level,' White confirms. 'In six months he could have gone for his black belt but he just disappeared. In the three years he came to classes he didn't really talk to me but I had no problems with him. He was polite and a nice guy, a very quiet guy.' I ask White if at any time in his three years with him Millar happened to mention that he had been a professional cyclist. 'No, I didn't know about his cycling career until afterwards,' White replies. Naturally, then, he didn't know that one of his pupils was – is – Britain's best ever Tour de France cyclist. 'No, I didn't know that. I did see him out on his bike one day. I was driving past and as I overtook him I realized it was Robert so I tooted my horn – and he gave me the two fingers . . . I don't think he realized it was me.'

The rumour that he was having a sex change reached White, too. 'I heard that after he disappeared. He did seem like a feminine guy; people would ask if he was a female, because you've got your [tae kwon do] suit on, and you can't really distinguish between men and women – they're unisex outfits.' And Millar is only five feet six inches tall, nine stone, and by then he was wearing his hair long and in plaits, sometimes beads, so it's hardly surprising. White adds, though, that 'he wasn't aggressive; he was gentle. He had the physique to be strong but he was a very gentle bloke. I don't think he was very interested in fighting, in the competition side of it. He liked the physical side to it, but he wasn't into the aggressive side. I was surprised that he just left, though, because for most students black belt is their first goal.' Another instructor in Daventry, Wayne Kent, has similar recollections. 'The strange thing about Robert was that he used to get a lift to training from one of the guys, but he would never let him pick him up from his house. He used to meet him at a petrol station. Even if it was tipping down with rain he would get dropped off there, too. He would never give out his phone number, either. It was only later that we found out that he lived on the other side of Daventry from the garage where he used to get picked up!' Kent says that 'he was one of these people who always turned up, trained very hard, and seemed to enjoy it. He had big legs, which was good for kicking, but he wasn't the most flexible of blokes.

'He brought his son and his daughter along to one session,' Kent continues. 'His son didn't speak any English I don't think. I didn't know about Robert's cycling career until I mentioned him to some cycling friends of mine and they said, "What . . . ? *The* Robert Millar?"' As for the sex change rumour, Kent notes that Millar continued training with him for at least two years after the story appeared. 'There was no sign of anything like that. We never really knew anything about him. He was quiet, but he could speak his mind; he'd say, "That's crap!" He could be humorous but people didn't really get the gist of his humour, I don't think.'

About three weeks after Millar moved to Dorset, Rutherford received a phone call from a female. 'Where is Robert?' she asked. 'He's gone missing.' Rutherford presumes the female was Linda, but he wasn't able to tell her where Millar was – he had no idea. He has only had occasional email contact since.

And so it is with everyone else. Brian Smith sends regular emails and only occasionally gets a response. Fotheringham hadn't heard from him for a couple of years until January 2005, when Millar emailed him with some answers to questions Fotheringham had put to him for his book *Roule Britannia*. Wayne Bennington says 'it was 2003 when I last spoke to him, when I called to tell him I was getting married again. He said, "What are you doing that for?" I asked if he was still riding his bike and he said one hour a day, and if it was a nice day he rode out by the sea. I think he was in Dorset or Devon at that time.' Others have claimed that he has spent time in Australia, New Zealand, Spain, and various places in the south of England. One 'sighting' I am aware of was in Spain in the middle of 2003, when one of Patrick Valcke's mechanic friends bumped into Millar. He was riding his bike and his hair was dyed red. Bafflingly, Jack Andre claims to have received a phone call from Millar in mid-2005, having not heard from him for the best part of a decade. 'He called to recommend an English cyclist,' says Andre. 'It was a brief call. All he said was, "You wouldn't recognize me if you saw me now."'

Brian Smith is in no doubt as to the cause of his friend's disappearance, but wonders about Millar's motivations. 'I defend Robert all the time and I just don't understand what goes through people's minds when they spread these rumours. I try to contact him and he doesn't get back to me, and I think it's because of this shit. He doesn't trust anybody now. But it's typical of Robert to just disappear.' With a half-smile, Smith adds, 'He's playing with people's minds. He knows that.'

Epilogue

More than four months had passed since my first direct email to Millar, but there had been no response. It seemed that he really had gone into hiding, which in some respects seemed both predictable and logical – 'I knew he wanted to hide,' said Bennington, 'he just wanted to be Robert Millar' – but in other respects didn't. After all, it was Millar himself who, after winning one of his three Tour de France stages, said, 'You feel that maybe ten million people are watching. It makes you feel you are making history.' So he wanted to make history; he didn't want to be forgotten. 'I don't want to be remembered as someone who won the King of the Mountains one year and nothing else,' he said on another occasion. Yet two decades on there seemed a very real possibility that he wouldn't even be remembered for that, let alone for being second in the Tour of Italy, twice second in the Tour of Spain, King of the Mountains in the Tour of Italy, winner of the Dauphiné Libéré, the only British rider to win stages in the three major tours . . . Millar hadn't simply disappeared, he had vanished, leaving no discernible trace.

When, in 2004, a group of British cyclists began a 'Backing Bob' campaign and travelled en masse to the Pyrenees in retro Peugeot jerseys, to celebrate the 20-year anniversary of his King of the Mountains success, their efforts to contact Millar proved futile. Similarly, when Sport Scotland tried to inform him of his induction to the Scottish Sport Hall of Fame in 2003, he didn't respond; and the organizers couldn't even find him to invite him to a get-together of all Britain's Tour de France cyclists in Sheffield in 2005. Millar's only real 'presence' these days is thanks to an unofficial web-based fan club run from the small island of Islay off the west coast of Scotland – which somehow seems suitably obscure. Meanwhile, not only is there no Robert Millar Square, or similar, in Scotland, but in a cruelly ironic twist one of the country's top bands, inspired indirectly by Millar's feats, named themselves after his nemesis, Pedro Delgado. 'The Delgados' were one of Scotland's finest musical exports, and favourites of the late John Peel, until they disbanded, after five albums (including *Domestiques* and *Peloton*), in 2005.

Had Millar just turned his back on cycling, was there something that had driven him away, or did he feel that the sport had rejected him? When he told *The Sunday Times* in 2000 that he'd 'walked away' from the sport, did he mean that literally, and finally? 'I'll reject you before you reject me', was Graeme Obree's interpretation of his 'survival strategy'. Well, it seemed clear that Millar, who had given so much to the sport of cycling, had done just that. But why?

In early August 2006 I was driving through Glasgow city centre when my phone rang. It was Brian Smith.

'I think you'd better sit down,' he said.

'I'm driving.'

'Then pull in. Robert's just emailed me.'

Millar had responded to a thread on 'Veloriders', a UK website with a very active discussion forum. A conversation had been running for several days, to several pages, entitled 'Robert Millar', and eventually matters turned to the circumstances surrounding his departure from the post of national coach at British Cycling. Reading this, Smith had felt that some misinformation was being peddled, so he forwarded the link to Millar, wanting to alert him to it, but also keen to coax any kind of response out of him. Within a day Millar responded to Smith, and also logged on to the site – registering with the memorable handle 'Gottheteeshirt' – to set the record straight.

Finally it seemed he might be ready to communicate. I tried another email, asking him again to contact me. And the next day there was a response:

From: Robert Millar
To: Richard Moore

Sorry Richard, but I can't help with your book, it's not personal so don't take it that way. Call it self-protection, a quirk of character or whatever, it's not something I've done in the past and it won't be in the future. As I've said to Brian [Smith] and others – people/journalists have the right to give their own opinions and make their own judgements concerning my cycling career. The who, where, when, ifs and buts of it.

Initially I was delighted to get any kind of reply. Then a suspicion crept up on me that it wasn't Millar, but someone pretending to be him. I emailed again: 'I have a nagging suspicion that this isn't Robert. Can I speak to you, either on the phone or in person?' The response was unequivocal: 'I'm not doing any media stuff at all.' I tried again, but got the email equivalent of a clip around the ears: 'Like I said, I don't do media stuff now.'

I left it for a month. Then I tried again, brazenly dispatching yet another email:

From: Richard Moore
To: Robert Millar

Hi Robert,

I've been working on the book. I think I've got your career just about covered . . . The ending to the book will cover, for want of a better word, your disappearance. As I said before, I have no desire to expose you – you have every right to disappear and I respect that.

But it leaves me with a dilemma in writing about it. I don't need to spell out why you have chosen to cut your ties with cycling, but I would like to explain your choice, if I can.

It would be great if you had the last word on this, so that it is on your terms. It doesn't have to be long or detailed, but I think it would end the book in a good way.

Would that be possible?

Best wishes,

Richard

From: Robert Millar
To: Richard Moore

Maybe I lost the belief that UK road cycling could have some kind of better future. It certainly hasn't progressed, but you don't need me to point that out. Somehow that's not the kind of happy ending I think you had in mind.

From: Richard Moore
To: Robert Millar

I take it you're referring to the circumstances of your leaving British Cycling and the job of national coach . . . I get the impression that episode upset you . . . I don't want to dismiss its importance, but I don't see it as very significant when compared with your achievements, and your standing, as a cyclist. The respect you deserve for that far outweighs anything that happened with British Cycling.

Any chance I could speak to you, or you could answer some questions by email?

From: Robert Millar
To: Richard Moore

That depends on the question.

As for the BCF [British Cycling Federation] thing . . . Appointed in March [1997], told to take my time to settle into the job, learn how things have been done but make no decisions until the performance director is chosen in the autumn. There are no decisions to be made anyway. The race programmes are already decided for the season, who is going on what race as manager/mechanic etc. usually all decided as well. (No wonder it was called the travel club.) Spares needed, cars used, tyres supplied, everything is decided, even if those choices aren't the best for the purpose, it's all pre-arranged. All the budgets are allocated so it's just a question of dealing with minor people problems until Mr Performance is named.

The only input during the season I have is choosing where to stay for the world [championship] in San Sebastian and selecting the riders. The only people who complained about the hotel choice are Peter Keen and Chris Boardman, apparently it wasn't plush enough! Well it's all that the budget allowed – if they wanted better then stay within their pro team structure, it's what I always did when I went to the Worlds.

So after six months of dealing with 'wait until the performance director is appointed' finally he's named . . . and at the end of the first meeting with Mr Keen I'm told by him that he has no budget for my position the following year and my contract won't be renewed. I think the best laugh was when he followed up with, if I apply to be a team manager (i.e. car driver) in the usual way then I may be considered for a few races, but he then points out most of those spaces are filled already.

So I've wasted my time waiting for my 'boss' to be appointed, then I'm told that I'm not part of the plan at the first meeting.

You might ask what use was made of my time from when I was told I was not needed until the end of the contract? Absolutely none at all.

Oh well . . . after waiting half the year doing nothing useful or constructive how was another six months of doing even less going to affect me?

So when I look back at it now what has changed at the BCF . . . it's now called British Cycling aaaaaand that's about it. The same people are back there in the same seats, going on the same trips with the same results, making the same plans with their same ideas of how things are done.

You can't change unless you want to.

From: Robert Millar
To: Richard Moore

You'll have received a long reply about the BCF stuff . . . You're right, it isn't what my career was about but it kind of sums up the different commitment and passion needed to do well in top-level road racing.

There's no creativity, it's all numbers and figures, which is great in a fixed environment like track racing . . . i.e. if you have this number of watts you'll go this fast and we'll know you can reach this level of competition. It's like painting by numbers, fill in the boxes and you'll complete the picture . . . wooohooooo isn't that clever.

Trouble is, road racing isn't that controllable and if Picasso turned up for a job at the BCF paint school they'd tell him he was barking up the wrong tree.

When I read about coaching tips and the like I get the impression that people involved in just about every aspect of training and racing in the UK have forgotten they are racing with other people.

From: Richard Moore
To: Robert Millar

Is what happened with the BCF/British Cycling the reason why you have chosen to cut your ties? I keep using the word 'disappear' but perhaps it's just cycling that you've disappeared from?

I suppose the questions I'd like to ask are: where are you living and what are you doing? Do you still ride your bike? Do you still follow the sport at all?

From: Robert Millar
To: Richard Moore

I didn't consider driving a car around cycle races three times a year a future for me . . . it wasn't what I had to offer and I don't find it particularly interesting, so when I was told quite clearly I wasn't going to be part of this big World Class Performance Plan being put together by Peter Keen, the chapter was closed.

Disappeared? . . . not really. Moved on, relaxed, chilled, or only doing things that please me is more realistic. I have different interests now, I cycle occasionally but not fast and not far.

I haven't grown up with a small-minded attitude, most of my actual learning time as an adult has been in Europe, so it's normal that my values are different to those I might have acquired in the UK.

I spent a lot of time living an extra-ordinary life so now a bit of ordinary peace and quiet is appreciated.

From: Richard Moore
To: Robert Millar

How do you feel about a book being written?

Why did you never respond to those rumours a few years ago? I know you were around for a bit after that, at the Commonwealth Games in Manchester and Tour of the Peak . . . I mean, I think that not responding was a pretty brave thing to do. Did you feel that they weren't worth a response?

From: Robert Millar
To: Richard Moore

My opinion about the book . . . people are entitled to their opinion about my cycling career, if they want to write about [it] I can't stop them. I wouldn't encourage anyone to do it.

The stories, tales and general rubbish I see written aren't a surprise given that there's a whole morbid attitude to privacy in this country. Most European countries don't care what you had for breakfast, what kind of house or car you own, where you shopped or went on holiday. They really aren't interested in knowing the intimate details of some person that they saw on television. It's bizarre the need to diminish other people so that they can feel better about themselves. I'm not putting myself up for election, saying you ought to do this or that, so I don't have to justify what I do or who my friends are. I've shared a part of my life as a professional cyclist, now that career is finished I have the same right to privacy and a quiet time as the next person.

From: Richard Moore
To: Robert Millar

That's fair enough. I understand your point of view and respect it . . . But thinking about what you say about privacy . . . I get the impression that you are uncomfortable with the idea that others are interested in your life beyond your life as an athlete – it's just so difficult to separate the athlete and the person, I suppose . . . for me, like the majority of the population, our total failure to be anywhere near as good as our 'heroes' only emphasizes to us how special and exceptional they are . . . which only makes us more interested in them, and in trying to understand them. I had another question – I suppose it depends if you still follow cycling, and I'm not sure if you do, but do you have any opinions/thoughts on all the doping scandals to hit cycling, especially this year? They've really damaged the sport, of course, and it has certainly affected the public's view of it. Are you surprised/shocked/saddened to see this? Or could you see it coming?

From: Robert Millar
To: Richard Moore

You're right about people having difficulty separating the athlete from the daily person . . . it's as if the level of aggression and commitment used in competition is the way you behave with your family and friends. Lots of cyclists don't get that bit.

As for heroes . . . exceptional at what they do certainly but waiting in the queue at the supermarket they seem perfectly ordinary somehow. Heroes have the same life stuff to deal with as everyone else, they usually turn out to be smaller than they appear on TV too.

The doping scandal? Well you have to ask yourself why

have a 50% blood limit[*] when less than 5% of the population get anywhere near that figure. Those blood values go down with training and racing, fairly dramatically too, so there's no chance of maintaining such a level as a pro bike rider without help from somewhere.

Why isn't it 54% like cross country skiing? They all have near that limit so how come their levels are so high. It's not rocket science to work it out.

I wouldn't fancy dying in my sleep at a young age because my heart couldn't pump round blood that thick just so I could have a medal or big cup on my mantelpiece.

Historically there has always been cheating, it's human nature and it's not limited to just sport. Work, rest or play, people cheat.

Drugs are available in every walk of life so if some kid does a few drugs to have what he or she thinks will be a better night out what would be morally different about that same person taking something to improve their performance when they do a sport or a maths test? Being an athlete doesn't turn you into some kind of morally superior being – it's all a reflection of the society we live in.

The UCI and IOC know what the normal blood values are; if you do any kind of basic research you discover it's somewhere between 41% and 44% . . . that's for sedentary people! As soon as you do exercise of any intensity the level goes down not up like I've seen passed off as an excuse.

Look at what changed after the Festina scandal [in 1998] . . . nothing. A couple of scapegoats took the blame but there

---

* The '50%' refers to a cyclist's haematocrit level – the concentration of red cells in the blood. A level above that can be caused by the use of EPO, though not in all cases. The UCI set 50 per cent as the limit, with riders above this not punished for doping but suspended for two weeks, after which they are allowed to race again if their haematocrit is below 50 per cent.

would have been more than a few people thinking it could have been them.

I am not surprised the general public is disappointed, I am too, but it's not as simple as blaming just the riders because everyone involved, from the team management all the way up to the ruling bodies, have some responsibility.

When you look at other sports it's the same crap wrapped up in different outfits . . . steroids for recovery, cortisone injections, painkillers, blood spinning, altitude training in Africa (yeah right, more like no one near enough to do a surprise control). So ask yourself why there aren't positives in certain big-money sports. They have sports doctors on every team too. Someone employed them to do a job which isn't only putting elastoplasts on blisters or dealing with insect bites.

So am I surprised . . . no.

Am I disappointed . . . yes.

Will anything change . . . history has the answer.

From: Richard Moore
To: Robert Millar

Thanks for the response to that last one – really interesting. Did you never fancy going into sports science? It's obviously something you have great knowledge of. I remember the appreciation you did in *Cycle Sport* for Dr Bellocq – does a lot of your knowledge come from him?

From: Robert Millar
To: Richard Moore

As an athlete your body is your tools, you have to learn how it functions, maximize your strengths and work on your weaknesses. I read lots of books on diet, training methods used in other sports, etc. For example, I'm not a vegetarian for ethical reasons, it's because that diet suits my intestines better. Humans have a digestion system which allows a meat-eating or vegetable intake, I just happen to feel better as a vege' eater. Speaking with team doctors helped [me] learn things relating to how and why you react to certain situations and training methods, the medical care stuff is mostly about using your physical potential to its maximum. You can't compete if you aren't 100% healthy. If you look after yourself you'll maintain that health . . . if you abuse it then you don't last very long. It all comes down to choices.

When you compete at world level the differences are so small between each athlete that small percentage gains gleaned here and there can be crucial.

Maybe I should do a degree in sports science . . . it can't be that hard after seeing some of the people who turn up waving them. There's often a world of difference between the theory and the practical application.

From: Richard Moore
To: Robert Millar

There was a famous quote of yours – after a British journalist asked you what you did when you weren't cycling, did you have a full-time job . . . can you remember what you said in response to that?

What are you doing now – I take it you don't work?! You mentioned other interests. Do you still do tae kwon do? Are you still a motorbike fanatic?

From: Robert Millar
To: Richard Moore

I think I replied that professional cycling was a full-time job on the continent and there wasn't any getting drunk after

games or smoking and holding betting circles on training
camps in the off-season.

No I don't work . . . I'm retired (kind of earned the right).
I do own a motorbike but I'm not and never was fanatical,
and I do a little bit of taekwondo to broaden my horizons.

From: Richard Moore
To: Robert Millar

I was talking to Graeme Obree, who said the key to succeeding
in something – really succeeding – was to have no back-up
plan . . . It occurred to me that when you went to France you
probably had a similar mindset – that you went to become a
cyclist with no back-up plan, whereas perhaps others had at the
back of their mind the option of coming home if it didn't work
out, or doing something else. Would you agree that it was an
all-or-nothing type scenario for you?

I also wonder about your feelings towards Glasgow and
Scotland – it always seemed to me that you got a bad press
from some people because they just didn't 'get' the dry and
often cynical Scottish sense of humour. Although you could
be quite down on Glasgow and Scotland, you seemed to me
to be a typical Scot in a lot of ways . . . how true do you think
that is? Do you ever return to Scotland these days?

From: Robert Millar
To: Richard Moore

I didn't consider failing, it wasn't an option even though I
would probably have done something else if I had not been
a pro bike rider. What? . . . I have no idea.

Proud to be Scottish, proud to be from Glasgow. I haven't
been in Scotland since that time I was at the Tour of Britain

[the 1998 Prutour] . . . I've grown used to warmer and drier places.

I don't think I've ever read a piece of journalism from an English language sports writer that doesn't criticize or put down the person they are writing about eventually . . . sure it starts all nice, how good they are, how they struggled etc., then the crap starts by the time you come to the end of the story.

Often I've read stuff (not necessarily about me) and it's so obviously just made up, but then again it's not the mentality of the press in the UK to sell good news.

A couple of the press guys covering cycling in Europe were what I'd consider good at their job, they didn't change your words or say useless crap just to make people look bad. It's hard to be tolerant when someone just makes up stuff to cover their back when either they couldn't be bothered or were asleep all afternoon in the press room because they had a heavy night drinking the night before.

I know I had bad days in doing my job, I could read about it in all its glory the next day, but the same standards ought to apply to poor reporting. Funnily enough most journalists can't quite get their head around the idea that the subject of the story they had just written might form an opinion of them based on their work.

From: Richard Moore
To: Robert Millar

It's funny – I think a lot of journalists would have had the opinion that you didn't care what they thought, or wrote . . . but I guess, from what you say there, that the opposite is true. In other words, some might have formed the impression that you were very thick-skinned when, in reality, you might have been more sensitive to criticism, etc. than many imagined. You obviously had some bad experiences with the press, which perhaps made you cynical . . . but would you say the cynicism was also a self-protection strategy on your part?

I had heard you spent some time in Spain and Australia recently – and England. Do you travel about rather than live in one place? Is there anywhere you call home?

From: Robert Millar
To: Richard Moore

Lots of journalists probably write stuff just to get a reaction. What you notice during a day and what affects you are two entirely different things.

Most journalists aren't as good at dealing with having their work examined or commented upon as they would have you believe either.

From: Robert Millar
To: Richard Moore

No more questions.

Afterword

'No more questions' was such a perfect ending to the Robert Millar story, not least in fulfilling my aim of giving Millar the final word. A pity, then, that a month after this book was first published, a tabloid newspaper tracked Millar down. They had apparently been tipped off by a neighbour after a review of the book appeared in the newspaper.

What appeared in the news pages of the *Daily Mail*, on the day that the 2007 Tour de France started in London, was a similar article to the one that had featured in the *Mail on Sunday* in August 2000. There was a new – but grainy – picture, and some new information; information which arguably, and certainly in Millar's view, constituted an invasion of privacy.

It had never been my intention to physically track Millar down – the search being far more interesting than the discovery – but rather, and if possible, to engage him and communicate with him on his terms, and by whatever method suited him. Email, as it turned out, was his preferred medium, and I could understand why. The method didn't matter. The important thing was to get Millar's words, his input, however limited. Significantly, but hardly surprisingly, that is more than any tabloid journalist has achieved by hunting him down and appearing unannounced on his doorstep.

Suffice to say that Millar was not happy. He believed that I had tipped off the newspaper as to his whereabouts. I had not. I don't think he had, at that point, read the book. I'm not sure if I expected him to.

But then, clearly, he did read it. In subsequent correspondence he seemed to object, in particular, to the tale, told by Allan Peiper, Stephen Roche and Dag Otto Lauritzen, alleging that he had avoided paying French *péage* tolls with the help of a set of heavy-duty bolt cutters, claiming that 'you need to be six foot six and built like a brick shithouse to even think about using bolt cutters.' In his email Millar adds, however, that, 'Driving through an already open gate is a whole different affair to stopping, getting out the bolt cutters, and causing criminal damage. You might get away with saying you've made an error with using the wrong exit, but I don't think when you got searched that the giant bolt cutters would go down that well . . . ' He is not, he adds, 'some tight-assed maniac' and dismisses the story as 'a piss poor attempt at a funny anecdote.'

Originally, Millar gave his blessing to the book – kind of. Some months after 'No more questions,' I emailed again to seek permission to include the correspondence within these pages. And a couple of days later came the response: 'As long as you correct my spelling you have my permission to use the emails.' (There were no spelling mistakes.)

Following the tabloid intrusion, however, Millar asked me to make it clear that he neither sanctioned nor endorsed the book. I am happy – though of course sad – to make this clear. I remain hopeful, however, that any reader takes a sympathetic view of Millar. In researching and writing this book my admiration for Millar, for all his quirks and foibles – possibly because of his quirks and foibles, for his insistence in being true and answerable only to himself – increased hugely. But regardless of that, the very least he deserves is respect, which naturally should extend to respecting his very obvious desire for privacy.

Perhaps one day Robert Millar will re-emerge. Perhaps he won't. One thing is sure: whatever he does or doesn't do, it'll be on Robert Millar's terms. Which is exactly as it should be. In the meantime, the enigma remains intact. 'Remaining unknowable is the only true way to be known.'

No more questions.

Robert Millar Palmares

Amateur
1976: Scottish junior RR champion; six wins.
1977: Six wins.
1978: British National championship; Tour of the Peak; Scottish Hill-climb championship; eight wins.
1979: ACBB: British national championship; 4th, World Championships; Merlin Plage Trophy for best amateur in France; Paris-Evreux; Route de France; GP de la Beucherie; Chrono Madaleine; six wins in France.

Professional
Teams: 1980–1985 Peugeot; 1986–1987 Panasonic; 1988 Fagor; 1989–1991 Z; 1992–1994 TVM; 1995 Le Groupement.

1980: no wins; 3rd Tour of Vaucluse; 8th Tour of Romandie; 5th National Championship; 11th World Championship.
1981: No wins; 7th Tour of Romandie; 7th Dauphiné Libéré; 5th Tour de l'Aude; 5th GP Gippingen; 14th World Championship.
1982: no wins; 7th Tour of Romandie; 2nd Tour de l'Avenir.
1983: 1 win; Stage 10 Tour de France; 3rd Dauphiné Libéré; 14th Tour de France; 37th World Championship; 25th Tour of Lombardy.

1984: 3 wins; Stage two, Tour of Romandie; Stage four, Midi Libre; Stage 11, Tour de France – Mountains Jersey, Tour de France; 2nd Nice-Alassio; 2nd Tour of Haut Var; 6th Paris-Nice; 15th Liège-Bastogne-Liège; 5th Tour of Romandie; 4th Midi Libre; 4th Tour de France; 6th World Championship; 7th Tour of Catalonia.

1985: 1 win; Tour of Catalonia overall; 7th Tour of Haut Var; 6th Paris-Nice; 6th Criterium International; 6th Tour Midi-Pyrénées; 2nd Tour of Spain; 9th Dauphiné Libéré; 11th Tour de France; 10th World Championship; 4th GP Wallonia; 3rd Tour of Piedmont.

1986: 1 win; Stage six, Tour of Spain; 2nd Tour of Spain; 6th Tour of Aragon; 2nd Tour of Switzerland; 10th GP d'Isbergues; 13th Tour of Lombardy; 7th Montjuich hill-climb.

1987: 2 wins; Stage, Tour of the Mediterranean; Stage 21, Giro d'Italia; 6th Tour of the Mediterranean; 7th Catalan Week; 12th Flèche Wallone; 5th Liège-Bastogne-Liège; 4th Tour of Romandie; 2nd Tour of Italy; 19th Tour de France; 21st Tour of Lombardy.

1988: no wins; 9th Paris-Nice; 3rd Criterium International; 3rd Liège-Bastogne-Liège; 6th Tour of Spain; 3rd Route du Sud; 2nd Bicicleta Vasca; 8th Tour of Catalonia.

1989: 4 wins; Stage four, Tour of Romandie; Stage seven, Dauphiné Libéré; Stage ten, Tour de France; Tour of Britain overall; 7th GP Bessèges; 8th GP Cannes; 8th Paris-Camembert; 8th Tour of Vaucluse; 2nd GP Wallonia; 3rd Tour of Romandie; 2nd Dauphiné Libéré; 6th National Championship; 10th Tour de France; 9th GP of Americas; 30th World Championship.

1990: 2 wins; Stage four, Tour of Romandie; Dauphiné Liberé overall; 4th Tour of Andalucia; 7th GP Rennes; 9th Flèche Wallone; 15th Liège-Bastogne-Liège; 2nd Tour of Switzerland; 14th Wincanton Classic; 2nd Tour of Britain;

4th GP Ouest France; 13th GP of Americas; 4th Tour of Lombardy; 19th World Cup.

1991: 1 win; Stage five, Tour of Switzerland; 10th Sicilian Week; 2nd Tour of Romandie; 2nd Classique des Alpes; 4th Dauphiné Libéré; 5th Tour of Switzerland; 72nd Tour de France; 22nd Wincanton Classic; 4th Tour of Britain; 5th GP of Americas.

1992: no wins; 9th Catalan Week; 9th Liège-Bastogne-Liège; 20th Tour of Spain; 18th Tour de France; 21st San Sebastian Classic; 9th Tour of Britain; 6th Tour of Lazio; 7th Tour of Piedmont.

1993: no wins; 15th Tour of Spain; 9th Classique des Alpes; 7th Tour of Asturias; 6th Midi Libre; 2nd Tour of the Mining Valleys; 5th National Championship; 24th Tour de France; 22nd San Sebastian Classic.

1994: no wins; 9th Tour of Galicia; 4th Climber's Trophy; 6th Coppa Piacci; 7th Coppa Sabatini; 16th Tour of Lombardy.

1995: one win; National Championship; 9th Classique des Alpes; 14th Route du Sud.

This list of results originally appeared in the 1997 issue of *Cycle Sport* magazine edited by Robert Millar, though he pointed out that it was not his idea to include any positions lower than third. Millar's reasoning was that if you weren't on the podium, you didn't do anything worth remembering.

Acknowledgements

Thanks to Robert Garbutt and the staff of *Cycling Weekly* for providing invaluable access to the archives of *Cycling Weekly*, *Cyclist Monthly* and *Cycle Sport*; thanks also to all at Procycling; and to Peter Carr, Alasdair Fotheringham, Doug Gillon, Rupert Guinness, Wayne Kent, Kenny Pryde, Frank Quinn, Shawlands Academy, Neil Storey and Jackson White. I gratefully consulted work by Samuel Abt, Martin Ayres, Philippe Bouvet, Robin Magowan, David Walsh, John Wilcockson, Les Woodland, and Adrian Bell and Lucy Brzoska, whose book, *Viva la Vuelta*, was useful in researching chapter 8.

Many thankyous to many cyclists, all of whom gave their time willingly and generously: Phil Anderson, Jack Andre, Graham Baxter, Wayne Bennington, Roland Berland, Billy Bilsland, Jimmy Dorward, Willie Gibb, Sandy Gilchrist, Harry Hall, Andy Hampsten, Graeme Herd, John Herety, Peter Johnstone, Graham Jones, Peter Keen, Sean Kelly, Atle Kvalsvoll, Dag Otto Lauritzen, Roger Legeay, Phil Liggett, Freddy Maertens, Gerry McDaid, Jamie McGahan, Alasdair MacLennan, Neil MacLeod, Bobby Melrose, Graeme Obree, John Parker, Gary Paterson, Allan Peiper, Ronan Pensec, Cees Priem, Stephen Roche, Theo de Rooy, Alan Rushton, Jimmy Rutherford, Jock Shaw, Paul Sherwen, Pascal Simon, John Storrie, Ian Thomson, Patrick Valcke, David Whitehall and Sean Yates.

Sadly, a few weeks after this book was first published, Arthur Campbell passed away, aged 89. Arthur devoted as much of his life to cycling – and to helping those such as Robert Millar – as any other individual. Happily, he was able to attend the launch of this book, where he appeared in robust health and good humour. He even managed to give as good as he got in a (good-natured) argument! This book remembers Arthur Campbell with respect and admiration.

I'd like to thank Mark 'Stan' Stanton, my literary agent, who proposed the idea to Michael Doggart and Tom Whiting at HarperCollins, both of whom were enthusiastic and supportive.

I am hugely indebted to Justin Davis – a Jock in Paris – for helping to ensure that contributions from France weren't lost in translation, but also for becoming as fascinated by Robert Millar as I was. Much of the material from France was gathered and/or translated by Justin. I'd also like to thank another interpreter extraordinaire, Iciar Gomez, for her kindness in translating emails by Spanish cycling legends.

Special thanks to the Brydie family – Alison, Andy and Chris, and their other halves, Andy, Jo and Gillian – for allowing me to spend many weeks in their Highland hideaway. Thank you, too, to my very good friends the Tylers – James, Rachel, Sophie, Edward and Tom – and to Tasha Baylis.

For his help in trying to contact Robert Millar, thanks to Brian Smith. For their feedback at various stages, I am very grateful to my father, Brian, and my brothers Robin and Peter; and to Alan Pattullo, Julia Fields, William Fotheringham, Brian Palmer of the unofficial Millar fan club, the Washing Machine Post, and Dr Brian Walker of the Scottish Institute of Sport. I would also like to thank Kirsten Speirs and her team at KDMedia; Donald Walker, Graham Bean and Richard Bath. Almost finally, thanks to Belle and Sebastian, another original Glasgow talent (who prove that it isn't always grey).

Finally, of course, thanks to Robert Millar – for doing it his way.

Index